John Wilson

A treatise on English punctuation

Designed for letter-writers, authors, printers

John Wilson

A treatise on English punctuation
Designed for letter-writers, authors, printers

ISBN/EAN: 9783337107789

Printed in Europe, USA, Canada, Australia, Japan

Cover: Foto ©Paul-Georg Meister /pixelio.de

More available books at **www.hansebooks.com**

A

TREATISE

ON

ENGLISH PUNCTUATION;

DESIGNED FOR

LETTER-WRITERS, AUTHORS, PRINTERS, AND
CORRECTORS OF THE PRESS;

AND FOR

THE USE OF SCHOOLS AND ACADEMIES.

With an Appendix,

CONTAINING RULES ON THE USE OF CAPITALS, A LIST OF ABBREVIATIONS,
HINTS ON THE PREPARATION OF COPY AND ON PROOF-READING,
SPECIMEN OF PROOF-SHEET, ETC.

BY JOHN WILSON

TWENTY-FIFTH EDITION.

POTTER, AINSWORTH, & COMPANY,

NEW YORK AND CHICAGO.

Entered according to Act of Congress, in the year 1871, by
JOHN WILSON,
In the Office of the Librarian of Congress at Washington.

University Press: John Wilson & Son, Cambridge.

PREFACE TO THE TWENTIETH EDITION.

IN 1826, an edition of this work, designed solely for printers, was first published. In 1850, the second edition appeared, greatly enlarged, and designed for letter-writers, authors, printers, and correctors of the press.

In 1855, the author, in his Preface to the third edition, says: "In presenting anew the following treatise, the author would say, that, agreeably to the admission contained in the closing paragraph of the Preface to the second edition, he has embraced the opportunity of making what is conceived to be further improvements, by changing occasionally the modes of expression, enlarging the remarks and exercises, rewriting and extending the section on compound and derivative words, drawing up a more copious list of abbreviations, offering to young authors some considerations on the preparation of 'copy,' and appending a full and minute Index. He feels justified in affirming, that not only in its present form, but in its past, this book is the most complete of any on the subject that he has seen."

And now, three years after the author's death, this edition — the twentieth — is offered to the public, in the hope that it may still continue to merit the approval awarded to former editions.

CAMBRIDGE, Mass.
1871.

PREFACE TO THE SECOND EDITION

THE work that follows is a new edition of one published by the writer in England, about six years ago, under the title of "A Treatise on Grammatical Punctuation;" the difference consisting, not in their fundamental principles, but in the mode in which these are stated, in the divisions of the subjects treated of, in the augmentation of the exercises, and in the insertion of matter which is entirely new.

The proper manner of using the book will depend altogether on the capabilities of the learner. If unversed in Punctuation, or but slightly acquainted with the art, it is recommended, that, after a careful study of Sect. II. of the "Introduction," he confine his attention to the leading principles laid down in the definitions and rules, all of which are printed in a larger character, and may be readily seen; and also to their illustrations, which are given under the head of "Examples" and of "Oral Exercises," — in that portion which applies merely to the rules. When he has gone through this course, he will have been furnished with as much information as will enable him to comprehend the exceptions or the additional principles contained in the "Remarks," and to explain or write and punctuate the remaining or second series of exercises in accordance both with the rules and the remarks.

These modes of studying the book, it is conceived, may be advantageously adopted in schools, with more or less variation, to suit the capacity of each individual in a class. The Italic lines, under the heads termed "Exercises," are mere general directions, which the teacher may modify according to his own taste and judgment. But, beyond these brief hints, the writer has not prescribed any questions for examination, because he thinks that such a procedure, common as it is in elementary books, either offers a premium to sloth and ignorance on the part of an instructor, or implies an insult to his understanding and his talents, as if he were less capable than an author of knowing what to ask of those under his charge.

Though written in a manner which specially adapts it to instruction in schools, the work is also designed for printers and private students, all of whom must have some previous acquaintance with English literature; and also for young authors, who can have little difficulty in mastering an art so intimately connected with their tastes or profession. For this class of students, the exercises termed "Oral" will be found peculiarly serviceable; tending, as they do by a variety of examples, to impress on the mind the practical applications of the rules and remarks to which they refer.

At the request of friends, the writer has introduced into the Appendix a short article on Proof-reading, the insertion of which will, he trusts, be found of some use to authors and printers, if not to general readers.

With respect to the mode in which the work has been executed, its author asks no indulgence but that of candor and good feeling. He has ventured, as in the former edition, to call the book a "Treatise," because he professes to have gone somewhat thoroughly into the subject with which it deals; but he does not flatter himself, that he has cleared away every obstacle which has beset one small but requisite pathway to literary excellence. On the contrary, he feels that in a production of this nature, which requires so much experience and accuracy, and for the preparation of which so little aid, comparatively speaking, can be derived from other writers, all is not yet effected that can be done to simplify, and to put on a firm basis, that despised but useful art, — the art of Punctuation.

BOSTON, May, 1850.

CONTENTS.

CHAP. I. — INTRODUCTION.

Page

SECT. I. — THE IMPORTANCE AND USES OF CORRECT PUNC-
TUATION 1
SECT. II. — PLAN OF THE WORK, AND DEFINITIONS OF THE
TERMS USED 19

CHAP. II. — THE GRAMMATICAL POINTS.

Introductory Observations 26

SECT. I. — THE COMMA.

Remarks on the Use of the Comma 27
Two Words, of the same Part of Speech, connected by the
Conjunctions *and, or, nor* 28
Two Words, of the same Part of Speech, not connected by a
Conjunction 33
Series of Words of the same Part of Speech 37
Words or Phrases in Apposition 41
Words or Phrases in Contrast 45
The Subject and the Predicate 50
Relative Pronouns and Relative Clauses 57
Parenthetical Phrases and Clauses 64

viii CONTENTS.

Page.

Vocative Words, Phrases, and Clauses 68
Adjectival, Participial, and Absolute Phrases 69
Adverbs and Adverbial Phrases 72
Phrases at the End of Sentences or Clauses 78
Inverted or Transposed Expressions 83
One Clause depending on Another 89
Correlative Words, Phrases, and Clauses 93
Phrases and Clauses in the same Construction 98
Clauses having a Verb understood 104
Clauses consisting of Short Quotations or Remarks 108
Numeral Figures and Words 112

SECT. II. — THE SEMICOLON.

A Sentence consisting of Two Conjoined Clauses 113
Expressions divided into Simpler Parts 116
A Series of Expressions having a Common Dependence . . . 120
Short Sentences slightly Connected 125
Lists of Words, Phrases, and Numbers 128

SECT. III. — THE COLON.

Remarks on the Use and Abuse of the Colon 129
Two Clauses not joined by a Conjunction 130
Conjoined Members of Sentences 134
Quotations, Remarks, &c., formally Introduced 138
The Chanting Service in the Liturgy 141
Terms in the Rule of Three 141
Concluding Remarks 141

SECT. IV. — THE PERIOD.

Complete and Independent Sentences 142
Headings, Subheads, Phrases in Titlepages, &c. 147

CONTENTS. IX

                Page
Names, Titles, and other Words, abbreviated 148
Marks or Figures used instead of Words 150
Letters used for Figures or Words 150

CHAP. III. — THE GRAMMATICAL AND RHETORICAL POINTS.

Introductory Observations 153

SECT. I. — NOTES OF INTERROGATION AND EXCLAMATION.

Remarks on the Notes of Interrogation and Exclamation . . 154
Expressions in the Form of Questions 155
Expressions indicating Passion or Emotion 159

SECT. II. — MARKS OF PARENTHESIS.

Observations on Parentheses, and Marks of Parenthesis . . . 167
Words thrown obliquely into the Body of a Sentence 168

SECT. III. — THE DASH.

Remarks on the Use and Abuse of the Dash 174
Broken and Epigrammatic Sentences 175
A Concluding Clause on which other Expressions depend . . 178
The Echo, or Words repeated Rhetorically 182
A Parenthesis coalescing with the Main Passage 186
Ellipsis of the Adverb " Namely," &c. 191
Subheads, &c., to Paragraphs 194
Omission of Letters, Figures, or Words 195

CHAP. IV. — LETTER, SYLLABIC, AND QUOTATION POINTS.

Page.
Introductory Observations 197

SECT. I. — THE APOSTROPHE.

Elision of Letters, or Shortening of Words 198
The Genitive or Possessive Case 204

SECT. II. — THE HYPHEN.

Remarks on the Uses of the Hyphen 208
Compound Words 209
Prefixes in Derivative Words 219
The Division of Words into Syllables, according to their Pronunciation 224
The Division of Words into Syllables, according to their Form, Derivation, or Meaning 225

SECT. III. — MARKS OF QUOTATION.

Words borrowed from a Speaker or an Author 228
One Quotation within Another 230
Extracts composed of Successive Paragraphs 232

CHAP. V. — MISCELLANEOUS MARKS.

Brackets, or Crotchets 235
A Comma Inverted; Two Commas 236
The Index, or Hand; Three Stars; the Caret; the Brace . . 237
Marks of Ellipsis; Leaders 238
Accents; Marks of Quantity; the Cedilla; the Tilde 239
Marks of Reference 240

CHAP. VI. — GENERAL EXERCISES.

	Page.
Introductory Observations	241
Pride and Humility, by Thomas Brown	242
Abou Ben Adhem, by Leigh Hunt	244
Panegyric on England, by Edward Everett	245
The Pen and the Press, by John Critchley Prince	247
A Taste for Reading, by George S. Hillard	248
Relative Perfection, by John James Tayler	250
Labor not Lost, by R. C. Trench	251
Ancient and Modern Writers, by Charles Sumner	252
The True Source of Reform, by E. H. Chapin	253
Great Men generally Good, by John Logan	254

APPENDIX.

Uses of Capital Letters	257
The First Word of a Book, Tract, &c.	258
The First Word after a Full Point	258
Appellations of God and Christ	259
Titles of Honor and Respect	261
Names of Persons, Places, &c.	262
Nouns and Adjectives derived from Proper Names	263
Words of Primary Importance	264
The Pronoun *I*, and the Interjection *O*	265
Commencement of Lines in Verse	266
Prosopopœia, or Personification	266
Quotations, Examples, &c.	267
Capitals used instead of Figures	268
Titlepages, Inscriptions, &c.	268

CONTENTS.

	Page.
ITALIC CHARACTERS	269
TERMS RELATING TO BOOKS	270
Captions, Subheads, Sideheads, and Running Titles	270
Signatures	271
Names of Various Sizes of Books	271
ABBREVIATIONS AND REPRESENTATIVE LETTERS	272
Various Modes of Forming Abbreviations	272
Table of Abbreviations	277
MEDICAL AND MATHEMATICAL SIGNS	301
ASTRONOMICAL CHARACTERS	302
The Twelve Signs of the Zodiac	302
The Planetary Signs	302
The Lunar Signs	302
Aspects of the Planets	302
HINTS ON PREPARING COPY, AND ON READING PROOFS	303
EXPLANATION OF PROOF-MARKS	316
SPECIMEN OF PROOF-SHEET	320
INDEX	323

ENGLISH PUNCTUATION.

CHAPTER I.

INTRODUCTION.

SECT. I.—THE IMPORTANCE AND USES OF CORRECT PUNCTUATION.

No one will hesitate to admit, that next in value to the capacity of discerning or discovering truth, and of feeling the blessed relations which we sustain to the Being who made us, and to our fellow-creatures, particularly those with whom we are more immediately connected, is the power. by which intelligence and emotion are communicated from one mind to another. By it the great and the gifted of past times have bequeathed to us many a rich legacy of thought and deed; and by it those of the present either re-create the old materials, or fashion new ones, for the delight and improvement of their own generation; and transmit to the future — to beings yet unborn — their treasures of wisdom, of genius, and of love. This power, it is needless to say, is language, oral and written, especially the latter.

But as oral speech has its tones and inflections, its pauses and its emphases, and other variations of voice, to give greater expression to the thoughts which spoken words represent, and to produce on the mind of the hearer a more rapid and intense impression than lifeless enunciation could effect; so written or printed language is usually accompanied by marks or points, to enable the reader to comprehend at a glance the precise and determinate sense of the author, — a sense which, without these marks, would in many instances be gathered only by an elaborate and painful process, and very often be misunderstood. It therefore obviously follows, that the art which serves to elucidate the meaning of a writer, to bring out his ideas with more facility, and to render his expressions a genuine transcript of the feelings and sentiments which he would convey to the hearts and the minds of others, is entitled to no small degree of attention.

Now, it is indisputable that Punctuation *does* conduce to make written language more effective, by exhibiting with greater precision and definiteness the ideas, feelings, and emotions of an author, than could be accomplished by a mass of words, however well chosen, if brought together without those peculiar marks which show the multifarious varieties of union or of separation existing in thought and expression. For what is Punctuation, and what its aim? It is the art of dividing a literary composition into sentences, and parts of sentences, by means of points, for the purpose of exhibiting the various combinations, connections, and dependencies of words. And what is this process but a means of facilitating that analysis and combination which must be made, consciously or unconsciously, before we can penetrate to the very core of an author's thoughts, and appropriate them as food for the life and growth of our own minds? We would not overrate the importance of Punctuation, or deny that many subjects are worthy of a higher regard, and have a more immediate and vital influence on the well-being of society. But we would emphatically say, that this subject ought to be understood by all who are led, by the bent of their tastes, the force of their genius, or their condition in life, to enter upon any of the walks of literature, whether they would tread an humble and a beaten track, or wander into paths adorned by flowers and fruit. It is related to philology and metaphysics, and indeed, more or less, to every science or art communicated by the instrumentality of written language. It is intimately connected with the principles of grammar; subservient to the purposes of syntax; essential to the clearing-up of ambiguities, which so often obscure composition; and useful to the more ready understanding even of those sentences whose construction is not liable to the charge of obscurity. By the omission or the improper insertion of points, not only would the beauties and elegances of literature, but even its advantages, be faintly discerned and enjoyed, except by the most attentive readers, or by men of superior taste and information: the sense of even the more simple and familiar class of productions — such as the narrative, the essay, or the epistle — would be liable to be misapprehended, or, at least, to be imperfectly understood. Indeed, the perusal of a single page of any work will bear testimony to the comparative value of a just punctuation. Nay, scarcely can a sentence be perused with satisfaction or interest, unless pointed with some degree of accuracy. The well-known speech of Norval, for instance, in the tragedy of " Douglas," may, by an erroneous use of the pauses, be delivered in such a manner as to pervert or destroy the meaning ; as, - -

> " My name is Norval on the Grampian hills.
> My father feeds his flock a frugal swain;
> Whose constant cares were to increase his store.
> . . . .
> We fought and conquered ere a sword was drawn.
> An arrow from my bow, had pierced their chief
> Who wore that day the arms which now I wear."

But the insertion of the right stops will restore the sense of these passages, and render them conformable to the conceptions of the dramatist:—

> "My name is Norval. On the Grampian hills
> My father feeds his flock; a frugal swain,
> Whose constant cares were to increase his store.
> . . . .
> We fought and conquered. Ere a sword was drawn,
> An arrow from my bow had pierced their chief,
> Who wore, that day, the arms which now I wear." *

Notwithstanding, however, its utility, Punctuation has not received that attention which its importance demands. Considered merely as the plaything of the pedant, or as the peculiar function of the printer, it is often neglected or perverted by those who have occasion to present to the eye either their own thoughts or the thoughts of others. The man of science, the mental philosopher, and the philologist seem to regard it as too

---

* In the note at the end of this section, page 18, will be found a few other instances of erroneous pointing, which, though in their nature sufficiently ludicrous, show in a forcible manner the necessity of paying a due regard to punctuation. Many happy illustrations of the importance of correct marks may also be seen in Day's valuable little work, entitled " Punctuation reduced to a System," pp. 33—45.

trifling, amid their grander researches into the laws of the universe, the internal operations of the human mind, and its external workings by means of language. The grammarian passes it by altogether unheeded, or lays down a few general and abstract principles; leaving the pupil to surmount the difficulties of the art as well as he may. The lawyer engrosses in a character which is perfectly legible; but, by its deficiency in sentential marks, it often proves, like the laws of which he is the expounder, " gloriously uncertain" as to the meaning intended to be expressed. The painter, the engraver, and the lithographer appear to set all rules at defiance, by either omitting the points or misplacing them, when required in certain departments of their work. The letter-writer, with his incessant and indiscriminate dashes, puts his friend, his beloved one, his agent, or his employer, to a *little* more trouble, in conning over his epistle, than is absolutely necessary. Even the author — who, of all writers, ought to be the most accurate — not unfrequently puts his manuscript into the printer's hands, either destitute of grammatical points, or so badly punctuated as to create a needless loss of time to the compositor.

But though an acquaintance with the principles of the art in question has been deemed the peculiar province of the printer, who might therefore be expected to have the requisite qualifications for the performance of his task; yet it must be admitted, that from the press are issued many books, grossly erroneous in sentential marks; and perhaps not a few, which, though distinguished for elegance of style, accuracy of orthography, or beauty of printing, are unworthy of being held up as models of good taste and judgment in the use of points. It is a fact well known to those connected with the press, that compositors in general have a very deficient knowledge of Punctuation, considered as a branch of science; and that they acquire what they do know of it as an art, chiefly by mechanical habit, or by the correction of innumerable blunders, marked on the proof-sheets.

To make these observations, however, without granting many exceptions, would savor more of the petulance of presumption than of the candor of true criticism. There are numerous masterpieces of composition, in which the writer, the compositor, and the corrector of the press, have, either separately or together, inserted points with taste and propriety.

But enough has been said to demonstrate the necessity for an increased attention to the subject, and to prove a very obvious, though not an acknowledged, truth, that the principles of Punctuation must be duly learned, before they can be understood, or brought into systematic and perfect use. The question, then, will naturally arise, How is the desired improvement to be effected? how are the theory and practice of the art to be attained? We answer, By the most simple means; by the very means which are so well adapted to other subjects of learning. Let Punctuation form a branch of academical instruction; let it be studied, after a competent knowledge of English etymology and syntax has been acquired; let the rules be thoroughly comprehended by the pupil, — be explained to him, if necessary, in the teacher's language, and re-explained by himself in his own words. Let him also write copious exercises, in order to bring into further play his judgment and taste; and let him present to his teacher these trials of his skill, to be examined and approved or corrected. By this means will he soon be capable of so punctuating his own compositions as to be read by others with ease, pleasure, and advantage.

This is an age of authors, as well as of readers. Young aspirants after fame, some of them of considerable merit, meet us at every step, and in every department of literature. But surely, if they are capable of enlightening the world by their wisdom, or dazzling it by their genius, *they* can have no difficulty in writing so as to be understood. If they have thoughts worthy of being communicated through the agency of the pen and the press, they surely cannot with justice regard it as any degradation of their powers to submit to the task of indicating, as accurately as possible, what they do really intend to say. If there is beauty in their style; if there is pathos in their sentiments; if there is moral and intellectual vigor in the thoughts that burn for utterance; if their discourse is calculated to refine the taste, to improve the heart, and ennoble the mind, of the reader, — surely they should be careful that *that* beauty be not marred, that *that* pathos be not unfelt, that *that* vigor be not weakened, that *that* discourse be not shorn of half its power over the character and happiness of others, from the petty motive of saving themselves the trouble of learning what, of all men, from the very nature of their pursuits, they are the best able and most bound to learn. Besides, it is worthy of remark, that, by habituating themselves to the practice of pointing, their attention will naturally be directed to clearness of thought, and accuracy of expression. They will be more apt to regard words as but of little value, except as representatives of ideas, and as an instrument by which these may gain access to the human soul. If involved in the difficulty of punctuating a badly formed sentence, such as the following, " God heapeth favors on his servants ever liberal and faithful," — supposing this to imply that the Divine Being is ever liberal and faithful, — they will almost necessarily be led to reconstruct it, that they may rid themselves of their perplexity, and leave no doubt as to the sense meant to be conveyed; for, beyond all question, facility in punctuation is generally in proportion to the perspicuity and the good arrangement of words. Let authors, therefore, turn a little of their attention to the elements of this art, trifling and undignified as it may seem to be. Let them not transfer to their printer that department of duty which as authors it is their own province to fill. With some few boasted exceptions, no doubt much overrated, neither compositors nor correctors of the press are immaculate; for they do not understand all the subjects treated of in books, and cannot with accuracy punctuate what they do not comprehend.

It was in bygone times a preliminary requisite, that printers should be acquainted with what are termed the learned languages. But though, in this age of a more general and superficial literature, a profound knowledge of Hebrew points, Greek accents, and Latin quantities, is no longer required, it is necessary that compositors be acquainted with the principles of their native tongue, and with the functions of the peculiar marks used for setting off sentences, clauses, and phrases. Were every author to write his work in a fair, legible character, and so punctuate his language as to convey the sense clearly and correctly, then might compositors act as mere machines, and " follow " their " copy." But, until writers for the press condescend to use the stops systematically and accurately, the humble workmen who put together the world-enlightening types must be more than unconscious machines: they must, to some degree, enter into the conceptions of those on whose works they are employed, and develop the sense of their manuscripts, with the greatest possible discrimination, by the help and service of the poor, despised, but useful handmaids, — the commas, the semicolons, and other little points. We know well the feeling which very naturally and properly exists in the minds of compositors, that the " copy " put into their hands should be prepared with an accuracy which would preclude the necessity, on their part, of losing time by pondering over the manuscript in order to render it intelligible to the reading public. But this we know also, that, in the actual state of things, the time thus apparently lost is, when employed aright, a comparative gain, by reason of the far greater consumption of unprofitable labor in the insertion and extraction of points, after the proof-sheet has been returned by the corrector of the press. If the manuscript be defective or erroneous in its sentential marks, the compositor must either take a little trouble in pointing it himself, or have it done for him afterwards by the proof-reader, to the serious diminution of his professional character, his good temper, and his weekly wages. But, further, we would ask, Is not the operative who comprehends the principles of his calling, — who really knows what he is about, —

a happier and a nobler being than he who works at mere random, and stumbles at every petty obstruction in his way? Does not his daily toil become a pleasure, when it brings into play the exercise of a fine taste and a cultivated understanding? Do not his very difficulties become a source of satisfaction, when he himself can solve them, without being forced for ever to ask the aid of his fellow-workmen, or to submit to the painful process of undoing what he has already done, — of altering and improving what he has ignorantly and blunderingly executed? Do not, indeed, these difficulties become less and less, the more frequently he is successful in removing them? Does he not, by his endeavors to perform his work in a skilful manner, acquire habits of discrimination, that will enable him, in cases at which others would fret and foam or idly stand, to see, as it were intuitively, the very thing required, and the mode in which it should be done? These questions may be asked in relation to manual labor of any kind. They may be asked, too, in respect to all the branches of work in which a compositor may be engaged. But they are put here chiefly in reference to his knowledge and appliance of the art of Punctuation; and we feel assured, that, if desirous of being able to insert points with skill and propriety, he will also aim to perform well all the duties pertaining to his sphere of toil. If, therefore, the compositor would lose as little as possible of that time which is so valuable to him; if he would have at his command greater pecuniary resources than he can have by ignorance of his art, or by habits of carelessness; if, by the exercise of his intellectual powers, he would deprive physical toil of no small share of its pain or lassitude,—let him, if now ignorant of the subject, never rest contented till he is able both to understand the principles on which Punctuation is based, and to bring them into full practice.

The remarks just made have the strongest claim on the attention of youths learning the art of type-setting; many of whom, stimulated by a love of change or by false views of independence, soon break loose from those steady and regular habits which are necessary for mastering the difficulties of any occupation; moving about from one employer to another, without having a disposition or sufficient time to attain a knowledge even of the first principles of the craft by which they are to earn a living. But if desirous of perfecting themselves in the various branches of typography, one of which we have shown to be the art of Punctuation, it is of the greatest moment that they resolve to remain with a person whom they can regard as a friend as well as an employer; and receive from him, or at their leisure hours from the study of books designed for the purpose, such instruction as will conduce to their improvement, and render them, when of age, competent to discharge, with honor to themselves and with satisfaction to others, the duties pertaining to their profession.

If a knowledge of Punctuation is admitted to be requisite to the setter of types, there will be the utmost reason for regarding it as indispensable to a reader of proof-sheets. Besides the multiform duties devolving on or expected from him,—of correcting and improving the work of compositors, which is seldom, if ever, a faithful representation of the "copy;" of rectifying the orthography of inexperienced writers, and drawing the attention of others to errors in grammar and construction, into which the most accurate will sometimes fall, — the professional corrector is generally required, in the existing state of authorship, to devote a great part of his attention to the proper insertion of points, and thus to present to the public eye in a readable condition what would otherwise be an ill-digested mass of letters and words. When it is considered that he has not unfrequently to perform this task amid doubts and difficulties arising from manuscript almost illegible, it will be seen how necessary it is for correctors of the press to possess that kind of knowledge which is so easily within their reach, and which at present forms an essential and a peculiar feature of their calling, — an accurate knowledge of the theory and practice of Punctuation. It would not be right to expect from them, even if they were better remunerated, perfect accuracy in their work; but, so long as they hold so responsible a situation, their ignorance of this branch of their profession should be regarded as inexcusable.

It may be, and has been, objected to the study of this art, that it is not subject to any fixed or determinate principles; that scarcely two writers follow the same mode of punctuating sentences. Where one author or printer uses a comma, another would insert a semicolon; and, where one thinks a semicolon ought to be employed, another prefers a colon, if not a comma. One teacher embarrasses the learner with an additional pause (the semicomma), by giving it "a local habitation and a name;" while a different one discards the colon altogether as a useless point. Some grammarians would unfeelingly lop off the dash, as an excrescence on a printed leaf; but others, again, are so partial to its form and use as to call in its aid on every possible occasion.

The objection has, on purpose, been strongly stated. But might not similar objections be adduced against the orthography, the etymology, and the syntax of the English language; against, indeed, the general principles of English Grammar? Might it not be demonstrated, that grammarians and lexicographers differ in spelling, in pronunciation, in the classification of the parts of speech, in modes of derivation and of construction, and in the position of relatives and adverbs? Might not a plausible treatise be written against grammatical principles, — as plausible, but just as illogical and unconvincing, as are the common and startling objections against a system of Punctuation? Might it not be shown, that Johnson and Lowth, Blair, Murray, and Crombie, have attacked the dicta of others, and have had their own attacked in turn? Might it not be proved, that kings and queens, statesmen and historians, poets and essayists, nay, even professed grammarians, have written false English, and violated the most generally acknowledged canons of syntax? But surely it would not be a fair conclusion to draw, from this diversity of opinion and from the employment of inelegant or incongruous English, that there are no determinate principles in the language; that there is no authority to which an appeal can be made; that authors may send forth their compositions into the world, without any regard whatever to law or usage. Neither is it, we contend, a legitimate conclusion, that, because some writers disagree in their system of pauses, and others point their works at random, therefore Punctuation is too trifling to demand serious attention, — too unsettled to be treated as a branch of science, or practised with any degree of uniformity as an art.

The writer, then, of the present work can have no hesitation in asserting, that the art of Punctuation is not more varied or changeable in its character than that of composition ; and that its *essential* principles are as fixed and determinate as those canons in syntax, which, though sometimes violated by our best authors, are universally acknowledged to be indisputable. Diversities in the application of these principles will no more prove that modes of punctuating sentences are altogether arbitrary, than diversities in styles of composition will demonstrate that the labors of grammarians to ascertain the laws of language must go for nought, and that every writer may take whatever liberties he chooses, in opposition to reputable usage. As various modes of expressing a thought may be justifiably used, when they do not affect the principles of grammar; though, as respects beauty, elegance, or force, one mode may be preferable to another: so also different methods of pointing a sentence may be allowable, when they do not violate the fundamental laws of Punctuation; though they may be objectionable or otherwise, just as they are less or more calculated to please the eye, and bring out the sense of the passage.

Perhaps one reason why Punctuation has been generally undervalued or neglected is, that grammarians have devoted so little of their attention to the subject. The books, too, professedly written to elucidate its principles, are, so far as have been observed by the writer of the present work, deficient either in an explanation of exceptions and difficulties; in examples and exercises; or in rules and remarks, illustrative of the diversified functions of the notes of interrogation and exclamation, the marks of parenthesis, the dash, the apostrophe, the hyphen, and the quotation-marks. For though these may be regarded as minor points, when compared to others of a more grammatical nature, yet they occur so frequently that no work on Punctuation which passes them over with only a few brief and hasty remarks can be considered practically and generally useful.

Another cause of the neglect and misapprehension to which correct Punctuation is subject, arises probably from the false light in which it is regarded. Many persons seem to consider points as being the representatives *only* of rhetorical pauses; as showing merely those places, in the utterance of a composition, at which time for breathing is required; as indicating the definite proportions of the stops made in reading aloud. Hence not a few writers and authors point their manuscript exactly as they would recite it, in accordance with their power of enunciation, with the quickness or slowness of their perceptions, or with their particular views as to the influence of pauses on the minds of their hearers. Elocutionists themselves disagree in respect to the precise cessations of the voice which should be made in delivery. Granting, however, that there were no differences of opinion on this subject, and that all good speakers would make the same pauses in the reading of any given discourse, it might even then be easily shown, that the points in common use would not be sufficient for rhetorical purposes; and that, if thus employed, they would tend, by the necessity of perpetually repeating them, and the consequent minute separations of words and phrases, rather to perplex the judgment of the reader, than to facilitate his comprehension of the writer's meaning. Let us suppose, for instance, that the following passage were so punctuated as to correspond in some measure with the peculiar notation adopted by Mr. Vandenhoff, in his excellent work on the "Art of Elocution," pp. 73, 74, and with the real pauses demanded by an accurate and effective delivery, it would stand thus: —

"Men of superior genius; while they see the rest of mankind, painfully struggling, to comprehend obvious truths; glance, themselves, through the most remote consequences; like lightning, through a path, that cannot be traced; they see the beauties of nature, with light and warmth, and paint them forcibly, without effort; as the morning sun, does the scenes he rises upon; and, in several instances, communicate to objects, a morning freshness, and unaccountable lustre, that is not seen in the creations of nature. The poet, the statuary, the painter, have produced images, that left nature far behind."

But let the same sentence be punctuated by the rules of grammar, and not by those of rhetoric, and with the sole view of indicating the sense of the passage, it would appear as follows: —

"Men of superior genius, while they see the rest of mankind painfully struggling to comprehend obvious truths, glance themselves through the most remote consequences, like lightning through a path that cannot be traced. They see the beauties of nature with light and warmth, and paint them forcibly without effort, as the morning sun does the scenes he rises upon; and, in several instances, communicate to objects a morning freshness and unaccountable lustre that is not seen in the creations of nature. The poet, the statuary, the painter, have produced images that left nature far behind."

By comparing the two modes of punctuation adopted in the passage under notice, — namely, the rhetorical or close, and the grammatical or free, — it will be obvious, that, while the latter tends to elucidate the aim of the writer, and to some extent assist the delivery, the former throws nothing but obscurity on his meaning; and, though showing the various pauses of the voice with greater accuracy, imparts no information whatever on matters which in delivery are as important, — the inflections, the intonations, the emphases, the calm, equable flow, or the wild torrent, of a good reader or an eloquent speaker.

That grammatical and rhetorical punctuation are not one and the same, is acknowledged by the best elocutionists. Thus the writer just quoted says,* that "the grammatical pauses, which are addressed to the eye of the reader, are insufficient for the speaker, who addresses himself to the understanding ' through the porches of the ear.' ... We have, therefore, rhetorical pauses, which are independent of, though consistent with and assistant to, the grammatical pauses."

It must, however, be admitted that some of the points — namely, the mark of admiration and of exclamation, the parenthesis, and the dash — partake more of a rhetorical character than the common and principal points; and in this light we will consider them in the following pages. But, on the whole, it will be found that the art of Punctuation is founded rather on grammar than on rhetoric; that its chief aim is to unfold the meaning of sentences, with the least trouble to the reader; and that it aids the delivery, only in so far as it tends to bring out the sense of the writer to the best advantage.

* "Art of Elocution," p. 63.

INTRODUCTION.

NOTES

ILLUSTRATING THE VALUE OF CORRECT PUNCTUATION.

1. The following request is said to have been made at church: "A sailor going to sea, his wife desires the prayers of the congregation for his safety." But, by an unhappy transposition of the comma, the note was thus read: "A sailor, going to see his wife, desires the prayers of the congregation for his safety."

2. A blacksmith, passing by a hair-dresser's shop, observed in the window an unpointed placard, which he read as follows: —

>"What do you think? —
>I'll shave you for nothing,
>And give you some drink."

The son of Vulcan, with a huge black beard on his chin and a little spark in his throat, considered the opportunity too good to be lost. He accordingly entered; and, after the operation had been duly performed, asked, with the utmost *sang froid*, for the liquor. But the shaver of beards demanded payment; when the smith, in a stentorian voice, referred him to his own placard, which the barber very good-humoredly produced, and read thus: —

>"What! do you think
>I'll shave you for nothing,
>And give you some drink?"

3. Another example of the ludicrous will tend still better to show the value of just punctuation: —

>"Every lady in this land
>Hath twenty nails upon each hand;
>Five and twenty on hands and feet.
>And this is true, without deceit."

If the present points be removed, and others inserted as follow the true meaning of the passage will at once appear: —

>"Every lady in this land
>Hath twenty nails: upon each hand
>Five; and twenty on hands and feet.
>And this is true, without deceit."

Sect. II. — Plan of the Work, and Definitions of the Terms used.

In the preceding section, Punctuation was defined to be the art of dividing a written or printed discourse into sentences, and parts of sentences, by means of certain marks called *points*, for the purpose of exhibiting the various combinations, connections, and dependencies of words. Its uses also were found to consist primarily in developing, with as much clearness as possible, the sense and the grammatical constructions of a composition; and secondarily in showing, to some extent, the various pauses which are requisite for an accurate reading or delivery.

We now proceed to enter on the practical mode of attaining the information required; and, for the sake of order and of clearness of conception, it is proposed to regard the subject as separable into branches. We will treat, in the first place, of the marks pertaining to SENTENCES, which may be divided into two kinds, — the common or principal points, which are chiefly of a *grammatical* nature; and the less common but equally necessary points, which, occurring as they often do in animated composition, and being used for the twofold purpose of bringing out the sense and aiding the delivery, are entitled to be spoken of as both *grammatical and rhetorical.* We will, lastly, speak of other marks, which either bear a more intimate relation to LETTERS and SYLLABLES than to words and sentences, or are of a varied and mixed character; and hence these may be termed *letter, syllabic, quotation,* and *miscellaneous points.*

Before, however, commencing the study of the laws which regulate the use of these marks, the learner should know at least as much of grammar as will enable him to distinguish, with tolerable accuracy, the different parts of speech into which language is resolvable. Besides this, it is essential that he be in some measure acquainted with the various kinds of sentences, their usual constructions, and the mode in which they may be analyzed into their component parts. Taking, therefore, for granted that he is not entirely ignorant of the principles of the English language, we will intrude into the province of the grammarian, only so far as may be necessary for the student to form correct notions of the meaning of a few terms, relating to sentences, which will frequently occur in the rules and remarks, and without a due knowledge of which he would be unable fully to comprehend the laws of Punctuation. The terms alluded to, then, are defined and illustrated as follow:—

DEFINITIONS.

I. A SENTENCE is an assemblage of words, so arranged as to form a proposition, or two or more related propositions; making, directly or indirectly, complete sense.

II. A SIMPLE SENTENCE expresses only a simple proposition. It consists of one nominative, subject, or thing spoken of, and of a single predicate, or affirmation concerning the subject; as,—

1. Calumny | destroys reputation.   2. The Creator | is good.
3. Kings | reign.

In these propositions, the words that precede the perpendicular lines are the subjects or nominatives, and those that follow are the predicates.

A logician would define a proposition by stating it to be a sentence consisting of a subject; of the copula, or sign of predication; and of the predicate. But the explanation given will be found sufficiently correct for grammatical purposes.

III. A COMPOUND SENTENCE consists of two or more simple sentences in combination, and therefore contains more than one nominative and finite verb, either expressed or understood; as, —

1. Virtue refines the affections; but vice debases them.
2. To err is human; to forgive, divine.
3. Age, though it lessens the enjoyment of life, increases our desire of living.

That these sentences are compound will be seen at once by resolving each into two simple sentences: " Virtue refines the affections. Vice, on the other hand, debases the affections." — "To err is human. To forgive is divine." — "Age lessens the enjoyment of life. It, however, increases our desire of living."

IV. MEMBERS. — When a sentence consists of several clauses, admitting of a union of some and a separation of others, those which are combined may together be called *members*; as, —

The ox knoweth his owner, | and the ass his 'master's crib: | but Israel doth not know; | my people do not consider.

In this example there are four clauses: the first two forming one member; the latter two, another member.

In many books, however, the word *member* is used in its primary and more extensive sense, as denoting any portion of a sentence, whether a single clause, a phrase, or a word.

V. A CLAUSE is a simple sentence, or part of a sentence, united to another, and contains a nominative and a finite verb, either expressed or understood; as, —

1. That high moral excellence is true greatness | cannot be denied.
2. Candor is a quality | which all admire.
3. Though he slay me, | yet will I trust in him.
4. The smile of gayety may be assumed, | while the heart aches within.
5. Gentleness often disarms the fierce, | and melts the stubborn.

When the subject of a proposition is itself a sentence, or contains a finite verb, as in No. 1, above, it is called a *nominative clause;* when a clause begins with a relative pronoun, as the last in No. 2, it is termed a *relative clause;* when clauses are introduced by corresponding words, as "though" and "yet" in No. 3, they are named *correlative;* when one clause is subject to another for completeness of sense, as those in No. 4, they are called *dependent;* and when one is simply added to another, *co-ordinate or consecutive clauses,* as exemplified in No. 5.

VI. A PHRASE consists of at least two words, being a form of expression, or part of a sentence, which has no finite verb, expressed or understood; and which therefore does not of itself make any assertion, or form complete sense; as, —

1. In haste.
2. Of all our senses.
3. By infinite wisdom.
4. Awkward in person.
5. Studious of praise.
6. Useful to artists.
7. To confess the truth.
8. Law and order.
9. A man of wisdom.

In works on grammar, these and similar expressions are usually called *imperfect phrases;* but the definition just given will preclude the necessity of using the epithet. An article or any unemphatic word and a noun, or the simple infinitive, — as, *a book, the man, to love,* — will, to avoid circumlocution, be treated in the following pages, not as a phrase, but as a word.

A nominative phrase consists of several words, standing as the subject of a proposition. An adjectival, a participial, a prepositional phrase, are phrases severally beginning with an adjective, a participle, or a preposition. Those phrases, however, which, though commencing with a preposition, are used instead of single adverbs, are commonly spoken of as adverbial phrases, as, "*In* haste," for *hastily.*

VII. TERMS and EXPRESSIONS. — To avoid repetition, a word or a phrase is sometimes called *a term;* and a phrase or a clause, *an expression.*

VIII. PARENTHETICAL WORDS or EXPRESSIONS are intermediate words, phrases, or clauses, which, though required by the sense of the passage in which they occur, are not essential to the construction. Of these a fuller description, with illustrations, will be given under the rule which treats of the mode of punctuating them.

IX. CORRELATIVES. — When two words express reciprocal relations, or correspond one to another, they are termed *correlative words;* as, "Pompey was not *so* brave a general *as* Cæsar." — "*Though* the man was intellectually rich, *yet* he was morally poor."

Correlatives may be nouns, adjectives, or adverbs; but those to which reference will be made in this work are chiefly of a conjunctive nature, denoting relations of various kinds, — sometimes that of connection, dependence, or consequence; and sometimes of comparison, similitude, or equality.

X. APPOSITION. — Nouns, pronouns, or phrases, or a noun or pronoun and a phrase, are said to be in apposition, when put in the same case, and signifying the same thing, or when one is used as explanatory of the other; as, " The river Thames."

XI. A SERIES denotes a succession of three or more words, phrases, or clauses, joined in construction; as, —

1. The hermit's life is private, calm, devotional, and contemplative.
2. Fire of imagination, strength of mind, and firmness of soul, are rare gifts.
3. God's love watcheth over all, provideth for all, maketh wise adaptations for all.

The first example exhibits a series of words; the second, of phrases; the third, of clauses. What are termed by elocutionists the members of a series will in this work be called *particulars*.

XII. A COMPOUND WORD consists of two or more simple or primitive words; as, —

1. Fireside.
2. Nevertheless.
3. Self-conceit.
4. Fellow-workman.

The simple words in compounds may, in general, be known from their being separately current in the language. For the sake of brevity, they are sometimes called *simples* or *primitives*.

The term DERIVATIVE is restricted to a compound word, the portions of which are not each separately used in English; as, *manly, excitement, consciousness, generalization: prospectus, circumstance, philosopher, theology*.

XIII. The CONSTRUCTION of a sentence is the mode in which its materials — its words, phrases, and clauses — are combined and arranged. When two or more phrases or expressions qualify others, or are qualified by them; when they act as nominatives to the same verb; when they govern the same words or phrases, or are governed by the same verbs, participles, or prepositions, — they are said to be in the same construction.

After the pupil has acquired a knowledge of the meaning of the terms just explained, or revived the impressions which he had previously received from his study of syntactical principles, he should state, in his own words, the nature and object of Punctuation, and then analyze the following extracts, or any other piece of composition, into sentences, and their various parts:—

EXERCISE.

ATHENS.—If we consider merely the subtlety of disquisition, the force of imagination, the perfect energy and elegance of expression, which characterize the great works of Athenian genius, we must pronounce them intrinsically most valuable. But what shall we say when we reflect that from hence have sprung, directly or indirectly, all the noblest creations of the human intellect; that from hence were the vast accomplishments and the brilliant fancy of Cicero, the withering fire of Juvenal, the plastic imagination of Dante, the humor of Cervantes, the comprehension of Bacon, the wit of Butler, the supreme and universal excellence of Shakspeare? All the triumphs of truth and genius over prejudice and power, in every country and in every age, have been the triumphs of Athens. Wherever a few great minds have made a stand against violence and fraud, in the cause of liberty and reason, there has been her spirit in the midst of them, inspiring, encouraging, consoling,—by the lonely lamp of Erasmus, by the restless bed of Pascal, in the tribune of Mirabeau, in the cell of Galileo, on the scaffold of Sidney. But who shall estimate her influence on private happiness? Who shall say how many thousands have been made wiser, happier, and better by those pursuits in which she has taught mankind to engage; to how many the studies which took their rise from her have been wealth in poverty, liberty in bondage, health in sickness, society in solitude? Her power is, indeed, manifested at the bar, in the senate, in the field of battle, in the schools of philosophy. But these are not her glory. Wherever literature consoles sorrow, or assuages pain; wherever it brings gladness to eyes which fail with wakefulness and tears, and ache for the dark house and the long sleep,—there is exhibited, in its noblest form, the immortal influence of Athens.

The dervise, in the Arabian tale, did not hesitate to abandon to his comrade the camels with their load of jewels and gold, while he retained the casket of that mysterious juice which enabled him to behold at one glance all the hidden riches of the universe. Surely it is no exaggeration to say, that no external advantage is to be compared with that purification of the intellectual eye which gives us to contemplate the infinite wealth of the mental world; all the hoarded treasures of its primeval dynasties, all the shapeless ore of its yet unexplored mines. This is the gift of Athens to man. Her freedom and her power have, for more than twenty centuries, been annihilated; her people have degenerated into timid slaves; her language, into a barbarous jargon; her temples have been given up to the successive depredations of Romans, Turks, and Scotchmen: but her intellectual empire is imperishable. And when those who have rivalled her greatness shall have shared her fate; when civilization and knowledge shall have fixed their abode in distant continents; when the sceptre shall have passed away from England; when, perhaps, travellers from distant regions shall in vain labor to decipher on some mouldering pedestal the name of our proudest chief,— shall hear savage hymns chanted to some misshapen idol over the ruined dome of our proudest temple, and shall see a single naked fisherman wash his nets in the river of the ten thousand masts,— her influence and her glory will still survive, fresh in eternal youth, exempt from mutability and decay, immortal as the intellectual principle from which they derived their origin, and over which they exercise their control. — T. B. MACAULAY: *Critical and Miscellaneous Essays*, vol. iii. pp. 402, 403.

THE VOCATION OF POETRY. — It is the high and glorious vocation of Poesy as well to make our own daily life and toil more beautiful and holy to us by the divine ministerings of love, as to render us swift to convey the same blessing to our brother. Poesy is love's chosen apostle, and the very almoner of God. She is the home of the outcast, and the wealth of the needy. For her the hut becomes a palace, whose halls are guarded by the gods of Phidias, and kept peaceful by the maid-mothers of Raphael. She loves better the poor wanderer whose bare feet know by heart the freezing stones of the pavement, than the delicate maiden for whose dainty soles Brussels and Turkey have been overcareful; and I doubt not but some remembered scrap of childish song hath often been a truer alms than all the benevolent societies could give. — J. R. LOWELL: *Conversations, &c.*, p. 133.

CHAPTER II.

THE GRAMMATICAL POINTS.

In accordance with the plan proposed in the last section, this chapter will be devoted to the consideration of the principal sentential marks, namely, —

1. The COMMA . . . . [,]
2. The SEMICOLON . . . . [;]
3. The COLON . . . . [:]
4. The PERIOD . . . . [.]

The Comma marks the smallest grammatical division of a sentence, and usually represents the shortest pause; the Semicolon and the Colon separate those portions which are less connected than those divided by commas, and admit each of a greater pause; and the Period is, what its name denotes, a full stop, which commonly terminates a sentence.

REMARK.

The names of the points have been borrowed by grammarians from the terms which rhetoricians employed to indicate the various kinds of sentences, and the parts of which they consist. Thus the Period signified a complete circuit of words; a sentence, making, from its commencement to its close, full and perfect sense. The Colon was the greatest member or division of a period or sentence; and the Semicolon, the greatest division of a colon; while the Comma indicated a smaller segment of the period, — the least constructive part of a sentence.

Sect. I. — THE COMMA.

The COMMA [,] marks the smallest grammatical division in written or printed language, and commonly represents the shortest pause in reading or delivery.

REMARKS.

a. Agreeably to the principles contended for in the Introduction, it will be noticed that the comma is here said, not to mark the smallest segment of a composition, but only the least *grammatical* division ; that is, the least portion into which a sentence can be divided, when regard is had to the sense, and not to the delivery. But many sentences do not at all admit of being divided grammatically; as, " The great use of books is to rouse us to thought;" though, when considered in a rhetorical or elocutionary light, they should be separated into parts, or groups of words, as in reading the example just given : " The great use of books | is | to rouse us | to thought."

b. It is usual for grammarians to say, that the comma represents the shortest pause, and that that pause is equal to the time required for counting *one;* but the remark admits of so many exceptions as to be without any practical value. Numerous instances occur in which the comma is so far from indicating the shortest pause, that a cessation of the voice equal to the time of counting *one, two,* if not *three,* is demanded both by the nature of the sentiment and the construction of the language; as, for instance, after the words " vice " and "undertake " in the following sentences: " Virtue is always advantageous; *vice,* never." — " Nations, like men, fail in nothing which they boldly *undertake,* when sustained by virtuous purpose and firm resolution." In other instances, the comma does not exhibit any pause whatever, but merely the grammatical division, as in the expression, " Yes, sir ; " where, in common or unemphatic discourse, no pause can be made between the words.

c. On this subject all *elocutionists* are agreed. Mr. Maglathlin, in the " National Speaker," p. 30, says that " the comma occurs sometimes where there should be no pause in reading or speaking ; nor can the length of any required stop be inferred with much certainty from the common stop-mark used." Dr. Mandeville, in his " Elements of Reading and Oratory," p. 32, remarks that "the comma does not necessarily represent a pause;" that "it suspends the voice, in unimpassioned reading or speaking, sufficiently long to draw breath;" but that, "under the influence of emotion, its time is indefinite." And the celebrated Walker, in "Rhetorical Grammar," p. 36 (Boston edition, 1814), when speaking of all the points, admits that "these marks sufficiently answer the purposes of written language, by keeping the members of sentences from running into each other, and producing ambiguity; but, when we regard them as guides to pronunciation, they fail us at almost every step."

RULE I.

Two Words, of the same Part of Speech, connected by the Conjunctions AND, OR, NOR.

Two words, belonging to the same part of speech, or used as such, when closely connected by one of the conjunctions *and*, *or*, *nor*, are not separated by a comma from each other.

EXAMPLES.

1. Pay supreme and undivided homage to goodness and truth.
2. Grand ideas and principles elevate or ennoble the mind.
3. Benefits should be long and gratefully remembered.
4. Virtue or vice predominates in every man and woman.
5. Some monks may be said to be neither of nor in the world.
6. The necessity and the use of physic have been much exaggerated.
7. It is natural to compassionate those who are suffering and alone.

REMARKS.

a. In these examples, it will be seen that the comma is regarded as inadmissible, not only between two words united by a conjunction, but also *after* them. Here no point should be used, except when they come at the end of a clause or sentence, or form such phrases as, from their construction with others, require to be punctuated; as, "To the intelligent and *virtuous*, old age presents a scene of tranquil enjoyments."

b. Some writers distinguish two connected prepositions by the insertion of commas, and would point the fifth example thus: " Some monks may be said to be neither *of*, nor *in*, the world." But there seems to be no valid reason for deviating from the rule; though, when prepositions are removed from, and at the same time connected with, each other, and are dependent on one and the same term (as in the sentence we are just writing, and as in the eighth example under Rule V.), a comma is required after each to bring out the sense.

c. By referring to p. 22, Definition VI., it will be found that the insertion of an article between connected words, as in the sixth example, does not at all affect the validity of the rule. — In the seventh example, the words united by the conjunction are not of the same part of speech, unless the phrase be treated elliptically, so as to mean "suffering and *being* alone;" but instances of this or a similar kind are obviously subject to the same principle as words of one sort.

d. When the first of two connected words is qualified by a preceding adjective or adverb which is inapplicable to the second, or when the latter is followed by a term not belonging to the former, a comma is usually required before the conjunction; as, " Donations will be *thankfully* received, and applied to the benefit of the suffering poor." — " 'Twas certain he could write, and cipher *too*."

e. The comma, however, is not inserted between the conjoined words, when the latter is immediately preceded by a qualifying or governing word, and both refer to one and the same term; as, " The world has confidence in the judgment and *wise* conduct of a truly honest man."

f. When two phrases, the former ending and the other beginning with a noun, are joined by the conjunction *and*, *or*, or *nor*, they may be separated by a comma; as, " Integrity of *understanding*, and *nicety* of discernment, were not allotted in a less proportion to Dryden than to Pope." — " So shall sweet *thoughts*, and *thoughts* sublime, my constant inspiration be." The comma is also placed after the last phrase, when, as in these examples, it relates, equally with the first, to the remainder of the sentence.

g. If, however, the first phrase is preceded by one of the correlatives *both*, *either*, *neither*, or the second by an article, or when the phrases are introduced into the body of a sentence necessarily requiring the insertion of commas, they should be left unpointed; as, "*Both* integrity of understanding *and* nicety of discernment were allotted in a no less proportion," &c. — " Man is the child of God and *the* heir of immortality." — " As we do, and we must as Protestants, consider

Romanism a false and vicious *system of religion* or *form of Christianity*, whatever we can lawfully and morally do to stay its progress, we not only have a right, but it is our duty, to do." In the last example, the two Italicized phrases are not separated by a comma, because the advantage of this mode of pointing in a more simply constructed sentence would be counterbalanced here by the disadvantages resulting from all the phrases being set off alike.

h. When the second of two words, united by the conjunction *and* or *or*, is elliptical, or is inserted as an after-thought or for the sake of emphasis, it may be pointed off by commas; as, "A sense of personal propriety would often interrupt, *and exclude*, an imputation of unworthy motives to those who hold opinions opposite to our own:" the sense being, "would interrupt, *if it would not exclude*, an imputation," &c.; or "would interrupt, *and indeed exclude*." The awkwardness of the punctuation, which forms an exception to the rule, might usually be avoided by a happier construction of such sentences.

i. When the conjunction *or* stands between two nouns, or between a noun and a phrase, which are synonymous, or of which the latter is explanatory of the former, they may be separated by a comma from each other; as, "The dwelling of Norma was not unaptly compared to the eyry of the ospray, or *sea-eagle*." If the explanatory term is intermediate or parenthetical, a comma should be placed after each of the terms; as, "Sin, or *moral evil*, should excite the greatest abhorrence."—See Rule VIII.

j. Some punctuators would apply the preceding remark as a rule to all instances in which one of two words, coupled by the conjunction *or*, is explanatory of the other. In nouns, we think, the comma is usually required, to show that the terms, which might otherwise be regarded as significant of two ideas or things, are designed to represent only one and the same; but the pointing of adjectives and adverbs similarly situated would, in many cases, tend, by the breaking-up of the connection, to confuse, instead of assisting, the reader. Besides, it should be remembered that qualifying words are seldom, if ever, perfectly synonymous; and that, even if they were exactly of the same signification, the omission of the commas could scarcely affect the sense. For instance, this sentence, "He who is devoutly or piously disposed to God is also benignant or kind to men," is as easily understood as if it were punctuated, "He who is devoutly, or piously, disposed to God is also benignant, or kind, to men;" and, in the unpointed form, is more agreeable to the eye.

TWO CONJOINED WORDS.

ORAL EXERCISES.

After describing the nature and uses of the comma, as mentioned in page 27, state the first Rule, and assign the reason why the connected words in the following sentences are unpointed :—

Liberty and eloquence have been united in all ages.
Some children learn early to sing and to dance.
We often see rank or riches preferred to merit or talent.
Let us cherish an earnest and a reverential love of truth.
The liberal arts soften and harmonize the temper.
An unjust merchant is neither loved nor respected.
Be vitally and practically interested in the well-being of all.
Let nothing be done insincerely or hypocritically.
Let neither indolence nor vice canker the promise of the heart.
Within and without us are many foes to rectitude.

According to Remarks in pages 28—30, state the reasons for the omission or the insertion of commas between conjoined words in the following sentences :—

The youth wrote letters both to and concerning the lady.
Socrates was a virtuous and a wise man.
A convenient spot, and surprise, effected his purpose.
The prophet went, and addressed the people.
He, and he only, is worthy of our supreme affections.
Piety and unsullied virtue are venerated even by the wicked.
Money is the bane of bliss, and source of woe.
Have both soundness of faith and activity of benevolence.
Neither purity of aim nor goodness of deed was attributed to him.
Regard the rights of persons and the rights of property.
It may, and must, exist under the circumstances of the case.
Would you escape, and live; remain, or die? Speak, or perish.
The laverock, or lark, is distinguished for its singing.
Parenthetical or intermediate words are often used.

EXERCISE TO BE WRITTEN.

Write the following sentences, and punctuate those only which, agreeably to the Remarks, should have commas :—

An ellipsis or omission of words is found in all kinds of composition. (Remarks *d* and *i*.)

How many a knot of mystery and misunderstanding would be untied by one word spoken in simple and confiding truth of heart!

A distinction ought to be made between fame and true honor (Remark e.)

The balmy influences of neither sea nor sky could revive or restore him.

Refinement of mind and clearness of thinking usually result from grammatical studies. (Remark f.)

The greatest genius is never so great as when it is chastised and subdued by the highest reason.

In composition there is a transposed or inverted order of words, as well as a convcutional or common arrangement. (Remark j.)

The first end to which all wisdom or knowledge ought to be employed is to illustrate the wisdom and goodness of God.

Morality and religion itself is degraded by the use of unmeaning terms. (Remark d.)

Is it sickness or selfishness that spreads most misery through our homes?

A quickness of observation and an ingenuousness of character are often found in very young children. (Rule, and Remarks c, g.)

The Greek and Roman writers were once understood and relished in a remarkable degree.

Some have neither the resolution nor the power of carrying their projects to a completion. (Rule, and Remarks c, g.)

Pope examined lines and words with minute and punctilious observation.

The nineteenth century has been and is a time of extraordinary mental activity. (Remark h.)

I would calmly and humbly submit myself to the good and blessed will of God.

Let us greet and take by the hand those who were our youthful companions. (Remark d.)

The human heart beats quick at the sight or hearing of courageous and disinterested deeds.

The senses or sensibility of one body may be radically more acute than those of another. (Remark i.)

The most ferocious conflicts have been brightened by examples of magnanimous and patriotic virtue.

It was the greatest act ever done either by or for human beings. (Rule, and Remark b.)

Whenever, therefore, we divide Christianity into doctrines of faith and doctrines of practice, we must remember that the division is one of our own fabrication. (Rule, and last portion of Remark g.)

RULE II.

Two Words, of the same Part of Speech, not connected by a Conjunction.

Two words, of the same part of speech and in the same construction, if used without a conjunction between them, are separated from each other by a comma.

EXAMPLES.

1. Lend, lend your wings.
2. The dignity of a man consists in thought, intelligence
3. Can flattery soothe the dull, cold ear of death?
4. The discipline of suffering nourishes, invigorates virtue.
5. We are fearfully, wonderfully made.
6. Their search extends along, around the path.
7 Never was beheld a child fairer, more beautiful.

REMARKS.

a. The adverbs *more* and *most,* the former of which occurs in the seventh example, are considered here as united with the adjectives or the adverbs which they qualify. Thus, "more beautiful" is equivalent to the single but antiquated word *beautifuller.*

b. Besides the comma inserted between two nouns, or between two words equivalent to nouns, the same point is put after the last, when it does not end a sentence or a clause; as, "Thought, *thought,* is the fundamental distinction of mind." — "Reason, *virtue,* answer one great aim." — "The earth is filled with the labors, the *works,* of the dead." In these and similar instances, the comma is required to show that both nouns are equally related to what follows.

c. But the comma should be omitted after the second of the nouns, if it alone is connected in sense with the last portion of the clause; as, "The miseries of war bear the impress of cruelty, of *hardness* of heart."

d. Strict accuracy seems to require the insertion of a comma after the last of the governing and qualifying words in the examples under the rule; namely, after "lend," "cold," "invigorates," "wonderfully," "around." But this mode of punctuating is opposed to the most reputable usage, and is seldom needed to bring out the sense; not to mention the uncouth appearance which *modifying* or *governing* words have when standing alone, or in disruption from the context:

as, "All great works of genius come from deep, *lonely*, thought." Contrast the sentence, thus pointed, with "All great works of genius come from deep, *lonely* thought," and the superiority of the latter form will be obvious.

e. When, however, the adjectives or adverbs are used to qualify a word that precedes them, a comma should be placed after the second, if the clause is unfinished; as, "The world that is outward, *material*, is the shadow of that which is spiritual." A comma should also be placed after the second of two governing words, when they precede, not a single word, but a phrase or clause; as, "To deny ourselves is to deny, *to renounce*, whatever interferes with our convictions of right."

f. The comma should be omitted between two adjectives, when the first qualifies the second adjective and a noun; as, "The emperor possessed a beautiful *white horse;*" that is, the emperor had a white horse that was beautiful. Were a comma placed between the adjectives, the sense would be that he possessed a horse that was beautiful *and* white.

g. When two adjectives that are not synonymous precede a noun, and convey only one idea, they are treated as a compound epithet, and united by a hyphen; as, "The maidens danced amid the *festal-sounding* shades."

h. If two nouns are used as a compound, whether so written or not, or if the former partakes of the nature of an adjective, they are not separated by a comma; as, "*Walter Scott* ranks high as a *fiction-writer.*" — "Ward Room, Franklin Schoolhouse, Washington Street." Words similar to those mentioned in this and the preceding remark will be explained under the "Hyphen."

i. When a word iterated is the resumption of a sentiment broken off, a dash is used before the repetition, instead of a comma; as, "But I fear — I fear Richard hardly thought the terms proposed were worthy of his acceptance." The punctuation of broken sentences will be more fully treated of under the "Dash."

j. A comma may be put after two adverbs, or after an adverb repeated, as well as between them, when they qualify a clause; as, "Verily, *verily*, I say unto you." But when one adverb is followed by another, the former qualifying the latter, no comma is admissible; as, "The part was *remarkably well* performed."

k. The last of two verbs, participles, or prepositions, if used without governing the words that follow them, is set off with a comma; as, "On, *on*, when honor calls."

l. It not unfrequently happens, that two prepositions or conjunctions come together, without requiring any separation by a marked pause; as, "He walks *up towards* the hill." — "The pupil of a docile disposition not only loves, *but also* venerates, his preceptor." In respect, however, to the former example, it may be observed that the first preposition is not in construction with the second, but forms part of the verb "walk," which is compound, and would in some languages be expressed by a single word; and, as to the latter, that the conjunctions "but" and "also" are so closely connected in sense as to be inseparable in construction.

ORAL EXERCISES.

Explain how Rule II. *requires the insertion of commas between words of the same part of speech in the following sentences:* —

Nothing is so intelligible as sincere, disinterested love.
Sound, sound the tambourine! Strike, strike the mandaline!
Men live abroad in regions which are milder, more temperate.
Socrates and Plato were philosophers, sages.
The outward, material world is the shadow of the spiritual.
Genius is not a quality of idle, lazy men.
Rash, fruitless war is only splendid murder.
Fairly, rightly regarded, religion is the great sentiment of life.
Storms purge the air without, within the breast.

State how the reasons given in the Remarks for the insertion or the omission of commas (pp. 83, 84) *will apply to the following sentences:* —

It is a matter of the finest, the most deliberate calculation.
The only test of goodness, virtue, is moral strength.
Virtue, religion, is the one thing needful.
Woe, woe, to the rider that tramples them down!
A steady, durable good cannot be derived from an external cause.
Work that is easy, pleasant, does not make robust minds.
Remove, expel the blustering, blundering blockhead!
The history of the humblest human life is a tale of marvels.
How delightful to gaze at the dark-blue sky!
Behold that crowd of keen, anxious-looking men.
Some village Hampden here may rest.
Mirthfully, wildly, the bright waves flash along.
A benevolent man is very much esteemed, respected.
Fallen, fallen, is the mighty Babylon!

THE COMMA.

EXERCISE TO BE WRITTEN.

In writing the following sentences, punctuate those words only which require commas, in accordance with the second Rule and the Remarks:--

The young shepherd promised to buy me a pretty brown ribbon. (Remark *f.*)

The man of true refinement will not object to enter into the honest heartfelt enjoyments of common life. (Rule, and Remark *d.*)

The rosy-crowned Loves, with their many-twinkling feet, frisk with antic Sports and blue-eyed Pleasures. (Remark *g.*)

A good that is steady durable cannot be derived from an external cause. (Rule, and Remark *e.*)

The intellect and the conscience are intimately indissolubly bound together. (Rule, and Remark *d.*)

Employment activity is one of the fundamental laws of human happiness. (Rule, and Remark *b.*)

Not a few of the wisest grandest spirits have toiled at the work bench and the plough. (Rule, and Remarks *d, h.*)

A hardy honest peasantry are the glory of an agricultural country. (Rule, and Remark *d.*)

Weeping sighing the mother hid the children in her gory vest. (Rule, and Remark *k.*)

The human mind spreads its thoughts abroad into the immeasurable the infinite.

Does not every man feel, that nothing nothing could induce him to consent to become a slave? (Rule, and Remark *b.*)

All all conjure us to act wisely faithfully in the relation which we sustain. (Rule, and Remarks *b, j.*)

We should have a deeper a more vivid conviction of the importance the sacredness of our work. (Rule, and Remarks *a, b.*)

Of intellectual gifts, the rarest the most glorious is great inventive genius. (Rule, and Remarks *a, e, f.*)

Who will deny that imagination refines elevates the other mental powers? (Rule, and last sentence in Remark *e.*)

The most abandoned men have sometimes professed courage contempt of mere bodily suffering. (Rule, and Remarks *c, f.*)

A desolate lonely feeling springs up of having exchanged their home for a distant foreign country. (Rule, and Remarks *d, l.*)

All things must work together for certain good, so long as we continue in free unconditional self-surrender to the service of God. (Rule, and Remarks *d, h.*)

RULE III.

Series of Words of the same Part of Speech.

In a series of words, all of the same part of speech, a comma is inserted between each particular.

EXAMPLES.

1. Industry, honesty, and temperance are essential to happiness.
2. Alfred the Great was a brave, pious, and patriotic prince.
3. Happy is the man who honors, obeys, loves, or serves his Creator.
4. The discourse was beautifully, elegantly, forcibly delivered.
5. The spirit of the Almighty is within, around, and above us.

REMARKS.

a. Some punctuators omit the comma between the last two particulars, when united by either of the conjunctions *and, or, nor*. But the propriety of using the comma will perhaps be obvious to any one who examines the nature of such sentences: for the last two words of a series are not more closely connected in sense and construction with each other than with the preceding words; as, "Infancy, childhood, youth, *manhood, and age* are different stages in human life."

b. When, however, three words of the same part of speech are in juxtaposition, the last being preceded by *and* or *or*, but do not form a series, the comma is omitted before the conjunction; as, "By the wise arrangement of nature, *infancy and childhood* last long." Here the noun "nature" is governed by the preposition "of;" and the two following nouns, "infancy and childhood," are of themselves the compound nominative to the succeeding verb. The punctuation, therefore, differs from that of a sentence in which three words are used in a series, or in the same construction; as, "Childhood, youth, and maturity last longer or shorter in different individuals."

c. In a series of three nouns preceded by an adjective qualifying only the first, the comma should be omitted before the conjunction; as, "The characteristics of Mr. Mason's mind were *real* greatness, strength and sagacity."

d. A comma should be put after the last noun in a series, if it is not joined to the others by a conjunction, and does not end a sentence or clause; as, "Reputation, virtue, *happiness*, depend greatly on the choice of companions." — "The good man is alive to all the sympathies, the sanctities, *the loves*, of social existence." When, however, *and, or,* or *nor* occurs, the comma is unnecessary after the last noun, because the conjunction shows that all the particulars have, either separately or together, a relation to what follows in the sentence; as, "Reputation, virtue, *and happiness* depend greatly on the choice of companions." — "The good man is alive to all the sympathies, the sanctities, *and the loves* of social existence."

e. When the last particular is one of several qualifying words, it must not be separated by a point from that portion of the sentence on which it acts; as, "Too much of our love is an instinctive, ungoverned, narrow, *selfish* feeling." — See p. 33, Remark *d*.

f. But a comma should be put after the last adjective or adverb, not preceded by a conjunction, when it is separated by the other particulars of the series or by a verb from the word qualified, and does not finish the clause or sentence; as, "There is something real, substantial, *immortal*, in Christian virtue." — "Exalted, tender, *beneficent*, is the love that woman inspires."

g. When the last governing word in a series is preceded by a conjunction, a comma is unnecessary after it; but, if written without a conjunction, the comma should be inserted; as, "God's design is to recover, exalt, and *bless* the guiltiest of our race." — "Endeavor to elevate, refine, *purify*, the public amusements." When, however, the term governed is only a monosyllabic word, the comma may in such cases be omitted; as, "Teach, urge, threaten, *lecture* him."

h. When three or more words of the same part of speech, and in the same construction, are severally connected by means of *and*, *or*, or *nor*, the comma may be omitted after each of the particulars; as, 'Let us freely drink in the soul of love and beauty and wisdom from all nature and art and history." Some writers separate all such serial words by a comma; but a mode of punctuation so stiff as this seldom aids in developing the sense, and, in sentences requiring other commas, is undoubtedly offensive to the eye, if it does not obscure the meaning itself. A correct reader will, however, as a matter of course, pause more or less after each particular, in accordance with the nature of the sentiment.

i. But, when a series of nouns is resolvable into two or more phrases, each having two coupled words, a comma should be used between the phrases; as, "A Christian spirit may be manifested to Greek or Jew, male or female, friend or foe."

j. When, in two or more pairs, only the last pair depends on a concluding term, the comma should be omitted after it; as, "The true Christian is a man of principle, of truth and integrity, of kindness and modesty, of *reverence and devotion* to the Supreme Glory."

SERIES OF WORDS.

ORAL EXERCISES.

Recite the Rule (p. 37) *for the insertion of commas in the following sentences:*—

Learn patience, calmness, self-command, disinterestedness, love.
The mind is that which knows, feels, and thinks.
Honor, affluence, and pleasure seduce the heart.
Milton's poetry is always healthful, bright, and vigorous.
The child can creep, skip, walk, or run.
Let great principles be wrought into the mind, the heart, the life.
The work was neither dexterously, quickly, nor well done.
The love that woman inspires is exalted, tender, and beneficent.

Agreeably to the Remarks (pp. 37, 38), *state the reasons for the insertion or the omission of commas in the following sentences:*—

Aristotle, Cicero, and Quintilian are high authorities in rhetoric.
The tendency of poetry is to refine, purify, expand, and elevate
God is the source, object, model, of perfect love.
The air, the earth, the water, teem with delighted existence
His reign is that of a great, godlike, disinterested being.
Wise, eloquent, cautious, intrepid, was Ulysses.
The arts prolong, comfort, and cheer human life.
Charity beareth, believeth, hopeth, all things.
The man professed neither to eat nor drink nor sleep.
The poor and rich, and weak and strong, have all one Father

Say why the omission of a comma between the last two conjoined nouns in the following sentences does not accord with the Rule, but with Remark b:—

In Paradise, Adam and Eve reigned supreme. There was, in Eve's every gesture, dignity and love.
According to the Thompsonian philosophy, heat and cold are antagonist identities.
In two branches of science, chemistry and natural history, medical men have been the most successful laborers.
It is well calculated to render the timber impenetrable to the agents of decomposition,—air and moisture.
Dr. Twitchell's wonderful faculty often rendered the unintelligible plain and clear.
In reference to time, hours and days are of great importance: in respect to eternity, years and ages are nothing.

THE COMMA.

EXERCISE TO BE WRITTEN.

In putting commas between or after the serial words in the following sentences be guided by the third Rule and the Remarks (pp. 37, 38):—

Let holiness goodness virtue be to you the pearl of great price. (Rule, and first portion of Remark *d.*)

The recovery of our little darling dancing singing Mary is worth all the gold that ever was mined. (Rule, and Remark *e.*)

The hardships of a good life prove refine and exalt the human character. (Rule, and first portion of Remark *g.*)

No one can find peace but in the growth of an enlightened firm disinterested holy mind. (Rule, and Remark *e.*)

Ease indulgence luxury sloth are the sources of misery; making a man a poor sordid selfish wretched being. (Rule, and Remarks *d, e.*)

A great soul is known by its enlarged strong and tender sympathies. (Rule, Remark *e,* and last of *d.*)

All that charms the eye or the ear or the imagination or the heart is the gift of God. (Remark *h.*)

The Indian nut alone is clothing, meat and trencher drink and can. (Remark *i.*)

All have some conceptions of truth kindness honesty self-denial and disinterestedness. (Rule, and Remark *a.*)

In a city there is much to inflame imbitter degrade the minds of the poor. (Rule, and second portion of *g.*)

Let us every day become more pure kind gentle patient spiritual and devout. (Rule, and Remark *a.*)

Meekly truthfully disinterestedly the dying man had trod the path of life. (Rule, and Remark *f.*)

In heaven live the friends benefactors deliverers ornaments of their race. (Rule, and first of Remark *d.*)

True courage is the exercise result and expression of the highest attributes of our nature. (Rule, and last of Remark *d.*)

Some have unreasonably denied the strength and fervor and enduringness of human love. (Remark *h.*)

The Hebrew is closely allied to the Arabic the Phœnician the old Persian the Syriac and the Chaldee. (Rule, and Remark *a.*)

You are a parent or a child a brother or a sister a husband or a wife a friend or an associate of some kindred soul. (Remark *j.*)

Our present knowledge thoughts feelings characters are the results of former impressions passions and pursuits. (Rule, and Remarks *d a.*)

RULE IV.

Nouns or Phrases in Apposition.

§ I. Two nouns or personal pronouns, or a noun and pronoun, one in apposition with the other, should not be separated by a comma, if they may be regarded as a proper name or as a single phrase.

§ II. But a noun or pronoun and a phrase, or two or more phrases, when put in apposition, are separated by a comma from each other, and, if the sentence or clause is unfinished, from what follows.

EXAMPLES.
§ I.
1. The poet Milton wrote excellent prose and better poetry.
2. It is well known that the word "philosopher" signifies lover of wisdom.
3. He himself was the editor of the work; but he left it a botch.

§ II.
1. Homer, the greatest poet of antiquity, is said to have been blind.
2. We, the people of the United States, are lovers of republicanism.
3. The twin sisters, Piety and Poetry, are wont to dwell together.

REMARKS.

a. The term *noun* here is so used as to apply either to a single word of this character, or to an unemphatic word and a noun. Thus, both words, "the poet," in the first example, are, to avoid circumlocution, spoken of as a noun, and not as a phrase.

b. When two or more words can be treated as one compound name or as a single phrase, they do not admit a comma between them; as, "Alexander of Macedon; Sir William Jones; our Lord Jesus Christ; the Lord God Almighty." But if names, titles, or characteristics are so applied as to vary the thought, or produce a separate impression on the mind, they should be set apart by a comma; as, "Worship thy Creator, God; and obey his Son, the Master, King, and Saviour of men."

c. The word *brothers*, when put in apposition with a proper name in a firm, is left unpointed; as, "Smith Brothers and Co." But when used, either in the singular or plural number, to convey the notion of another person, it is not in apposition, and must therefore be distinguished by the comma; as, "Smith, Brother, and Co."

d. Proper names, when inverted, are separated by a comma; as, "*James*, Thomas; *Williamson*, John;" meaning Thomas James and John Williamson.

e. After the word *price*, when immediately preceding the value of any commodity, the comma may be omitted; as, "Price $5," or "Price fifty cents."

f. A comma is put between two nouns or pronouns if used synonymously, or if the latter expresses an illustrative or an additional thought; as, "Force of voice is strength, *energy;* vivacity is life, *animation.*" — " A son, *John*, was born after his father's death."

g. When a proper name is put after a phrase in apposition, the comma may be omitted; as, " The great orator *Cicero* was famed for many excellences." Unless where the noun is introduced by way of explanation or parenthesis; and, in such a case, it is preceded by a comma, and, in an unfinished clause, followed by the same point; as, "The wisest of the Jewish kings, *Solomon*, became a fool."

h. When the first of two nouns of the possessive case has the sign of possession, a comma should intervene between them; as, "The work will be found at *Appleton's*, the bookseller." But, if the possessive sign is omitted after the first noun, and put after the second, the comma may be dispensed with; as, "It will be seen at *Putnam* the publisher's." Should, however, this mode of writing be so constructed as to have, for the unmarked possessive, several names constituting a firm, a comma should be inserted before the noun ending with the *s* and apostrophe; as, "The young man is a clerk at Little, Brown, and *Company*, the publishers';" the awkwardness of the punctuation here arising from the clumsiness of the expression.

i. If a term, preceding a noun or a pronoun, is used absolutely, a comma is inserted only between them; as, "A trifling scholar, *he* heeds not the lessons of instruction."

j. When a pronoun of the second person immediately precedes a noun, a relative pronoun, or a word or phrase used for a noun, the comma is unnecessary between them; as, "*Thou* river, roll; *ye* who are aged, come; all *ye* high Powers." But if the pronoun, as the nominative to a verb, or as the antecedent of a relative, is separated from them, or if it is put in the objective case, a comma should be put before and after the intervening term; as, "*Thou*, Father, *markest* the tears I shed." "What art *thou*, execrable shape, *that* darest advance?" "*On thee*, beloved, I wait."

k. When the latter of two nouns or phrases is predicated of the former, the comma is not required between them; as, "Plutarch calls lying *the vice of slaves.*" — " The Romans thought Augustus Cæsar *a god.*" — " I consider Dr. Johnson *as an excellent moralist.*" So also if the subject spoken of be a pronoun; as, " The people elected *him* president of the United States."

ORAL EXERCISES.

Show how the following sentences exemplify the fourth Rule, in respect to the insertion or omission of commas : —

Friends, the beloved of my bosom, were near.
Mahomet was a native of Mecca, a city in Arabia.
The emperor Antoninus wrote an excellent work on morals.
The term " reason " has been variously defined.
Diogenes, the Greek philosopher, lived in a tub.
Bowditch the astronomer translated the " Mécanique Céleste."
Newton, the great mathematician, was very modest.
The butterfly, child of the summer, flutters in the sun.
Hope, the balm of life, soothes us under every misfortune.
Spenser the poet lived in the reign of Queen Elizabeth.
Art thou that traitor angel who first broke peace in heaven?
I Paul, the prisoner of Jesus Christ for you Gentiles.
I, thy father-in-law Jethro, am come unto thee.

Say why, according to the Remarks (pp. 41, 42), *commas are inserted or omitted in the following sentences :* —

The emperor Augustus was a patron of the fine arts.
The frigate " Jamestown " conveyed corn to the suffering Irish.
God is a Father-God, a God of paternal love.
To thee we bow, Friend, Father, King of kings!
" Adjunct" is derived from *adjunctum,* addition, something added.
Ease, rest, owes its deliciousness to toil.
William was slain; leaving one child, Alice.
The eloquent preacher Massillon was a Frenchman.
The author of " Paradise Lost," Milton, was a noble-minded man
At Thomson the hatter's store. At Thomson's, the hatter.
A brave boy, he could not injure others.
O Thou whose love can ne'er forget its offspring, man!
Ye powers and spirits of this nethermost abyss.
Thou, Lord, art the life and light of all this wondrous world.
All agree in designating Howard a philanthropist.

EXERCISE TO BE WRITTEN.

Insert commas where, according to pages 41–43, *they are required:—*

In Greek, the word "poet" denotes a maker a creator. (Rule, § I.; and Remarks *a*, *f*.)

The apostle John was peculiarly beloved by his divine Master Jesus Christ the Saviour of the world. (Rule, and Remark *b*.)

The capital of Turkey Constantinople is finely situated on the European side of the Bosphorus. (Last of Remark *g*.)

General Washington the first president of the United States was a true patriot a genuine lover of his country. (Rule, and Remark *b*.)

Marcus Aurelius Antoninus says, "Often return to your true mother philosophy." (Remark *b*, first portion; and Remark *f*.)

Much stress was laid upon pronunciation delivery by the most eloquent of all orators Demosthenes. (Remark *f*, and last of *g*.)

London the capital of Great Britain contains nearly three millions of inhabitants. (Rule, § II.)

A great and gloomy man the king sat upon the throne of his ancestors. (Remark *i*.)

I recommend the reading of good books as a source of improvement and delight. (Remark *k*.)

The first expedition of Columbus was fitted out by John of Anjou Duke of Calabria. (Rule, § II.; and Remark *b*.)

O Thou who hast at thy command the hearts of all men in thy hand! (First of Remark *j*.)

I Artaxerxes the king decree that whatsoever Ezra the priest the scribe of the law shall require, &c. (Rule, and Remark *b*.)

You blocks! you stones! you worse than senseless things! O you hard hearts! you cruel men of Rome! (First of Remark *j*.)

And, when the angel Death stands by, be thou my God my helper nigh. (Rule, Remark *b*, and last of *j*.)

When, as returns this solemn day, man comes to meet his Maker God. (Last of Remark *b*.)

The world-famed dramatist Shakspeare lived in the reign of the greatest of English queens Elizabeth. (Remark *g*.)

Adonijah the son of Haggith came to Bathsheba the mother of Solomon. (Rule, § II.)

In the firm of Graham Brother and Co. there are three persons in partnership,—James Graham, his younger brother, and John Jones; but I do not know how many there are in the firm of Kennedy Brothers,—whether there be two or more. (Remark *c*.)

RULE V.

Words or Phrases in Contrast.

Words or phrases contrasted with each other, or having a mutual relation to others that follow them, in the same clause, are separated by commas.

EXAMPLES.

1. False delicacy is affectation, not politeness.
2. The author of that work was a distinguished poet, but a bad man.
3. Many persons gratify their eyes and ears, instead of their understandings
4. Prudence, as well as courage, is necessary to overcome obstacles.
5. Strong proofs, not a loud voice, produce conviction.
6. One may utter many pompous, and speak but few intelligible, words
7. Avoid, or rather prevent the introduction of, so pernicious a fashion.
8. Good men are not always found in union with, but sometimes in opposition to, the views and conduct of one another

REMARKS.

a. Not a few authors would write the sixth example without a comma after the adjective "intelligible." But though it is well to avoid the use of the point after a qualifying or a governing word when its omission could effect no ambiguity, as in the phrase " deep, *lonely* thought," and others referred to in p. 33, Remark *d;* yet where, as in the instance under the present rule, the words or phrases, which have a common bearing on one and the same expression, are apart, and the first is properly set off by a comma, the insertion of a corresponding comma after the second seems requisite for an easy obtaining of the sense. And this, indeed, is the usage of the best, though perhaps not of the most numerous, punctuators.

b. The seventh and eighth examples are introduced here, not as models of composition, but to show that the harshness of their construction demands a corresponding rigor in the mode of punctuation. This, however, the student may sometimes avoid in his *own* composition, by giving to his style greater freedom and elegance. For instance, the seventh example might be thus constructed and pointed: "Avoid so pernicious a fashion, or rather prevent its introduction."

c. When two contrasted or related words, united by either of the conjunctions *but, though, yet, as well as,* qualify a following noun or phrase, or refer to the same preposition, the comma may be omitted: as, "Cæsar delivered his orations in *elegant* but *powerful* language."

"He was *a great* though *an erring* man." — "Hercules had *the strength* as well as *the courage* of the lion."

d. But if the adverb *not*, either with or without a conjunction, comes between two such words, a comma should be used after each, in accordance with the Rule, to indicate their common dependence on the last portion of the sentence; as, "The strong and violent emotions are the natural produce of *an early*, if not of *a savage*, state of society."

e. If the above-mentioned conjunctions unite not two words, but a word and a phrase, or two phrases, the commas should be inserted; as, "Intemperance not only wastes *the earnings*, but *the health and minds*, of men."

f. Two words or phrases connected by *but* or *yet*, or if either of these conjunctions be understood, are separated by a comma, when the first term is preceded by *not* or *though ;* as, "Not *beautiful*, but graceful." — "Though *black*, yet comely; and though *rash*, benign."

g. Commas should not be used between words contrasted in pairs, and having prepositions or conjunctions between them; as, "Let elevation *without* turgidness, purity *without* primness, pathos *without* whining, characterize our style." — "Nothing is more wise or more admirable in action than to be resolute *and yet* calm, earnest *and yet* self-possessed, decided *and yet* modest." .

h. When a negative word or phrase is put before an affirmative one, and does not commence the sentence, the phrases are separated by a comma, not only from each other, but from that portion of the sentence with which they are connected; as, "The greatest evils arise to human society, *not from wild beasts*, but from untamed passions."

i. If, however, the word expressing negation is not put in immediate connection with one of the phrases, but in that portion of the sentence on which they depend; or if a finite verb, active or neuter, immediately precedes the negative, the comma should be omitted before the first phrase; as, "The greatest evils do *not* arise to human society from wild beasts, but from untamed passions." — "The greatest evils to human society *arise not* from wild beasts, but from untamed passions." — "It *is not* from wild beasts, but from untamed passions, that the greatest evils arise to human society."

j. In some instances, where the insertion of a comma between contrasted phrases, used as a compound intermediate expression, would tend to obscure the connection subsisting between the parts of a sentence, the point between the phrases may be omitted; as,

"The wise and good of every name are, *with diversity of gifts* but *the same spirit*, striving, each in his own way, to carry society forward into a healthier condition than the present." By inserting a comma after "gifts," — a mode of pointing which is correct in itself, — the relation between the verb "are" and the participle "striving" would be in some measure concealed from the eye.

k. The principle of omission exemplified in the preceding remark may be occasionally applied to sentences of a different construction, where words or expressions, admitting a comma without its being essential to the sense, are united to others from which the commas cannot at all be excluded. If this principle is judiciously applied, the relations and dependencies of the several parts of a sentence will be often exhibited to much advantage.

ORAL EXERCISES.

Why, according to the fifth Rule, should certain words and phrases in the following sentences be set off by commas? —

Truth is not a stagnant pool, but a fountain.
Measure your life by acts of goodness, not by years.
Intrinsic worth, and not riches, ought to procure esteem.
Speak for, not against, the principles of love and peace.
You were paid to fight against, and not to rail at, Alexander.
Washington was the head of the nation, and not of a party.
Though deep, yet clear; though gentle, yet not dull.
Rhetoric is the science, and oratory the art, of speaking well.
There are few voices in the world, but many echoes.

State the principles, as given in the Remarks, for the omission or the insertion of commas in the following sentences: —

Philosophy makes us wiser, Christianity makes us better, men.
Milton burned with a deep yet calm love of moral grandeur.
He was not only the teacher but the model of his pupils.
Socrates was directed by a good, if not a divine, genius.
Learning is the ally, not the adversary, of genius.
The man suffered not only in his estate, but in his reputation.
It is the duty of a child, not to direct, but to obey, his parents.
Religion dwells not in the tongue, but in the heart.
To die for truth is not to die for one's country, but for the world
We ought not to betray, but to defend, our country.

THE COMMA.

EXERCISE TO BE WRITTEN.

Punctuate those sentences which require commas, in accordance with the principles laid down in the preceding Rule and Remarks (pp. 45-47): —

It is not the business of virtue to extirpate the affections but to regulate them. (Rule, and Remark *i.*)

We live in deeds not years; in thoughts not breaths; in feelings not in figures on a dial. (Rule.)

Novel-reading is generally calculated to weaken if not to debase the moral powers. (Rule, and Remark *d.*)

Punishments often shock instead of harmonizing with the common feeling and sense of justice. (Rule.)

Most of Homer's defects may reasonably be imputed not to his genius but to the manners of the age in which he lived. (Rem. *h.*)

He who is insensible to praise is either raised far above or sunk much below the ordinary standard of human nature. (Rule.)

Knowledge is conducive if not essential to all the ends of virtue. (Rule, and Remark *d.*)

Zeal without knowledge, prudence without courage, and peacefulness without principle, are dangerous qualities. (Remark *g.*)

Christians have cast away the spirit in settling the precise dignity of their Master. (Rule.)

The Pyrrhonists not only doubted of every thing they saw and heard but of their own existence. (Rule, and Remark *i.*)

A lofty rectitude marked every small as well as every great action of Washington's life. (Remark *c.*)

The treasures of wisdom are not to be seized with a violent hand but to be earned by persevering labor. (Rule, and Remark *i.*)

The literature of a nation is one of its highest and certainly one of its most refined elements of greatness and order. (Rule.)

Those who flatter the prejudices of others are the enemies not the friends of the improvement and happiness of mankind. (Remark *d.*)

God's love to us is not a technical dogma but a living and practical truth. (Rule.)

Christianity may harmonize with but it needs not the sanction of philosophy. (Rule, and Remark *b.*)

A man's self-reproach may be less for what one has than for what he has not done. (Rule.)

Whenever words are contrasted with contradistinguished from or opposed to other words, they are always emphatical. (Rule, and Remark *b.*)

Motives of the most sincere though fanciful devotion induced the old man to renew the half-defaced inscriptions on the tombs of his ancestors. (Remark *c.*)

Benevolence is not merely a feeling but a principle; not a dream of rapture for the fancy to indulge in but a business for the hand to execute. (Rule, and Remark *f.*)

The missionary went forth, not only with the wisdom of the serpent but with the simplicity of the dove, to do battle against every form of error and vice. (Remark *j.*)

Society proceeds from barbarity to refinement, from ignorance to knowledge, from wealth to corruption, and from corruption to ruin. (Remark *g.*)

Every one can distinguish an angry from a placid a cheerful from a melancholy a thoughtful from a thoughtless and a dull from a penetrating countenance. (Remarks *g, a*, and Rule.)

Though unavoidable calamities make a part yet they make not the chief part of the vexations and sorrows that distress human life. (Rule, and Remark *f.*)

The great object of education is not to store the mind with knowledge but to give activity and vigor to its powers. (Remark *i*, and Rule.)

We are so made as to be capable not only of perceiving but also of being pleased with or pained by the various objects by which we are surrounded. (Rule, and Remarks *h, b.*)

From the hour at which printing was invented, the brain and not the arm, the thinker and not the soldier, books and not kings, were to rule the world. (Remark *g.*)

A rhetorical sometimes a grammatical pause should be used after words in apposition with or in opposition to each other. (Rule, and Remarks *a, b.*)

Poetry is a voice that issues from and finds its echoes in the deep popular heart, where lies the source of all faith and of all enthusiasm for good. (Rule, and Remark *b.*)

> Contrasted faults through all their manners reign:
> Though poor luxurious; though submissive vain;
> Though grave yet trifling; zealous yet untrue;
> And, even in penance, planning sins anew. (Rule, and Remark *f.*)

By the side of man should stand woman, — not Amazonian but angelic; gentle yet godlike in works of knowledge and duty; meek yet mighty in all the miracles of charity and benevolence. (Rule, and Remark *f.*)

RULE VI.

The Subject and the Predicate.

No point, or pause-mark, is admissible between the subject or nominative and the predicate, or after any word that has a direct bearing on an expression which immediately follows.

EXAMPLES.

1. Poetry has a natural alliance with the best affections of the human heart
2. A grandee on the exchange may be a pauper in God's universe.
3. To be totally indifferent to praise or censure is a real defect in character.
4. The love which survives the tomb is one of the noblest attributes of the soul.

REMARKS.

a. In the above examples, the words "poetry," "grandee," "to be indifferent" (equivalent to the noun *indifference*), and "love," are the several *nominatives* to the verbs "has," "may be," and "is." Such phrases as "a grandee on the exchange," "to be totally indifferent to praise or censure," are sometimes called *nominative phrases;* and such an expression as "the love which survives the tomb," a *nominative clause.* (See pp. 21, 22; V., VI.) But, logically speaking, all these are the *subjects* of what are severally predicated of them.

b. In these examples, with a partial exception in the first, the nominatives and verbs are accompanied by certain modifying or limiting phrases, so strictly connected in sense with the former as to be grammatically *inseparable* from them. In other words, each of the sentences expresses an uninterrupted flow of thought, and therefore allows no marked division.

c. There is, however, a class of sentences in which the subject or the predicate is accompanied with expressions, qualifying or explanatory, that are *separable* from the portions with which they are connected; as, "The weakest reasoners, *especially on the subject of religion,* are, *generally speaking,* the most positive." — " Health, *which is God's gift,* should be preserved." Expressions of this kind are sometimes termed parenthetical or intermediate, and will be particularly considered under Rule VIII. In every such case, *two* commas must be used, as above, to show the relation of the nominative to its verb, and that of the verb to the chief words in the predicate.

d. In the rule, it is said that no pause-*mark* is admissible under certain circumstances, therein specified. This qualification of the principle laid down will be clearly understood, if the learner bear in mind that pauses are of two kinds: first, those which are *marked,* or represented to the eye, by the common grammatical points, exhibiting the constituent parts of sentences; and, second, those which are *unmarked,* — such rhetorical pauses as are omitted in writing and printing, but required in reading aloud. Thus, in the examples under the rule, the sense and the construction alike forbid the comma to interfere in separating the nominative or subject from the verb; and yet a correct elocution demands between them a slight pause.

e. From want of attending to the distinction between these two kinds of pauses, some writers would place a comma immediately before the verb, when its subject consists of a number of words, or, as it is commonly expressed, when the nominative is accompanied with an inseparable adjunct; as, " The good taste *of the present age,* has not allowed us to neglect the cultivation of the English language." But unless where, in any given sentence, the length of the subject would give rise to ambiguity or to difficulty in reading it, this mode of punctuation seems to be useless. Indeed the reason assigned on its behalf is a sufficient ground for its rejection; namely, that the nominative is accompanied with an *inseparable* adjunct. For if the adjunct cannot be separated from the nominative, and if the nominative is intimately joined in sense with the verb which it governs, surely the relation subsisting between them should not be broken up, except in cases where it is absolutely necessary. That such adjuncts, too, are as intimately and grammatically connected with the verb as they are with the nominative, and that they cannot well stand apart, will be obvious from the example already given, which means that " *the good taste of the present age* has not allowed us " — and not that " *the good taste* has not allowed us " — " to neglect the cultivation of the English language." Sentences of this kind are obviously very different from those in which adjuncts, or modifying words, are separable both from the nominative and from the verb, as in the examples cited in Remark *c,* where a comma, both before and after the intervening phrase, serves to bring together the parts related to each other. The pointing objected to is based on a theory which cannot be reduced to practice, — that every expression, separated from another by the smallest cessation of the voice, should be indicated by a mark; but we again repeat, that only by the sense and the grammatical form of a passage, and not by the rhetorical mode of its delivery, must the art of punctuation be regulated, at least so far as the common points are concerned.

f. To the rule here recommended, there are, however, several exceptions, required by the peculiar form in which a proposition is sometimes expressed, and by the fact that the insertion of a comma between the subject and the predicate tends occasionally to a clearer perception of an author's meaning. The exceptions are as follow: —

g 1. When a sentence is so constructed as to leave it uncertain whether a modifying word belongs to the subject or the predicate, — as in the passage, " The man of talent merely is strong for enterprise and execution," — a comma should be introduced where it will best develop the sense. If the aim of the writer was to speak of a man of mere talent, the comma should be inserted after the adverb " merely;" but, if of a man of talent who is strong only for enterprise and execution, it should be placed *before* the adverb. The sentence, indeed, might have been written in accordance with syntactic principles, which would have precluded the necessity of transgressing one of the chief laws in punctuation; but the province of the punctuator is not to change the construction of sentences, but to bring out their meaning in so far as his art will permit him.

g 2. When the subject consists of two or more nouns not united by a conjunction, a comma is required before the predicate; as, " Immensity, *sublimity*, are expressed by a prolongation of the voice." — " *Riches, pleasure, health*, become evils to those who do not know how to use them." If, however, the nouns are joined by a conjunction, the comma between the subject and the predicate is omitted; as, " Sculpture, painting, and *poetry* will always have admirers." — See pp. 33, *b ;* 37, *d.*

g 3. When the nominative is followed by two or more words which belong to it, and between which a comma must be inserted, a comma is required also before the verb; as, " A new *feeling* of what is due to the ignorant, the poor, and the depraved, *has* sprung up in society." — " *Worlds* above, around, and beneath, *arch* thee about as a centre."

g 4. When between the extremities, either of a nominative clause or of its predicate, occurs a word or an expression requiring to be marked off by commas, a comma should also be introduced immediately before the predicate; as, " The success with which Rousseau passed, *coarse and selfish as he was*, for a man of deep and tender feeling, *appears* to have been the signal for a procession of writers to withdraw the public attention from their own transgressions." —

"The evil which is intermixed in human society, *serves, without question*, to exercise the noblest virtues of the human soul." If, however, the subject is not a clause, but a phrase, it should not be separated by a comma from the predicate, though the latter contains a word or an expression enclosed by commas; as, "A sincere and honest man may, *in truth*, do such work as shall make him a benefactor to his neighborhood."

g 5. When the subject consists of a nominative clause, ending with a noun or pronoun, which is apt to be read so closely with the predicate as to confound the sense, a comma should precede the verb; as, "Who does *nothing*, knows nothing." — "That a peculiar state of the mere particles of the brain should be followed by a change of the state of the sentient *mind*, is truly wonderful." — "He that sees a building as a common *spectator*, contents himself with speaking of it in the most general terms;" a sentence which, if left unpointed, might, unless more than ordinary attention was given, be blunderingly read, "He that sees a building, as a common spectator contents himself with speaking of it," &c.

g 6. When a nominative clause contains two verbs, with one of which it ends, a comma is required before the predicate; as, "He that *places* himself neither higher nor lower than he ought to *do*, exercises the truest humility."

g 7. When the subject ends and the predicate begins with the same verb, or with two verbs of a like form, a comma should be placed between them; as, "Whatever *is, is* right." — "The defendant *served, moved* to set aside the summons."

g 8. When a subject is repeated in a different form before its verb, as sometimes ungrammatically occurs, a comma may be used, in solemn or forcible language, between the two forms; as, "The works that I do in my Father's name, *they* bear witness of me." But, when these modes of expression are used in familiar kinds of writing, it is better to omit the comma; as, "My flocks *they* do wander." In another part of the work, it will be seen that a dash (—) is employed in sentences of this construction, when they are highly rhetorical.

h. By a colloquial idiom, the subject is sometimes found both at the beginning and the end of a proposition. In such cases, a comma is inserted before the repeated subject; as, "*He* was a distinguished philosopher, *Socrates*."

i. The above exceptions may appear, from their number, to overthrow the rule; but some of them, it will be seen, are in opposition to it, only because the sentences themselves are contrary to the laws of good or elegant composition. As for the others, it may be remarked, that, if a competent person take up any well-written essay or discourse in the English language, he will perceive that the principle contained in the rule is applicable to so overwhelming a number of sentences, as to render the exceptions, were there ten times more than we have pointed out, quite insignificant.

j. A comma should not be inserted after any of the forms of the verb *to be*, when used as a copula, or connecting link, between the subject and the predicate; or before a verb in the infinitive mood, when preceded by another verb; as, " The sole object of importance *is* the moral development of society." — " It ill *becomes* wise and good men *to oppose* and degrade one another." Some writers would insert a comma; but the punctuating of such sentences as these, where the parts are so closely related, is unnecessarily stiff, though between them a correct delivery requires a pause

---

ORAL EXERCISES.

Explain how it is, that, according to the sixth Rule (p. 50), *commas are unnecessary in the following propositions:* —

Nature has given all men some conceptions of immortality.
The region beyond the grave is not a solitary land.
Simplicity of life and manners produces tranquillity of mind.
The Almighty sustains and conducts the universe
Human affairs are in continual motion and fluctuation.
To calculate shrewdly is different from meditating wisely.
An Epicurean world makes an Epicurean God.
The earth-clod of the globe has been divinely breathed upon.
Aptitude for business is not power of reason.
The best monuments of the virtuous are their actions.
Misery is the necessary result of a deviation from rectitude.
Sensitiveness to the approbation of virtuous men is laudable.
The streams of small pleasures fill the lake of happiness.
Intemperance is the grossest abuse of the gifts of Providence.
A desire of knowledge is natural to the mind of man.
" Know thyself" is a useful and comprehensive precept.
His being a scholar prevented any gross mistake in his style.
To be proud and inaccessible is to be timid and weak.
He who masters his passions conquers his greatest enemy.
Our intellectual powers may be indefinitely enlarged.

SUBJECT AND PREDICATE.

Mention why, in accordance with the Remarks on pages 50–54, the sentences that follow are pointed or unpointed with commas :—

Light, whether it be material or spiritual, is the best reformer.
He who teaches, often learns himself.
Those who were not so, became cringing and hypocritical
He who made it, now preserves and governs it.
A youth, a boy, a child, might understand the question.
Job, Hesiod, and Homer mention several of the constellations.
The idea of what ought to be, rises up from the bosom of what is
Whoever firmly wills, will be a good man.
Thy rod and thy staff, they comfort me.
The careless poet of Avon, was he troubled for his fame?
And Harry's flesh it fell away. — But John he cried in vain.
He seemed wanting in every good affection, Nero.
He groweth rich, that fawning and supple parasite.
It needs a divine man to exhibit any thing divine.
It is our duty to appropriate our time to valuable purposes.

EXERCISE TO BE WRITTEN.

Insert commas only where required by the preceding Remarks :—

Reason and true philosophy never attempt, in their conclusions, to separate God from his works. (Rule, and last of Remark *g* 4.)

Times of general calamity and confusion have ever been productive of the greatest minds.*

It is not in our power to change the established order of things. (Remark *j*, and Rule.)

Patience with the erring and offending is one of the holiest of all forms of character.

He who being master of the fittest moment to crush his enemy magnanimously neglects it is born to be a conqueror. (Rem. *c*, *g* 4.)

One of the arts that tend most to the improvement of human intellect is the art of language.

Philosophy, religion tend to promote just and honorable views of the Creator of the universe. (First of Remark *g* 2.)

The most sublime speculation of the contemplative philosopher can scarcely compensate for the neglect of the smallest active duty.

The highest art of the mind of man is to possess itself with tranquillity in the hour of danger. (Rule, and Remark *j*.)

---

* The sentences, in this exercise, to which no references are attached, may be compared with the Rule and with Remarks *a—e*, pp. 50, 51.

To mourn deeply for the death of another loosens from myself the petty desire for life. (Remark *g* 5.)

The vigorous character of composition depends on the decision with which the mind grasps a truth.

That our age holds an amount of refinement and civilization that preceding ages did not have seems evident. (Remark *g* 6.)

An excessive or indiscriminate reading of novels and romances is exceedingly injurious to the young.

To live soberly, righteously, and piously comprehends the whole of our duty. (Remark *g* 1 or 3.)

Sincere respect for the men of early times may be joined with a clear perception of their weaknesses and errors.

He who loves the bristle of bayonets only sees in their glitter what beforehand he felt in his heart. (Remark *g* 1.)

To walk beneath the porch is still infinitely less than to kneel before the cross.

The swan whose neck is out of all proportion to his body is the most beautiful of all birds. (Remark *c*.)

The great sources of intellectual power and progress to a people are its strong and original thinkers.

He who troubles himself more than he needs grieves also more than is necessary. (Remark *g* 6 or 7.)

The grammatical points are not sufficient to indicate either the number or the duration of the pauses.

Intelligence, beauty, and modesty are the principal charms of woman. (Remark *g* 2, last sentence.)

The impartial distribution of posthumous fame or censure must have some effect on the most callous and unprincipled.

He that shall endure unto the end the same shall be saved. (First of Remark *g* 8.)

He who follows the pleasures of the world is in constant search of care and remorse.

Joy, grief, love, admiration, devotion are all of them passions which are naturally musical. (Remark *g* 2, first portion.)

The highest literature and art of every age embody its highest spiritual ideal of excellence.

Silent and severe they sit those men of the old fearless time. (Remark *h*.)

He who has never studied the consequences of human actions perceives, in the great concourse of mankind, only a multitude of beings consulting each his own peculiar interest. (Remark *g* 4 or 5.)

RULE VII.

Relative Pronouns and Relative Clauses.

§ I. A comma is put before a relative clause, when it is explanatory of the antecedent, or presents an additional thought.

§ II. But the point is omitted before a relative which restricts the general notion of the antecedent to a particular sense.

EXAMPLES.
§ I.
1. Behold the emblem of thy state in flowers, which bloom and die.
2. Study nature, whose laws and phenomena are all deeply interesting.
3. Channing has set forth great and universal truths, that cannot perish.
4. These were small states, in which every man felt himself to be important.
5. The father of history was Herodotus, from whom we have an account of the Persian war.

§ II.
1. Every teacher must love a boy who is attentive and docile.
2. Happy are the people whose history is the most wearisome to read.
3. Urbanity often lends a grace to actions that are of themselves ungracious.
4. Some men engage in labors in which they afterwards take no delight.
5. It is barbarous to injure those from whom we have received a kindness.

REMARKS.

a. By comparing any of the examples in the first class with its corresponding one or any other in the second, it will at once be seen that they are essentially different as to the senses intended to be conveyed. In the former class, the clause at the beginning of the sentence, which contains the antecedent, is of a general character: that at the end — the relative clause — presents something additional, or explanatory of what has been said. In the latter class, the antecedent clause lays down a proposition which is restrained or limited in its sense by the relative.

b. If a relative clause which is explanatory of the antecedent be placed between the extremities of a sentence, a comma is required both after the antecedent word or phrase, and before that verb of which it is the nominative; as, " Slaves and savages, *who receive no education,* are proverbially indolent." — See p. 64.

c. But, if the nominative is accompanied by a limiting relative clause, — or, to speak more accurately, if the subject is composed of an antecedent and a relative clause, — both points should be omitted; as, "The man *who is faithfully attached to religion* may be relied on with confidence." For, were a comma placed after either "man" or "religion," or after words corresponding to these in similar sentences, a separation would be made between parts, which, from their restrictive character, are obviously inseparable. — See p. 51, *d, e.*

d. When, however, the antecedent consists of nouns or phrases between which commas are required, a comma should also be inserted before the relative clause, though restrictive; as, "There are many dreams, fictions, or theories, *which* men substitute for truth." Were the comma after "theories" omitted, the connection between "which" and the preceding noun would seem to be closer than that existing between the relative pronoun and the other particulars, to which it has an equal relation; and such an omission would, in many instances, tend to hinder a perception of the sense.

e. A comma may also be put before the relative pronoun, even when restrictive, if it is immediately followed by a word or an expression enclosed by commas, and especially if the antecedent is qualified by an adjective; as, "It was only a few *discerning* friends, *who*, in the native vigor of his powers, perceived the dawn of Robertson's future eminence." The reasons offered for this mode of punctuating are, that the adjective has some effect to loosen the restraining power of the relative over the antecedent; and that the omission of the comma between the two portions of such a sentence — between "friends" and "who" in the present example — would draw the pronoun more closely to the clause which precedes it, than to that of which it forms a part.

f. By some writers and printers, a comma is always put before the relative, though used restrictively, if separated by several words from its grammatical antecedent; as, "It is *power* of thought and utterance, *which* immortalizes the products of genius." — "*He* preaches sublimely, *who* lives a righteous and pious life." But we have little hesitation in saying, that the punctuation is in both examples erroneous. In the former, the antecedent "power" is accompanied with the inseparable modifying phrase, "of thought and utterance;" the sense being, not that *power*, but that *the power of thought and utterance*, immortalizes the products of genius. In the latter example, it will be seen that the proper construction is, "*He who* lives a righteous and pious life preaches sublimely;" and that, in this collocation of the words, the comma would be correctly left out between the antecedent and the relative. If, therefore, a separation be made in the construction between words which are closely united in sense, as in the instances given, that separation, instead of being increased by the introduction of a point, should be made as little as possible by omitting it.

g. To the preceding remark the only exception is when the relative might improperly be read so as to refer to a proximate term; as, "Creeds too often carry, in their ruins, the seeds of that faith in the divine and eternal, *without which* our nobler nature starves and perishes."

h. To prevent ambiguity, a comma is sometimes put before the words, *of which, of whom,* even when used restrictively, to distinguish the preposition from that which connects two nouns, one of which governs the other; as, "Compassion is an emotion, *of which* you should never be ashamed." — "No thought can be just, *of which* good sense is not the groundwork." — "No thought, *of which* good sense is not the groundwork, can be just." The insertion of the point will distinguish phrases of this kind from such as occu. in the following sentences: "Compassion is an *emotion of grief* for the sufferings of others." — "The actions of princes are like those great rivers, the *courses of which* every one beholds, but whose springs have been seen by few." It may be remarked too, that, when the relative pronoun does not immediately follow the clause containing the antecedent, the comma omitted before the relative is inserted between the two portions of the sentence, as after the word "rivers" in the last example.

i. The principles stated in both divisions of the rule are applicable to sentences in which an adverb is put for a relative pronoun; as, "The philosophers took refuge in Persia, *where* [in which country] they soon became dispersed." — "Mark the majestic simplicity of those laws *whereby* [by which] the operations of the universe are conducted."

j. Sentences in which the relative pronoun may be supplied are subject to the same rules as those in which it is expressed; as, "Genius is not a single faculty of the mind, *distinct* from all the rest." — "Genius is not a faculty of the mind *separate* from all the rest." In both forms of the example, the relative pronoun with the verb —*which is*—is understood after the word "mind;" but in the former the comma is used, because the first clause makes perfect sense of itself, and the second is explanatory. In the latter form, the comma is omitted, for the reason that both clauses are so blended as to be inseparable in sense; the first being restrained or limited in its meaning by the second. The following sentence contains past participles, used in both an explanatory and a restrictive sense, and punctuated accordingly: "Poets are by no means wingless angels, *fed* with ambrosia *plucked* from Olympus, or manna *rained* down from heaven."

k. When a present participle is put instead of a relative and a verb, the insertion or omission of the comma will also depend on the principle just stated; as, "The path of mere power is that of the cannon-ball, *destroying* [which destroys] every thing in its course." — "There are moral principles *slumbering* in the souls of the most depraved."

l. Sometimes, however, a restrictive clause of the kind mentioned in the two foregoing remarks should be preceded by a comma, when, its antecedent being removed at some distance from the relative pronoun, the latter is in danger of being connected too closely with a nearer noun; as, "Commercial nations have an *apathy* to amusement, *distinct* from mere gravity of disposition." A comma may also be inserted before and after a clause beginning with an adjective or a past participle, if introduced between the extremities of a sentence, in order to show the alliance of the nominative with its verb, or of one noun with another; as, "A man, *distinguished* for his virtues and attainments, *is* commonly respected."

m. When the ellipsis may be supplied with the adverb *when*, involving in its signification a nominative or a relative and a verb, a comma should be inserted before two adjectives or participles, restrictive or unrestrictive, or an adjective or participle with words depending on it; as, "Man, *ignorant* and *uncivilized*, is a ferocious savage." — "The death of Socrates, *philosophizing with his friends*, is the most pleasant that could be desired."

n. When only the relative pronoun is understood, the antecedent should be left unpointed; as, "The *laws* we reverence are our brave fathers' legacy;" that is, the laws *which* we reverence.

o. Such as, when equivalent to a demonstrative and a relative pronoun, is subject to the second division of the rule; as, "There is no *such* partition in the spiritual world *as* you see in the material;" that is, there is not *that* partition *which* you see.

p. A semicolon is sometimes used before a relative pronoun, particularly when it refers to an antecedent in a remote clause. But this mode of punctuating will be best exhibited hereafter.

RELATIVE CLAUSES.

ORAL EXERCISES.

State the principles in the seventh Rule (p. 57), and show how they may be applied to the sentences that follow:—

Avoid rudeness of manners, which must hurt the feelings of others.
Every good man must love the country in which he was born.
The child was much attached to Jane, who loved him dearly.
Those who are wealthy have great influence over others.
Virtue is that to which the man himself contributes.
What is more wonderful than the human eye, that sees all around?
The subject should be held up in every light of which it is capable.
Death is the season which brings our affections to the test.
Turn not back from the good path on which you have entered.
Cherish true patriotism, which has its root in benevolence.
Ambition is the germ from which all growth of nobleness proceeds.
Christianity is a religion whose origin is unquestionably divine.
He who reads in a proper spirit can scarcely read too much.
War is a tremendous evil, to which many have unhappily resorted.

Mention the reasons, given in the Remarks (pp. 57-60), for inserting or omitting commas in such sentences as the following:—

Satan, whom now transcendent glory raised above his fellows, spake
The eye, that sees all things, sees not itself.
Man, who is born of a woman, is of few days.
The credulity which has faith in goodness is a sign of goodness.
He that is slow to anger is better and nobler than the mighty.
Where is the philosopher, the man, who would thus live and die?
He questioned me of the battles, sieges, fortunes, that I have passed.
The large book, which I bought years ago, has not yet been read.
No faculty lives within us which the soul can spare.
Nothing is in vain that rouses the mind to thought and reflection.
There is a craving for enjoyment, which cannot be destroyed in man.
William left the city of New York, where he was doing well.
Here comes his body, mourned by Mark Antony.
Adopt a plan of life founded on religion and virtue.
A great mind gazeth on the sun, glorying in its brightness.
Genius addresses the consciousness existing in all men.
Physical science, separate from morals, parts with its chief dignity.
Socrates was one of the greatest sages the world ever saw.
Such as are careless of themselves are seldom mindful of others.

THE COMMA.

EXERCISE TO BE WRITTEN.

Punctuate, or leave unpointed, the following sentences, as required by the preceding Rule and Remarks (pp. 57–60): —

We should trace in all events the wisdom and benevolence of God from whom descendeth every good and perfect gift. (Rule, § I.)

We read, with a reverential love, of men devoting themselves to the interests of humanity. (Last of Remark *k*.)

The lever which moves the world of mind is emphatically the printing-press. (Rule, § II.; and Remark *c*.)

Youth is introductory to manhood to which it is a state of preparation. (Rule, § I.)

To the Father of lights in whom there is no darkness are we indebted for all the blessings we enjoy. (Rule, § I.; and Rem. *b, n*.)

There was nothing in the mind of Jesus of which you have not the principle and the capacity in yourself. (Remark *h*.)

Some countries are infested with bands of robbers who attack travellers in the open day. (Rule, § I.)

Set at nought the grosser pleasures of sense whereof others are slaves. (Remark *i*, compared with *h*.)

There is a philosophic spirit which is far more valuable than any limited acquirements of philosophy. (Rule, § II.)

The entrance on a new course awakens new energies and powers which rapidly unfold into life and vigor. (Rule, § I.)

Science and Poetry alike recognizing the order and the beauty of the universe are alike handmaids of Devotion. (Remark *m*.)

The brightest part of thy life is nothing but a flower which withers almost as soon as it has blown. (Rule, § I.)

Columbus was sent to the university of Padua where he acquired such knowledge as was then taught. (Remarks *i, o*.)

Does the sentiment of patriotism reign in the common soldier who hires himself to be shot at for a few cents a day? (Rule, § I.)

A government directing itself resolutely and steadily to the general good becomes a minister of virtue. (Remark *m*.)

May we be living flowers in those everlasting gardens of the Lord where angels and seraphs are the guardians! (Remarks *i* and *g*.)

What are the moral influences of poverty its influences on character which deserve our chief attention? (Remark *d*.)

The Greeks may well boast of having produced a Euclid whose works are esteemed even by the profoundest mathematicians in modern times. (Rule, § I.)

Go not from the world with the joyless consciousness of those to whom the fountains of its purest bliss have been sealed. (Rule, § 11.)

You may treat life as a problem which has to be wrought out to a successful result. (Rule, § 1.)

There is no charm in the female sex which can supply the place of virtue. (Rule, § 11.; and Remark *f.*)

Aid in reforming those social abuses the existence of which casts such a gloom and blight on the happiness of all. (Last of Rem. *h.*)

The benefit arising to us from an enlarged understanding cannot well be overrated. (Last of Remark *k.*)

The moral character is modified in some degree by the tastes and habits of feeling imbibed from the situation in which men are placed. (Remark *j*; and Rule, § 11.)

A good reader will often pause where no grammarian would insert a point; and, on the other hand, he will sometimes neglect the commas he finds inserted by the writer. (Remarks *i* and *n.*)

The memory of the eyes that hung over a man in infancy and childhood will haunt him through all his after-life. (Rule, § 11.; and Remark *c.*)

Macpherson who has given us some highly original images spoils half his work by forgetting that his bard was a Gaul. (Rule, § 1.; and Remark *b.*)

The superior wisdom of the present day consists in the better knowledge derived from experience of the limits of our faculties. (Remark *l*, last portion.)

Antiquity would have raised altars to that vast and mighty genius who, for the advantage of human kind, could tame the rage of thunder and of despotism. (Remark *e.*)

He only is filled with the true spirit of devotion who recognizes, in the outward forms of beauty, the mind of Him who has chosen this mode of intercourse with his trustful and adoring offspring. (Remark *f*; and Rule, § 11.)

A peace worth all the specious goods which this world has at its disposal will ever be found in a simple and contented mind, in an affectionate heart, and in a pure and honorable life. (Last of Remark *l*; and Rule, § 11.)

That the memories of those most justly venerable and dear should throng around us with a new vitality, as life's evening draws on, is scarcely reconcilable with the supposition, that the spirit of which such remembrances are the most precious possession is itself on the point of expiring for ever. (Rem. *j*, lines 8–11; and *h*, first portion.)

RULE VIII.

Parenthetical Phrases and Clauses.

Expressions of a parenthetical or intermediate nature are separated from the context by commas.

EXAMPLES.

1. The sun, with all its attendant planets, is but a very little part of the grand machine of the universe.
2. Books, regarded merely as a gratification, are worth more than all the luxuries on earth.
3. The man of refinement and sensibility finds himself, as it were, in accordance with universal nature.
4. A man of more than ordinary intellectual vigor may, for want of the faculty of expression, be a cipher in society.

REMARKS.

a. In punctuation there is perhaps no rule so well adapted as this for showing the construction and sense of passages, and yet none seems to be less understood or observed by writers and printers. To prevent, therefore, any mistake, on the part of the pupil, as to the meaning of a parenthetical phrase or clause, and to enable him to insert the right points by distinguishing it with some degree of accuracy from the parenthesis, from which it derives its name, we may have to anticipate a little what will be laid down and illustrated in the next chapter.

b. A parenthesis and a parenthetical expression are alike in this respect, that each is a sentence, or a part of a sentence, enclosed within another. But the difference between these two kinds of intermediate sentences or phrases is, that *parentheses* are so used as to be susceptible of omission, without affecting either the sense or the construction of the main passage; while *parenthetical expressions* cannot be omitted, without diminishing the force or changing the import of that by which they are preceded and followed. The following examples will illustrate the difference spoken of, and at the same time exhibit the proper modes of punctuation:—

1. It is probable that every planet (as the Creator has made nothing in vain) is inhabited.
2. The benevolent and pious man, even when persecuted, is, on the whole, a happy man.

The first of these sentences exemplifies the parenthesis, with its appropriate marks; the second, such expressions as are merely parenthetical or intermediate. In the former sentence, the main sentiment would be perfect, both as to its sense and the construction of the language, if the intermediate clause were thrown out from its present place; in the latter, the omission of the phrases between the commas — "even when persecuted," and "on the whole " — would sensibly affect the meaning intended to be conveyed. For the sake of distinction and convenience, this easy kind of parenthesis loses the more generic name, and is commonly termed a *parenthetical expression*.

c. Many short expressions which were formerly enclosed within marks of parenthesis, and which, on account of their construction differing from that of the other portions of the sentence, may properly be called parentheses, are now usually pointed off by commas; as, " Study, *I beseech you*, to store your minds with the exquisite learning of former ages." — "' Thirst for glory,' *says a great writer*, ' is often founded on ambition and vanity.'" As these short expressions interfere but slightly with the unity of thought conveyed in the context, commas are preferable to the parenthetical marks.

d. Many writers are accustomed to omit the comma, in all cases, after a conjunction; but it is evident, that, when a word of this or any other part of speech is divided by a phrase or clause from the portion of the sentence to which it belongs, such intervening expression should have a comma before as well as after it, as in the following example: " Agamemnon still lives before us in the 'tale of Troy divine;' *but*, were not his name embalmed in that imperishable song, there would not now be a wreck of it."

e. Short phrases of a parenthetical kind, when closely united in sense to the context, and particularly when introduced into what is itself parenthetical, should be left unpointed; as, " Poesy can portray *with much energy* the excesses of the passions." This is further exemplified in the intermediate clause of the remark just made, — " when closely united *in sense* to the context;" in which the Italicized words partake somewhat of the nature of a parenthetic phrase, but are better read in union with the words that precede and follow them.

f. Conjunctions, adverbs or adverbial phrases, words or expressions in a direct address, and absolute or other phrases, are sometimes used parenthetically; but, occurring as they do in a variety of ways, their punctuation will be best explained under different rules.

ORAL EXERCISES.

Assign the reason, as given in the eighth Rule, for the insertion of commas in the following sentences:—

A contract, to be valid, must be for some legal object or purpose.
Every passion, however base or unworthy, is eloquent.
Some men are refined, like gold, in the furnace of affliction.
It is mind, after all, which does the work of the world.
Nature, through all her works, delights in variety.
The ship leaps, as it were, from billow to billow.
A spiritual nature, to grow in power, demands spiritual liberty.
The ocean, in its mighty heavings, makes you serious.
Dismiss, as soon as may be, all angry and wrathful thoughts.
But, if education cannot do every thing, it can do much.
Let us send light and joy, if we can, to every one around us.
Man, in his highest mood of thought, aspires to God.
There, where knowledge ceases, faith should strongest prove.
Take your lot, as it is assigned you, without murmuring or complaint.
Christianity, in the highest sense, is the religion of sorrow.

Why, according to the Rule or the Remarks (pp. 64, 65), are the parenthetical expressions in the following sentences pointed or unpointed?—

Thou knowest, come what may, that the light of truth cannot be put out.

Of nothing may we be more sure than this, that, if we cannot sanctify our present lot, we could sanctify no other.

The travellers set out early, and, before the close of the day, arrived at the destined place.

But, in the formation of character, we know that man is to lay its foundations for himself.

Yet, after leaving school, Cowper threw away the next twenty or thirty years of his life almost in doing nothing.

We can sometimes trace extraordinary skill in the liberal arts to the existence of a quarry of fine marble.

Civilization, which on the whole has never gone backward, is new-shaped and modified by each particular people.

The greatest of all human benefits, that at least without which no other benefits can be truly enjoyed, is independence.

Burke and Paine were incarnations of the spirits whose conflict has for ages divided the world.

PARENTHETICAL EXPRESSIONS.

EXERCISE TO BE WRITTEN.

Punctuate the parenthetical expressions, except those to which Remark e, p. 65, will apply :—

A single hour in the day steadily given to the study of an interesting subject brings unexpected accumulations of knowledge. (Rule.)

Benevolence is on whatever side we may contemplate the subject a godlike virtue. (Rule.)

True it is, that were we cast from birth into solitude we should grow up in brutal ignorance. (Rule, and Remark *d*.)

Excellence is in any position almost the infallible result of the determination to excel. (Rule.)

"The virtuous man" it has been beautifully said "proceeds without constraint in the path of his duty." (Remarks *c, e*.)

In Dante for the first time in an uninspired bard the dawn of a spiritual day breaks upon us. (Rule.)

A people should honor and cultivate as unspeakably useful that literature which calls forth the highest faculties. (Rule.)

Simple truths when simply explained are more easily comprehended I believe than is commonly supposed. (Rule, and Remark *c*.)

I would stamp God's name and not Satan's upon every innocent pleasure. (Rule.)

Fanaticism in its ill sense is that which makes a man blind to perceive the falseness of an error. (Rule.)

> Cursed be the verse how well soe'er it flow
> That tends to make one worthy man my foe. (Rule.)

I maintain, that as knowledge extends the range of all imagery is enlarged; and what is far more important that the conception kindles by the contemplation of higher objects. (Remarks *c, d*.)

The love of the beautiful and true like the dewdrop in the heart of the crystal remains for ever clear and liquid in the inmost shrine of man's being. (Rule, and Remark *e*.)

Numerous instances there have been as every reader knows of those who have thrown down every obstacle in the way of their mental elevation. (Remark *c*.)

Without fairness of mind which is only another phrase for disinterested love of truth great native powers of understanding are perverted. (Rule.)

We cannot see an individual expire though a stranger or an enemy without being prompted by compassion to lend him every assistance in our power. (Rule, and Remark *e*.)

RULE IX.

Vocative Words, Phrases, and Clauses.

A word or an expression, denoting a person or an object addressed, is separated by a comma from the rest of the sentence.

EXAMPLES.

1. Antonio, light my lamp within my chamber.
2. Take these two savages to your care, Charon.
3. Boast not, my dear friends, of to-morrow.

REMARKS.

a. When the terms or expressions in a direct address indicate awe, wonder, or any other strong emotion, it is better to use after them the note of exclamation; as, "My sister! O my sister!"

b. For the punctuation of the personal pronoun in a vocative expression, see page 42, Remark *j*.

ORAL EXERCISE.

Assign the reason for the insertion of commas in the following sentences :—

Sir, I beg to acknowledge the receipt of your long-expected letter.
I am obliged to you, ladies, for the kindness you have shown.
Come hither, Moor. — What would you, Desdemona?
From childhood, seignior, you have been my protector.
Idle time, John, is the most ruinous thing in the world.
Come, companion of my toils, let us take fresh courage.
All hope abandon, ye who enter here. — I am, dear madam, yours.

EXERCISE TO BE WRITTEN.

Punctuate these sentences in accordance with the above Rule :—

Continue my dear James to make virtue your principal study.
Acquire my daughters the habit of doing every thing well.
Descend from heaven Urania. — You weep good Ethelbert.
Sir the declaration will inspire the people with increased courage.
This my lords is a perilous and tremendous moment.
Verres what have you to advance against this charge?
Morning is the best time to study my beloved children.
Thou who despisest the outward forms lose not the inward spirit.

RULE X.

Adjectival, Participial, and Absolute Phrases.

Adjectival, participial, and absolute phrases are each separated by a comma from the remainder of the sentence.

EXAMPLES.

1. Awkward in his person, James was ill qualified to command respect.
2. Cradled in the camp, Napoleon was the darling of his army.
3. Having approved of the plan, the king put it into execution.
4. Peace of mind being secured, we may smile at misfortune.
5. To speak candidly, I do not understand the subject.
6. Generally speaking, the conduct of that man is honorable.

REMARKS.

a. The first three examples show the punctuation of adjectival and participial phrases, each of these being separated by a comma from the clause which follows, and with which it is associated. The next three severally exhibit that of phrases containing the nominative, the infinitive, and the participle absolute; so called because they are grammatically independent of the rest of the sentence in which they occur.

b. The phrase which begins the following sentence may be treated as an example of the imperative absolute, and should therefore be pointed as the other independent phrases: " *Take him for all in all,* I shall not look upon his like again."

c. The nominative absolute when used pleonastically, or the expression to which it belongs, is also divided by a comma from what follows it; as, " *The captain,* I hope he will not act thus." — " *He that hath ears to hear,* let him hear."

d. Though followed by a participle, a nominative, if it be the subject of a verb, is not absolute or independent. In this construction, a comma should be inserted both before and after the participial phrase; as, " He, *being dead,* yet speaketh." — See p. 50, *c.*

e. All the phrases referred to, when used intermediately or parenthetically, are enclosed by commas; as, " James, *awkward in his person,* was ill qualified to command respect." — See p. 64.

f. The objective absolute or independent is subject to the same kind of punctuation; as, " Alfred, *than whom a greater king never reigned,* deserves to be held up as a model to all future sovereigns."

g. If placed at the end of the sentence, such phrases should each be preceded by a comma: as, "His conduct is honorable, *generally speaking.*" But elegance or perspicuity of style will seldom permit this change of position in phrases used independently.

h. In respect, however, to those adjectival and participial phrases before which a relative pronoun, in its restrictive sense, is understood, the comma should be omitted. — See p. 59, *j*, second example; and p. 60, *k*, last example.

i. The absolute phrases, *to proceed, to conclude,* &c., when placed at the beginning of a paragraph, to the whole of which they refer, are better pointed with a colon.

ORAL EXERCISES.

Recite the tenth Rule, which lays down the principle for inserting commas in the following and similar sentences :—

Shame being lost, all virtue is lost. — He being dead, we shall live.
Speaking in round numbers, he made fifty thousand dollars.
Crowded in filth, the poor cease to respect one another.
To confess the truth, I was greatly to blame for my indiscretion.
We being exceedingly tossed, they lightened the ship.
Partial in his affections, he was ill fitted to acquire general love.
H. Tooke having taken orders, he was refused admission to the bar.
The sun having risen, we departed on our journey.
His father being dead, the prince succeeded to the throne.
Raising his head from the earth, man looks before and after.
Incensed with indignation, Satan stood unterrified.

How do the Remarks apply to the punctuation of the following sentences?

Regard him as you may, I think that he is a dangerous man.
Timothy Taylor, may he always thus act and speak!
We, being exceedingly tossed, lightened the ship.
The prince, his father being dead, succeeded to the throne.
This is, to say nothing worse, highly reprehensible.
His conduct, generally speaking, is highly honorable.
We set out in the journey of life, full of spirit and high in hope.
The lady was agreeable, being formed with the qualities that we love.
We may smile at misfortune, peace of mind being secured.
Then came Jesus, the doors being shut, and stood in the midst.
I never sought an opportunity of meeting him, to tell you the truth.
Let them attend, all they who feel interested in this great subject.

EXERCISE TO BE WRITTEN.

Let the following sentences be pointed according to Rule X. or the Remarks :—

Full of desire to answer all demands the truly benevolent do not think it troublesome to aid the cause of the wretched. (Rule.)

There are to confess the truth few who are fully qualified for the high office of governing their fellows. (Remark *e.*)

Employed in little things an elevated genius appears like the sun in his evening declination. (Rule.)

Horne Tooke having taken orders was refused admission to the bar. (Remark *d.*)

Having the inward life men cannot conceal it; having divine treasures they will not hoard them. (Rule.)

A state of ease is generally speaking more attainable than a state of pleasure. (Remark *e.*)

Virtue being abandoned we become terrified with imaginary evils. (Rule.)

Those who are truly my friends let them come to my assistance. (Remark *c.*)

To supply this deficiency the Creator endowed him with nobler qualities of intellect. (Rule.)

Physicians the disease once discovered think the cure half wrought. (Remark *e.*)

Surpassing the boast of the too-confident Roman Napoleon but stamped on the earth, and a creation of enchantment arose. (Rule.)

This gentleman take him for all in all possessed a greater variety of knowledge than any man I ever knew. (Remarks *b, e.*)

Overwhelmed with shame and remorse the soul feels itself shut out from heaven. (Rule.)

    God, from the mount of Sinai, whose grey top
    Shall tremble he descending will himself
    Ordain their laws.   (Remark *e.*)

To take some men at their word you would suppose they believed that only one class in society was entitled to consideration. (Rule.)

Ores are called native or natural compounds being produced by nature. (Remark *g.*)

I being in the way, the Lord led me to the house of my master's brother. (Rule.)

There is no single period of history, which all things being taken into consideration will allow us to be indifferent to the progress of mankind. (Remark *e.*)

RULE XI.

Adverbs and Adverbial Phrases.

Adverbs or adverbial phrases, when used as connectives, or when they modify not single words, but clauses or sentences, are each followed by a comma; and, if used intermediately, they admit a comma before as well as after them.

EXAMPLES.

1. Why, these are testimonies of what the unfriended may do.
2. I proceed, thirdly, to point out the proper state of our temper.
3. On the other hand, let not the imagination be ungovernable.
4. Punctuality is, no doubt, a quality of high importance.
5. The most vigorous thinkers and writers are, in fact, self-taught.

REMARKS.

a. The following words, with others of a similar kind, are pointed in accordance with the rule: — Again, further, moreover, once more, as yet, yea, nay, why, well, first, secondly, finally, accordingly, consequently, unquestionably, indisputably, namely, at present, in truth, in short, in fine, in general, in particular, in the meantime, in the next place, in all probability, of late, of course, above all, nevertheless, doubtless, without doubt, true (used for *indeed*), that is (for *namely*), on the one hand, on the contrary, for the most part, now and then.

b. When any of the adverbs or adverbial phrases in the preceding list, or others of a like character, are used to qualify single words, the commas should be omitted; as, "The lecture was *again* delivered." — "Some men are *in the highest degree* mystical."

c. Besides the adverbs and adverbial expressions which qualify single words, many of those relating to the whole clause or sentence in which they occur are sometimes written and printed without commas; as, "*Perhaps* I will give it." — "He was *formerly* a wealthy citizen." The omission of the point is recommended wherever the adverb readily coalesces with the context, as it does in the examples just given.

d. If, however, there is any harshness in the construction or the collocation, the adverbial word or expression may be set off by commas; as, "Poverty, *perhaps*, has been the most fertile source of literary crimes" *e.* The insertion or the omission of commas in respect to such words as *hence, also,* seems, in general practice, to be a matter of taste or caprice. But, except when required by peculiar reasons, the points are better omitted; for, in general, these adverbs unite very readily with the context; as, "*Hence* have arisen dangerous factions." — "The earth is *also* clothed with verdure."

f. Here and *there,* when used antithetically before an adjective or a noun, and placed at the beginning of a clause or sentence, should be each followed by a comma; as, "*Here,* every thing is in stir and fluctuation: *there,* all is serene and orderly." Commonly, however, these words do not require to be punctuated.

g. When two intermediate adverbs, not qualifying any particular word, come together, that which coalesces least with the other portions of the sentence should alone have a comma both before and after it; as, "There were, *surely,* always pretenders in science."

h. Many words ranked as adverbs are sometimes employed conjunctively, and require a different treatment in their punctuation. When used as conjunctions, *however, now, then, too, indeed,* are divided by commas from the context; but when as adverbs, qualifying the words with which they are associated, the separation should not be made. This distinction will be seen from the following examples: —

1. HOWEVER. — We must, *however,* pay some deference to the opinions of the wise, *however* much they are contrary to our own.

2. Now. — I have *now* shown the consistency of my principles; and, *now,* what is the fair and obvious conclusion?

3. THEN. — On these facts, *then,* I *then* rested my argument, and afterwards made a few general observations on the subject.

4. Too. — I found, *too,* a theatre at Alexandria, and another at Cairo; but he who would enjoy the representations must not be *too* particular.

5. INDEED. — The young man was *indeed* culpable in that act, though, *indeed,* he conducted himself very well in other respects.

When placed at the end of a sentence or a clause, the conjunction *too* must not be separated from the context by a comma; as, "I would that they had changed voices *too.*"

i. The particle *therefore,* which is used sometimes as an adverb, and sometimes as a conjunction, may be set off by commas when it is of a parenthetical nature, or obstructs the flow of the composition, and left unpointed when it coalesces easily with the other parts of the sentence; as, "Music has charms, and *therefore* ought to be admired: if, *therefore,* you have an opportunity of learning that delightful art, study it with avidity."

j. Besides, when used as a preposition, should not be punctuated; but, when occurring as an adverb or a conjunction, a comma is required after, and, if occurring intermediately, also one before it; as, "*Besides* him, there was another man who acted in the same manner: there were present, *besides*, several ladies, who seemed to give their approbation." The same remark is applicable to the word *notwithstanding*.

k. Though the examples in Remarks *h, i, j,* are not to be regarded as models of composition, they probably illustrate the use of the comma, by the juxtaposition of the particles, much better than if these were put separately in sentences less liable to critical objection.

l. Used adverbially, *yesterday, to-day, to-morrow,* &c., are, like the adverbs of time, *now, then* (Remark *h*), not separated by points from the words with which they are connected; as, "John went *yesterday* to Cincinnati."

m. All adverbial words or phrases, if followed by a parenthetical expression, must, according to p. 64, have a comma after them; but, if finishing a sentence or a clause, they should have that point which is required by their position.

n. When an adverbial word or phrase comes between two phrases or clauses, it must be separated by a comma only from that expression which it does not qualify; as, "He was saved, for a time *at least*, from a relapse." — "Though Nature has given to all her children some conceptions of immortality, *still* her information is far from proving satisfactory."

ORAL EXERCISES.

Show how the punctuation in these sentences corresponds to Rule XI. : —

Lastly, let me repeat what I stated at the beginning of my lecture.
Such, undoubtedly, is the characteristic of genuine virtue.
On the contrary, I believe that truth is the great inspirer.
There is, now and then, a youth of more than youthful powers.
He made the most, mentally, of whatever came in his way.
Undoubtedly, the statement he has made is not correct.
There are many ends, doubtless, for which each thing exists.
But, lastly, let us examine the truth of these arguments.
In fact, modern civilization is a corrupted Christianity.
Such, in general, is the humiliating aspect of the tomb.
Accordingly, the chronicles of the middle ages teem with crimes.
The national life, in short, is to a certain extent diseased.
Well, proceed with the speech which you have so well begun.

ADVERBS AND ADVERBIAL PHRASES.

According to Remarks on pages 72-74, assign reasons for the punctuation of the adverbial or conjunctive words and phrases which occur in the following sentences, or for the omission of commas :—

At present, the individual is often crushed by circumstances.
True, the rooms of the poor are not lined with works of art.
Let us further consider the arguments on this subject.
My high-blown pride at length broke under me.
How inconceivably thin and tender are the threads of a spider!
Let us, in the first place, observe the inanimate world.
That is, there is a true way of expressing truth.
Well, I call conversation the sweet interchange of thought.
I do not well know why I should think of it in any other respect.
Ay, love the good and the beautiful. — Aye love the good, &c.
He first went to New York, and afterwards to Philadelphia.
Attend, first, to the literal sense; and, secondly, to the metaphorical.
Probably there are few who ever accomplish as much as they expected.
Few, probably, ever accomplish as much as they expected.
Why do you trust your character to be evolved by accident?
If I cannot perform my promise, why, I will regret having made it.
Hence all human laws are more or less imperfect.
Here also is the distinction between faith and mere assent.
I am inclined, however, to believe this to be a mistaken opinion.
However great Napoleon was as a general, he was not a good man.
Now, feudalism is the embodiment of Satanic pride.
Now I know in part; but then shall I know even as also I am known.
It is, then, a mark of wisdom to live virtuously and devoutly.
Have not you, too, gone about the earth like an evil genius?
We look at all things too exclusively from our own point of view.
If she trust the stars above, they can prove treacherous too.
True eloquence, indeed, does not consist in mere speech.
Professors Bentley and Porson were scholars indeed.
Our civilization, therefore, is not an unmixed good.
Therefore is our civilization not an unmixed good.
A certain degree of moral culture, therefore, must be presupposed.
A certain degree of moral culture must therefore be presupposed.
Besides this, it may be of the greatest advantage to you in business.
It may, besides, be of the greatest advantage to you in business.
They, notwithstanding, had much love to spare.
A man may be rich, notwithstanding pecuniary losses.
We shall perhaps leave the city to-morrow morning.
Yet, fair as thou art, thou shunnest to expose thyself to the public.

THE COMMA.

EXERCISE TO BE WRITTEN.

Insert commas only where required by Rule XI. *and Remarks* (pp. 72–74): —

Hence the organs of sense are probably in a state of the greatest sensibility in an early period of life. (Remarks *e*, *c*.)

Shakspeare was the most brilliant example unquestionably of a triumph over the defects of education. (Rule, and Remark *a*.)

The children of our cottagers too appear to derive peculiar pleasure from the soft breath of spring. (Remark *h* 4.)

As yet science has hardly penetrated beneath the surface of nature. (Rule, and Remark *a*.)

Characters endowed with great excellences will unfortunately often stand in need of great allowances. (Remark *g*.)

Do we in a word reduce the whole of human duty to a bald and punctilious discharge of worldly business? (Rule.)

However much he was persecuted, he loved his persecutors not the less. (Remarks *b*, *h* 1.)

The happiness of the dead however is affected by none of these considerations. (Remark *h* 1.)

First men of uncommon moral endowments may be expected to be men of uncommon intellectual powers. (Rule, and Remark *a*.)

If therefore you find that you have a hasty temper, watch it narrowly. (Remark *i*.)

The Greeks were great reasoners; and their language accordingly abounds in connectives. (Rule, and Remark *a*.)

This was the object to which the meeting first directed its attention. (Remark *b*.)

His prudent conduct may heal the difference; nay may prevent any misunderstanding in future. (Rule, and Remark *a*.)

Having now removed the objections made to our conduct, I shall take up very little more of your lordships' time. (Remarks *b*, *h* 2.)

There was great scarcity of corn, and consequently dearth of all other victuals. (Rule, and Remarks *a*, *d*.)

Every thing that grows is a world probably of uncounted myriads of beings. (Rule, and Remark *d*.)

Sooner or later insulted virtue avenges itself on states, as well as on private men. (Rule.)

The author therefore commences his undertaking by an analysis of names. (Remark *i*.)

Without being rash on the one hand or fearful on the other we shall find all things working together for good. (Remark *n*.)

ADVERBS AND ADVERBIAL PHRASES. 77

Christ stands immeasurably in advance of the moral attainments of the world. (Remark *b*.)

And hence perhaps it is that Solomon calls the fear of the Lord the beginning of wisdom. (Remark *g*.)

The lateral force of human action that is the influence of contemporaries, is great. (Rule, and Remark *a*.)

Meanwhile we do not believe in any infallible specific, in any sudden and unusual remedy. (Rule.)

But yesterday the word of Cæsar might have stood against the world. (Remark *b*.)

Sometimes doubts and apprehensions will haunt the mind in its searchings for truth. (Rule.)

But on the other hand do not suppose that poverty is altogether a waste and howling wilderness. (Rule, and Remark *c*.)

There is undoubtedly very often more happiness in the hut than in the palace. (Rule, and Remark *g*.)

Nature has indeed given us a soil which yields bounteously to the hand of industry. But what are lands, &c. (Remark *h* 5.)

Society must of course receive beauty into its character and feeling. (Rule, and Remark *a*.)

Let us contemplate then this connection, which binds the prosperity of others to our own. (Remark *h* 3.)

Still a great and fruitful idea dimly pervades the eccentric speculations of Fourier. (Rule, and Remark *b*.)

We should look on character acquired here as the condition of happiness hereafter. (Remark *c*, and last of *f*.)

At present innumerable prejudices obstruct a complete extraction of the mental and moral wealth latent in society. (Rule, and Remark *a*.)

Did I not see other and holier influences than the sword working out the regeneration of our race, I should indeed despair. (Remarks *c*, *h* 5.)

Again perfection requires that each quality should be without debasing alloy. Lastly perfection requires that all the graces be expanded to an unlimited degree. (Rule, and Remark *a*.)

De Foe soon however relinquished every thing else for literature and politics; for which indeed his temper and talents adapted him much better than for business. (Remarks *h* 1, 5.)

Now how does capital punishment operate? Why it cuts off the offender from all the chance of reformation. (Remarks *h* 2 and *b*; Rule, and Remark *a*.)

RULE XII.

Phrases at the End of Sentences or Clauses.

§ I. When a phrase beginning with a preposition, an adverb, or a conjunction, relates to or modifies a preceding portion of the sentence, a comma is unnecessary, if the parts are closely connected in sense.

§ II. But the point must be inserted when its omission would occasion ambiguity, or when the phrase begins with a particle obstructing the connection which subsists between the different portions of the sentence.

EXAMPLES.

§ I.

1. For that agency he applied without a recommendation.
2. Cultivate your intellectual powers by habits of study and reflection.
3. The idea is very happily applied under one of its forms.

§ II.

1. He applied for that agency, without a recommendation
2. Cultivate your intellectual powers, especially by habits of study, &c
3. The idea is very happily applied, at least under one of its forms.

REMARKS.

a. In the first three examples, the phrases beginning with the prepositions "without," "by," "under," are closely connected with both portions of the sentence in which they severally occur, and therefore should not be preceded by a comma.

b. If, in the first example of the second class, the comma were omitted before the preposition "without," the sentence might be wrongly understood to mean, that a person applied for an agency, without its having any recommendation in its favor. Of the next example, if written without the comma before the adverb "especially," the meaning might be, that, by habits of study and reflection, you should cultivate particularly your intellectual powers, that is, in preference to others; but this is not the sense. In both of these sentences, the insertion of the comma, as above, leads obviously to the true signification. In the last example, the sense is brought out more clearly by inserting a comma before the modifying words "at least," because they belong rather to the phrase than to the whole clause, and obstruct the connection between "applied" and "under one of its forms."

c. When the use of a word qualifying the phrase interrupts but slightly the connection between two parts of a sentence, the comma is better omitted. Thus, though susceptible of being pointed. the following sentences, where the final phrases are severally modified by the words *either, even,* may be written without the comma: " A good man will be happy *either* in this world or the next." — " The knowledge of nature cannot be exhausted *even* by the wisest."

d. But, if a final phrase conveys an additional thought, or is preceded by another phrase, with which it does not readily unite, the comma should be inserted; as, " A strong idea of religion has *generally* prevailed, *even* among the most uncultivated savages." — " The ode was frequently sung *at his request,* either in the church or at some occasional meeting of the choir."

e. The rule is applicable to a sentence ending with *two* phrases, each beginning with a particle, which may be taken either separately or as a compound phrase; the last or both referring to some portion of what precedes.

f. A phrase, at the end of a clause or sentence, of an antithetical character, is preceded by a comma; as, " Man's true destination is not perfection, *but* the unceasing perfecting of his nature." — See Rule V., p. 45.

g. No point is required before a final phrase beginning with *but*, in the sense of *except;* as, " None are poor *but* the mean in mind."

h. When a phrase begins with a verb in the infinitive mood, and its preposition signifies *in order to*, it should not be preceded by a comma; as, " We do not pray to God *to instruct* him." Unless where the omission of the point would too closely unite the latter portion of the clause with the phrase; as, " Our minds must go out into the infinite and immortal regions, *to find* sufficiency and satisfaction for the present hour."

i. If the words *in order* are expressed before the infinitive, the phrase is usually preceded by a comma; as, " We should be virtuous and devout, *in order* to refine and elevate our nature."

j. Final phrases, referring to time, measure, or distance, whether they begin with a preposition or are elliptical, should not be preceded by any point; as, " Byron was born *on Jan.* 22, 1788, and died *April* 19, 1824." — " The mason built the wall *a hundred feet high.*" — " Some men can easily walk *four miles an hour.*"

k. But when the last phrase consists of a date, and the preceding one ends with a noun, it is better to distinguish the phrases by a comma, unless they are connected by means of a preposition; as, "The mills were destroyed by *fire*, Sept. 28, 1854." — "Peace was concluded between England and France *in* February, 1763."

ORAL EXERCISES.

State why, in conformity with Rule XII. (p. 78), *commas are used in some of these sentences, and omitted in others :* —

He was a man of extraordinary powers, both of mind and body.
The fertile earth is fragrant after soft showers.
Take heed not to place thyself in the power of temptation.
View the path you are entering on, with an enlightened mind.
The grandeur of Rome has vanished like a spectre in the night.
Poisons are sweet in the moral world, as truly as in the natural.
Do thy best to pluck this crawling serpent from my breast.
Poverty of mind is often concealed under the garb of splendor.
Repentance is not a single act, but a habit of virtue.
Truth is not hidden from us by an impenetrable veil.
All great things are so, only by the assemblage of small things.
Call off the thoughts when running upon disagreeable objects.
Keep an inventory of your friends, rather than of your goods.

Mention why, in accordance with the above Remarks, commas are inserted or omitted in the following sentences : —

Thou art a soldier even to Cato's wishes.
I knew the facts of the case even when I wrote to you.
Judge not either capriciously or by a factitious standard.
He was a Columbus in a brave heart, if not in achievement.
Virtue is not the creature of will, but necessary and immutable.
Our best works are fractions, not complete and rounded unities.
Nothing remained but to throw himself on the mercy of Heaven.
Let me find a charter in your voice to assist my simpleness.
He left the room to see whether all was safe.
Cultivate the art of reading, in order to read well.
Patrick Kelly left Ireland seventeen years ago.
You will be sure to find me in the school at nine o'clock, A.M.
Adam Smith was born in Scotland, 1723, and died 1790.
The lyre was invented 1004 B.C.; and paper in China, 105 B.C.

EXERCISE TO BE WRITTEN.

In agreement with the Rule and the Remarks (pp. 78–80), *let commas be inserted or omitted in the following sentences:* —

A year is much in human life particularly to the very young and very old. (Rule, § II.)

Follow the perfections of your enemies rather than the errors of your friends. (Rule, § II.; and Remark *f*.)

The love of praise should be preserved under proper subordination to the principle of duty. (Rule, § I.)

The soul becomes great by the habitual contemplation of great objects. (Rule, § I.)

Do not employ your wit either to insult or to offend your associates. (Remark *c*.)

I often come to this quiet place to breathe the airs that ruffle thy face. (First of Remark *h*.)

A true philosopher is careful to preserve an evenness of mind both in prosperity and adversity. (Rule, § II.)

How superior is the man of forbearance and gentleness to every other man in the collisions of society! (Rule, § II.)

Christianity represents physical evil as the direct appointment of God's love. (Rule, § I.)

The active mind of man seldom or never rests satisfied with its present condition how prosperous soever. (Rule, § II.)

The saint owes much of the grace and elegance of his spirit to the influences of sorrow in some form. (Rule, § I.)

A great mind is formed by a few great ideas not by an infinity of loose details. (Rule, both sections; and Remarks *e*, *f*.)

The first indications of genius disclose themselves at a very early period. (Rule, § I.)

The knowledge of any one truth acts as an introducer and interpreter between us and all its kindred truths. (Rule, § I.)

We cannot bid farewell to so large a portion of human history without deep and earnest thought. (Rule, § II.)

Herbert always attracted friends and strangers by the elegance and benignity of his manners. (Rule, § I.)

Law should not be the rich man's luxury but the poor man's remedy. (Rule, § II.; and Remark *f*.)

There are Christians who defer to some perpetual and concurrent authority either in a living person or in a body of persons. (Rule, § II.; and Remark *d*.)

The intellectual powers may be exercised to the neglect and stifling of the moral and spiritual. (Rule, § II.)

Half of what passes among men for talent is nothing but strong health. (Rule, § I.; and Remark *g*.)

Sensible men show their good sense by saying much in a few words. (Rule, § I.)

Shake not the credit of others in endeavoring to establish your own. (Rule, § II.)

Ariosto, the eminent Italian poet, was born in the year of our Lord 1474, and died 1533. (Remark *j*.)

Let your affections be cultivated with ardor and purity through all the successive periods of life. (Rule, § I.; and Remark *e*.)

Let us not think of the departed as looking on us with earthly, partial affections. (Rule, § I.)

Who can look on this scene without an increase of love and reverence and trust? (Rule, § II.)

The dormant faculties of men seem only to be awaiting more favorable circumstances to disclose themselves. (First of Rem. *h*.)

The soul is nursed for heaven by the discipline of a sacred sorrow. (Rule, § I.)

The well-being of a community cannot flow from the simple effect of one great change however necessary or successful. (Rule, § II.)

The grandeur and vastness of human hope are corresponded to by a similar grandeur and vastness of human nature. (Rule, § I.)

Some men put on the appearance of virtue in order to succeed in their nefarious enterprises. (Rule, § II.; and Remark *i*.)

There are many topics on which individuals may hold the greatest diversity of opinion without any diminution of holy sympathy in the essential principles of religion. (Rule, § II.; and Remark *e*.)

Seek for distinction only among the honest and pious. Seek for distinction but only among the honest and pious. (Rule, §§ I., II.; and Remarks *c*, *d*.)

Let us employ the powers which our Creator has given us in such a manner as will be fitted to purify and elevate our nature. (Rule, § II.)

Moral light must be intermingled with intellectual light to conduct us safely through our mortal course. (Rule, § II.; and last portion of Remark *h*.)

No man can struggle, for years together, to evolve his character into pure moral manhood without shedding around him a benignant, life-giving influence. (Rule, § II.)

RULE XIII.

Inverted or Transposed Expressions.

Many phrases which, in their natural or usual order, do not require to be punctuated, are, when inverted, set off by a comma from the rest of the sentence.

EXAMPLES.

1. By Cowley, the philosopher Hobbes is compared to Columbus.
2. To the wise and good, old age presents a scene of tranquil enjoyment.
3. Of all our senses, sight is the most perfect and delightful.
4. In perusing the works of enlightened men, we ought to think much.

REMARKS.

a. The natural or usual order of words in English composition, if adopted in the above sentences, would run as follows: "The philosopher Hobbes is compared by Cowley to Columbus."—"Old age presents a scene of tranquil enjoyment to the wise and good."—"Sight is the most perfect and delightful of all our senses."—"We ought to think much in perusing the works of enlightened men." It will be seen, that the phrases which have been punctuated in the examples, are, when put in the usual order, written without commas, in accordance with the first part of Rule XII., p. 78.

b. In the inverted or rhetorical style in which these sentences are exemplified under the rule, it is obvious, that, if the comma were omitted, we could not read or understand them, without a greater exercise of the judgment than is required when that point is inserted after each transposed phrase.

c. But the rule, as commonly laid down by grammarians, is by no means universal in its application. The mere circumstance of the transposition of a word or phrase is not a sufficient reason for introducing a comma, as may readily be seen by inspecting either a single page of an author who adopts this style, or a few lines in any of the poets; and indeed, were all such inversions punctuated, both perspicuity and good taste would be in numberless instances violated. On the other hand, actual usage is so discordant, that, in many cases, it would seem to be a matter of mere choice, whether an inverted phrase should have a comma or not. By attention, however, to the various modes in which the sentences under notice are formed, most of the practical difficulties would be overcome.

d. In accordance with the remark just made, the comma should be dispensed with under the following circumstances, — unless the inverted portions of a sentence are both of them clauses, or severally end and begin with words of the same part of speech, with a noun and an adjective, or *vice versâ:* —

1. When the first inverted portion contains a noun governed by a verb in the last part of the sentence; as, " That interesting and valuable *history* he did not read." — " *Him and his actions* you will very probably *imitate.*" — " *The praise of judgment* has Virgil justly *contested* with Homer."

2. When the second portion of the sentence commences with a verb, whether principal or auxiliary, before its nominative; as, " At the bottom of the garden *ran* a little rivulet." — " Of the variegated mountain *shall* nought remain unchanged." — " Underneath our happiest mirth *is* a calm fountain of sober thought."

3. When a preposition is removed from the word to which it usually belongs, and placed at the beginning of the inverted phrase; as, " *With* that portion of the work he was the least *satisfied;*" instead of, " He was the least *satisfied with* that portion of the work." — " *To* egotists and pedants I have a strong *antipathy.*" — " *Of* all truly noble feelings they were quite *unsusceptible.*"

4. When the first of the inverted portions of a sentence begins with the words *it is*, or *only;* as, " *It is* in the sphere of intellect alone that men are becoming truly civilized." — " *Only* on a few slight occasions they felt disposed to be merciful."

5. When, though a distinct articulation may require a slight pause, an inverted phrase can be read in close connection with what follows it, without affecting the import of the sentence; as, " *In infancy* the mind is peculiarly ductile." — " *To each* the soul of each how dear!" — " *By these swords* we acquired our liberties." — " *In a lucid manner* the orator expressed his ideas."

6. When an expression precedes an inverted phrase which is connected more closely with the latter portion of the sentence than with the former; as, " However opposite may be the sides from which we start at the foot of the mountain, *in approaching its summit* we approach one another."

e. By carefully comparing the examples given under Remark *d* with those under the rule, and with a few additional ones, which, for the sake of reference, we shall now present, the student will be struck with the fact, that, though in some respects similar to each other, they are in other and various respects dissimilar; and he will also perceive, that, while the insertion of a comma in the examples belonging to Remark *d* would be of no advantage in bringing out the true meaning of the sentences, the omission of the point between the inverted portions of those about to be exhibited would operate to a greater or less extent in impeding an easy comprehension of the sense: —

1. That interesting and valuable history which you lent him, he did not read.
   Him whose actions you approve, you will very probably imitate.
   The praise of judgment, Virgil has justly contested with Homer.
2. At the bottom of the garden, a little rivulet ran.
   Of the variegated mountain, nought shall remain unchanged.
   Underneath our happiest mirth, there is a calm fountain of sober thought.
3. With that portion of the work, Jeffrey was the least satisfied.
   To egotists and pedants, sensible men have a strong antipathy.
   Of all feelings that are truly noble, they were quite unsusceptible.
4. In the sphere of intellect alone, men are becoming truly civilized.
   On a few slight occasions, they felt disposed to be merciful.
   By forgetfulness of injuries, we show ourselves superior to them.
5. In youth, shun the temptations to which youth is exposed.
   To each, honor is given. — By these, various opinions may be held.
   In a remarkably striking and lucid manner, the orator expressed his ideas.
6. In approaching the summit of a mountain, we approach one another.

f. When, however, no serious error would be produced by the omission of the comma, the briefer inverted phrases, even those belonging to the above class, may be left unpointed, if they occur in clauses set off by commas; as, "On *piety humanity* is built, and on *humanity much* happiness, and yet still more on piety itself." Instances of this kind are often met with in poetry.

g. But such inverted words as appear in the second and third examples of No. 5 above, where the omission of the comma would manifestly tend to confusion or error, must in all cases be punctuated. So also must any phrase that is equivalent to a clause, or into which it is easily convertible; as, "*In believing attainment impossible*, you will make it so;" that is, "If you believe," &c. (see Rule XIV., p. 89); the only exception to the use of the point here being when such a phrase is used under the circumstances specified in Remark *d* 6.

h. All inverted phrases, when preceded by other phrases or by clauses, are treated as parenthetical expressions, and punctuated according to Rule VIII. and the remarks thereon, pp. 64, 65.

THE COMMA.

ORAL EXERCISE.

Why, according to Rule XIII. and Remarks (pp. 83–85), are commas inserted or omitted between the transposed expressions in the following sentences? —

To most, religion is a mere tradition or a momentary feeling.
In fearless freedom he arose. — By vicious examples be not misled.
Of all ill habits, that of idleness is the most incorrigible.
The first-fruit of your daily thoughts consecrate to God.
In all sublime scenes, there is a mixture of the awful.
With earnest heart I humbly crave my latter end like his may be.
The history of past ages, men often read to little purpose.
Her crystal lamp the evening star has lighted.
To minds of a devout temper, the eternal is mirrored in the temporal.
In the British Museum is the original work of Copernicus.
Whom ye ignorantly worship, Him declare I unto you.
Only by degrees we turn our thoughts inwardly on ourselves.
Without much thought, books cannot be profitably read.
To public opinion all states must in a measure bow.
Of good delivery, distinct articulation is an essential requisite.
Against great force of reasoning it is in vain to contend.
By the faults or errors of others, wise men correct their own.
In early years the habits of industry are most easily acquired.
At his control, despair and anguish fled the struggling soul.
Through her rags do the winds of the winter blow bleak.
To study the science of spirit, I must enter my own soul.
All the appearances of nature I was careful to study.
By good nature, half the misery of human life is assuaged.
In silent and solitary places, genius is often found.
Into that glorious world he constantly beckons us to follow him.
Like a spectre in the night, the grandeur of Rome is vanished.
Scipio, Milton called "the height of Rome." — In thee I confide.
It is only by devotion to liberal pursuits that we can be truly liberal
Greater exploits than force, counsel and wisdom achieve.
To thee I pour my prayer. — In power and wealth exult no more.
What is the right path, few men take the trouble of inquiring.
This great error I wish to expose. — It is a place he aspires to hold.
In meeting with a madman, feign yourself a fool.
To those whose interests are in danger, time is valuable.
For want of this, genius has been a scourge to the world.
In eternity God dwelleth, free from anger and from pain.
With the many, life is one round of never-ceasing toil.

EXERCISE TO BE WRITTEN.

Punctuate the following sentences, or leave them unpointed, in accordance with the thirteenth Rule and the Remarks thereon:—

In the production and preservation of order all men recognize something that is sacred. (Rule, and Remark *e* 5.)

From the right exercise of our intellectual powers arises one of the chief sources of our happiness. (Remark *d* 2, 3.)

Through life truth ought to be one of the great objects of human pursuit. (Rule, and Remark *e* 5.)

In the attainment of all excellence in the arts patronage and genius should go hand in hand. (Rule.)

Education is at home a friend, abroad an introduction, in solitude a solace, in society an ornament. (Remark *d* 5.)

In every material action of your life consider well its probable result. (Rule, and Remark *e* 5.)

Of all our virtuous emotions those of kind regard are the most readily imitated. (Rule.)

In the solemn silence of the mind are formed those great resolutions which decide the fate of men. (Remark *d* 2.)

Before giving way to anger try to find a reason for not being angry. (Rule, and last portion of Remark *g*.)

In the acuteness of the external senses some of the inferior animals excel our species. (Rule, and Remark *e* 5.)

Over matchless talents probity should throw its brightest lustre. (Rule, and Remark *e* 3.)

It is from the spirit's own pearl that the good embellish their character. (Remark *d* 4.)

From the little root of a few letters science has spread its branches over all nature, and raised its head to the heavens. (Rule.)

Only in the light of a sublime faith can the history of our race be read without despondency. (Remarks *d* 2, 4.)

In the ruffled and angry hour we view every appearance through a false medium. (Remark *e* 5.)

It is through moral and spiritual power that the rivers of thought and feeling are to be turned. (Remark *d* 4.)

      Friend of the brave! in peril's darkest hour
      Intrepid Virtue looks to thee for power.   (Remark *d* 6.)

Of all treasons against humanity there is no one worse than his who employs great intellectual force to keep down the intellect of his less-favored brethren. (Rule.)

In these hours of golden leisure my chief haunt is the banks of a small stream. (Rule, and Remark *e* 5.)

This view of religion I propose to make the subject of some free discussion. (Remark *d* 1.)

In amusement and novel-reading only the girl spends all her evening hours. (Rule, and Remark *e* 4.)

On feelings allied to these priestcraft and sorcery have often fastened themselves. (Rule, and Remark *e* 3.)

In order to improve the mind we ought less to learn than to contemplate. (Rule, and last portion of Remark *g*.)

With what you have be satisfied. — All you hear believe not. (Remark *d*, third line.)

In the hurry and eagerness of selfish competition we underrate the silent influence of moral character. (Rule, and Remark *e* 5.)

When others are asleep, in its own contemplations the soul finds a source of solace and pleasure. (Remark *d* 6.)

In not learning your business perfectly you cannot give satisfaction to your employer. (Rule; and Remark *e* 6, and last of *g*.)

To every character its fitting position and appropriate function have been assigned. (Remark *d* 3.)

It is to the unaccountable oblivion of our mortality that the world owes all its fascination. (Remark *d* 4.)

By doing nothing we learn to do ill. — To command any subject adequately we must stand above it. (Rule, and last of Remark *g*.)

In this struggle his moral discipline consists. On no other terms could he be at once a dweller on earth and an heir of heaven. (Remark *d* 3, 2, 5.)

> On some fond breast the parting soul relies,
> Some pious drops the closing eye requires;
> Even from the tomb the voice of nature cries,
> Even in our ashes live their wonted fires.   (Rem. *d* 3, 1, 5, 2.)

Through the dim veil of the visible and perishing man catches a glimpse of the vast significance of the unseen and the eternal. (Rule, and Remark *e* 5.)

> On beds of green sea-flower thy limbs shall be laid,
> Around thy white bones the red coral shall grow,
> Of thy fair yellow locks threads of amber be made,
> And every part suit to thy mansion below.   (Rem. *d* 3, 5, and *f*.)

Into every human being has God breathed an immortal soul. — Into every human being God has breathed an immortal soul. (Remarks *d* 2 and *e* 2.)

RULE XIV.

One Clause Depending on Another.

Two clauses, one depending on the other, are separated by a comma.

EXAMPLES.

1. If you would be revenged on your enemies, let your life be blameless
2. Wealth is of no real use, except it be well employed.
3. Unless it blossoms in the spring, the tree will not bear fruit in autumn.
4. Till we can go alone, we must lean on the hand of a guide.
5. Fill thy heart with goodness, and thou wilt find that the world is full of good.

REMARKS.

a. Sentences containing dependent clauses are generally distinguished by one of them beginning with a particle expressive of condition, admission, purpose, causation, time, or place. They are not, however, necessarily so constructed, as is shown in the fifth example, the clauses of which depend, one on the other, not in form, but in sense; being equivalent to — "*If* thou fill thy heart with goodness, thou wilt find," &c.

b. A phrase having the import of a conditional clause, and put at the beginning of the sentence, is also distinguished by a comma; as, "*To be good*, you must do good;" that is, "That you may be good, you must do good." — See p. 85, last portion of *g*.

c. When, in a sentence relating to time, place, or manner, the clause beginning with an adverb is put last, and is closely connected in sense with what precedes it, the comma should not be inserted; as, "I love my kind *where'er* I roam." — "You will reap *as* you sow." Clauses like these may be regarded as akin to the restrictive relative. — See Rule VII., § II., p. 57.

d. But if the adverbs *when, where,* &c., have only a faint reference to time or place, or introduce an additional idea, they should be preceded by a comma; as, "Refrain not to speak, *when* by speaking you may be useful to others." — "Andrew sailed for California, *where* he does a flourishing business."

e. When the conjunctions *if* and *because* are used to bind closely together the two clauses between which they are severally placed, the comma is unnecessary; as "You may go *if* you will." — "Sin is not less dangerous *because* men are hardened by it."

f. No point should be introduced between two clauses united by the conjunction *that,* signifying purpose or design, if it is closely connected with the preceding verb; as, "He *visited* the springs *that* he might improve his health." But a comma must be inserted if the conjunction is separated at some distance from the verb; as, "Let us *consider* the following propositions, *that* we may fully understand the subject."

g. The comma is usually admissible between the clauses, when the words *in order* come before the conjunction *that,* unless they are preceded immediately by the verb; as, "Cæsar visited Britain, *in order that* he might conquer the inhabitants." — "The man *travelled in order that* he might regain his strength."

h. The distinction recommended in the punctuation of the first example under each of the Remarks *f* and *g* may seem rather nice; but, undoubtedly, the phrase *in order that* obstructs the flow of a sentence more than the simple conjunction *that.*

ORAL EXERCISES.

Show how Rule XIV. *is applicable to the punctuation of the sentences that follow:—*

Where thoughts kindle, words spontaneously flow.
The good which men do is not lost, though it is often disregarded.
If there were no cowardice, there would be little insolence.
Where the heart is well guarded, temptations cannot enter.
It were no virtue to bear calamities, if we did not feel them.
Make men intelligent, and they become inventive.
Though a civilization may die, it leaves imperishable records.
People are rude and unpolite, because they are ignorant.
Wherever we are, we are not forgotten by a kind Providence.
Were patrons more disinterested, ingratitude would be more rare.
Since none enjoy all blessings, be content with a few.
Go where a man may, home is the centre to which his heart turns.
As we grow older, life becomes dim in the distance.
We obey the laws of society, because they are the laws of virtue.
While the bridegroom tarried, they all slumbered and slept.
Dare to be good, whatever evil may surround you.
If their lungs receive our air, that moment they are free.
When beggars die, there are no comets seen.
Make up your mind to do a thing, and you will do it.
Every thing is beautiful, if left where nature meant it to be.

DEPENDENT CLAUSES.

How do the Remarks (pp. 89, 90) apply to the punctuation of the following sentences:—

Drop upon Fox's grave the tear, 'twill trickle to his rival's bier.
By playing with a fool at home, he'll play with you abroad.
I will see you when you arrive. — I will go whither thou goest.
He went away as soon as I came. — Use time as if you knew its value.
Do unto others as you would have them do unto you.
Quietness and peace flourish where justice and reason govern.
Let us live while we live. — Fear not, while acting justly.
He went to the city of Manchester, where he remained for a year.
The age of miracles is past, while that of prejudice remains.
Sense shines with the greatest lustre, when it is set in humanity.
I fled because I was afraid.—Speak clearly if you would be understood
Truth is to be loved, purely and solely because it is true.
Live well that you may die well. — We go that we may be in time.
Be studious and diligent, in order that you may become learned.

EXERCISE TO BE WRITTEN.

Point, or leave unpointed, the following sentences, according to the principles laid down in the fourteenth Rule and the Remarks:—

When the great man is laid in his grave lies of malice are apt to give way to lies of adulation. (Rule.)

Decide not by authoritative rules when they are inconsistent with reason. (Rule, and Remark d.)

A man may comfort himself for the wrinkles in his face provided his heart be fortified with virtue. (Rule.)

We cannot turn in any direction where the Creator's love does not smile around us. (Remark c.)

If theological gossip were the measure of religious faith we should be the devoutest of all human generations. (Rule.)

We cannot raise the moral standard of the depressed classes till we have first improved their social condition. (Rule, and Remark d.)

Unless he put a bridle on his tongue the babbler will soon shut himself out from all society. (Rule.)

Have respect for yourself that others may not disrespect you. (Rule, and last sentence of Remark f.)

We should be ashamed of many of our actions were the world acquainted with our motives. (Rule.)

By timely resisting them the greatest evils may be overcome. Rule, and Remark b.)

If there be nothing celestial without us it is only because all is earthly within. (Rule.)

Remember your own feelings in order that you may judge of the feelings of others. (Rule, and Remarks *g*, *h*.)

Where the whole is one dark blot of shade there can be no picture. (Rule.)

Breathe into men a fervent purpose and you awaken powers before unknown. (Rule, and Remark *a*.)

Some people endeavor to divert their thoughts lest their minds should reproach them. (Rule.)

We were present when General Lafayette embarked at Havre for New York. (Remark *c*.)

When we combat error with any other weapon than argument we err more than those whom we attack. (Rule.)

Let all dispose their hours till midnight when again we pray your presence. (Remark *d*.)

In how small a compass lie all the elements of man's truest happiness if society were only conducted in a rational spirit! (Rule.)

Suppress the first desires of evil as soon as they arise, and extinguish the spark before it spreads. (Remark *c*.)

Where true religion has prevented one crime false religions have afforded a pretext for a thousand. (Rule.)

Our hearts should be filled with gratitude when we contemplate the wonderful works of nature. (Rule, and Remark *d*.)

The lives of men should be filled with beauty even as the earth and heavens are clothed with it. (Rule.)

Rear stronger minds and they will lift up the race to sublimer heights of dignity and power. (Rule, and Remark *a*.)

There never is true eloquence except when great principles and sentiments have entered into the substance of the soul. (Rule.)

We live that we may die. — Attend that you may receive instruction. (Remark *f*, first sentence.)

If women fulfilled truly their divine errand there would be no need of reforming societies. (Rule.)

We compare the divine Mind with ours that we may have something within the grasp of our reason to dwell upon. (Last of Rem. *f*.)

We weep over the dead because they have no life, and over the living because they have no perfection. (Remark *e*.)

Give me a larger eye and I will reveal to you another rank of worlds marshalled behind those whose shining hosts you now behold. (Rule, and Remark *a*.)

RULE XV.

Correlative Words, Phrases, and Clauses.

§ I. Two correlative expressions, united by the conjunction *as* or *than*, are written without a point between them.

§ II. But, when united by any other word than these conjunctions, the correlative expressions are distinguished by a comma.

EXAMPLES.

§ I.

1. Men are never | so easily deceived || as when they plot to deceive others.
2. A child in the humblest walks of life is | as richly gifted || as in the highest.
3. Only | such repentance is beneficial || as makes us wiser and better.

Do not spend | more time in bed || than is required for sleep.

§ II.

1. But | though learned and methodical, || yet the teacher was not a pedant.
2. A great man will | neither trample on a worm, || nor cringe before a king.
3. All know that | as virtue is its own reward, || so vice is its own punishment.
4. Yes, | the more we see of a truly good man, || the better we love him.

REMARKS.

a. To indicate the true character of the sentences just quoted, we have put two perpendicular lines between each pair of correlative expressions, and a single line before the first expression, in each example. It will be seen, that the phrases or clauses beginning severally with the correlative words, "so—as," "as—as," "such—as," "more—than," which occur in the first class of examples, have a stronger attraction to each other than those commencing with the correlatives "though—yet," "neither—nor," "as—so," "the more—the better," in the second; and that, on this account, the expressions under the former division are properly written without commas, and those under the latter with them.

b. When the conjunction *but* is improperly used, after *so,* for *as* and a negative, the sentence is subject to the principle of punctuation contained in the first section of the rule; as, "There is no opinion *so* absurd *but* has [*as not* to have] some philosopher or other to produce in its support."

c. When, in sentences referable to the first division of the rule, the last of the correlative words requires a comma after it, a comma should also be inserted between the correlative expressions; as, "The mind that boasts of its rich endowments is *so* limited and cramped, *as*, in comparison with what it might enjoy, to be utterly poor and naked." It is evident, that, without the point before the conjunction *as*, this word would seem to be more closely united with the preceding than with the following portion of the sentence, to which it rather belongs.

d. Correlative expressions should be separated, if ambiguity of sense would be occasioned in any instance by the omission of the comma before the second correlative; as, "*Greater* is he that prophesieth, *than* he that speaketh with tongues." Without the point, the sentence might be improperly read so as to mean, — "Greater is he that prophesieth with tongues than he that speaketh with tongues."

e. So, also, in respect to the same class of sentences, the correlative expressions are better separated by a comma, when they consist of two or more phrases; as, "We can no *more* preserve a stationary attitude | in the moral world, *than* we can refuse to accompany the physical earth | in its rotation." Here, the insertion of the point, though not essential, shows more clearly those portions of the sentence to which each set of phrases belongs, and by this means serves to bring out the sense.

f. As an exception to the second division of the rule, it may be remarked, that the comma is better omitted between clauses containing the correlative words *so* or *such—that*, when they are closely connected; as, "John was *so* much injured *that* he could not walk." — "The earthquake produced *such* a shock *that* it awoke us all."

g. But if these correlatives are placed at or near the beginning of the clauses to which they respectively belong, or if the last correlative word has a comma after it, the clauses should be separated, agreeably to the rule; as, "*So* benevolent a man was he, *that* almost every act of his was devoted to the well-being of his race." — "Man is *so* created, *that*, let his wants be as simple as they will, he must labor to supply them."

h. Expressions beginning with *both—and, whether—or, either—or, neither—nor*, are generally separated by a comma when each is a clause, but left unpointed when one of them is a phrase; as, "*Neither* flatter yourselves, *nor* permit others to flatter you." — "We cannot trace *either* their causes *or* their effects."

CORRELATIVE EXPRESSIONS. 95

ORAL EXERCISES.

Agreeably to Rule XV. (p. 93), state why some of the following sentences are printed with, and others without, the comma: —

It is easier to rouse the passions than to direct the mind.
When pride cometh, then cometh shame. — She is as good as he.
No one is so much alone in the universe as a denier of God.
As we do to others, so shall it be done unto us.
Man gains wider dominion by his intellect than by his right arm.
Wherever man is, there are the elements of poetry.
Every one has as much vanity as he is deficient in understanding.
If you know that your object is good, then without hesitation seek it.
A good name is rather to be chosen than great riches.
Though truth is fearless and absolute, yet she is meek and modest.
I have returned to refute a libel as false as it is malicious.
The more industrious you are, the sooner will you learn a trade.
Be governed more by a regard to duty than by a prospect of gain.
Such as the tree is, such will be the fruit.
We can discover nothing so sublime as the spirit of self-sacrifice.
The better a proverb is, the more trite it generally becomes.

Show how the preceding Remarks will apply to the punctuation of correlative clauses and phrases in the following sentences: —

No errors are so trivial but they deserve to be mended, and no sin so slight but it should be repented of and renounced.

Our sympathy is always awakened more by hearing the speaker, than by reading his works in our closet.

Only such sorrow purifies and blesses, as comes to us in the pursuit of high and noble ends.

Better is a dinner of herbs where love is, than a stalled ox, and hatred therewith.

Virtue is so amiable that even the vicious admire it. — So frowned the mighty combatants, that hell grew darker at the sight.

Such was the rush of the people, that but few could be admitted to the lecture.

Grace of manners is so essential to rulers, that, whenever it is neglected, their virtues lose a great degree of lustre.

Whether my gift be liberal, or whether it be niggardly, is not the question. — Whether right or wrong, I am held responsible.

We can neither fly from the presence of God, nor escape his sight. — Virtue is neither a phantom nor a vain vision.

THE COMMA.

EXERCISE TO BE WRITTEN.

Let these sentences be punctuated or not, agreeably to the fifteenth Rule and the Remarks (pp. 93, 94):—

We are so afraid of each other's doctrines that we cannot cure each other's sins. (Rule, § II.; and Remark *g*.)

Does not the glorious sun pour down his golden flood as cheerily on the poor man's cottage as on the rich man's palace? (Rule, § I.)

We must not only avoid what God has forbidden but do what he has commanded. (Rule, § II.)

One angel's history may be a volume of more various truth than all the records of our race. (Rule, § I.)

Although men are accused for not knowing their own weakness yet perhaps as few know their own strength. (Rule, § II.)

He is a better man who wisely speaks than he who talks at random. (Remark *d.*)

No sublimity is so real as that which makes itself deeply felt in union with beauty. (Rule, § I.)

Though he were as rich as Crœsus still would man be dissatisfied with his condition. (Rule, §§ I., II.)

Better live an honest poor man than die a selfish and grasping millionnaire. (Rule, § I.)

What thou forbiddest us that will we shun and abhor: what thou commandest us that will we love and pursue. (Rule, § II.)

My engagements are of such a character as will deprive me of partaking the festivities of the day. (Rule, § I.)

Such is the course of nature that whoever lives long must outlive those whom he loves. (Rule, § II.; and Remark *g*.)

The doll-shop is as fit a place for studying character as the fashionable dinner-party, the assembly, or the ball-room. (Remark *e*.)

The rarer the beauty of the external scene the deeper should be the impression of the unseen God. (Rule, § II.)

Of things invisible, the evidence can never be such as those who rely on purely intellectual assurance will demand. (Rule, § I.)

The more a man speaks of himself the less he likes to hear another spoken of. (Rule, § II.)

Nothing appears to us so beautiful in human experience as the reciprocal affection of parents and children. (Rule, § I.)

The gigantic genius of Shakspeare so far surpassed the learning and penetration of his time that his productions were little read and less admired. (Rule, § II.; and Remark *g*.)

Rather do good than seem to be. — So live with men as if God saw you. (Rule, § I.)

The progress of some men is so rapid that they keep ahead of common sense. (Remark *f.*)

Neither could he obtain the benefits which he desired nor avert the calamities which he feared. (Rule, § II.; and first of Remark *h.*)

I am as much known to God as if I were the single object of his attention. (Rule, § I.)

Art is capable of not only imitating nature in her graces but even of adorning her with graces of her own. (Rule, § II.)

Either the mere will of the magistrate or the conscience of the individual must decide in the case. (Remark *h*, second portion.)

The more the love of poetry is cultivated and refined the more do men strive to make their outward lives rhythmical and harmonious. (Rule, § II.)

There is no part of social life which affords more real satisfaction than those hours which one passes in rational and unreserved conversation. (Rule, § I.)

Not more do we discern in the writings of Shakspeare the greatest manifestation of human genius than in the reality of Christ the highest expression of the Divine. (Remark *e.*)

The more highly we cultivate our minds here the better shall we be prepared for the nobler pursuits of the next stages of our existence. (Rule, § II.)

It had been better for them not to have known the way of righteousness than, after they have known it, to turn from the holy commandment delivered unto them. (Remark *c* or *e.*)

> As no cause
> For such exalted confidence could e'er
> Exist so none is now for fixed despair. (Rule, § II.)

The age in which George II. reigned was not by any means marked by such striking features of originality or vigor as some of the preceding eras. (Rule, § I.)

There is nothing which employs the mind and the heart so attractively as the close study of character in all its smaller peculiarities. (Rule, § I.)

The universe at large would suffer as little in its splendor and variety by the destruction of our planet as the verdure and sublime magnitude of a forest would suffer by the fall of a single leaf. (Remark *e.*)

RULE XVI.

Phrases and Clauses in the same Construction.

Two or more phrases or clauses, when in the same construction, are separated by a comma from each other, and, when they do not complete a proposition, from the remainder of the sentence.

EXAMPLES.

1. No one ought unnecessarily to wound the feelings of his neighbors, or to insult their religious prepossessions.
2. Regret for the past, grief at the present, and anxiety respecting the future are plagues which affect the generality of men.
3. Beauty haunts the depths of the earth and sea, and gleams out in the hues of the shell and the precious stone.
4. Crafty men contemn studies, simple men admire them, and wise men use them.

REMARKS.

a. The first and second of these sentences exemplify the use of *phrases* in the same construction; the third and fourth, that of *clauses.* Both kinds of expressions are said to be in the same construction, for these reasons, — that, in the first example, the infinitives "to wound," "to insult," are each governed by one and the same verb, "ought;" that, in the second, the whole series of phrases forms a compound nominative to the verb "are;" that, in the third, the verbs "haunts" and "gleams," occurring respectively in the two clauses, have the same nominative, "beauty;" and that, in the fourth, the clauses are all formed alike, and have a mutual relation. In the second example, the co-ordinate expressions do not conclude the proposition; and therefore a comma is put after the last of these, in order to point out their common dependence on what follows.

b. When two brief phrases are formed alike, and united by either of the conjunctions *and, or, nor,* the comma is better omitted between them; as, "A healthy body *and* a sound mind should be preserved as real blessings." — "The pastimes of youth have a tendency to invigorate the body *or* to expand the mind." The omission of the point is particularly recommended, when two phrases form a compound parenthetical expression, or belong to one; as, "We must file a protest against the practice of destroying the birds of the garden; for, besides depriving us of *the beauty of their appearance* and *the music of their song*, it lets in a flood of insects, whose numbers the birds were commissioned to keep down." — See p. 46, *j*.

c. If, however, by omitting the comma, two such phrases might be read so as to obscure or pervert the meaning, the point must be inserted; as, " Receive blessings with thankfulness, *and* afflictions with resignation." — See also p. 29, *f.*

d. When two connected phrases are different in form or in the number of words, their relation to the context is better seen when they are set off by commas; as, " Undue susceptibility, and the preponderance of mere feeling over thoughtfulness, may mislead us."

e. The same mode of punctuation is adopted for a word and a phrase, or for a series consisting partly of words and partly of phrases; a comma, however, being put after the last particular, when it does not end the clause; as, " Calmness, modesty, candor, forgetfulness of self, *and love of others*, are all required for the occasion."

f. But, to prevent ambiguity, a little care is sometimes necessary to discriminate phrases from single words, as in the following sentence: " Their depravity, *their spiritual ignorance and destitution*, are awfully great." Were a comma put after "ignorance," the sentence would be analyzed improperly, and convey a wrong meaning; whereas the sense of the passage requires the Italicized portion to be viewed, not as a phrase and a word, but as a mere phrase, and punctuated as above. By omitting the adjectival words, " their spiritual," which qualify both of the nouns " ignorance " and " destitution," the punctuation would, according to Rule III., p. 37, be thus exhibited: " Their depravity, ignorance, and destitution are awfully great."

g. When a series consists both of words and phrases, all connected by one of the conjunctions *and*, *or*, *nor*, the comma should be omitted between the single words, but inserted between the phrases; as, " Some men would be distinguished in their occupation *or* pursuit *or* profession, *or* in the style of living, *or* in the dignity of office, *or* in the glare *and* pride *and* pomp of power." — See p. 38, *h.*

h. When a series consists of phrases or clauses, united by either of the conjunctions just named, the particulars are separated from one another by a comma; as, " Reach the goal, *and* gain the prize, *and* wear the crown." But, if the series is used parenthetically, the commas may be omitted; as, " Through the soul we have direct access to God, and, *by a trustful heart* and *a submissive will* and *a devoted service*, may spiritually unite ourselves with him." — See *b.*

i. Pairs of words are regarded as phrases, and punctuated in accordance with the rule; as, " Anarchy *and* confusion, poverty *and* distress, follow a civil war." — " Whether we eat *or* drink, labor or sleep, we should be moderate."

j. It is very usual, particularly in the United States, to omit the comma between the number of a house or shop and the street, and after the name of a month when preceding that of the year to which it belongs; but, as these words are employed neither adjectively nor in apposition, the point should, beyond all doubt, be inserted; as, " *No.* 140, Broadway, New York, *January*, 1855." — " Thomas Tegg, bookseller, 73, Cheapside." In accordance with the same principle, a comma should be put after a reference made to any of the sacred books, when it is followed immediately by the chapter and verse; as, " John, xvi. 20: " unless the references to Scripture are numerous, when, for the sake of neatness, the comma is better omitted.

k. Consecutive or co-ordinate clauses, if not joined by a conjunction, are sometimes better distinguished by a semicolon or a colon than by a comma; as, " Death is certain; time, uncertain." — " Death is certain: time is uncertain." — See Rule XVII., p. 104.

l. To exhibit the limits of the rule, it may not be improper to anticipate what will be more fully treated of in the next section; namely, that clauses, when separable into smaller portions requiring the comma, are separated from each other by a semicolon; as, " How strange it seems, that the passion of love should be the supreme mover of the world; that it is this which has dictated the greatest sacrifices, and influenced all societies and all times; that to this the loftiest and loveliest genius has ever consecrated its devotion; that but for love there were no civilization, no music, no poetry, no beauty, no life beyond the brute's!" The sentences given to exemplify the rule are not thus divisible, and are therefore punctuated only by means of the comma.

ORAL EXERCISES.

Say why, according to Rule XVI., commas are inserted in these sentences: —

To cleanse our own opinions from falsehood, our hearts from malignity, and our actions from vice, is our first concern.

Speak as you mean, do as you profess, and perform what you promise.

Great moral principles, pure and generous dispositions, cannot be confined to this or that spot.

The true worshipper of beauty sees it in the lowliest flower, meets it in every path, enjoys it everywhere.

Eloquence is to be attained by the full culture, the general enriching, of the heart and mind.

Has God provided for the poor a coarser earth, a thinner air, a paler sky?

The voice of merriment and of wailing, the steps of the busy and the idle, have ceased in the deserted courts.

Man was created to search for truth, to love the beautiful, to desire what is good, and to do the best.

You may dazzle men's eyes with large enterprises in philanthropy, but possess nothing of the philanthropic spirit.

Beauty flows in the waves of light, radiates from the human face divine, and sparkles in the pathway of every child.

The devil loves nothing better than the intolerance of reformers, and dreads nothing so much as their charity and patience.

Infinite space, endless numbers, and eternal duration, fill the mind with great ideas.

———

Assign the reasons given in the Remarks (pp. 98, 99) *for the insertion or the omission of commas in such sentences as the following :—*

It is education that characterizes mental power as the talent of an angel or the capacity of a fiend.

Eminent talent and distinguished attainment are sometimes connected with obliquity of character.

The student may, by close application and by proper culture, attain ease and grace in his composition.

Some persons mistake abhorrence of vice for uncharitableness, and piety for enthusiasm.

Suffering often calls forth our best feelings, and the highest energies of the mind.

Fraud, enthusiasm, and narrowness of view, often shape the premises to fit the conclusion.

The beauty of his moral character, his generous impulses and sympathies, were the theme of every tongue.

Babylon and Troy and Tyre, and even early Rome, are passing already into fiction.

Age never dims their sight, nor slackens their speed, nor weakens their force, nor abates their fidelity.

Perfection of mind consists of firmness and mildness, of force and tenderness, of vigor and grace.

On the rich and the eloquent, on nobles and priests, the Puritans looked down with contempt.

THE COMMA.

EXERCISE TO BE WRITTEN.

Let the punctuation of such of the following sentences as require to be pointed accord with the Rule and Remarks (pp. 98–100):—

Joint effort conquers nature hews through mountains rears pyramids dikes out the ocean. (Rule.)

With a callous heart, there can be no genius in the imagination or wisdom in the mind. (Rule, and Remark *c.*)

Genius deals with the possible creates new combinations discovers new laws and acts from an insight into principles. (Rule.)

Refined manners and polite behaviour must not be deemed altogether superficial. (First of Remark *b.*)

To be wise in our own eyes to be wise in the opinion of the world and to be wise in the sight of our Creator seldom coincide. (Rule.)

Thou art capable of something purer nobler infinitely better than thou hast become. (Remark *e.*)

Familiarity with the world's vices can never reveal to you the world's great truths or enable you to fathom its deep realities. (Rule.)

It should be the first object of education to form a pure heart high principle an earnest and ingenuous spirit. (Rule.)

We live in times that call for wisdom in contemplation and virtue in action. (Rule, and Remark *c.*)

Every human being has a work to carry on within duties to perform abroad influences to exert which are peculiarly his. (Rule.)

Resolute thoughts find words for themselves and make their own vehicle. (Rule.)

The man of enlightened understanding and persevering ardor has many sources of enjoyment which the ignorant man cannot reach. (First of Remark *b.*)

The only distinctions in society which should be recognized are those of the soul of strong principle of incorruptible integrity of usefulness of cultivated intellect of fidelity in seeking for truth. (Rule.)

To the poor and the desolate the timid and the anxious the weary and the aged the idea of a common brotherhood must be full of light. (Rule, and Remark *i.*)

The pure, kind, trustful heart, intent on duty and only ambitious of usefulness, bears, in the beaming eye and open brow and gladsome voice, unfailing evidence of inward peace and joy. (Last of Rem. *h.*)

Do the voice of the wise and the arm of the brave and the blood of the patriot go for nothing in the wild conflict that is desolating the earth? (Rule, and first of Remark *h.*)

I know of no great expounder of moral principle I know of no eloquent teacher of divine truth who is more useful in God's world, than a business-man that carries his religion into his business. (Rule.)

Can we imagine that God's highest gifts of intelligence imagination and moral power were bestowed to provide only for animal wants? (Remark *e.*)

Ancient superstition introduced the fine arts into her train called the powers of genius to her aid and employed the painter and the poet to hold out her charms to the world. (Rule.)

Want and anxiety and habitual discontent and hate of fancied oppression can never raise a class and excite it to noble efforts. (Rule, and Remarks *i*, *g*.)

How often, in surveying the great man's splendid mansion and wandering through his ancient woods and beautiful gardens, have we met with some touching memorial of human affection! (Remark *b*, both sentences.)

That fortitude which has encountered no dangers that prudence which has surmounted no difficulties that integrity which has been attended by no temptations can at best be considered but as gold not yet brought to the test. (Rule.)

Surely this is a world of plenteousness and beauty and gladness of loves and friendships of blessed homes and holy altars of sacred communions and lofty aspirations and immortal prospects. (Rule, and Remarks *g*, *b*, and first of *h*.)

Faith is the root and foundation of whatever is noble and excellent in man of all that is mighty and admirable in his intellect of all that is amiable and praiseworthy in his affections of all that is sound and stable in his moral being. (Rule.)

Put holy truth in every false heart; instil a sacred piety into every worldly mind and a blessed virtue into every fountain of corrupt desires; and the anxieties of philanthropy might be hushed and the tears of benevolent prayer and faith might be dried up and patriotism and piety might gaze upon the scene and the prospect with unmingled joy. (Rule, and Remarks *d*, *h*, *k*, *l*.)

The culture of the intellect is an unmixed good, when it is sacredly used to enlighten the conscience to feed the flame of generous sentiment to perfect us in our common employments to throw a grace over our common actions to make us sources of innocent cheerfulness and centres of holy influence and to give us courage strength stability amidst the sudden changes and sore temptations and trials of life. (Rule, and Remarks *b*, *e*.)

RULE XVII.

Clauses having a Verb understood.

When, in a compound sentence, the clauses have each a different nominative, but have only one verb, expressed in the first clause and understood in the others, the ellipsis, or place of the verb, should be supplied by a comma.

EXAMPLES.

1. A wise man seeks to shine in himself; a fool, to outshine others.
2. The wise man considers what he wants; the fool, what he abounds in.
3. The wise man is happy in his own approbation; the fool, in the applause of his fellows.

REMARKS.

a. In the above examples, a comma is inserted after the second nominative, "fool," to indicate, in the first sentence, the ellipsis of the verb "seeks;" in the second, that of the verb "considers;" and, in the third, that of the verb and adjective, "is happy." Hence a semicolon is required before the second nominative to divide each sentence into the two larger portions of which it consists, and to show the relation of its various parts.

b. But, if two clauses have a bearing on a final expression, the comma should be omitted after the second nominative, and the semicolon before it changed into a comma; as, "Herder had more of the Oriental fancy, *Schleiermacher* more of the European acuteness, *in his composition.*" For, were a semicolon put after "fancy," and a comma after "Schleiermacher," as in the rule, the phrase "in his composition" would seem to be connected only with the last clause, though it belongs equally to both.

c. So, also, when two short clauses are joined by either of the conjunctions *and, or, nor, but,* and any word but a noun follows the second nominative, the comma should be omitted where the verb is understood, and the semicolon after the first clause exchanged for a comma; as, "Life is precarious, *and* death *certain.*" If a semicolon were placed after the word "precarious," it would be necessary to separate "death" and "certain" by a comma; as, "Life is precarious; and death, certain." But such a mode of punctuation would be too rigid, and is not required for bringing out the sense.

d. When, too, in a series of clauses, each ellipsis is followed by a preposition or by the comparative *as*, the free style of pointing seems more appropriate; as, "Mathematicians have sought knowledge in figures, philosophers *in* systems, logicians *in* subtilties, and metaphysicians *in* sounds."

e. If, however, obscurity would arise, either in two clauses or in a series, from the omission of the comma,—as, for instance, when the preposition *of* is used,—the punctuation adopted in the examples under the rule must be followed. Thus: "Power reminds you *of* weakness; permanency, *of* change; life, *of* death; light, *of* darkness; and the true, *of* the false."

f. When lightness or vivacity characterizes the style, the free mode of pointing is preferable to the other, if no ambiguity would arise from its use, as in the following passage: "There is a magic in the sound of 'Stop thief! stop thief!' The tradesman leaves his counter, and the carman his wagon; the butcher throws down his tray, the baker his basket, the milkman his pail, the errand-boy his parcels, the school-boy his marbles, the paver his pickaxe, the child his battledoor: away they run pellmell, helter-skelter."

ORAL EXERCISES.

Why, according to Rule XVII., *are commas inserted in these sentences?*—

Curiosity allures the wise; vanity, the foolish; and pleasure, both
The Grecians excelled in precepts; the Romans, in examples.
Homer was the greater genius; Virgil, the better artist.
Passion overcomes shame; boldness, fear; and madness, reason.
Anger prompts men to contention; avarice, to oppression.
The benevolent man is esteemed; the penurious, despised.
A robber employs violence; and a thief, cunning and guile.
The young are slaves to novelty; the old, to custom.
War is the law of violence; peace, the law of love.
The Doric dialect was broad and rough; the Ionic, smooth.
Semiramis built Babylon; Dido, Carthage; and Romulus, Rome.
Labor brings pleasure; idleness, pain.
Plants are formed by culture; men, by education.
One murder makes a villain; millions, a hero.
Pleasant recollections promote cheerfulness; and painful ones, gloom
Crowns were the playthings of Napoleon; thrones, his footstool.
Truth belongs to the man; error, to his age.
Benevolence is allied to few vices; selfishness, to fewer virtues.

Assign the reasons for the punctuation of the following sentences, agreeably to the Remarks (pp. 104-5):

Our existence has no support, our life no aim, our spiritual weakness no power to lean upon, without God.

Shakspeare was the greatest poet, Newton the most distinguished mathematician, that England ever produced.

The coarse worm yields us a beautiful fly, and the thorny bush a lovely flower.

The notions of Dryden were formed by comprehensive speculation, but those of Pope by minute attention.

Shakspeare died in 1616, Milton in 1674, Dryden in 1700, Pope in 1744, and Goldsmith in 1774.

Bonaparte was a man of unbounded ambition; and Washington, of disinterested patriotism.

EXERCISE TO BE WRITTEN.

Punctuate those sentences to which no references are given, in accordance with Rule XVII.; and the others agreeably to the Remarks :—

The character of Milton was peculiarly distinguished by loftiness of thought; that of Dante by intensity of feeling.

Concession is no humiliation nor admission of error any disgrace. (Remark *c.*)

Among the ancient critics, Longinus possessed most delicacy; Aristotle most correctness.

The sculptor sees a statue and the philosopher a principle, where, to the general eye, all is " without form, and void." (Remark *b.*)

Homer's imagination is by much the most rich and copious; Virgil's the most chaste and correct.

The cupola is taken from the human skull pillars from legs thatching from hair and tiling from the scales of fish. (Remark *d.*)

Reading maketh a full man; conference a ready man; and writing an exact man.

Avarice must come to the hour of utter destitution and pride to the hour of utter prostration. (Remark *c.*)

The quality the most difficult to be found in public situations is probity; the least difficult confidence.

Some men are eminent for what they possess some for what they achieve and others for what they are. (Remark *d.*)

The first ingredient in conversation is truth; the next good sense; the third good-humor; and the fourth wit.

All our mental perceptions suggest their opposites, — the finite the infinite; the seen the unseen; time eternity; creation a God.

A pictured landscape recalls a familiar scene and a portrait a familiar countenance. (Remark c.)

Talent is full of thoughts; genius of thought. One has definite acquisitions; the other indefinite power.

Addison taught the intellect and fancy and Richardson the passions, to move at the command of virtue. (Remark b or c.)

Nature had no obstacles that he did not surmount; space no opposition that he did not spurn.

Among the ancient critics, Longinus possessed most delicacy Aristotle most correctness, of judgment. (Remark b.)

To mourn without measure is folly; not to mourn at all insensibility. — Foresight is simple; retrospect multiform.

The young are slaves to novelty the old to custom the middle-aged to both the dead to neither. (Remark d.)

Custom respects things which are done by the majority; habit those which are done by individuals.

A man's true prosperity often begins when he is said to be ruined and his ruin when he is said to be prospering. (Remark c.)

Genius is the intuitive perception of what is; moral sentiment the feeling of what ought to be.

Chaucer most frequently describes things as they are Spenser as we wish them to be Shakspeare as they would be and Milton as they ought to be. (Remark d.)

Delicacy leans more to feeling; correctness more to reason and judgment. The former is the gift of nature; the latter more the product of culture and art.

Rashness is the error of youth; and timid caution of age. — Hurry is the mark of a weak mind; despatch of a strong one. (Rule, and Remark e.)

> All nature is but art, unknown to thee;
> All chance direction which thou canst not see;
> All discord harmony not understood;
> All partial evil universal good.

The wise man is happy when he gains his own approbation and the fool when he recommends himself to the applause of those about him. (Remark c.)

Fear urges us to action; terror to flight. — The idle want steadiness of purpose; the indolent power of exertion. — Children have understandings; men intellect.

RULE XVIII.

Clauses consisting of Short Quotations or Remarks.

A short quotation, or any expression that resembles a quotation, is separated by a comma from the clause which precedes it.

EXAMPLES.

1. Dr. Thomas Brown truly says, "The benevolent spirit is as universal in its efforts as the miseries which are capable of being relieved."
2. One of the first lessons of a judicious education is, Learn to think and to discriminate.
3. It may be laid down as a sacred maxim, that every man is wretched in proportion to his vices.

REMARKS.

a. By a short quotation is meant a single sentence, containing the remark of another writer. By an expression resembling a quotation is indicated a remark, of some degree of importance, to which attention is called in the introductory clause. Such a remark is not unfrequently preceded by the conjunction "that," as in the third example; and, in these cases, the comma is usually inserted before the particle.

b. Some writers annex a dash [—] to the comma; but this is unnecessary, except before emphatic or long passages. If, however, quotations or remarks extend to two or more sentences, and are formally or specially introduced, a colon is preferable.

c. When an *indirect* quotation or a remark is preceded by a very brief clause, the comma is not required; as, "*Andrew says* he loves me." — "*I doubt not* that mind is immortal." — "*It is impossible* that we should make Walter fully understand his ignorance."

d. But, if the remark or quotation consists of phrases which require to be punctuated, a comma should precede the conjunction, even when the introductory part of the sentence is quite short; as, " *Ossian says,* that sorrow, like a cloud on the sun, shaded the soul of Clessamour." A comma should also be inserted after the conjunction, if an inverted or an adverbial phrase begins the remark; as, "It is certain, *that,* in the declension of taste and science, language will degenerate." The reason for the punctuation in such instances is, that the omission of the comma would bring the word "that" into too close a contact with that part of the sentence with which it has the least affinity. For the sentence is obviously divisible into two portions, less connected than others which require to be pointed; the first ending, in the former of these examples, with the verb "says," and, in the latter, with the adjective "certain."

e. The comma may be omitted before *that*, when the clause on which the conjunction depends does not precede the remark, but is thrown in between its parts; as, "In the ancient world, *it is well known that* the name of poet was the same as that of prophet." This omission takes place because a comma is put after the first portion of the sentence, and because the repetition of the point would tend to give a false view of the construction, and thereby obscure the sense.

f. But when, in similar sentences, the conjunction is omitted, the comma should be substituted, agreeably to the principle adopted in parenthetical expressions; as, "In the ancient world, *it is well known*, the name of poet was the same as that of prophet." — See page 64, Rule VIII.

g. A clause which begins with *what, when, where, if*, or *how*, indicating an indirect question or remark, is not usually separated from its antecedent clause; as, "Will no one tell me *what* she sings?" — "Revelation clearly informs us *how* we may obtain happiness."

ORAL EXERCISES.

Say why, according to Rule XVIII., the following sentences are punctuated: —

Patrick Henry commenced by saying, "It is natural to man to indulge in the illusions of hope."

The great and decisive test of genius is, that it calls forth power in the souls of others.

I am not now to discuss the question, whether the souls of men are naturally equal.

The very correct remark has been made, that "it is a great loss to lose an affliction."

I reply, I do and must regard heaven as a world of intercourse and sympathy.

His grand excellence was this, that he was a true man. — There is much in the proverb, "Without pains, no gains."

Such seems to be the disposition of man, whatever makes a distinction produces rivalry.

It is a law of man's nature, that he should endeavor to act beforehand the part to which he is destined in a higher state of being.

How do the preceding Remarks (pp. 108–9) *apply to the insertion or the omission of commas in the sentences that follow ?* —

St. John says that God is love. — Swift asserts that no man ever wished himself younger.

Every one knows James is a very prolific writer. — I trust you feel the importance of the subject.

It cannot be questioned, that we are, as yet, only in the rudiments of the great science of education.

Wirt writes, that, as a statesman, Alexander Hamilton was distinguished for the great extent of his views.

Ere another day pass, I hope that you will find yourself surrounded by your wife and children.

By the sweat of our brow, I say, we have to earn the little which we possess.

We all know how a man of mighty genius can impart himself to other minds.

EXERCISE TO BE WRITTEN.

Insert commas or not between the clauses of the following sentences, in accordance with the eighteenth Rule and the Remarks : —

Seneca tells us " There is a settled friendship, nay, a near relation and similitude, between God and good men." (Rule.)

In the great science of society, it must be confessed that we have much to learn. (Remark *e.*)

They know not what they say who cry out " Let us build tabernacles of rest." (Rule.)

Thou knowest that virtue can never be despoiled of its deathless crown. (Remark *c.*)

It may be laid down as an unfailing and universal axiom that " all pride is abject and mean." (Rule.)

We know it is wrong. — I tell you that I have not your book. - He said she bought it. (Remark *c.*)

The true ennoblement of our nature consists in the feeling that our existence stretches beyond the bounds of this globe. (Rule.)

It is well known what strange work there has been in the world under the name and pretence of reformation. (Remark *g.*)

Thou shalt take up this proverb against the king of Babylon, and say " How hath the oppressor ceased ! " (Rule.)

In the din and bustle of business, it may be the voice of conscience and duty speaks unheard. (Remark *f.*)

I say unto all Watch. — It is a true saying that we are never too old to be taught. (Rule.)

Coleridge said he had the habit of seeking for the " good and beautiful " in all his eyes beheld. (Remark c.)

There is no foundation for the popular doctrine that a state may flourish by arts and crimes. (Rule.)

> Some dream that they can silence, when they will,
> The storm of passion, and say "Peace, be still." (Rem. c, and Rule.)

It has long been a subject of inquiry whether there existed in nature a universal language. (Rule.)

Keep it in view that the great object of study is to fit the mind to be an instrument of usefulness in life. (Rule.)

It is not enough that we have great qualities: we must also have the management of them. (Remark c.)

A celebrated modern writer says "Take care of the minutes, and the hours will take care of themselves." (Rule.)

We affirm that, without some portion of enthusiasm, no person ever became a true poet or painter. (Remark d, second sentence.)

It was said of Socrates that he brought philosophy down from heaven to dwell among men. (Rule.)

I may say that, of all the men we meet with, nine parts of ten are what they are, good or evil, useful or not, by their education. (Remark d, second sentence.)

Tell me when was it that you felt yourself most strongly inclined to go astray? — Tell me when it was that you felt yourself most strongly inclined to go astray. (Rule, and Remark g.)

It is one among the pious and valuable maxims which are ascribed to Francis de Sales " A judicious silence is always better than truth spoken without charity." (Rule.)

In delineating the character of Dr. Bowditch, it deserves to be mentioned that he was eminently a self-taught and self-made man. (Remark e.)

Let me ask you are your resolutions as firm as when you first set out in the spiritual life? — Let me ask you if your resolutions are as firm, &c. (Rule, and Remark g.)

The poet Gray, one of the most intellectual and fastidious of men, says "Happy they who can create a rose-tree, or erect a honeysuckle!" (Rule.)

Thou knowest that principle, grounded in the eternal laws of mind and emanating from the unchangeable essence of God, cannot perish. (Rule, and first of Remark d.)

RULE XIX.

Numeral Figures and Words.

With the exception of dates, figures consisting of four or more characters are pointed with a comma before every three from the end, or between each class of hundreds.

EXAMPLE.

The population of China in 1743, according to the French missionaries, was 150,029,855; in 1825, according to Dr. Morrison, 352,866,002.

REMARKS.

a. Properly speaking, the comma, as here used, is neither a grammatical nor a rhetorical point; but, for the easy understanding of the value of sums, it is exceedingly useful. The rule is inserted in this place, merely because a more appropriate situation could not be found for it in the book.

b. When put in words, numbers are usually left unpointed; as, to take the first calculation in the example, "The population of China in 1743 was fifteen millions twenty-nine thousand eight hundred and fifty-five."

c. When round numbers are used, and no comparison is made between one sum and another, words are preferable to figures; as, "According to Balbi, the entire population of Africa is thirty-nine millions."

EXERCISE TO BE WRITTEN.

Punctuate the figures, except those expressive of dates:—

The sun is 883210 miles in diameter, about 2774692 miles in circumference, and distant from the earth about 95000000 of miles.

The Rocky Mountains rise 12500 feet above the level of the ocean; the Andes, 21440 feet.

On April 17, 1790, Dr. Franklin died at Philadelphia, aged eighty-four, and bequeathed $4444 to the people of Boston, for the benefit of young married artificers.

Population of the city of New York in 1790 was 33131; in 1800, 60489; in 1810, 96373; in 1820, 123706; in 1830, 202589; in 1840, 312710; in 1850, 515507.

Sect. II. — THE SEMICOLON.

The SEMICOLON [;] is used to separate such parts of a sentence as are somewhat less closely connected than those separated by a comma.

RULE I.

A Sentence consisting of Two Conjoined Clauses.

When two clauses are united by either of the conjunctions *for, but, and,* or an equivalent word, — the one clause perfect in itself, and the other added as a matter of inference, contrast, or explanation, — they are separated by a semicolon.

EXAMPLES.

1. Economy is no disgrace; for it is better to live on a little than to outlive a great deal.
2. Genius breaks from the fetters of criticism; but its wanderings are sanctioned by its majesty and wisdom.
3. Modesty is one of the chief ornaments of youth; and it has ever been esteemed a presage of rising merit.

REMARKS.

a. When a conjunction unites two clauses incapable of being subdivided by a comma, in the last of which the nominative is understood, the insertion of a comma between the clauses is preferable to that of the semicolon. Thus, were the nominative " it," in the third example, omitted, the sentence would be punctuated as follows: " Modesty is one of the chief ornaments of youth, *and* has ever been esteemed a presage of rising merit." — See page 98.

b. When a sentence consists of three or more clauses, united by a conjunction, none of which are susceptible of division, a semicolon should be put between those which are least connected in sense, and a comma only between the others; as, "The woods may disappear, *but* the spirit of them will never now; *for* it has been felt by a poet, *and* we can feel for ever what he felt."

ORAL EXERCISE.

Repeat the preceding Definition and Rule, and say why semicolons are inserted in the following sentences:—

All cannot be great; and nobody may reasonably expect all the world to be engaged with lauding his merits.

Idleness is the parent of every vice; but well-directed activity is the source of every laudable pursuit and worldly attainment.

Examinations are formidable even to the best prepared; for the greatest fool may ask more than the wisest man can answer.

An entire retreat from worldly affairs is not what religion requires; nor does it even enjoin a long retreat from them.

Religion must be the spirit of every hour; but it cannot be the meditation of every hour.

A clownish air is but a small defect; yet it is enough to make a man disagreeable.

We have carved a cross upon our altars; but the smoke of our sacrifice goes up to Thor and Odin still.

Reasoning implies doubt and uncertainty; and therefore God does not reason.

Endless existence is a great truth; but an immortality of pure affections and holy employments is far greater.

Men must have recreation; and literature and art furnish that which is most pure, innocent, and refining.

Do not think yourself perfect; for imperfection is natural to humanity.

Pope had perhaps the judgment of Dryden; but Dryden certainly wanted the diligence of Pope.

Life is felt to be a great and gracious boon by all who enjoy its light; and this is not too much felt.

Never value yourself upon your fortune; for this is the sign of a weak mind.

Virtue is a real honor; whereas all other distinctions are merely titular.

Distracted and surprised with deep dismay
At these sad tidings; but no time was then
For long indulgence to their tears or grief.

TWO CONJOINED CLAUSES.

EXERCISE TO BE WRITTEN.

Let the following sentences be punctuated agreeably to the preceding Rule and Remarks:—

Make a proper use of your time for the loss of it can never be regained.

Truth will pass down in fragments to posterity but posterity will collect and compose them into a whole.

Ivy is the beauty of old ruins and your faith is not unlike it for it springs up so strongly from amidst fallen hopes. (Remark *b*.)

Mere knowledge may be idle but belief and love will, and must, go forth in action.

> He is a freeman whom the truth makes free
> And all are slaves beside.

Chaucer followed nature everywhere but never went beyond her. (Remark *a*.)

Good and evil are inseparable companions but the latter often hides behind the back of the former.

Liberal dealing is better than almsgiving for it tends to prevent pauperism, which is better than to relieve it.

The proud have no friends in prosperity for then they know nobody and none in adversity for then no one knows them. (Rem. *b*.)

Property left to a child may soon be lost but the inheritance of virtue will abide for ever.

Outward suffering is the lot of human nature and it is cheering to see it bravely borne even on the battle-field.

A good conscience is a continual feast and proves a spring of joy amidst the greatest distresses. (Remark *a*.)

The study of truth is perpetually joined with the love of virtue for there is no virtue which derives not its original from truth.

A little philosophy inclineth men's minds to atheism but depth in philosophy bringeth men's minds to religion.

Infidelity is not always built upon doubt for this is diffident nor philosophy always upon wisdom for this is meek. (Remark *b*.)

Some persons make a long story short but most persons make a short story long. — Scott built a castle but he broke his heart.

We promise according to our hopes but perform according to our fears. (Remark *a*.)

The esteem of wise and good men is the greatest of all temporal encouragements to virtue and it is the mark of an abandoned spirit to have no regard to it

RULE II.

Expressions divided into Simpler Parts.

A semicolon is placed between two or more parts of a sentence, when these, or any of them, are divisible by a comma into smaller portions.

EXAMPLES.

1. Men are not to be judged by their looks, habits, and appearances; but by the character of their lives and conversations, and by their works.
2. The noblest prophets and apostles have been children once; lisping the speech, laughing the laugh, thinking the thought, of boyhood.
3. As we perceive the shadow to have moved, but did not perceive it moving; so our advances in learning, as they consist of such minute steps, are perceivable only by the distance.

REMARKS.

a. It is obvious, that, if the smaller portions of a sentence require to be separated by a comma from each other, the construction and sense of the whole passage will be more readily perceived, if the larger divisions are set apart by the insertion of a point indicating a less intimate connection. This will show the propriety of putting a semicolon, in the first example, between the negative and the affirmative portion of the sentence; in the second, between the clause and the series of phrases; and, in the third, between the members.

b. When, however, in a sentence resolvable into two or more larger portions that require to be separated by a semicolon, the last ends with a series of phrases, of which only the final one is capable of subdivision, the comma will usually be found sufficient to distinguish all the final terms. Thus: " As, with a small telescope, a few feet in length and breadth, man learns to survey heavens beyond heavens, almost infinite; so, with the aid of limited senses and faculties, does he rise to the conception of what is beyond all visible heavens, beyond all conceivable time, *beyond all imagined power, beauty, and glory.*"

c. When the insertion of a semicolon would tend to break up the harmony or the dependencies of the thought expressed, the larger portions of a sentence, though its smaller parts are susceptible of being grammatically divided, should be separated only by a comma, as in the following passage: "Like one of those wondrous rocking stones reared by the Druids, which the finger of a child might vibrate to its centre, yet the might of an army could not move from its place, | our Constitution is so nicely poised and balanced, that it seems to sway with every breath of opinion, yet so firmly rooted in the heart and affections of the people, that the wildest storms of treason and fanaticism break over it in vain." This sentence, though containing seven grammatical parts, or pointed groups of words, is divisible into two main portions, the first ending with the word "place;" but these larger portions cannot be more separated from each other than the smaller ones, because they are so compactly and finely bound together, that any other mark than a comma would tend to loosen their connection, and to mar the unity which runs throughout the whole passage.

ORAL EXERCISE.

Assign the reason for the insertion of semicolons in the following sentences:—

Prosperity is naturally, though not necessarily, attached to virtue and merit; adversity, to vice and folly.

The furnace of affliction may be fierce; but, if it refineth thy soul, the good of one meek thought shall outweigh years of torment.

Every thing that happens is both a cause and an effect; being the effect of what goes before, and the cause of what follows.

There is a fierce conflict of good and evil throughout the universe; but good is in the ascendant, and must triumph at last.

Argument, as usually managed, is the worst sort of conversation; as it is generally, in books, the worst sort of reading.

The creation of a thousand forests is in one acorn; and Egypt, Greece, Rome, Gaul, Britain, America, lie folded already in the first man.

He was respectful, not servile, to superiors; affable, not improperly familiar, to equals; and condescending, not supercilious, to those beneath him.

The little, bleak farm, sad and affecting in its lone and extreme simplicity, smiled like the paradise of poverty; when the lark, lured thither by some green barley-field, rose ringing over the solitude.

As a malicious censure, craftily worded and pronounced with assurance, is apt to pass with mankind for shrewd wit; so a virulent maxim in bold expressions, though without any justness of thought, is readily received for true philosophy.

It is the first point of wisdom to ward off evils; the second, to make them beneficial.

The look that is fixed on immortality wears not a perpetual smile; and eyes, through which shine the light of other worlds, are often dimmed with tears.

The golden rule is a protest against selfishness; and selfishness, cleaving as it does to the inmost core of our being, is the besetting sin of the world.

Books are standing counsellors and preachers, always at hand, and always disinterested; having this advantage over oral instructors, that they are ready to repeat their lesson as often as we please.

EXERCISES TO BE WRITTEN.

Agreeably to the Rule (p. 116), *insert semicolons in the following sentences:*—

By granting that intellectual improvement was unfavorable to productions of the imagination, we should look to the least cultivated minds for bolder flights than to Milton, Pope, or Byron the absurdity of which is seen by the mere statement of it.

Wordsworth, in his poetry, works out wisdom as it comes from the common heart of man, and appeals to that heart in turn causing us to recognize the truth, that there is something in humanity which deserves alike our love and reverence.

The most precious of all possessions is power over ourselves power to withstand trial, to bear suffering, to front danger power over pleasure and pain power to follow our convictions, however resisted by menace and scorn the power of calm reliance in scenes of darkness and storms.

There, cold and lifeless, is the heart which just now was the seat of friendship there, dim and sightless, is the eye whose radiant and enlivening orb beamed with intelligence and there, closed for ever, are those lips on whose persuasive accents we have so often and so lately hung with transport.

> But who the melodies of morn can tell? —
> The wild brook, babbling down the mountain-side
> The lowing herd the sheepfold's simple bell
> The pipe of early shepherd, dim descried
> In the lone valley echoing far and wide,
> The clamorous horn along the cliffs above
> The hollow murmur of the ocean-tide
> The hum of bees the linnet's lay of love
> And the full choir that wakes the universal grove.

Insert commas and semicolons in the following sentences, where they are required by the references:—

Be not anxious impatient over-inquisitive but thoughtful serious and calm. (Page 116, Rule; and p. 37, Rule.)

If ever Christianity appears in its power it is when it erects its trophies upon the tomb when it takes up its votaries where the world leaves them and fills the breast with immortal hope in dying moments. (Page 116, Rule; p. 89, Rule and *d*; p. 98, Rule.)

When we look up to heaven and behold the sun shining in glory or the moon and the stars walking in brightness untaught nature prompts us to adore Him that made them to bow down and worship in the temple not made with hands. (Page 116, Remark *c*; p. 98.)

Every particle of dust every grain of sand every minutest atom is an active agent in the mighty whole making itself felt through all the masses in our solar system and through this on all systems in the universe. (Rule, p. 116; and Rule, p. 98.)

When the virtuous father of a family stands before us great in native worth of soul amidst all the outward tokens of poverty and an humble calling what a feeling of honor and sympathy goes forth spontaneously from our hearts to greet that truest expression of human respectability! (Page 116, Remark *c*; p. 64; p. 79, *h*.)

As we trust the long-tried affection of a human friend when for reasons satisfactory to him he now and then withholds from us his ultimate purposes so pious souls acquiescing in ignorance and conscious of absolute dependence on the Parent Mind dissolve their fears and their doubts in perfect faith. (Page 116, Rule; p. 89, Rule and *d*; and p. 64.)

There also are the eloquence the literature the poetry of all times and tongues,— those glorious efforts of genius that rule with a never-dying sway over our sympathies and affections commanding our smiles and tears kindling the imagination warming the heart filling the fancy with beauty and awing the soul with the sublime the terrible the powerful the infinite. (Page 116, Rule and *b*; pp. 37, 57, 61, 98.)

Though sometimes on passing from the turmoil of the city and the heats of restless life into the open temple of the silent universe we are tempted to think that *there* is the taint of earth and *here* the purity of heaven yet sure it is that God is seen by us through man rather than through nature and that without the eye of our brother and the voices of our kind the winds might sigh and the stars look down on us in vain. (Page 116, Rule; p. 64; p. 98, Rule and *b*.)

RULE III.

A Series of Expressions having a Common Dependence.

When, in a series of expressions, the particulars depend on a commencing or a concluding portion of the sentence, they should be separated from each other by a semicolon, if they are either laid down as distinct propositions, or are of a compound nature.

EXAMPLES.

1. Philosophers assert, that Nature is unlimited in her operations; that she has inexhaustible treasures in reserve; that knowledge will always be progressive; and that all future generations will continue to make discoveries, of which we have not the slightest idea.

2. To give an early preference to honor above gain, when they stand in competition; to despise every advantage which cannot be attained without dishonest arts; to brook no meanness, and stoop to no dissimulation, — are the indications of a great mind, the presages of future eminence and usefulness in life.

3. If we think of glory in the field; of wisdom in the cabinet; of the purest patriotism; of the highest integrity, public and private; of morals without a stain; of religious feelings without intolerance and without extravagance, — the august figure of Washington presents itself as the personation of all these ideas.

REMARKS.

a. The first sentence exemplifies a series of clauses, being each a distinct proposition, but depending all on the words that precede them, namely, "philosophers assert." The second example illustrates a series of expressions, the first two consisting each of a phrase and a clause; the third, of two coupled phrases; and all depending on the portion which concludes the sentence, — on the predicate, "are the indications of a great mind," &c. The third example exhibits a series of phrases, which, according to Rule XVI., p. 98, would be punctuated only with a comma, were it not for the compound phrase, "of the highest integrity, public and private," the subdivision of which requires to be distinguished by a point less significant than that between the other phrases.

b. Commas are sometimes preferable to semicolons, when none of the particulars in a series of clauses, except perhaps the last, are divisible into simpler portions. This mode of punctuation should be adopted when the particulars begin each with a verb, and have a common nominative on which they depend, as in the following passage: "*Poetry* | *reveals* to us the loveliness of nature, *brings* back the freshness of early feeling, *revives* the relish of simple pleasures, *keeps* unquenched the enthusiasm which warmed the spring-time of our being, *refines* youthful love, *strengthens* our interest in human nature by vivid delineations of its tenderest and loftiest feelings, *spreads* our sympathies over all classes of society, *knits* us by new ties with universal being, and, through the brightness of its prophetic visions, *helps* faith to lay hold on the future life." — See page 98.

c. If a series of phrases, of which some at least are compound, though none of them parts of clauses, depends on the commencing or the concluding portion of a sentence, and any of them are capable of being subdivided by means of a comma, all the depending portions should be separated from each other by a semicolon; as, "By doing, or at least endeavoring to do, our duty to God and man; by acquiring an humble trust in the mercy and favor of God, through Jesus Christ; by cultivating our minds, and properly employing our time and thoughts; by correcting all unreasonable expectations from the world and from men; and, in the midst of worldly business, habituating ourselves to calm retreat and serious recollection, — by such means as these, it may be hoped, that, through the divine blessing, our days shall flow in a stream as unruffled as the human state admits."

d. Accordingly, such phrases as those which occur in the following sentence, though dependent on another expression, are punctuated better by the comma: "The world is still renewed with fresh life and beauty, with a constant succession of trees and plants, with a new race of animals, with a new generation of men."

e. Some punctuators insert a dash, instead of a semicolon or a comma, between clauses or phrases dependent on other expressions. But, though it is not denied that in the more rhetorical kind of such sentences, this mark may be adopted, the semicolon or the comma is usually preferable, because the frequent recurrence of dashes, thence ensuing, would be unpleasant to the eye, without affording a proportionate aid to the understanding, and would mar the effect which they have when properly and necessarily used.

f. The dash, however, appended to a comma, as in the second and third examples under the rule, is suitably put after the last particular, that the relation of all the particulars to the portion on which they depend may be more clearly shown. — See Chap. III., Sect. III.

THE SEMICOLON.

ORAL EXERCISE.

Show how the Rule (p. 120) *may be applied to the insertion of the semicolons in the following sentences :—*

To have even our earthly being extended in everlasting remembrance; to be known wherever the name of virtue can reach; and to be known as the benefactors of every age, by the light which we have diffused, or the actions which we have performed or prompted, — who is there that does not feel some desire of this additional immortality?

Is there any splendor to be found in distant travels beyond that which sets its morning throne in the golden east; any dome sublimer than that of heaven; any beauty fairer than that of the verdant and blossoming earth; any place, though invested with all the sanctities of old time, like that home which is hushed and folded within the embrace of the humblest wall and roof?

Leighton is great by the magnificence of thought; by the spontaneous emanations of a mind replete with sacred knowledge, and bursting with seraphic affections; by that pauseless gush of intellectual splendor, in which the outward shell, the intermediate letter, is eclipsed and almost annihilated, that full scope may be given to the mighty effulgence of the informing spirit.

Happy, thrice happy, he who relies on the eternity of the soul; who believes, as the loved fall one after one from his side, that they have returned to their native country; who feels that each treasure of knowledge he attains, he carries with him through illimitable being; who sees in virtue the essence and the element of the world he is to inherit.

There are men whose powers operate in leisure and in retirement, and whose intellectual vigor deserts them in conversation; whom merriment confuses, and objection disconcerts; whose bashfulness restrains their exertion, and suffers them not to speak till the time of speaking is past; or whose attention to their own character makes them unwilling to utter at hazard what has not been considered, and cannot be recalled.

That benevolence which prompted Jesus to incessant exertion; which supported him through unparalleled suffering; which was alike the soul of his discourses, his actions, and his miracles; which shone through his life and his death; whose splendors were around his brow when he expired on the cross, and when he sat down on the right hand of the Majesty on high, — what is it but a glorious revelation of the glorious truth, that God is love?

SERIES OF EXPRESSIONS. 123

EXERCISES TO BE WRITTEN.

Insert semicolons or commas between the particulars of each series in these sentences, in accordance with the Rule and Remarks (pp. 120-21): —

The great tendency and purpose of poetry is to carry the mind above and beyond the beaten, dusty, weary walks of ordinary life to lift it into a purer element and to breathe into it more profound and generous emotion. (Rule, and Remark *c*.)

He was framed to enjoy equally the fire of poetic or the abstruseness of philosophical writings to watch the meteor-flash of oratory or to trace in history's page the even course of milder eloquence. (Remark *d*.)

Benevolence remembers the slave pleads his cause with God and man recognizes in him a human brother respects in him the sacred rights of humanity and claims for him, not as a boon but as a right, that freedom without which humanity withers, and God's child is degraded into a tool or a brute. (Remark *b*.)

If thou hast never tasted the holy peace which descends into the simplest heart, when it fervently realizes the presence of God if no gleam from the future life ever brightens thy earthly way if the sores and irritations of thy contact with the world are never soothed and softened by the healing consciousness of a divine love, — thou hast studied to little purpose, and the fountains of a true happiness are yet sealed up to thee. (Rule.)

The bad phenomenon of character, which is mainly to be traced to impulse, is that of uncertainty of a being on whom no dependence can be placed who is driven hither and thither by every wind that blows who receives impressions one day from one quarter, another day from another who has neither fixed principles in his intellect, nor harmony and consistency in his conduct. (Rule.)

No matter in what language the stranger's doom may have been pronounced no matter what complexion, incompatible with freedom, an Indian or an African sun may have burned upon him no matter in what disastrous battle his liberty may have been cloven down no matter with what solemnities he may have been devoted upon the altar of slavery, — the first moment he touches the sacred soil of Britain, the altar and the god sink together in the dust his soul walks abroad in her own majesty his body swells beyond the measure of his chains, that burst from around him and he stands redeemed, regenerated, and disenthralled by the irresistible Genius of Universal Emancipation. (Rules, pp. 120, 116.)

Let the following paragraphs be punctuated throughout, in consistency with the Rules and Remarks (pp. 120–21), and with preceding portions of the work:—

Wherever on this earth an understanding is active to know and serve the truth wherever a heart beats with kind and pure and generous affections wherever a home spreads its sheltering wing over husband and wife and parent and child — there under every diversity of outward circumstance the true worth and dignity and peace of man's soul are within reach of all.

In the light of beauty that floats over the changing aspects of the material universe in the grand interpreting thought which pervades the broken story of the ages and translates it into coherency in the spirit which comes to you from the smiles of gladness and the tears of sorrow and softens your heart in genial sympathy with human weal and human woe in the interchange of ideas which kindles enthusiasm and draws a higher meaning and purpose out of life — acknowledge realities which transcend the limits of sense own a spiritual world whose mysteries encompass you on every side by whose laws you are bound and in whose issues of endless unfolding you are yourself perhaps destined to be involved.

Those who have shone in all ages as the lights of the world the most celebrated names that are recorded in the annals of fame legislators the founders of states and the fathers of their country on whom succeeding ages have looked back with filial reverence patriots the guardians of the laws who have stemmed the torrent of corruption in every age heroes the saviours of their country who have returned victorious from the field of battle or more than victorious who have died for their country philosophers who have opened the book of nature and explained the wonders of almighty power bards who have sung the praises of virtue and of virtuous men whose strains carry them down to immortality — with a few exceptions have been uniformly on the side of goodness and have been as distinguished in the temple of fame. It was one of the maxims which governed their lives that there is nothing in nature which can compensate wickedness that although the rewards and punishments which influence illiberal and ungenerous minds were set aside that although the thunders of the Almighty were hushed and the gates of paradise were open no more they would follow religion and virtue for their own sake and co-operate with eternal Providence in perpetual endeavors to favor the good to depress the bad and to promote the happiness of the whole creation.

RULE IV.

Short Sentences slightly Connected.

When several short sentences follow one another, slightly connected in sense or in construction, they should be separated by a semicolon.

EXAMPLES.

1. Stones grow; vegetables grow and live; animals grow, live, and feel.
2. Every thing grows old; every thing passes away; every thing disappears.
3. She presses her child to her heart; she drowns it in her tears; her fancy catches more than an angel's tongue could describe.

REMARKS.

a. Without instituting any comparison between the merits of a concise and a diffuse style of composition, — which, indeed, is out of our province, — we may observe, that a printed page, when crowded with short sentences, and having, in consequence, a great number of capitals and large spaces, is offensive to the eye. As a matter of taste, therefore, as well as of propriety, it is recommended, that, wherever a number of short successive sentences are evidently allied to one another in thought, expression, or construction, as in the examples under the rule, semicolons be substituted for full points.

b. In poetry very often occur short sentences which could not be separated by a full point, without destroying the connection which subsists between them; for, hampered by the peculiar structure of verse, and more attentive to the fineness of his thoughts, the harmony of his numbers, and the appropriateness of his imagery, than to any regular train of ideas, the poet is frequently obliged to omit the connecting and disjunctive particles, so useful in prose composition in knitting together parts of sentences which are closely related in sense, and in separating those which are distinct. Especially in the more common kinds of verse, consisting of stanzas regularly formed, as used in songs, ballads, and hymns, it is better to point the sentences, of which they consist, with semicolons or colons, according to their various relations, except where the distinctions in thought and expression are prominent; for, in all such cases, periods must be used.

c. When, in a series of short sentences, each particular is constructed exactly alike, and the last is preceded by the conjunction *and*, the separation may be indicated by a comma, instead of a semicolon, agreeably to the rule on page 96; as, "The pride of wealth is contemptible, the pride of learning is pitiable, the pride of dignity is ridiculous, and the pride of bigotry is insupportable."

ORAL EXERCISE.

What is the reason for the insertion of semicolons in these sentences?—

The wind and rain are over; calm is the noon of day; the clouds are divided in heaven; over the green hill flies the inconstant sun.

The old men sit at their doors; the gossip leans over her counter; the children shout and frolic in the streets.

There is good for the good; there is virtue for the faithful; there is victory for the valiant; there is spirituality for the spiritual.

The evidences of religion have been collected; its doctrines have been elucidated; the attacks of its enemies have been repelled; the morals of its professors, upon the whole, have been purified.

When a writer reasons, we look only for perspicuity; when he describes, we expect embellishment; when he decides or relates, we desire plainness and simplicity.

The Christian orator speaks the truth plainly to his hearers; he awakens them; he shows them their impending danger; he excites them to action.

The temples are profaned; the soldier's curse resounds in the house of God; the marble pavement is trampled by iron hoofs; horses neigh beside the altar.

The epic poem recites the exploits of a hero; tragedy represents a disastrous event; comedy ridicules the vices and follies of mankind; pastoral poetry describes rural life; and elegy displays the tender emotions of the heart.

> Full many a gem of purest ray serene
> The dark, unfathomed caves of ocean bear;
> Full many a flower is born to blush unseen,
> And waste its sweetness on the desert air.

We pay no homage at the tomb of kings to sublime our feelings; we trace no line of illustrious ancestors to support our dignity; we recur to no usages, sanctioned by the authority of the great, to protract our rejoicing. No: we love liberty; we glory in the rights of men; we glory in independence.

EXERCISE TO BE WRITTEN.

Separate these short sentences by means of semicolons, in accordance with the Rule and Remarks (p. 125):—

He is poor perhaps his plans have been defeated he finds it difficult to provide for the exigencies of life sickness is permitted to invade the quiet of his household long confinement imprisons his activity.

When we read a classical poet, we feel as if we had entered a marble temple, where a cool silence reigns a few quiet statues gleam around us, pure and naked a few short inscriptions tell of the deeds of heroes all is calm, grand, and simple, to the highest perfection of art.

> There is a pleasure in the pathless woods
> There is a rapture on the lonely shore
> There is society, where none intrudes,
> By the deep sea, and music in its roar.

The world is fair around thee the bright and blessed sun shineth on thee the green and flowery fields spread far, and cheer thine eye, and invite thy footstep the groves are full of melody ten thousand creatures range freely through all the paths of nature; but thou art not satisfied as they are.

Genius, mental power, has surrounded your homes with comfort it has given you the command of the blind forces of matter it has exalted and consecrated your affections it has brought God's immeasurable universe nearer to your hearts and imaginations it has made flowers of paradise spring up even in poor men's gardens.

It is pleasant to be virtuous and good, because that is to excel many others it is pleasant to grow better, because that is to excel ourselves it is pleasant to mortify and subdue our lusts, because that is victory it is pleasant to command our appetites and passions, and to keep them in due order within the bounds of reason and religion, because that is empire.

Saints have established our religion by their lives martyrs have confirmed it by their deaths hypocrites have added strength to it by their dissimulation tyrants have purified it by their persecutions infidels have corroborated it by their opposition the arrows of its enemies have served for its protection the resistance which it has met with from the combined wit and genius and malice of mankind have brought forth those illustrious and immortal defences which establish its truth upon the basis of demonstration.

RULE V.

Lists of Words, Phrases, and Numbers.

A semicolon is put before *as, viz., to wit, namely, i. e.,* or *that is,* when they precede an example or a specification of particulars, or subjects enumerated; and also between these particulars, when they consist each of a disjunct pair of words, or of a single word or phrase but slightly connected with the others.

EXAMPLES.

1. Many words are differently spelled in English; as, "Inquire, enquire; jail, gaol; sceptic, skeptic."
2. To Greece we are indebted for the three principal orders of architecture; namely, the Doric, the Ionic, and the Corinthian.
3. De Quincey's Philosophical Writers, 2 vols. Vol. 1. Hamilton; Mackintosh; Kant; Herder; Richter; Lessing. Vol. 2. Bentley; Parr.

REMARK.

When *as, namely, that is,* &c., with the terms after them, are used parenthetically, they should be preceded only by a comma; as, "The word 'reck,' that is, *care*, denotes a stretching of the mind." — "Of the three cardinal virtues, namely, faith, hope, and charity, the greatest is charity." — See pp. 64, 72.

ORAL EXERCISE.

Say why semicolons are used in the following sentences:—

The inseparable preposition *pre* is derived from the Latin *præ;* as in "prefix, prejudice, predetermine."

Some men distinguish the period of the world into four ages; viz., the golden age, the silver age, the brazen age, and the iron age.

Logicians say that the operations of the mind are three; namely, 1. Simple apprehension; 2. Judgment; 3. Discourse, or reasoning.

Our duties to individuals are classed under four heads; viz., as arising from affinity; friendship; benefits received; contract.

Find the increase in the population from 1790 to 1800; to 1810; 1820; 1830; 1840; 1850; from 1800 to 1810; 1810 to 1850.

Sect. III. — THE COLON.

The COLON [:] is used in a sentence between parts less connected than those which are divided by a semicolon, but not so independent as separate, distinct sentences.

REMARKS.

a. It is to be regretted that some grammarians have expressed a wish to discard the use of the colon, and that others have ventured even to expel it from their systems of punctuation. But, though in former times it was common to employ this point where the semicolon or the period might have been more serviceable, there are in composition well-ascertained cases in which the insertion of the colon tends to bring out the idea of a writer with greater facility. The truth of this remark may be tested by a comparison of the sentences which will now be exhibited to illustrate the proper use of the colon, with those which have been cited in pp. 113-28 in exemplification of the semicolon, and with others, of a different character, requiring the period, which will be treated of in the next section.

b. On the other hand, some writers are accustomed to insert colons between clauses or phrases, where, both from the construction and the sense, semicolons should be used. Thus, in a work recently published, which, though remarkable for the excellence of its thoughts and the beauty of its style, is very inaccurately punctuated, the larger portions of the following passages are separated by the colon, instead of the semicolon: "There are sorrows that affect a more private sphere of *action:* and these, too, have their appropriate compensations." — " We must not violate the first principles of eternal *reason:* we must not disregard those instinctive promptings of our spiritual nature which are as much fundamental realities of our being, and as essential conditions of all truth, as the principles of reason *itself:* and, in our earnest efforts to find out God and understand his ways, we must admit no view inconsistent with the highest notion that we can form of a perfect Spirit."

THE COLON.

RULE I.

Two Clauses not joined by a Conjunction.

A colon should be put after a clause that is complete in itself, but is followed, without a conjunction, by some remark, inference, or illustration.

EXAMPLES.

1. Virtue is too lovely and useful to be immured in a cell: the world is her sphere of action.
2. Nor was the religion of the Greek drama a mere form: it was full of truth, spirit, and power.
3. In business there is something more than barter, exchange, price, payment: there is a sacred faith of man in man.

REMARKS.

a. The chief difference between this rule and that on page 113 is, that the semicolon is used between two clauses when they are united by a conjunction, and the colon when the particle is omitted. Thus, —

Avoid affectation; for it is a contemptible weakness.
Avoid affectation: it is a contemptible weakness.

In many cases, however, the insertion of the connective would injure the beauty or force of the sentiment, as in the examples under the rule.

b. When the conjunction is omitted between clauses having only one verb, a semicolon is preferable, because, by the ellipsis of the verb, the portions of the sentence are dependent in their construction, and more closely allied; as, "The path of truth is a plain and safe path; that of falsehood, a perplexing maze." — See page 104.

c. Two clauses, of which the former raises the expectation of the latter, or which express a comparison or a contrast one with the other, but without the use of a connecting word, are subject to the rule; as, "Anger is like rain: it breaks itself upon that on which it falls." — "Cowards die many times: the valiant never taste of death."

d. Conformably also to the rule, a colon is put after the adverbs *yes, no,* or after the vocative case when following them, if they are equivalent to a sentence answering a question previously asked or implied; as, " Will he pretend to say that this is an offensive war, —

a war of conquest? *Yes:* the gentleman has dared to make this assertion, and for reasons no less extraordinary than the assertion itself." — " Can Rolla's words add vigor to the virtuous energies which inspire your hearts? *No:* you have judged, as I have, the foulness of the crafty plea by which these bold invaders would delude you." These words are, indeed, often found with a mark of exclamation after them; but they are merely abbreviated, though forcible, modes of expressing approval or denial, and have the signification of the sentence, " I emphatically answer in the affirmative," or " in the negative."

e. When placed at the beginning of several sentences, to all of which they refer, the adverbial words *again, once more, in conclusion,* and the absolute phrases *to proceed, to conclude,* &c., which have the import of clauses, may be distinguished by a colon; as, " *To sum up all:* My friends, the time is short. We are as guests in a strange land, who tarry but one night. We wander up and down," &c.

ORAL EXERCISES.

After reciting the Definition of the colon, mention why that point is inserted in the following sentences: —

Harbor no malice in thy heart: it will be a viper in thy bosom.
Men's evil manners live in brass: their virtues we write in water.
Be on thy guard against flattery: it is an insidious poison.
Do not insult a poor man: his misery entitles him to pity.
Never flatter the people: leave that to such as mean to betray them.
Endeavor to excel: much may be accomplished by perseverance.
Study to acquire the habit of thinking: no study is more important.
Reading is but an instrument: education is to teach its best use.
To rule one's anger is well: to prevent it is better.
The word must be spoken: we want more justice, and less charity.
It is a miserable thing to live in suspense: it is the life of a spider.

There is no mortal truly wise and restless at the same time: wisdom is the repose of the mind.

A human heart throbs beneath the beggar's gabardine: it is no more than this that stirs with its beating the prince's mantle.

The present life is not wholly prosaic, precise, tame, and finite: to the gifted eye, it abounds in the poetic.

To be free, to have the mind of a freeman, is not to consider liberty as a privilege which a few only are to enjoy, and which, like some narrow and limited good, would become less by distribution: it is to wish, and to wish ardently, that all partook of the blessing.

Selfishness is the poison of a true devotion: love is its only fitting instrument.

Birth and death have an indissoluble correlation: they presuppose each other.

It is unworthy of one great people to think falsely of another: it is unjust, and therefore unworthy.

The passionate are like men standing on their heads: they see all things the wrong way.

Pride is increased by ignorance: those assume the most who know the least. — Do not despise human life: it is the gift of God.

He who receives a good turn should never forget it: he who does one should never remember it.

All reasoning is retrospect: it consists in the application of facts and principles previously known.

Real goodness does not attach itself merely to life: it points to another world.

Laziness grows on people: it begins in cobwebs, and ends in iron chains. — The prodigal robs his heir: the miser robs himself.

Nothing is denied to well-directed labor: nothing is ever to be attained without it.

The silence of nature is more impressive, would we understand it, than any speech could be: it expresses what no speech can utter.

Good temper is like a sunny day: it sheds a brightness over every thing. — Insist on yourself: never imitate.

Satire should not be like a saw, but a sword: it should cut, and not mangle.

The philosophies of antiquity addressed themselves to the intellect: the simple words of Jesus lay hold of the heart.

The actions of men are like the index of a book: they point out what is most remarkable in them.

Character is like stock in trade: the more of it a man possesses, the greater his facilities for making additions to it.

Men are often warned against old prejudices: I would rather warn them against new conceits.

The greatness of a gift cannot be determined by its absolute amount: it can be truly ascertained only by a moral standard.

> Music resembles poetry: In each
> Are numerous graces which no methods teach,
> And which a master-hand alone can reach.

EXERCISE TO BE WRITTEN.

Let colons be inserted between the clauses of these sentences, in accordance with the Rule or the Remarks (pp. 130–31) : —

For the training of goodness, the ancient reliance was on the right discipline of habit and affection the modern is rather on illumination of understanding.

But no the Union cannot be dissolved its fortunes are too brilliant to be marred; its destinies, too powerful to be resisted. (Rule, and Remarks *d, b.*)

There is a true eloquence, which you cannot too much honor it calls into vigorous exercise both the understanding and the heart of the hearer.

As the pupil is often obliged to bend all his faculties to the task before him, and tears sometimes fall on the page he is studying; so it is in the school of God's providence there are hard lessons in it.

This is certain nothing can be done without a recurrence, before every thing else, to strict justice in all the departments of human intercourse.

Strive to be a simple, honest, faithful man whatever hidden talent you possess will then come forth in its genuineness, and exert all its power. — Proceed I am all attention.

Are these to be conquered by all Europe united? No, sir no united nation can be, that has the spirit to resolve not to be conquered. (Remark *d.*)

The prophet gives the incentives to action the philosopher supplies matter for reflection. One recurs to the heart and the conscience as his medium of influence the other addresses himself to pure intellect.

It is with narrow-souled people as with narrow-necked bottles the less they have in them, the more noise they make in pouring it out. — A little praise is good for a shy temper it teaches it to rely on the kindness of others.

As the fire-fly only shines when on the wing, so it is with the human mind when at rest, it darkens. — Cotemporaries appreciate the man, rather than his merit posterity will regard the merit, rather than the man.

> I care not, Fortune, what you me deny
> You cannot rob me of free Nature's grace;
> You cannot shut the windows of the sky,
> Through which Aurora shows her brightening face

RULE II.

Conjoined Members of Sentences.

When a sentence consists of two members which are united by a conjunction or an adverb, and either of them is divisible into clauses separated by semicolons, a colon should be used before the connecting word.

EXAMPLES.

1. As we perceive the shadow to have moved along the dial, but did not see it moving; and it appears that the grass has grown, though nobody ever saw it grow: so the advances we make in knowledge, as they consist of such minute steps, are perceivable only by the distance.

2. Without the capacity of suffering, we might have been what the world, in its common language, terms happy; the passive subjects of a series of agreeable sensations: but we could not have had the delights of conscience; we could not have felt what it is to be magnanimous, to have the toil and the combat and the victory.

REMARKS.

a. These sentences are obviously divisible each into two portions. But, as they are susceptible of being subdivided into smaller parts, some of which should be separated by the semicolon, according to the rule on page 116; so, by reason of the principle that a remoter connection requires a point indicating a greater separation, the colon is introduced between the members; namely, before the connecting words " so " and " but."

b. In a long sentence, crowded with distinct clauses, of which several are united by conjunctions, it is better to insert a period than a colon between the two members, or largest portions; as in the following passage from Sir Humphrey Davy: " I envy no quality of mind or intellect in others, be it genius, power, wit, or fancy; but, if I could choose what would be most delightful, and I believe most useful, to me, I should prefer a firm religious belief to every other blessing. *For* it makes life a discipline of goodness; creates new hopes when all earthly hopes vanish; and throws over the decay, the destruction, of existence, the most gorgeous of all lights; awakens life even in death, and from corruption and decay calls up beauty and divinity; makes an instrument of fortune, and shame the ladder of ascent to Paradise; and, far above all combinations of earthly hopes, calls up the most delightful visions of palms and amaranths, the gardens of the blest, the security of everlasting joys, where the sensualist and the sceptic view only gloom, decay, annihilation, and despair."

c. The mode of punctuation recommended in the last remark is worthy of being adopted in the generality of the long passages, whose parts are joined by connecting or disjunctive words, which sometimes appear in the writings of the present day. But in the compositions of the old English writers, which, with much excellence of matter, are usually characterized more by unwieldiness than refinement of style, sentences often occur, whose members are united either by a relative pronoun, which is sometimes preceded by a preposition, or by an adverb or participle equivalent to the pronoun. In such cases, it is seldom that the members, however lengthened, can be separated by a period, without injuring the texture of the parts. However painful, therefore, it may be to the eye of the reader to fall on a page unrelieved by periods and corresponding breaks, the editor or the printer of a work of that kind should conform his punctuation to the nature of the composition; never deviating from the original by substituting a full point for the semicolon or the colon, unless where the character of the sentiments or the form of expressing them obviously admits of such a separation. Thus, the colon should be preserved between the members, or larger parts, of the following sentences; the first being taken from Dean Swift, and the second from an earlier writer, George Sandys: "I swore and subscribed to these articles with cheerfulness and content, although some of them were not so honorable as I could have wished; which proceeded wholly from the malice of Skyresh Bolgolam, the high admiral: *whereupon* my chains were immediately unlocked, and I was at full liberty." — " The parts I speak of are the most renowned countries and kingdoms: once the seats of most glorious and triumphant empires, the theatres of valor and heroical actions, the soils enriched with all earthly felicities; the places where Nature hath produced her wonderful works; where arts and sciences have been invented and perfected; where wisdom, virtue, policy, and civility have been planted, — have flourished; . . . where the Son of God honored the earth with his beautiful steps, wrought the works of our redemption, triumphed over death, and ascended into glory: *which* countries, once so glorious and famous for their happy estate, are now, through vice and ingratitude, become the most deplored spectacles of extreme misery; the wild beasts of mankind having broken in upon them, and rooted out all civility, and the pride of a stern and barbarous tyrant possessing the thrones of ancient and just dominion."

ORAL EXERCISE.

Why are colons inserted between the members of these sentences? —

Every one must, of course, think his own opinions right; for, if he thought them wrong, they would no longer be his opinions: but there is a wide difference between regarding ourselves as infallible, and being firmly convinced of the truth of our creed.

> He sunk to repose where the red heaths are blended;
> One dream of his childhood his fancy passed o'er:
> But his battles are fought, and his march it is ended;
> The sound of the bagpipe shall wake him no more.

How many things are there which a man cannot, with any face or comeliness, say or do himself! A man can scarce allege his own merits with modesty, much less extol them; a man cannot sometimes brook to supplicate or beg; and a number of the like: but all these things are graceful in a friend's mouth, which are blushing in a man's own.

When once our labor has begun, the comfort that enables us to endure it is the prospect of its end: for though, in every long work, there are some joyous intervals of self-applause, when the attention is recreated by unexpected facility, and the imagination soothed by incidental excellences not comprised in the first plan; yet the toil with which performance struggles after idea is so irksome and disgusting, and so frequent is the necessity of resting below that perfection which we imagined within our reach, that seldom any man obtains more from his endeavors than a painful conviction of his defects, and a continual resuscitation of desires which he feels himself unable to gratify.

> Patriots have toiled, and in their country's cause
> Bled nobly; and their deeds, as they deserve,
> Receive proud recompense. We give in charge
> Their names to the sweet lyre. The historic Muse,
> Proud of the treasure, marches with it down
> To latest times; and Sculpture, in her turn,
> Gives bond in stone and ever-during brass,
> To guard them, and to immortalize her trust:
> But fairer wreaths are due, though never paid,
> To those who, posted at the shrine of truth,
> Have fallen in her defence.

CONJOINED MEMBERS.

EXERCISE TO BE WRITTEN.

Insert both the semicolon and the colon wherever required in these sentences:—

The republic may perish the wide arch of our ranged union may fall star by star its glories may expire stone after stone its columns and its Capitol may moulder and crumble all other names which adorn its annals may be forgotten but as long as human hearts shall anywhere pant, or human tongues shall anywhere plead, for a true, rational, constitutional liberty, those hearts shall enshrine the memory, and those tongues shall prolong the fame, of George Washington.

We are not merely to transmit the world as we receive it to teach, in a stationary repetition, the arts which we have received as the dove builds, this year, just such a nest as was built by the dove that went out from the ark, when the waters had abated but we are to apply the innumerable discoveries, inventions, and improvements which have been successively made in the world,— and never more than of late years,— and combine and elaborate them into one grand system of condensed efficacy and quickened vitality, in forming and bringing forward our successors.

We may abound in meetings and movements enthusiastic gatherings in field or forest may kindle all minds with a common sentiment great revivals may bear away thousands on a torrent of sympathy but it is all in vain, if men do not retire from the tumult to the silent culture of every right disposition and the quiet practice of every duty in vain, unless they patiently engrave the commandments on inward tables, unless they hear a still voice in the soul, and retain a steady warmth there, when the noise has ceased and the flames have died away, as on the ancient mount of revelation.

As water, whether it be the dew of heaven or the springs of the earth, doth scatter and lose itself in the ground, except it be collected into some receptacle, where it may by union comfort and sustain itself and, for that cause, the industry of man hath framed and made spring-heads, conduits, cisterns, and pools, which men have accustomed likewise to beautify and adorn with accomplishments of magnificence and state, as well as of use and necessity so knowledge, whether it descend from divine inspiration or spring from human sense, would soon perish, and vanish to oblivion, if it were not preserved in books, traditions, conferences, and places appointed, as universities, colleges, and schools, for the receipt and comforting the same.

RULE III.

Quotations, Remarks, &c., formally introduced.

A colon should be placed before a quotation, a speech, a course of reasoning, or a specification of articles or subjects, when formally introduced.

EXAMPLES.

1. The air was sweet and plaintive; and the words, literally translated, were these: "The winds roared and the rains fell, when the poor white man, faint and weary, came, and sat under our tree."

2. Let us take, in illustration, three poets, in an ascending scale of intellectual precedence: Keats, the representative of sensitiveness; Byron, of wilfulness; Shakspeare, of self-direction.

REMARKS.

a. By a formal introduction to a quotation, &c., is meant the use of any phrase, or mode of expression, drawing the attention of the reader to what is about to be said.

b. Some writers put a dash after the colon, in order to distinguish more clearly the quotation from the introductory matter; as, "The words, literally translated, were these: — 'The winds roared,'" &c. But this seems unnecessary, unless the words cited begin a new paragraph, which usually occurs when they consist of more than one sentence.

c. When a quotation is short, and closely connected with the words preceding it, a comma between the parts is sufficient. — See page 108.

d. When quotations or remarks are introduced by one of the connective and explanatory words, *as, namely, that is,* a semicolon before and a comma after it are preferable to the colon; as, "I purchased the following articles; *namely,* tea, sugar, coffee, and raisins." The reason is, that the connection between the introductory remark and the example, or the articles enumerated, is rendered more intimate by the use of the explanatory word. — See page 128.

e. When the subjects or things specified consist of words or phrases in apposition with a preceding noun, or with that which is equivalent to it, without any formal introduction, a comma and a dash are used; as, "Energy and audacity of will characterize all ruling men, — statesmen, generals, reformers, orators."

QUOTATIONS FORMALLY INTRODUCED. 139

ORAL EXERCISE.

Say why colons are inserted before quotations, &c., in the following sentences:—

All our conduct towards men should be influenced by this important precept: "Do unto others as ye would that others should do unto you."

The discourse consisted of two parts: in the first was shown the necessity of exercise; in the second, the advantages that would result from it.

Speaking of party zeal, Pope makes this judicious remark: "There never was any party, faction, sect, or cabal whatsoever, in which the most ignorant were not the most violent; for a bee is not a busier animal than a blockhead."

Be our plain answer this: The throne we honor is the people's choice; the laws we reverence are our brave fathers' legacy; the faith we follow teaches us to live in bonds of charity with all mankind, and die with hope of bliss beyond the grave.

The philosopher Malebranche makes this curious remark: "It is possible that some creatures may think half an hour as long as we do a thousand years, or look upon that space of duration which we call a minute as an hour, a week, a month, or a whole age."

It is only necessary to make the experiment to find two things: one, how much useful knowledge can be acquired in a very little time; and the other, how much time can be spared, by good management, out of the busiest day.

In a letter from Oxford to my brother Amos, his late pupil, for whom John Henderson always entertained the highest esteem, he thus expresses himself: "See that you govern your passions. What should grieve us but our infirmities? what make us angry but our own faults?"

The words with which Beattie concludes one of the most beautiful stanzas of his principal poem, express a sentiment with which it is impossible for us not to sympathize: —

"Oh! how canst thou renounce the boundless store
Of charms that Nature to her votary yields?
The warbling woodland, the resounding shore,
The pomp of groves, and garniture of fields;
All that the genial ray of morning gilds,
And all that echoes to the song of even;
All that the mountain's sheltering bosom shields,
And all the dread magnificence of heaven; —
Oh! how canst thou renounce, and hope to be forgiven?"

EXERCISE TO BE WRITTEN.

Let these sentences be punctuated agreeably to the preceding Rule and Remarks (p. 138): —

We all admire this sublime passage "God said 'Let there be light;' and there was light." (Rule, and Remark *c.*)

Now, pray, remember this Unmixed carbonic acid gas, when inhaled, is a deadly poison. (Rule.)

The infinitive mood is often used as the nominative to a verb as, "To err" that is, error, "is human." (Remark *d;* and p. 128, Remark.)

When the Roman historians describe an extraordinary man, this always enters into his character as an essential part of it he was of incredible industry and of remarkable application. (Rule.)

Ye who still linger on the threshold of life, doubting which path to choose, remember that, when years shall be passed, and your feet shall stumble on the dark mountain, you will cry bitterly, but cry in vain "O youth! return: oh! give me back my early days." (Remark *c.*)

Silvio Pellico, in his excellent work on the "Duties of Men," thus remarks "To love our country with truly elevated feeling, we ought to begin by supplying it, in ourselves, with citizens, of whom that country need not feel ashamed." (Rule.)

Listening intently at the chimney, which communicated with that below, I distinctly heard the husband utter those words "Well, come now: must we kill them both?" To which the woman replied "Yes;" and I heard nothing more. (Rule, and Remark *c.*)

When the love of fame acts upon a man of genius, the case appears to stand thus The generality of the world, distinguished by the name of readers, observe, with a reluctance not unnatural, a person raising himself above them. All men have some desire of fame, and fame is grounded on comparison. (Rule.)

One of the best writers of the present day, but perhaps one of the least known, — John James Tayler, — says, when comparing the labors of the philosopher with those of the prophet "The philosopher, on the other side, cautiously accepting the material transmitted to him, explores it with the keen edge of his analysis, and pares off from the vital substance of truth the impure accretions which it has contracted in the grosser atmosphere of the popular belief, and which must check its growth and expansion when placed in the thin, pure air of a higher region." (Rule.)

RULE IV.

The Chanting Service in the Liturgy.

A mark similar to a colon is inserted in every verse of the Psalms used in the "Book of Common Prayer," and in works of a like nature; as, "My tongue is the pen : of a ready writer."

REMARK.

This mark does not represent a grammatical point, but is inserted for the use of choirs, where the Psalms, and other portions of the Liturgy, are chanted; and serves only to divide a verse into two parts.

RULE V.

Terms in the Rule of Three.

In arithmetical works, the terms used in the Rule of Three are set off by colons. Thus, the expression, "As 111 lbs. is to $6.45, so is 37 lbs. to $2.15," is put in the form, — "111 lbs. : $6.45 : : 37 lbs. : $2.15."

CONCLUDING REMARKS.

a. Some of the rules on the proper application of the colon and the dash ought to be rejected in works where their observance would occasion ambiguity; as in books of arithmetic, where colons are used for proportion, and where the dash is put as a mark for subtraction. Should these marks frequently occur, it will not be improper to substitute a semicolon where the construction requires the grammatical colon or the dash.

b. In works printed prior to this century, the colon was sometimes used to denote abbreviation; and, even at the present day, it is occasionally so employed in writing. This mode of punctuation, however, may be justly regarded as erroneous; the period being almost universally preferred as the mark denoting the contraction of words.

Sect. IV. — THE PERIOD.

The PERIOD, or Full Point [.], serves to indicate the end of a sentence which is assertive in its nature, and independent of any following sentence.

RULE I.

Complete and Independent Sentences.

When a sentence is complete in itself, and is neither connected in construction with what follows, nor of an interrogatory or exclamatory nature, its termination is marked with a period.

EXAMPLES.

1. Truth is the basis of every virtue. It is the voice of reason. Let its precepts be religiously obeyed. Never transgress its limits.
2. The right is the supreme good, and includes all other goods. In seeking and adhering to it, we secure our true and only happiness.

REMARKS.

a. For the mode of pointing short sentences which are slightly connected with each other, see page 125.

b. A full point is admissible between two parts of a long sentence, though they are closely connected in sense by a particle, when either of them can be divided into more simple parts, separated from one another by a semicolon or a colon; as in the following passage, in which the writer treats of Shakspeare: " Other men may have led, on the whole, greater and more impressive lives than he; other men, acting on their fellows through the same medium of speech that he used, may have expended a greater power of thought, and achieved a greater intellectual effect, in one consistent direction; other men, too (though this is very questionable), may have contrived to issue the matter which they did address to the world, in more compact and perfect artistic shapes. *But* no man that ever lived said such splendid extempore things on all subjects universally; no man that ever lived had the faculty of pouring out, on all occasions, such a flood of the richest and deepest language."

c. When the two larger portions of a continuous passage are joined by a conjunction, they may be separated by a period, if several of the minor parts are united to each other also by conjunctions. — See p. 134, Remark *b.*

d. A full point should be used between two sentences, joined by a conjunction, though their parts are incapable of being separated by a semicolon or a colon, if they do not depend one on the other in construction, and are not directly connected; as, "There are thoughts and images flashing across the mind in its highest moods, to which we give the name of inspiration. *But* whom do we honor with this title of the inspired poet?"

e. From the last remark and example, it is evident that the kind of point used depends less on the connecting word than on the construction and nature of the sentences. Accordingly, we find numerous instances, particularly in the Bible, of not only sentences, but paragraphs and chapters, beginning with *and*, and other conjunctions; as, "*For* the kingdom of heaven is like unto a man that is a householder, who went out early in the morning to hire laborers into his vineyard. *And*, when he had agreed with the laborers for a penny a day, he sent them into his vineyard. *And* he went," &c.

ORAL EXERCISES.

Mention the grammatical use of the period, and the reason for inserting that point in the sentences that follow :—

The benefits of conversation greatly depend on the previous attainments of those who are supposed either to communicate knowledge or to receive it. If, therefore, instruction be neglected, conversation will grow trifling; if perverted, dangerous.

Knowledge is not only pleasant, but useful and honorable. The liberal student will therefore endeavor to collect ideas on subjects which can enrich the understanding. Languages, and a taste for elegant letters, will form but a small part of his literary objects. He will dedicate a great portion of his time to the sciences properly so denominated. He will search for knowledge, not only in books, but in the exchange, the manufactory, the world at large. From these various sources, he will collect food for the mind, on which he will afterwards ruminate.

There lies upon the other side of the wide Atlantic a beautiful island, famous in story and in song. Its area is not so great as that of the State of Louisiana, while its population is almost half that of the Union. It has given to the world more than its share of genius and of greatness. It has been prolific in statesmen, warriors, and poets. Its brave and generous sons have fought successfully all battles but their own. In wit and humor, it has no equal; while its harp, like its history, moves to tears by its sweet but melancholy pathos.

Be servants of truth and duty, each in his vocation. Be sincere, pure in heart, earnest, enthusiastic. A virtuous enthusiasm is always self-forgetful and noble. It is the only inspiration now vouchsafed to man. Blend humility with learning. Ascend above the present in place and time. Regard fame only as the eternal shadow of excellence. Bend in adoration before the right. Cultivate alike the wisdom of experience and the wisdom of hope. Mindful of the future, do not neglect the past: awed by the majesty of antiquity, turn not with indifference from the future.

I would say to the people, You cannot, without guilt and disgrace, stop where you are. The past and the present call on you to advance. Let what you have gained be an impulse to something higher. Your nature is too great to be crushed. You were not created what you are, merely to toil, eat, drink, and sleep, like the inferior animals. If you will, you can rise. No power in society, no hardship in your condition, can depress you, keep you down, in knowledge, power, virtue, influence, but by your own consent. Make yourselves worthy of your free institutions, and strengthen and perpetuate them by your intelligence and your virtues.

This world is full of beauty,—full of innocent gladness. Open your inmost sense to all the influences of what is brightest and happiest in the scenes around you. Let the spirit be clear and transparent, to receive and transmit these blessed influences of the Creator's love, and send out the light of them on other hearts. Only a pure and gentle soul can feel them. Keep yours so that they do not come to you in vain. There is impiety in letting all this beauty rise and set on us daily unfelt. To sympathize with the loveliness which blooms and sparkles in every aspect of this terrestrial paradise is silent praise,—that worship of the heart, more audible to the ear of God than the chanted litany of the cathedral.

INDEPENDENT SENTENCES. 145

In accordance with the Rule and the Remarks (pp. 142-3), say why periods are inserted in the following passages:—

Legitimate reasoning is impossible without severe thinking; and thinking is neither an easy nor an amusing employment. The reader who would follow a close reasoner to the summit and absolute principle of any one important subject has chosen a chamois-hunter for his guide. Our guide will, indeed, take us the shortest way, will save us many a wearisome and perilous wandering, and warn us of many a mock road, that had formerly led himself to the brink of chasms and precipices, or at least in an idle circle to the spot from whence he started. But he cannot carry us on his shoulders: we must strain our own sinews as he has strained his, and make firm footing on the naked rock for ourselves by the blood of toil from our own feet.

There is no one, of ever so little understanding in what belongs to a human constitution, who knows not, that without action, motion, and employment, the body languishes and is oppressed; its nourishment runs to disease; the spirits, employed abroad, help to consume the parts within; and nature, as it were, preys upon herself. For although an inclination to ease, and moderate rest from action, be as natural and useful to us as the inclination we have towards sleep; yet an excessive love of rest, and a contracted aversion to employment, must be a disease in the mind, equal to that of a lethargy in the body.

This calamity is peculiar to man. The inferior tribes know nothing of it. They obey the laws of their life, and so they have no dread of what is to come. The lamb gambols alike through the green pastures or to the place of slaughter. Up to the last flutter of her wings, the bird ceases not to trill her matins upon the air. But the only immortal being upon the earth lives in dread of death. The only being to whom death is an impossibility fears every day that it will come. And if we analyze the nature of this fear, and explore the cause of it, we shall not be at all certain that it will not follow the mere natural man into a future life, and have an important part in its retributions.

When we look at different races of animals, though all partake of that mysterious property, life; yet what an immense and impassable distance is there between the insect and the lion! They have no bond of union, no possibility of communication. During the lapse of ages, the animalcules which sport in the sunbeams a summer's day, and then perish, have made no approximation to the king of the forests. But in the intellectual world there are no such barriers. All minds are essentially of one origin, one nature, kindled from one divine flame; and are all tending to one centre, one happiness. This great truth, to us the greatest of truths, which lies at the foundation of all religion and of all hope, seems to me not only sustained by proofs which satisfy the reason, but to be one of the deep instincts of our nature.

In whatever way, and in whatever century, the Homeric poems might be created and fashioned, they place before us a time when the heroic age was on the decline, or had perhaps already gone by. For there are two different worlds which both exist together in the compositions of Homer, — the world of marvels and tradition, which still, however, appears to be near and lively before the eyes of the poet; and the living circumstances and present concerns of the world, which produced the poet himself.

EXERCISE TO BE WRITTEN.

Insert periods in their respective places, and substitute capitals for small letters at the beginning of the sentences. —

The character of Washington is among the most cherished contemplations of my life it is a fixed star in the firmament of great names, shining, without twinkling or obscuration, with clear, steady, beneficent light it is associated and blended with all our reflections on those things which are near and dear to us.

Truly good books are more than mines to those who can understand them they are the breathings of the great souls of past times genius is not embalmed in them, as is sometimes said, but lives in them perpetually but we need not many books to answer the great ends of reading a few are better than many; and a little time, given to a faithful study of the few, will be enough to quicken thought and enrich the mind.

We stand on the threshold of a new age, which is preparing to recognize new influences the ancient divinities of violence and wrong are retreating to their kindred darkness the sun of our moral universe is entering a new ecliptic, no longer deformed by images of animal rage, but beaming with the mild radiance of those heavenly signs, Faith, Hope, and Charity the age of chivalry has gone: an age of humanity has come the horse, which gave the name to the first, now yields to man the foremost place in serving him, in doing him good, in contributing to his welfare and elevation, there are fields of bloodless triumph nobler far than any in which warriors ever conquered here are spaces of labor wide as the world, lofty as heaven.

RULE II.

Headings, Subheads, Phrases in Titlepages, &c.

A period is put after a heading or a subhead, indicating the kind of matter treated of; after any term placed over a column of contents or figure-work; after the address of a person or of persons, as used in epistolary and other writings; after every signature to a document; after the name of a book or its description, preceding the author's name, in a titlepage; and after any word or phrase used in imprints, catalogues, &c., when it is not intimately related to what follows. Thus: —

1.
CONTENTS.

CHAP. I. — INTRODUCTION.   Page.

Sect. I. — The Importance and Uses of Correct Punctuation 1
    Notes illustrating its Value 18
Sect. II. — Plan of the Work, and Definitions of the Terms used . . . 19
    Definitions of Sentences, &c. 20

2.
To Mr. Solomon Piper.

Dear Sir, — We hereby acknowledge the receipt of your favor of the 25th instant, addressed to our society, in which you are pleased, for reasons assigned, to present an organ to be placed in our new meeting-house for the purpose of aiding in public worship. Be pleased, dear sir, to accept the thanks of the society.

Very gratefully and respectfully, yours, &c.,

JONATHAN K. SMITH.
ASA H. FISK.
ASA HEALD.

DUBLIN, Feb. 22, 1856.

3. The First-class Standard Reader, for Public and Private Schools. By Epes Sargent. Boston: Phillips, Sampson, and Company. 1854.
  Mill (John Stuart). A System of Logic, Ratiocinative and Inductive. Third edition. London, 1851.
  Christmas with the Poets; a Collection of Songs, Carols, and Descriptive Verses, relating to the Festival of Christmas.

REMARKS.

a. No point should be attached to the name of any article or subject which is followed, as in the first example, by leaders, or several points serving to lead the eye to a term or figure put at the end of the line, and completing the sense.

b. When the subjects of a chapter or section, specified in a heading or in the contents or index of a book, are distinct, they should be separated by a period; but, if closely connected in sense, they are more appropriately marked by a minor point, according to the degree of connection subsisting between them; as, "Chap. II. America.— Discovery and Settlement: Columbus, Americus, Cabot, &c. Conquest of Mexico: Cortez, Pizarro, &c."

c. When the names in signatures are followed each by an explanatory term, the full point should be placed after the latter; as, —

JAMES MARSHALL, President.
TIMOTHY TOMPKINS, Treasurer.

JOHN THOMSON, } Committee.
WILLIAM PARK, }

RULE III.

Names, Titles, and other Words, abbreviated.

The period must be used after every abbreviated word.

EXAMPLES.

1. The age of MSS. is, in some instances, known by dates inserted in them.
2. Dr. H. Marsh, F.R.S., &c., Bishop of Peterborough; b. 1757, d. 1839.
3. The Plays of Wm. Shakspeare are sometimes printed from the text of Geo. Stevens, Esq., and Edw. Malone, Esq.

REMARKS.

a. When an abbreviated word ends a sentence, only one period is used to show the omission of the letters, and the termination of the sentence; but any other point required by the construction should be inserted after the period, as exemplified above in the abbreviations "F.R.S., &c.," and the "Esq." which appears after the name of George Stevens. In such lists of words, however, as contain many abbreviations, the period only may be used, if no obscurity, or doubtfulness of meaning, would be produced by the omission of the grammatical point. — See p. 151, Remark *c.*

b. In books printed at Edinburgh, the period is omitted after an abbreviated word which retains the last letter; as, " *Dr* Combe; *Mr* Buckingham." But this does not seem to be a sufficient reason for deviating from general usage.

c. Some printers use the apostrophe to indicate an ellipsis of intermediate letters in words which are fully pronounced; as, " Cha's; W'm," — a style of pointing that should never be resorted to, except in abbreviations of long and unusual words, and where saving of space is essential, as in headings to columns of figure-work.

d. Words derived from a foreign language, and introduced into the English, may be written or printed without the period, when they are uniformly used as contractions, and pronounced accordingly; as, " Two per *cent* is but small interest." Here, "cent," the abbreviation of the Latin *centum*, being now an English word, and pronounced as such, the period is unnecessary.

e. Such words as 1st, 2dly, 12mo, 8vo, 8°, are not, strictly speaking, abbreviations; for the figures represent the first letters of each word. The period, therefore, should not be used, unless any of these terms come at the end of a sentence. When several subjects are specified, or when particular days of a month or various sizes of books are often mentioned, words of this form are perhaps unobjectionable; but, in the usual kinds of composition, it would be better to write them in full; as, " The command of the army was given in 1796 to Napoleon Bonaparte, then in the *twenty-seventh* year of his age."

f. When the letters of the alphabet (A, B, C; *a, b, c*, &c.) are employed as significant signs, or for the purpose of reference, it is better to point them, not as abbreviations, but as ordinary words, in accordance with the construction of the sentences in which they occur; as, " The dominical letters for 1776 were G, F: therefore the first Sunday in January was the 7th of the month. Then, A representing the 7th January, D would represent the 7th February; D, the 7th March; G, the 7th April; B, the 7th May; E, the 7th June; and G, the 7th July." When placed at the beginning of a line, they are treated as subcaptions or sideheads, which, agreeably to Rule II., p. 147, require to be followed by a period, and which, in the Italic form, are so used throughout the present work.

g. Proper names, when shortened and meant so to be pronounced, should not, except at the end of a sentence, be written or printed with a full point; as, " On the poet's tombstone were inscribed the words, ' O rare *Ben* Jonson!' "

h. Lists of abbreviated words will be given in Appendix, No. IV.

RULE IV.

Marks or Figures used instead of Words.

When either marks or Arabic figures are substituted for words, the period should not be used, except at the end of a sentence; but the full point is inserted before decimals, and between pounds and shillings.

EXAMPLES.

1. He borrows $5,000, and agrees to pay interest at 6 per cent per annum
2. As an illustration of our remarks, see § 2, ¶ 10, notes * and †.
3. $8 + 9 + 7 \times 13 - 5 + 10 \times 6 - 12 \times 2 + 5 + 21 = 777$.
4. £1. 10s. 6d. sterling is equivalent to $6.78, United-States money.

REMARKS.

a. Marks and figures are considered as representative signs, not abbreviations. Hence the propriety of the rule.

b. When figures are put in a tabular or columnar form, periods are not inserted; but, when they occur in regularly constructed sentences or in dates or headings, that point should be used which would be adopted if they were written in words.

RULE V.

Letters used for Figures or Words.

When numerals are written in characters of the alphabet, instead of words or Arabic figures, it is usual to insert periods after them in all situations; and, when employed as dates, to separate by periods the portions into which they are divided when audibly read.

EXAMPLES.

1. In proof of his position, the learned divine referred to Gen. vi. 12, 13. Ps. lxv. 2; lxxviii. 39. Acts ii. 17. 1 Cor. i. 29.
2. In the titlepages of books and in inscriptions, dates are sometimes put in capitals, instead of figures; as, M.DCCC.LV. for 1855.

REMARKS.

a. A full point is, in the first example, put after chapters vi., lxv., lxxviii., ii., and i.; and, in the second, after M., DCCC., and LV., — not as being equivalent to the grammatical period, but merely because, of all the marks, it is the least offensive to the eye, and has been generally employed in such cases.

b. In referring to the chapters of the Bible, some writers use the Arabic figures; as, " Gen. 6. 12, 13," or " 6: 12, 13;" putting after them a colon or a period. But the mode exhibited in the first example under the rule is supported by the best usage, and is, we think, much preferable in its more clearly distinguishing the chapters from the verses.

c. Bible and other references are sometimes made by the insertion of a comma after the period; as, " Gen., vi., 12, 13;" " Vol. i., part iv., sect. ii., § 3." But, though this mode of punctuation is more accurate than that which omits the comma, it is less simple; and, because uncouth in its appearance, should not be adopted, unless, as in Remark *a*, it is essential to a clear discerning of the sense. - See p. 100, second portion of Remark *j*.

ORAL EXERCISE.

Assign the reasons given in the four preceding Rules and the Remarks for the punctuation of headings, names of books, abbreviations, marks, figures, and numeral capitals, as they occur in the following sentences : —

What will £100 amount to in 84 years, at $4\frac{1}{2}$ per cent per annum, compound interest? (Rule IV.; and Remark *d*, under Rule III.)

The train leaves New York at 9 o'clock, A.M., and $4\frac{1}{4}$, P.M.; returning at 10 in the evening. (Rules IV. and III.)

But the seasons are not alike in all countries of the same region, for the reasons already given. See chap. vi. § xii. ¶ 4, p. 530. (Rule III.; and Rule V., Remark *c*.)

Poetical Works. Mark Akenside. Lond. 1855. 2 vols. 12mo . . . 4533
   (Rule II. and Rem. *a*; Rule III., last of Rem. *a*, Rem. *e*; Rule IV.)

To R. H. Dana, jun., Esq., the well-known author of " Two Years before the Mast," the community are greatly indebted. (Rule III. and first of Remark *a*.)

Titus died in the third year of his reign, and the 41st year of his age, not without suspicion of being poisoned by his brother Domitian, who succeeded him. (Remark *e*, under Rule III.)

Young as he was, the gentleman earned the approbation of his friends, and at length became M.D., F.R.S., F.A.S. (Rule III. and first of Remark *a*.)

Constantine the Great was advanced to the sole dominion of the Roman world, A.D. 325, and soon after openly professed the Christian faith. (Rule III.; Rule IV., last portion of Remark *b*.)

LECTURE II.—The later Literature of the Greeks.—Their Sophists and
    Philosophers.—The Alexandrian Age 29
              (Rule II. and Remark *a*.)

Thomas Campbell wrote some beautiful lines on the Scottish king, James IV., who fell at the battle of Flodden. (Rule III.; and Remark *a*, first portion.)

The sentiments which chivalry inspired had a wonderful influence on manners and conduct during the 12th, 13th, and 14th centuries. (Remark *e*, under Rule III.)

    " Why so crusty, good sir?"—"Zounds!" cries Will, in a taking,
    " Who wouldn't be crusty with half a year's baking?"
                                      (Remark *g*, under Rule III.)

There are only two common principles on which every work of imagination must more or less proceed, — 1st, On the expression of those feelings which are common to all men of elevated thinking; and, 2d, On those patriotic feelings and associations peculiar to the people in whose language it is composed, and on whom it is to exert its nearest and most powerful influence. (Remark *e*, under Rule III.)

INTRODUCTION. 1. The Early Years of Elizabeth's Reign; Summary of their Literature.—2. Literary Greatness of the next Eighty Years; Division into Three Eras.——REIGN OF ELIZABETH FROM 1580.—3. Social Character of the Time; its Religious Aspect; Effects on Literature.—4. Minor Elizabethan Writers; their Literary Importance; the Three Great Names. (Rule II. and Remark *b*.)

The following are some of the marble statues, in the Museum of Naples, which most impressed me:—

    Psyche; a fragment, but full of feeling, grace, and beauty; by some, ascribed to Praxiteles.
    A bust of Caracalla, animated and lifelike.
    Two equestrian statues of Balbus and his son, found at Herculaneum; simple, noble, and dignified.
    A beautiful bas-relief of Dædalus and Icarus.
    A fine head of Alexander.   (Rule II.)

CHAPTER III.

THE GRAMMATICAL AND RHETORICAL POINTS.

BESIDES the Comma, the Semicolon, the Colon, and the Period, which are properly regarded as the most essential points in bringing out the sense of a written or printed composition, there are a few other marks, partly grammatical and partly rhetorical, well deserving the attention of those who desire to have their writings, whether of an epistolary or of a more elaborate nature, easily understood : —

  1. The NOTE OF INTERROGATION . . . [?]
  2. The NOTE OF EXCLAMATION . . . . [!]
  3. The MARKS OF PARENTHESIS . . . ( )
  4. The DASH . . . . [—]

In classifying these points as both grammatical and rhetorical, we mean to imply, not that those which have come under consideration afford no facilities in delivery, but that the Marks of Interrogation, Exclamation, and Parenthesis, and the Dash, have a more direct bearing on that art. They are rhetorical, in proportion to the degree in which they exhibit the force and intensity of a style that is rhetorical in its structure; but they are also grammatical, because they often serve to indicate, in connection with other marks, the nature, construction, and sense of the passages in which they occur.

Sect. I.—THE NOTES OF INTERROGATION AND EXCLAMATION.

1. The NOTE OF INTERROGATION [?] shows that a question is denoted by the words to which it is annexed.

2. The NOTE OF EXCLAMATION [!] indicates passion or emotion.

REMARKS.

a. The notes of interrogation and exclamation do not mark the relative pauses of the voice; occupying, as they do, sometimes the place of the comma or the semicolon, and sometimes that of the colon or the period. But they are usually put at the end of sentences, and are equivalent to a full point; requiring, therefore, in the majority of instances, the word that follows to begin with a capital letter, as after the period.

b. In some cases, it is difficult to distinguish the difference between an interrogative and an exclamatory sentence. As a general rule, however, it may be observed, that after words in which an answer is implied, or to which one is expected to be given, the note of interrogation is added; and after those, though apparently denoting inquiry, where no answer is involved or intended, the note of exclamation is the proper and distinctive mark. If the writer of such passages has a clear conception of his own meaning, he can be at no loss which of the points should be used; but if the language is ambiguous, and requires to be punctuated by a printer or an editor, either of the marks may, under the circumstances, be regarded as admissible.

c. In treating of the interrogative and exclamative marks, writers on punctuation, laying too much stress on the rhetorical character of these points, are wont to say that they cause an elevation of the voice. But, though it must be acknowledged that they assist much in the proper delivery of the passages in which they occur, it will not be denied that this results only from a knowledge of a writer's meaning, and from the kind of phraseology which he employs. That the notes of interrogation and exclamation have far less to do with the inflections of the voice than is commonly imagined, will be fully apparent from the following sentences, some of which require a rise, and others a fall, in their pronunciation: " Shall we in your person crown' the author of the public calamities, or shall we destroy` him ? " — " What is the happiness that this world can give`? Can it defend us from disasters´? " — " Oh that these lips had language´! " — " How mysterious are the ways of Providence`! "

RULE I.

Expressions in the Form of Questions.

An *interrogative* mark is placed at the termination of every question, whether it requires an answer, or, though in its nature assertive, is put, for the sake of emphasis, in an interrogative form.

EXAMPLES.

1. Why, for so many a year, has the poet or the philosopher wandered amid the fragments of Athens or of Rome; and paused, with strange and kindling feelings, amid their broken columns, their mouldering temples, their deserted plains? It is because their day of glory is past.

2. How can *he* exalt his thoughts to any thing great or noble who only believes, that, after a short term on the stage of existence, he is to sink into oblivion, and to lose his consciousness for ever?

REMARKS.

a. The first of these passages exemplifies a sentence expressive of direct inquiry; the second, one that is assertive in its meaning, but interrogative in its structure or form.

b. The mark of interrogation should not be used when it is only affirmed that a question has been asked, and the expression denoting inquiry is put in any other shape than that of a direct question; as, "I was asked if I would stop for dinner." If put in the interrogative form, this sentence would be read and punctuated according to the rule: "I was asked, ' Will you stop for dinner?' "

c. In some instances, however, a question may be assertive in its form, but interrogative in its sense; as, " You will stop for dinner?" In order to distinguish a sentence of this kind from one that is affirmative both in form and signification, it is obvious that the note of interrogation should be employed.

d. It is a common error, both with writers and printers, to make one interrogative mark represent several successive questions, which, though connected in sense, are in construction distinct and separate; and to substitute semicolons or dashes where notes of interrogation should be used. In the following passage, therefore, each question should be distinguished by its appropriate mark, and not by dashes, which are used in the original: " What is civilization? Where is it? What does it consist in? By what is it excluded? Where does it commence? Where does it end? By what sign is it known? How is it defined? In short, what does it mean?"

e. When, however, the expressions denoting inquiry cannot be separated, and read alone, without materially injuring the sense, one mark of interrogation, placed at the end of all the questions, will be sufficient; as, " Ah! whither now are fled those dreams of greatness; those busy, bustling days; those gay-spent, festive nights; those veering thoughts, lost between good and ill, that shared thy life?"

f. When sentences or expressions which were affirmative when spoken or originally written are quoted by a writer in the form of a question, the interrogative point should be put *after* the marks of quotation [" "], and not before them; as, —

"The passing crowd" is a phrase coined in the spirit of indifference. Yet, to a man of what Plato calls " universal sympathies," and even to the plain, ordinary denizens of this world, what can be more interesting than " the passing crowd"?

But, for the sake of neatness, any of the four grammatical points, when required, should be put *before* the quotation-marks, as they are not likely to give a false meaning to the words cited.

g. The interrogative mark should be inserted immediately after a question which formally introduces a remark or a quotation; as, " Who will not cherish the sentiment contained in the following words of Washington? ' The nation which indulges towards another an habitual hatred or an habitual fondness is, in some degree, a slave. It is a slave to its animosity or to its affection, either of which is sufficient to lead it astray from its duty and its interest.' "

ORAL EXERCISES.

After mentioning the distinctive uses of the notes of interrogation and exclamation, say why interrogative marks are inserted in these sentences:—

Are there not seasons of spring in the moral world? and is not the present age one of them?

Who can look only at the muscles of the hand, and doubt that man was made to work?

The past, the mighty past, the parent of the present,— where is it? What is it?

Are the palaces of kings to be regarded with more interest than the humbler roofs that shelter millions of human beings?

If a wicked man could be happy, who might have been so happy as Haman?

Who would tear asunder the best affections of the heart, the noblest instincts of our nature?

Have you more liberty allowed you to wound your neighbor's character than you have to shed his blood?

A gaudy verbosity is always eloquence in the opinion of him that writes it; but what is the effect on the reader?

Bion, seeing a person who was tearing the hair of his head for sorrow, said, "Does this man think that baldness is a remedy for grief?"

Is the celestial fire which glowed in their hearts for ever quenched, and nought but ashes left to mingle with the earth, and be blown around the world?

You say you will repent in some future period of time; but are you sure of arriving at that period of time? Have you one hour in your hand? Have you one minute at your disposal?

What but the ever-living power of literature and religion preserved the light of civilization, and the intellectual stores of the past, undiminished in Greece, during the long and dreary ages of the decline and downfall of the Roman empire?

Who shall sunder me from such men as Fenelon and Pascal and Borromeo,— from Archbishop Leighton, Jeremy Taylor, and John Howard? Who can rupture the spiritual bond between these men and myself? Do I not hold them dear? Does not their spirit, flowing out through their writings and lives, penetrate my soul? Are they not a portion of my being? Am I not a different man from what I should have been, had not these and other like spirits acted on mine? And is it in the power of synod or conclave, or of all the ecclesiastical combinations on earth, to part me from them?

Show how the Rule or the Remarks (pp. 155–6) *apply to the punctuation of these sentences:* —

"Honest man," says I, "be so good as to inform me whether I am in the way to Mirlington."

The question is not what we might actually wish with our present views, but what with juster views we ought to wish.

When a king asked Euclid the mathematician, whether he could not explain his art to him in a more compendious manner, he was answered that there was no royal way to geometry.

"The sun not set yet, Thomas?" — "Not quite, sir. It blazes through the trees on the hill yonder, as if their branches were all on fire."

The Phœnicians invented letters; but what did they do with them? Apply them to the record, the diffusion, transmission, and preservation of knowledge?

You do not expect me to leave my family, when we are all so comfortable, and brave the perils of a long passage and sickly climate, for the mere chance of getting gold?

> To purchase heaven, has gold the power?
> Can gold remove the mortal hour?
> In life can love be bought with gold?
> Are friendship's pleasures to be sold? —
> No: all that's worth a wish or thought,
> Fair virtue gives unbribed, unbought.

Can gray hairs make folly venerable? and is not their period to be reserved for retirement and meditation?

Are the stars, that gem the vault of the heavens above us, mere decorations of the night, or suns and centres of planetary systems?

Where be your gibes now; your gambols; your songs; your flashes of merriment, that were wont to set the table in a roar?

Are you conscious of a like increase in wisdom, — in pure endeavors to make yourself and other men what you and they ought to be?

Greece, indeed, fell; but how did she fall? Did she fall like Babylon? Did she fall "like Lucifer, never to hope again"?

Is there any man so swelled by the conceit of his union with the true church, as to stand apart, and say, "I am holier than thou"?

What do you say? What? I really do not understand you. Be so good as to explain yourself again. Upon my word, I do not. — Oh! now I know: you mean to tell me it is a cold day. Why did you not say at once, "It is cold to-day"?

RULE II.

Expressions indicating Passion or Emotion.

An *exclamative* mark is put after expressions denoting an ardent wish, admiration, or any other strong emotion; after interjections, words used as interjections, or clauses containing them; and after terms or expressions in an address, corresponding to the vocative case in Latin, when emphatic.

EXAMPLES.

1. Would that we had maintained our humble state, and continued to live in peace and poverty!
2. How sweet are the slumbers of him who can lie down on his pillow, and review the transactions of every day, without condemning himself!
3. What a fearful handwriting upon the walls that surround the deeds of darkness, duplicity, and sensual crime!
4. Bah! that's the third umbrella gone since Christmas. What were you to do! Why, let him go home in the rain, to be sure.
5. Away, all ye Cæsars and Napoleons! to your own dark and frightful domains of slaughter and misery!
6. Friends, countrymen, and lovers! hear me for my cause, and be silent that you may hear.

REMARKS.

a. With the exception of the dash, there is probably no point respecting which more vague and inaccurate conceptions are entertained than in regard to the applying of the note of exclamation. Some writers freely make use of this mark where the sentiments do not contain one iota of emotion, and foist it in on every possible occasion, sometimes in a twofold or a triplicate form; thus vainly trying to hide their lack of pathos or of passion by a bristling array of dagger-like points. Others, again, indulge a questionable taste for the same mark, by using it wherever their diction is capable of conveying emotion to others, but where neither the structure of the expressions employed, nor the tones or inflections of the voice required in reading, will admit of the point. On this subject, we quote the judicious remarks of the Rev. Joseph Robertson, in his "Essay on Punctuation," third edition, Lond. 1791, p. 113: "It may not be improper to caution the young and inexperienced writer against the immoderate use of exclamations. Whenever we see a page in prose profusely interspersed with points of admiration, we generally find it full of unnatural reveries, rant, and bombast. The Sacred Writings, and particularly the Psalms, abound with expressions of the warmest piety, and the most elevated descriptions of the Divine nature; .... but our translators, in conformity to the sober majesty of the original, have seldom introduced the note of admiration."

b. Generally speaking, only those sentences, clauses, or phrases should have the note of exclamation, which demand a fervid, passionate mode of delivery; or which commence with any of the interjections; with verbs in the imperative mood, adverbs, or prepositions, uttering a stern command or forcibly calling attention; with the adverbs *how, what,* unless they denote affirmation or inquiry; or with the case of address, when used in a solemn style, or emphasized by the use of the word *O.*

c. Between the interjections *O* and *oh* there exists an essential difference, which is frequently neglected even by some of our best writers. The former is properly prefixed to an expression in a direct address; but the latter ought never to be so employed. *O* should be used without the mark of exclamation *immediately* after it; but *oh,* sometimes with and sometimes without it, according to the construction and sense of the passage in which the word occurs. The following sentences will illustrate the difference spoken of, and the true mode of punctuation: —

1. The heavens and earth, O Lord! proclaim thy boundless power.
2. When, O my countrymen! will you begin to exert your vigor?
3. O blessed spirit, who art freed from earth! rejoice.
4. Oh! nothing is further from my thoughts than to deceive you.
5. Oh, what a glorious part you may act on the theatre of humanity!
6. Oh that all classes of society were both enlightened and virtuous!

In the first three examples, the particle *O* may be justly regarded as the sign of the case of address, which with its assistance conveys a feeling of greater emphasis or passion than it usually does without the sign: the note of exclamation being, in the first instance, put after the vocative word; in the second, after the vocative phrase; and, in the third, after the vocative clause. In the last three examples, the interjection, according to the form adopted (*oh*) and the manner in which it is applied, is obviously a different word. In the example numbered 4, the word *oh* is followed immediately by the mark denoting exclamation, because it is independent of the next expression, which closes merely with a period, there being nothing characteristic of emotion in the structure of the language used. In the fifth example, the interjection is pointed with a comma, because this word is grammatically separable from the part of the sentence beginning with " what;" but the note of exclamation, which would have been put after *oh* if the following expression had been simply affirmative, is placed at the end of all, to show the unity of strong feeling which runs throughout. In the sixth and last example, the interjection is not separated by any point from the conjunction " that," on account of its intimate relation to what follows; and the mark denoting an ardent wish is therefore, as in the preceding example, placed at the close of the sentence.

d. In accordance with the mode of punctuation adopted in the examples illustrating Remark *c*, it is recommended, that wherever interjections, or any other words indicative of deep emotion or fervid passion, are not meant to be significant in themselves, but to form part of a phrase, clause, or sentence, the mark of exclamation be put not after each of these words, but only at the end of each expression; as, " Ah me!" — " Alas, my noble boy! that thou shouldst die!" — " All hail, ye patriots brave!" — " Rouse, ye Romans! rouse, ye slaves!" This simple style of pointing seems much preferable to — " Ah! me!" " Alas! my noble boy! that thou shouldst die!" &c.; is sufficiently expressive for all the purposes of animated composition; and tends to preclude, what every author must dread, the charge of affectation or of quackery.

e. A remark similar to what is applied to the note of interrogation, p. 156, Remark *f*, may be made here. When expressions which were assertive in their original state are quoted, and used in an exclamatory manner, the point indicating astonishment, irony, or any other feeling, should be put after the marks of quotation; as, —

"It is perfectly allowable," says Lord Suffolk, "to use all the means which God and nature have put into our hands." . . . . My lords, we are called upon, as members of this house, as men, as Christians, to protest against such horrible barbarity. "That God and nature have put into our hands"! What ideas of God and nature that noble lord may entertain, I know not; but I know that such detestable principles are equally abhorrent to religion and humanity.

This is evidently the fair mode of pointing such extracts; the notes of interrogation and exclamation denoting sentiments quite different from those felt by the persons to whom the words quoted belong.

ORAL EXERCISES.

Why are notes of exclamation inserted in the following examples? —

Alas, poor Yorick! — Alas for the man who has not learned to work
We shall be so happy! — Live, live, ye incomparable pair!
Behold the daughter of Innocence! — How peaceful is the grave!
O Freedom! thou art not, as poets dream, a fair young girl.
How dear to this heart are the scenes of my childhood!
All hail, thou noble land, our fathers' native soil!
Praise to the men for whose writings I am the better and wiser!
What! kill thy friend who lent thee money, for asking thee for it!
The secret I implore: out with it! speak! discover! utter!
Farewell, a long farewell, to all my greatness!
Down, soothless insulter! I trust not the tale. — Ha, ha, ha!
Charge, Chester, charge! on, Stanley, on! — Out, out, Lucetta!
Oh the great deep of suffering in every human breast!

How often, in an instant, doth a hand unseen shift the scene of the world! — Alas! those happy days are gone.

When we pass from the living world to the dead, what a sad picture do we behold! Oh the grave! the grave!

Happy were it for us, did we constantly view the great Creator and Preserver of all continually manifesting himself in his works!

May the sun, in his course, visit no land more free, more happy, more lovely, than this our own country!

What mighty and remote revolutions hath the human mind predicted by observing the present positions of the heavenly bodies!

How pleasant will it be to mark the soul thus moving forward in the brightness of its course!

Tremble, O man! whosoever thou art, who art conscious to thyself of unrepented sins. Peace of mind thou shalt never enjoy.

What a multitude of that living host, now glorious in the blaze of arms and burning with desires of conquest, will fall and perish!

On you and on your children be the peril of the innocent blood which shall be shed this day!

I know not what course others may take; but, as for me, give me liberty, or give me death!

What noble institutions! what a comprehensive policy! what wise equalization of every political advantage!

How beautiful is all this visible world! how beautiful in its action and itself! — The will of God be done!

Show how the Remarks (pp. 160–61) *apply to the punctuation of the following sentences:* —

O Providence! how many poor insects of thine are exposed to be trodden to death in each path!

This, O men of Athens! my duty prompted me to represent to you on this occasion.

O sacred, wise, and wisdom-giving plant, mother of science! now I feel thy power within me.

O thou who future things canst represent as present, heavenly instructor! I revive at this last sight; assured that man shall live.

Oh! I could be bounded in a nutshell, and count myself a king of infinite space, were it not that I have had bad dreams.

Oh! you are wounded, my lord. — Oh! many a dream was in the ship an hour before her death.

Oh, how seldom has a pang shot through our hearts at the sight of our ruined fellow-creatures!

Oh, bloodiest picture in the book of time! Sarmatia fell, unwept, without a crime.

Oh that men should put an enemy into their mouths to steal away their brains!

Oh the insupportable anguish of reflecting that they died of hunger, when there was bread enough and to spare!

Alas for his poor family! — Alas that folly and falsehood should be so hard to grapple with!

Daughter of Faith, awake! arise! illume the dread unknown, the chaos of the tomb!

Alas, poor creature! I will soon revenge this cruelty upon the author of it.

Ugh! I look forward with dread for to-morrow. — Up, comrades, up! — Away with him to prison!

Fie, fie, fie! pah, pah! Give me an ounce of civet, good apothecary, to sweeten my imagination: there's money for thee.

Ah the laborious indolence of him who has nothing to do! the preying weariness, the stagnant ennui, of him who has nothing to obtain!

> But hail, ye mighty masters of the lay,
> Nature's true sons, the friends of man and truth!

How exceedingly prepossessing must have been the appearance of this young man, which made an impression upon Jesus so strong and evident as to cause it to be remarked that " Jesus loved him "!

164   INTERROGATIVE AND EXCLAMATIVE MARKS.

EXERCISE TO BE WRITTEN.

Let notes of interrogation and exclamation be inserted in the following sentences agreeably to the principles laid down in the two preceding Rules, and the Remarks under them (pp. 155-161): —

Peace to their manes May the turf lie lightly on their breast, and the verdure over their grave be as perpetual as their memories (Rule II.)

Is he who triumphed in the hope of immortality inferior to the worm, his companion in the tomb Will light never rise on the long night of the grave (Rule I.)

What a piece of work is man How noble in reason how infinite in faculties in form and moving how express and admirable in action how like an angel in apprehension how like a god (Rule II.)

Triptolemns asked Mordaunt, with a voice which faltered with apprehension, whether he thought there was any danger. (Remark *b*, under Rule I.)

How many bright eyes grow dim how many soft cheeks grow pale how many lively forms fade away into the tomb — and none can tell the cause that blighted their happiness. (Rule II.)

You do not think, I hope, that I will join in conversation with such a man, or that I will so far betray my character as to give countenance to such desperate proceedings (Remark *c*, under Rule I.)

How happy the station which every minute furnishes opportunities of doing good to thousands how dangerous that which every moment exposes to the injury of millions (Rule II.)

Where is the man who is entitled to set a boundary to himself in the path of righteousness, saying, " Hitherto shall I go, but no further " (Rule I. and Remark *f.*)

Wherever an agonizing people shall perish, in a generous convulsion, for want of a valiant arm and a fearless heart, they will cry, in the last accents of despair, " Oh for a Washington, an Adams, a Jefferson " (Rule II. and Remark *c.*)

What words can declare the immeasurable worth of books what rhetoric set forth the importance of that great invention which diffused them over the whole earth to glad its myriads of minds (Rule I. and Remark *d.*)

By what inconceivable perversion of taste and of labor has he framed, for the sentiments of his religion, a mode of expression so uncongenial with the eloquence of his country, and so adapted to dissociate them from all connection with that eloquence (Rule I.)

It is good to make earth and ocean, winds and flames, sun and stars, tributary to our present well-being: how much better to make them minister to our spiritual wants, teachers of heavenly truth, guides to a more glorious Being than themselves, bonds of union between man and his Maker (Rule II.)

Why is it that the names of Howard and Thornton and Clarkson and Wilberforce will be held in everlasting remembrance Is it not chiefly on account of their goodness, their Christian philanthropy, the overflowing and inexhaustible benevolence of their great minds (Rule I. and Remark *e.*)

Victims of persecution how wide an empire acknowledges the sway of your principles Apostles of liberty what millions attest the authenticity of your mission Meek champions of truth no stain of private interest or of innocent blood is on the spotless garments of your renown. (Rule II.)

Whither shall I turn Wretch that I am to what place shall I betake myself Shall I go to the capitol — alas it is overflowed with my brother's blood; or shall I retire to my house — yet there I behold my mother plunged in misery, weeping and despairing. (Rules I. and II.)

What is it only in dreams that beauty and loveliness have beamed on me from the human countenance; that I have heard tones of kindness which have thrilled through my heart; that I have found sympathy in suffering, and a sacred joy in friendship Are all the great and good men of past ages only dreams (Rule II.; Rule I. and Remark *e.*)

Does not the mind, after all, spread its own hue over all the scenes of life Does not the cheerful man make a cheerful world Does not the sorrowing man make a gloomy world Does not every mind make its own world Does it not — as if indeed a portion of the Deity were imparted to it — does it not almost create the scene around it (Rule I. and Remark *d.*)

Why has God placed man amidst this boundless theatre, revealed around him this endless creation, touched his heart with the love of beauty, and given him this delightful and awful interest in all that meets his eye, if he is merely a creature of the earth, soon to shut his eyes on these majestic scenes, and to be buried for ever in a narrow grave Does this love of the infinite, this attachment to the universe, seem suitable to so frail a nature Do they not suggest the idea of a being who belongs to the universe, and who is to fill an ever-widening sphere (Rule I.)

O Pascal thou wert pure in heart in this world, and now thou art in full sight of God. O John Milton thou art among the angels and the seraphs that were once thy glorious song; and this world is dear to them for what thou thyself wert in it. Oh, how sublimely dost thou move in heaven, the love of saints and heroes, and spirits multitudinous (Rule II. and Remark c.)

> O Nature how in every charm supreme (Rule II.)
>
> Can storied urn or animated bust
> Back to its mansion call the fleeting breath
> Can honor's voice provoke the silent dust,
> Or flattery soothe the dull, cold ear of death (Rule I.)

A crippled and suffering child, looked at from without, seems the heaviest of domestic afflictions. Yet, once confided to our care, what an object of tender interest it becomes What gentle and holy affections hover over it What a web of soft and fostering duty is woven round it It gives new beauty and value to life. We would fain keep it with us for ever. What a void is left when it is removed by the hand of death (Rule II.)

What must sound reason pronounce of a mind, which, in the train of millions of thoughts, has wandered to all things under the sun, to all the permanent objects or vanishing appearances in the creation, but never fixed its thought on the Supreme Reality; never approached, like Moses, to "see this great sight" (Remark *f*, under Rule I.)

Oh the littleness of man's heart, capable of loving only by units and in successive emotions, and therefore contracting the infinite heart of God to the narrowness of his own Oh the meanness of man's thoughts, when he takes the foot-rule, by which he measures his earthly dwelling, as his base-line of triangulation for measuring the amplitude of the heavenly temple (Rule II., Remark c.)

Who is the man whom you select from the records of time as the object of your special admiration Is it he who lived to indulge himself; whose current of life flowed most equably and pleasurably; whose desires were crowned most liberally with means of gratification; whose table was most luxuriantly spread; and whom fortune made the envy of his neighborhood by the fulness of her gifts Were such the men to whom monuments have been reared, and whose memories, freshened with tears of joy and reverence, grow and flourish and spread through every age Oh, no (Rule I. and Remark *e*; Rule II., Remark *d*.)

Sect. II. — MARKS OF PARENTHESIS.

Marks of Parenthesis consist of two curved lines ( ), which serve to indicate that an expression is inserted in the body of a sentence, with which it has no connection in sense or in construction.

REMARKS.

a. These two curves are sometimes called *parentheses*, or *a paren thesis*, — the same word that indicates the kind of phrase or clause which they enclose. But, as this designation tends to produce ambiguity or confusion of ideas, it would be better to name them "*marks* of parenthesis," and to restrict the term "parenthesis" to signify, what it properly means, those words which are *put between* such portions of a sentence as are intimately connected in sense and in construction.

b. Marks of parenthesis were once used in greater abundance than they are at the present day; many phrases and clauses now pointed with commas having been formerly enclosed by curved lines. This probably arose from the fact, that the older writers were more accustomed to an involved style of composition, which could not be read without the frequent use of parenthetical marks; whereas modern authors, many of them with less beauty and justness of sentiment, are wont to adopt a freer and an uncomplicated mode of writing. Hence, the eye being but little habituated to marks of parenthesis, there is a growing tendency to dispense with them, even when the structure of a sentence demands their insertion. Those intermediate expressions, indeed, which are less harsh or abrupt, or do not hinder the flow of the sentence into which they are thrown, are more easily read by means of commas than with the help of marks of parenthesis; but, on the other hand, it is evident, that a whole sentence, or a part of a sentence, introduced into the body of another, with which it does not harmonize, is more clearly distinguished, and that the eye is better able to connect the main portions, when the proper parenthetical marks are introduced. — See pp. 64, 65.

RULE.

Words thrown obliquely into the Body of a Sentence.

The marks of parenthesis enclose only those words which break the unity of the sentence into which they are thrown, and which may therefore be omitted without injury to its sense or its construction.

EXAMPLES.

1. The Egyptian style of architecture (see Dr. Pocock, not his discourses, but his prints) was apparently the mother of the Greek.
2. If we exercise right principles (and we cannot have them unless we exercise them), they must be perpetually on the increase.

REMARKS.

a. If a point would not be required between those parts of a sentence in which a parenthesis occurs, none should be used along with the parenthetical marks; as, " Are you still (I fear you are) far from being comfortably settled?" Here these marks are unaccompanied by any point, because, in its simple state, the sentence would be without it; as, " Are you still far from being comfortably settled?"

b. But, when a comma or any other point is necessary where the incidental clause is thrown in, it should be placed *after the last* mark of parenthesis; as, " Pride, in some disguise or other (often a secret to the proud man himself), is the most ordinary spring of action among men." Some writers would punctuate this and similar sentences with the same point before each of the marks; as, " Left now to himself, (malice could not wish him a worse adviser,) he resolves on a desperate project." But the former mode of pointing is preferable, as it connects the parenthesis more closely with the preceding part of the sentence, to which it is usually most related.

c. Sometimes the parenthetical portion of a sentence is designed to express either inquiry or an emotion of wonder, astonishment, delight, &c., when the main passage is in its nature affirmative. In cases of this kind, the point required, if there were no parenthesis, is to be inserted *before the first* mark under consideration, and that which belongs to the enclosed portion *before the second;* as, " While the Christian desires the approbation of his fellow-men, (and why should he not desire it?) he disdains to receive their good-will by dishonorable means."

d. On the other hand, the parenthesis is sometimes explanatory or affirmative; and the portion of the sentence with which it is connected, interrogative. Thus: "The righteousness which is of faith speaketh on this wise: Say not in thine heart, Who shall ascend into heaven? (that is, to bring Christ down from above;) or, Who shall descend into the deep? (that is, to bring up Christ again from the dead.) But what saith it?" In this passage, the points used with the marks of parenthesis are applied differently from those inserted in the example illustrating Remark *c*; but the principle is the same.

e. Before the first parenthetical mark, however, no point should be used, if not required in case the parenthetical words were omitted; as, "The rocks (hard-hearted varlets!) melted not into tears, nor did the trees hang their heads in silent sorrow."

f. Occasionally, the parenthesis is so little connected with the portion that follows it, that a period is required before the last mark, though no point whatever, or only a comma, is necessary to unite the parts before and after the parenthesis; as, —

> The path to bliss abounds with many a snare:
> Learning is one, and wit, however rare.
> The Frenchman, first in literary fame,
> (Mention him, if you please. Voltaire? — The same.)
> With spirit, genius, eloquence, supplied,
> Lived long, wrote much, laughed heartily, and died.

g. Though, strictly speaking, a parenthesis is an interruption of the sense of a passage, yet the marks indicating it may sometimes be used to enclose a word, phrase, or clause, placed at the *end* of a sentence; as, "The next night we were introduced at the Prince of Craon's assembly (he has the chief power in the grand duke's absence). The princess," &c. But such a mode of punctuation is seldom needed in a style characterized either by unity or elegance.

h. In the Scriptures, particularly in the Letters of the Apostle Paul, parentheses are found consisting of distinct sentences, which require to be separated by full points from the context, as in the following example: "Brethren, be followers together of me, and mark them who walk so as ye have us for an ensample. (For many walk, of whom I have told you often, and now tell you even weeping, that they are the enemies of the cross of Christ; whose end is destruction, whose god is their belly, and whose glory is in their shame; who mind earthly things.) For our conversation is in heaven; from whence also we look for the Saviour, the Lord Jesus Christ."

i. In reports of speeches, where a particular reference is sometimes made either to the present or a former speaker, or where the sense of the auditors is expressed by approbation or disapprobation, it is usual to enclose the inserted words within marks of parenthesis; as, "The lucid exposition which has been made of the object of the meeting by the Right Reverend Bishop (M'Ilvaine) lightens the task of recommending it to an audience like this. I do not know but I should act more advisedly to leave his cogent and persuasive statement to produce its natural effect, without any attempt on my part to enforce it. (No.)"

j. Some writers would put within parenthetical marks such words as are thrown into sentences to correct grammatical errors; as, "I am now as well as when you was (were) here." But, as will be shown hereafter, it is better to use brackets, that the language introduced may be clearly distinguished from the original; as (to take the same example), "I am now as well as when you was [were] here."

k. Sometimes marks of parenthesis are used to enclose an expression standing apart from the context, and added by way of explanation, or in reference to some other passage. Examples of this kind may be seen in the "Exercises to be written," which occur in the present treatise. The same marks are also used, particularly in dictionaries and in didactic and scientific works, to enclose the Arabic figures or the letters of the alphabet, when enumerating definitions of words, or subjects treated of; as, "(A.) The unlawfulness of suicide appears from the following considerations: (1.) Suicide is unlawful on account of its general consequences. (2.) Because it is the duty of the self-murderer to live in the world, and be useful in it. (3.) Because he deprives himself of all further opportunity to prepare for happiness in a future state." But, unless it is necessary to distinguish the letters or figures from the simpler modes of specification, the marks of parenthesis are better omitted.

l. When a parenthetical expression is short, or coincides with the rest of the sentence, the marks of parenthesis may be omitted, and commas used instead; as, "Every star, *if we may judge by analogy*, is a sun to a system of planets." The intervening words *says I, says he*, and others of a similar character, should all be written only with commas. — See p. 65, Remark *c.*

ORAL EXERCISE.

Show how the Rule and the Remarks apply to the punctuation of these sentences: —

I have seen charity (if charity it may be called) insult with an air of pity.

The Tyrians were the first (if we may believe what is told us by writers of high antiquity) who learned the art of navigation.

> Pleasure (whene'er she sings, at least) 's a siren,
> That lures, to flay alive, the young beginner.

The profound learning and philosophical researches of Sir William Jones (he was master of twenty-eight languages) were the wonder and admiration of his contemporaries.

> Know, then, this truth (enough for man to know):
> Virtue alone is happiness below.

Whether writing prose or verse (for a portion of the work is in prose), the author knows both what to blot, and when to stop.

Do we, then (for this one question covers the whole ground of this subject), — do we observe the strict conditions of our vast and unsurpassably momentous work?

The most remote country, towards the East, of which the Greeks had any definite knowledge (and their acquaintance with it was, at the best, extremely imperfect), was India.

While they wish to please, (and why should they not wish it?) they disdain dishonorable means.

I am so ill at present, (an illness of my own procuring last night: who is perfect?) that nothing but your very great kindness could make me write.

She had managed this matter so well, (oh, how artful a woman she was!) that my father's heart was gone before I suspected it was in danger.

> Perhaps (for who can guess the effects of chance?)
> Here Hunt may box, or Mahomet may dance.

Consider (and may the consideration sink deep into your hearts! the fatal consequences of a wicked life.

> Edward, lo! to sudden fate
> (Weave we the woof: the thread is spun.)
> Half of thy heart we consecrate.
> (The web is wove; the work is done.)

The air was mild as summer, all corn was off the ground, and the sky-larks were singing aloud (by the way, I saw not one at Keswick, perhaps because the place abounds in birds of prey).

> She was one
> Fit for the model of a statuary
> (A race of mere impostors when all's done:
> I've seen much finer women, ripe and real,
> Than all the nonsense of their stone ideal).

A certain man was sick, named Lazarus, of Bethany, the town of Mary and her sister Martha. (It was that Mary who anointed the Lord with ointment, and wiped his feet with her hair, whose brother Lazarus was sick.) Therefore his sisters sent unto him, saying, Lord, behold, he whom thou lovest is sick.

From an original and infinitely more lofty and intellectual state of existence, there remains to man, according to the philosophy of Plato, a dark remembrance of divinity and perfection.

Yet, in the mere outside of nature's works, if I may so express myself, there is a splendor and a magnificence to which even untutored minds cannot attend without great delight.

"You say," said the judge, "that the bag you lost had a hundred and ten dollars in it?" — "Yes, sir." — "Then," replied the judge, "this cannot be your bag, as it contained but a hundred dollars."

EXERCISE TO BE WRITTEN.

Introduce the marks of parenthesis into their respective places:—

Not a few are the incitements of the working classes would they were greater! to the accumulation of property, and even to the investment of land. (Remark *e.*)

The finest images which Joseph Hall conjures up and many of them are wonderfully fine never displace the great truths for the sake of which they are admitted. (Remark *a.*)

There is nothing that we call a *good* which may not be converted into a curse that is, nothing that is providential or external, and not of the soul; nor is there an evil of that nature which is not thoroughly a good. (Remark *b.*)

There is a power have you not felt it? in the presence, conversation, and example of a man of strong principle and magnanimity, to lift us, at least for the moment, from our vulgar and tame habits of thought, and to kindle some generous aspirations after the excellence which we were made to attain. (Remarks *e, L*)

Under God, and by those spiritual aids which are ever vouchsafed in exact proportion to our endeavors to obtain them, how gracious and glorious is this truth! we are morally and religiously, as well as intellectually, the makers of ourselves. (Remark *c*.)

Sir, I hope the *big* gentleman that has just sat down Mr. Francis Archer will do me the justice to believe, that, as I receive little satisfaction from being offended, so I am not sedulous to find out cause for offence. Applause. (Remark *i*.)

I mention these instances, not to undervalue science it would be folly to attempt that; for science, when true to its name, is true knowledge, but to show that its name is sometimes wrongfully assumed, and that its professors, when not guided by humility, may prove but misleading counsellors. (Remark *b*.)

And he said unto them that stood by, Take from him the pound, and give it to him that hath ten pounds. And they said unto him, Lord, he hath ten pounds. For I say unto you, that unto every one who hath shall be given; and from him that hath not, even that which he hath shall be taken away from him. (Remarks *l, h*.)

"Young master was alive last Whitsuntide," said the coachman. "Whitsuntide! alas!" cried Trim, extending his right arm, and falling instantly into the same attitude in which he read the sermon, "what is Whitsuntide, Jonathan" for that was the coachman's name, "or Shrovetide, or any other tide or time, to this?" (Remark *b*.)

No lesson of a practical kind and all lessons ought to be practical requires to be so often repeated as that which enjoins upon the mind a state of passivity; for what an electrical thing is it! How does it dart forth after this and that, flitting from sweet to sweet for it never willingly tastes of bitter things, and "feeding itself without fear"! (Remarks *a, b*.)

Inquiring the road to Mirlington, I addressed him by the name of Honesty. The fellow whether to show his wit before his mistress, or whether he was displeased with my familiarity, I cannot tell directed me to follow a part of my face which, I was well assured could be no guide to me, and that other parts would follow of consequence. (Remarks *a, b*.)

Socrates has often expressly said, that he considered human life in general and without doubt the state of the world in his day must have eminently tended to make him so consider it in the light of an imprisonment of the soul, or of a malady under which the nobler spirit is condemned to linger, until it be set free and purified by the healing touch of death. (Remark *a*.)

Sect. III. — THE DASH.

The DASH [—] is a straight horizontal line, used for the purposes specified in the following rules.

REMARKS.

a. Notwithstanding the advantages resulting from the proper use of the dash, the most indistinct conceptions have been formed in regard to its nature and its applications. Many authors, some of them of high standing in the literary world, as well as a majority of letter-writers, are wont to employ this mark so indiscriminately as to prove that they are acquainted neither with its uses, nor with those of the other points whose places it is made to supply. Some use it instead of a comma; others, instead of a semicolon; not a few, where the colon is required; and a host, between every sentence and after every paragraph. Others go even further, by introducing it between the most commonplace words and phrases, apparently to apprise the reader, through the medium of his eye, what perhaps he could not discover by his judgment, that the composition before him is distinguished for brilliance of diction, tenderness of sentiment, or force of thought. But surely the unnecessary profusion of straight lines, particularly on a printed page, is offensive to good taste, is an index of the *dasher's* profound ignorance of the art of punctuation, and, so far from helping to bring out the sense of an author, is better adapted for turning into nonsense some of his finest passages.

b. From these abuses in the application of the dash, some writers have strongly questioned its utility in any way as a sentential mark. So long, however, as modes of thought are different, and the style of composition corresponds with the peculiarities of an author's mind, so long will it be necessary occasionally to use the dash. The majestic simplicity of Scripture language may dispense with the use of this mark; but the affected and abrupt style of a Sterne, the broken and natural colloquialisms of a Shakspeare, the diffusive eloquence of a Chalmers, and the parenthetical inversions of a Bentham or a Brougham, will scarcely admit of being pointed only with the more common and grammatical stops.

RULE I.

Broken and Epigrammatic Sentences.

The dash is used where a sentence breaks off abruptly, and the subject is changed; where the sense is suspended, and is continued after a short interruption; where a significant or long pause is required; and where there is an unexpected or epigrammatic turn in the sentiment.

EXAMPLES.

1. Was there ever a bolder captain of a more valiant band? Was there ever — but I scorn to boast.
2. Then the eye of a child — who can look unmoved into that "well undefiled," in which heaven itself seems to be reflected?
3. You have given the command to a person of illustrious birth, of ancient family, of innumerable statues, but — of no experience.
4. HERE LIES THE GREAT — False marble! where? Nothing but sordid dust lies here.

REMARKS.

a. In the preceding examples, no grammatical point is used with the dash, because, in the first two and the last one, none would seem to be required if the sentences broken off had been finished; and because, in the third, the word "but," before the mark showing the suspensive pause, is intimately connected in sense with the phrase that follows it. But if the parts of a sentence, between which the pause of suspension is to be made, are susceptible of being grammatically divided, their proper point should be inserted before the dash; as, "He sometimes counsel *takes*, — and sometimes snuff."

b. Passages of the following kind, in which an unfinished question is taken up immediately afterwards in an alternate form, may be brought under the operation of the present rule; the dash, with a comma before it, being placed after the commencing portion of the sentence: "Who could best describe to you a country, — he who had travelled its entire surface, or he who had just landed on its shores? Who could best breathe into you the spirit of Christian love, — he who had scarcely learned to control his own passions, or Jesus of Nazareth?"

ORAL EXERCISE.

Why are dashes inserted in the following sentences? —

Men will wrangle for religion, write for it, fight for it, any thing but — live for it.

Greece, Carthage, Rome, — where are they? The pages of history — how is it that they are so dark and sad?

If you will give me your attention, I will show you — but stop! I do not know that you wish to see.

Leonidas, Cato, Phocion, Tell, — one peculiarity marks them all: they dared and suffered for their native land.

If thou art he, so much respected once — but, oh, how fallen! how degraded!

The good woman was allowed by everybody, except her husband, to be a sweet-tempered lady — when not in liquor.

I take — eh! oh! — as much exercise — eh! — as I can, Madam Gout. You know my sedentary state.

Hast thou — but how shall I ask a question which must bring tears into so many eyes?

When Jesus saw his mother, and the disciple standing by whom he loved, he saith unto his mother, Woman, — behold — thy son! Then saith he to the disciple, Behold — thy mother!

When the poor victims were bayoneted, clinging round the knees of the soldiers, would my friend — but I cannot pursue the strain of my interrogation.

> "Lord Cardinal! if thou think'st on heaven's bliss,
> Hold up thy hand; make signal of that hope." —
> He dies, and makes no sign.

Approaching the head of the bed, where my poor young companion, with throat uncovered, was lying, with one hand the monster grasped his knife, and with the other — ah, cousin! — with the other he seized — a ham.

> Good people all, with one accord,
> Lament for Madam Blaize,
> Who never wanted a good word —
> From those who spoke her praise.

A "Hamlet," a "Paradise Lost," and a St. Peter's Church, — are they not, each after its kind, creations to which nothing can be added, and from which nothing can be taken away, without disturbance of their serene, absolute completeness?

EXERCISE TO BE WRITTEN.

In the following sentences, insert dashes wherever necessary :—

"I forgot my" "Your portmanteau?" hastily interrupted Thomas. "The same."

Horror burst the bands of sleep; but my feelings words are too weak, too powerless, to express them.

To reward men according to their worth alas! the perfection of this, we know, amounts to the millennium.

"Please your honor," quoth Trim, "the Inquisition is the vilest" "Prithee, spare thy description, Trim. I hate the very name of it," said my father.

Frankness, suavity, tenderness, benevolence, breathed through their exercise. And his family But he is gone: that noble heart beats no more.

> Thou dost not mean
> No, no: thou wouldst not have me make
> A trial of my skill upon my child!

What beside a few mouldering and brittle ruins, which time is imperceptibly touching down into dust, what, beside these, remains of the glory, the grandeur, the intelligence, the supremacy, of the Grecian republics, or the empire of Rome?

In thirty years the western breeze had not fanned his blood: he had seen no sun, no moon, in all that time; nor had the voice of friend or kinsman breathed through his lattice. His children but here my heart began to bleed, and I was forced to go on with another part of the portrait.

The people lifted up their voices, and blessed the good St. Nicholas; and, from that time forth, the sage Van Kortland was held in more honor than ever for his great talent at dreaming, and was pronounced a most useful citizen and a right good man when he was asleep.

I now solemnly declare, that, so far as personal happiness is concerned, I would infinitely prefer to pass my life as a member of the bar, in the practice of my profession, according to the ability which God has given me, to that life which I have led, and in which I have held places of high trust, honor, respectability, and *obloquy.*

> At church, in silks and satins new,
> With hoop of monstrous size,
> She never slumbered in her pew
> But when she shut her eyes.

RULE II.

A Concluding Clause on which other Expressions depend.

A dash should be used after several words or expressions, when these constitute a nominative which is broken off, and resumed in a new form; and after a long member, or a series of phrases or clauses, when they lead to an important conclusion.

EXAMPLES.

1. That patriotism which, catching its inspirations from the immortal God, and leaving at an immeasurable distance below all lesser, grovelling, personal interests and feelings, animates and prompts to deeds of self-sacrifice, of valor, of devotion, and of death itself, — that is public virtue; that is the noblest, the sublimest, of all public virtues.

2. When ambition practises the monstrous doctrine of millions made for individuals, their playthings, to be demolished at their caprice; sporting wantonly with the rights, the peace, the comforts, the existence, of nations, as if their intoxicated pride would, if possible, make God's earth itself their football, — is not the good man indignant?

3. The infinity of worlds, and the narrow spot of earth which we call our country or our home; the eternity of ages, and the few hours of life; the almighty power of God, and human nothingness, — it is impossible to think of these in succession, without a feeling like that which is produced by the sublimest eloquence.

REMARKS.

a. Instead of a comma and a dash, which are used in these examples immediately before the finishing clause of the sentence, some writers and printers would insert a semicolon or a colon; but the punctuation adopted above seems to exhibit the construction and sense to more advantage, and to be more in harmony with the rhetorical character of such passages.

b. On the other hand, many would put dashes, in the third example, instead of the semicolons which we have introduced. The mode of punctuation here exhibited seems to be preferable, on account of its greater definiteness; showing, as it does, by the insertion, between the particulars of the compound series, of a point different from that used before the last portion of the sentence, both the similarities and the distinction which exist between its various parts. — See p. 120, Rule; p. 121, *c, e, f.*

A CONCLUDING CLAUSE.

ORAL EXERCISE.

State why dashes are inserted in the following sentences:—

To pull down the false and to build up the true, and to uphold what there is of true in the old, — let this be our endeavor.

At school and at college, the great vision of Rome broods over the mind with a power which is never suspended or disputed: her great men, her beautiful legends, her history, the height to which she rose, and the depth to which she fell, — these make up one-half of a student's ideal world.

The noble indignation with which Emmett repelled the charge of treason against his country, the eloquent vindication of his name, and his pathetic appeal to posterity, in the hopeless hour of condemnation, — all these entered deeply into every generous bosom; and even his enemies lamented the stern policy that dictated his execution.

That gush of human sympathy which brought tears into Charles Lamb's eyes, when he mingled in the living tide which pours through the streets of London, and he felt his heart beat responsive to the warm pulse of joy as it throbbed past him, — what was it but the vivid consciousness of God; the breath of the Father, softening the bosom over which it swept, and filling it with his own merciful tenderness towards the great family of man?

The grasp of a child's little hand around one of our fingers; its mighty little crow, when excited by the playfulness of its nurse; its manful spring upon the little woolpack legs that refuse to bear its weight, — are all traits of more or less pleasantness. Every step in the attainment of physical power; every new trait of intelligence, as they one by one arise in the infantine intellect, like the glory of night, starting star by star into the sky, — is hailed with a heart-burst of rapture and surprise, as if we had never known any thing so clever or so captivating before.

The affections which spread beyond ourselves, and stretch far into futurity; the workings of mighty passions, which seem to arm the soul with an almost superhuman energy; the innocent and irrepressible joy of infancy; the bloom and buoyancy and dazzling hopes of youth; the throbbings of the heart, when it first wakes to love, and dreams of a happiness too vast for earth; woman, with her beauty and grace and gentleness, and fulness of feeling, and depth of affection, and blushes of purity, and the tones and looks which only a mother's heart can inspire, — these are all poetical.

THE DASH.

EXERCISES TO BE WRITTEN.

Let dashes be introduced into these sentences, in accordance with the Rule:—

The collision of mind with mind; the tug and strain of intellectual wrestling; the tension of every mental fibre, as the student reaches forth to take hold of the topmost pinnacle of thought; the shout of joy that swells up from gladsome voices, as he stands upon the summit, with error under his feet, these make men.

The modest flower, nestling in the meadow-grass; the happy tree, as it laughs and riots in the wind; the moody cloud, knitting its brow in solemn thought; the river that has been flowing all night long; the sound of the thirsty earth, as it drinks and relishes the rain, these things are as a full hymn when they flow from the melody of nature, but an empty rhythm when scanned by the finger of art.

If we would see the foundations laid broadly and deeply on which the fabric of this country's liberties shall rest to the remotest generations; if we would see her carry forward the work of political reformation, and rise the bright and morning star of freedom over a benighted world, let us elevate the intellectual and moral character of every class of our citizens, and especially let us imbue them thoroughly with the principles of the gospel of Jesus Christ.

Above all the fret and tumult of actual existence, above the decrees of earth's nominal sovereigns, above all the violence and evil which render what is called history so black a record of folly and crime, above all these, there have ever been certain luminous ideas, pillars of fire in the night of time, which have guided and guarded the great army of humanity, in its slow and hesitating, but still onward, progress in knowledge and freedom.

When, at God's decree, human greatness from all its state falls to the ground like a leaf; when death, usually doing its work in silence, seems to cry out over the bier of the high and distinguished; when some figure, that has moved with imposing tread in our sight, towers still more out of the dark valley; when the drapery of mourning unrolls itself from private chambers to line the streets, darken the windows, and hang the heavens in black; when the stroke of the bell adds a sabbath solemnity to the days of the week, and the boom of guns, better fired over the dead than at the living, echoes all through our territory; while the wheels of business stop, and labor leans its head, and trade foregoes its gains, and communication, save on one theme, ceases, we may well ask the meaning and cause.

Insert both semicolons and dashes in their respective places:—

Wherever on this earth an understanding is active to know and serve the truth wherever a heart beats with kind and pure and generous affections wherever a home spreads its sheltering wing over husband and wife, and parent and child, there, under every diversity of outward circumstance, the true worth and dignity and peace of man's soul are within reach of all.

When, in addition to the mere spectacle and love of nature, there is a knowledge of it too when the laws and processes are understood which surround us with wonder and beauty every day when the great cycles are known, through which the material creation passes without decay, then, in the immensity of human hopes, there appears nothing which need stagger faith it seems no longer strange that the mind which interprets the material creation should survive its longest period, and be admitted to its remoter realms.

The infinite importance of what he has to do the goading conviction that it must be done the utter inability of doing it the dreadful combination, in his mind, of both the necessity and incapacity the despair of crowding the concerns of an age into a moment the impossibility of beginning a repentance which should have been completed, of setting about a peace which should have been concluded, of suing for a pardon which should have been obtained, all these complicated concerns without strength, without time, without hope with a clouded memory, a disjointed reason, a wounded spirit, undefined terrors, remembered sins, anticipated punishment, an angry God, an accusing conscience, all together intolerably augment the sufferings of a body which stands in little need of the insupportable burthen of a distracted mind to aggravate its torments.

If thou art a child, and hast ever added a sorrow to the soul, or a furrow to the silvered brow, of an affectionate parent if thou art a husband, and hast ever caused the fond bosom that ventured its whole happiness in thy arms to doubt one moment of thy kindness or thy truth if thou art a friend, and hast ever wronged, in thought, word, or deed, the spirit that generously confided in thee if thou art a lover, and hast ever given one unmerited pang to that true heart that now lies cold and still beneath thy feet, then be sure that every unkind look, every ungracious word, every ungentle action, will come thronging back upon thy memory, and knocking dolefully at thy soul then be sure that thou wilt lie down sorrowing and repentant on the grave, and utter the unheard groan, and pour the unavailing tear, more deep, more bitter, because unheard and unavailing.

RULE III.

The Echo, or Words repeated Rhetorically.

The dash is used before what is termed by elocutionists the *echo;* that is, before a word or phrase repeated in an exclamatory or an emphatic manner.

EXAMPLES.

1. Shall I, who was born, I might almost say, but certainly brought up, in the tent of my father, that most excellent general — shall I, the conqueror of Spain and Gaul, and not only of the Alpine nations, but of the Alps themselves — shall I compare myself with this half-year captain? — a captain, before whom should one place the two armies without their ensigns, I am persuaded he would not know to which of them he is consul.

2. Newton was a Christian; — Newton! whose mind burst forth from the fetters cast by nature on our finite conceptions; — Newton! whose science was truth, and the foundation of whose knowledge of it was philosophy; not those visionary and arrogant presumptions which too often usurp its name, but philosophy resting on the basis of mathematics, which, like figures, cannot lie; — Newton! who carried the line and rule to the utmost barriers of creation, and explored the principles by which, no doubt, all created matter is held together and exists.

REMARKS.

a. Before the iteration of the words "shall I," in the first example, dashes are put without any other point, to show that what precedes is unfinished. After the expression, "this half-year captain," a note of interrogation is placed, because the question terminates here.

b. In the second example, semicolons are introduced before the dashes, in order to separate with greater clearness the various members, some of which are divisible into clauses. But, in the more simple kinds of sentences (as in the first five under the Oral Exercise, p. 183), a comma will be sufficient before the dash.

c. After expressions of the kind under consideration, it is seldom necessary to put the exclamatory mark; as, "Edmund Burke was a man who added to the pride, not merely of his country, but of his species; — a man who robed the very soul of inspiration in the splendors of a pure and overpowering eloquence." The construction of the language used, and the nature of the sentiment, will readily indicate what point, if any, should be inserted.

d. When a parenthesis is introduced before an iterated expression, the dash should both precede and follow the parenthetical marks: as, —

> When I am old — (and, oh, how soon
> Will life's sweet morning yield to noon,
> And noon's broad, fervid, earnest light
> Be shaded in the solemn night!
> Till like a story well-nigh told
> Will seem my life, when I am old), —
> When I am old, this breezy earth
> Will lose for me its voice of mirth;
> The streams will have an undertone
> Of sadness not by right their own.

e. The dash is also sometimes used before that which is merely an echo of the *thought* previously expressed; or, in other words, when the same idea is repeated in a different form in the same sentence; as, "Our own nature is the first and nearest of all realities, — *the corner-stone* of the entire fabric of truth." In many of these passages, however, when they are of a less rhetorical nature, the dash may be omitted; as, "There is nothing more prejudicial to the grandeur of buildings than to abound in angles; *a fault* obvious in many, and owing to an inordinate thirst for variety, which, whenever it prevails, is sure to leave very little true taste"

ORAL EXERCISE.

Explain the reason why dashes are inserted in these sentences:—

You speak like a boy, — like a boy who thinks the old, gnarled oak can be twisted as easily as the young sapling.

Never is virtue left without sympathy, — sympathy dearer and tenderer for the misfortune that has tried it, and proved its fidelity.

There are, indeed, I acknowledge, to the honor of the human kind, — there are persons in the world who feel that the possession of good dispositions is their best reward.

The faithful man acts not from impulse, but from conviction, — conviction of duty, — the most stringent, solemn, and inspiring conviction that can sway the mind.

All great discoveries, not purely accidental, will be gifts to insight; and the true man of science will be he who can best ascend into the thoughts of God, — he who burns before the throne in the clearest, purest, mildest light of reason.

Man is led to the conception of a Power and an Intelligence superior to his own, and adequate to the production and maintenance of all that he sees in nature; — a Power and Intelligence to which he may well apply the term *infinite.*

Can Parliament be so dead to its dignity and duty as to give its sanction to measures thus obtruded and forced upon them? — measures, my lords, which have reduced this late-flourishing kingdom to scorn and contempt.

He hears the raven's cry; and shall he not hear, and will he not avenge, the wrongs that his nobler animals suffer? — wrongs that cry out against man, from youth to age, in the city and in the field, by the way and by the fireside.

The voices in the waves are always whispering to Florence, in their ceaseless murmuring, of love; — of love eternal and illimitable, not bounded by the confines of this world or by the end of time, but ranging still, beyond the sea, beyond the sky, to the invisible country far away.

> 'Twas my cradle in childhood, — that ocean so proud;
> And in death let me have its bright waves for my shroud;
> Let no sad tears be shed, when I die, over me;
> But bury me deep in the sea, — in the sea.

Then I told what a tall, upright, graceful person their great-grandmother Field once was, and how in her youth she was esteemed the best dancer — (here Alice's little right foot played an involuntary movement, till, upon my looking grave, it desisted) — the best dancer, I was saying, in the county, till a cruel disease, called a cancer, came, and bowed her down with pain; but it could never bend her good spirits, or make them stoop, but they were still upright, because she was so good and religious.

Harriet complied, and read; — read the eternal book for all the weary and the heavy-laden; for all the wretched, fallen, and neglected of this earth; — read the blessed history in which the blind, lame, palsied beggar, the criminal, the woman stained with shame, the shunned of all our dainty clay, have each a portion that no human pride, indifference, or sophistry, through all the ages that this world shall last, can take away, or by the thousandth atom of a grain reduce; — read the ministry of Him who, through the round of human life, and all its hopes and griefs, from birth to death, from infancy to age, had sweet compassion for and interest in its every scene and stage, its every suffering and sorrow.

EXERCISE TO BE WRITTEN.

Let dashes be inserted before the echoes in the following passages :—

We must take a wakeful and active interest, that seeks them out; an interest that examines into the causes of their degradation, and labors to raise them to a more just social position; an interest that comes from faith in man as the child of God, and from faith in God as the heavenly Father; an interest that never despairs of the fallen or the lost, but makes Him who was the friend of publicans and sinners its model.

Truth should be enshrined in our inmost hearts, and become the object of our fervent contemplation, our earnest desire and aspiration. Consecrate, above all things, truth, whatever prejudices it may proscribe, whatever advantages it may forfeit, and whatever privileges it may level; truth, though its recompense should be the privations of poverty or the darkness of the dungeon; truth, the first lesson for the child, and the last word of the dying; truth, the world's regenerator, God's image on earth, the essence of virtue in the character, the foundation of happiness in the heart; truth, the whole truth, and nothing but the truth.

It is the sorrow which draws sweetness from the affections, and is hallowed by conscience, the sorrow that mingles its sanctifying drop in the cup of virtuous love and pure-souled friendship, the sorrow which mortifies young ambition, and tempers presumptuous enthusiasm, the sorrow which makes us feel our weakness and inefficiency, when we have put forth earnest efforts to serve the truth and aid human progress, this is the sorrow which chastens and exalts the spirit, and fills it with a noble seriousness, and binds it by holier ties to that ideal of perfection and blessedness which never perishes from the trust and the aspiration of the true servants of God.

It remains with you, then, to decide, whether that freedom at whose voice the kingdoms of Europe awoke from the sleep of ages, to run a career of virtuous emulation in every thing great and good; the freedom which dispelled the mists of superstition, and invited the nations to behold their God; whose magic torch kindled the rays of genius, the enthusiasm of poetry, and the flame of eloquence; the freedom which poured into our lap opulence and arts, and embellished life with innumerable institutions and improvements, till it became a theatre of wonders; it is for you to decide, whether this freedom shall yet survive, or be covered with a funeral pall, and wrapped in eternal gloom.

RULE IV.

A Parenthesis coalescing with the Main Passage.

When parentheses or intermediate expressions, that easily coalesce with the construction of the sentences in which they occur, are separable into portions requiring points, dashes may be used instead of the common marks of parenthesis.

EXAMPLES.

1. The whole deportment of a child is delightful. Its smile — always so ready when there is no distress, and so soon recurring when that distress has passed away — is like an opening of the sky, showing heaven beyond.

2. The archetypes, the ideal forms of things without, — if not, as some philosophers have said, in a metaphysical sense, yet in a moral sense, — exist within us.

REMARKS.

a. When a sentence, being assertive, can be read without a point between the parts into which a parenthesis is introduced, — that is, on the supposition of its being excluded, — none will be requisite along with the dashes; as in the first example under the rule, which, if the parenthesis were omitted, would read thus: "Its smile is like an opening of the sky, showing heaven beyond."

b. But when, without the parenthesis, such a sentence would require a comma or any other grammatical mark at the place where the parenthesis occurs, both the dashes must be preceded by that mark, as in the second example.

c. The parenthetical portion, even though incapable of subdivision, is enclosed by dashes, when it contains an echo of what precedes, or is thrown in by way of explanation; as, "It was under the influence of impulse — the impulse of nature on his own poetic spirit — that Burns went forth singing in glory and in joy on the mountain-side."

d. If the parenthesis is expressive of inquiry or emotion, a note of interrogation or of exclamation should be used before the second dash, whatever may be the point, if any, required before the first; as, "How little — may it not be? — the most considerate feel the import of a grateful acknowledgment to God!" "In conformity with a rule of the Trotters, 'never to flinch from duty,' I stand here, not to make a speech, — for who would expect me to make a speech? — but to thank you for the honor you have done us, and to give you some reminiscences of the Trotter family."

e. The following passage, which, as requiring a dash before the echoed word "not," belongs to Rule III., p. 182, should, though perhaps it does not contain a strictly parenthetical expression, have the same mark before the conjunction "but," in accordance with the examples under the present rule, in order to show the relation of the first two larger portions of the sentence to the latter: " Luther entered Rome, not in the mood of the scholar or the poet, — not to study inscriptions, or muse over the ruins of fallen grandeur, — but with the burning zeal of a devout pilgrim, who hoped to find there a fountain which would slake the deep thirst of his soul."

f. Though but partially embraced by the rule, the following is a sentence which requires for its elucidation a similar mode of pointing: " The finest displays of power, — such as those which delineate Prometheus blessing mankind, and defying the thunder of Jove, even when fastened to the barren rock, with the vulture tugging at his heart, — what are they but the principles which have animated men who have struck for freedom; braving the dungeon, the stake, and the scaffold, in their enthusiasm for liberty, and their determination to emancipate themselves and their fellow-creatures?" Here, it will be seen, the nominative case is interrupted by the parenthesis, and then repeated in an interrogative form. (See Rule II., p. 178.) To exhibit this interruption and change, made with a view of imparting intensity to the language, the parenthetical dashes, preceded each by a comma, are used.

g. Where one parenthetical clause is contained within another, both of which should be distinctly perceived, that which is less connected in construction, whatever the order, may be enclosed by the usual marks, and the other set off by dashes, as in the following lines: —

> " Sir Smug," he cries (for lowest at the board —
> Just made fifth chaplain of his patron lord;
> His shoulders witnessing, by many a shrug,
> How much his feelings suffered — sat Sir Smug),
> " Your office is to winnow false from true:
> Come, prophet, drink, and tell us what think you."

h. For the merely grammatical mode of pointing parentheses and parenthetical expressions, see pp. 64, 65; 167–170.

ORAL EXERCISE.

Show how these sentences exemplify the Rule and the Remarks (pp. 186-7): —

There are times — they only can understand who have known them — when passion is dumb, and purest love maintains her whole dominion.

The true test of a great man — that, at least, which must secure his place among the highest order of great men — is his having been in advance of his age.

In youth — that is to say, somewhere between the period of childhood and manhood — there is commonly a striking development of sensibility and imagination.

To Andersen — a young man of vivid fancy, fine senses, and cordial sympathies, who had been reared in the blessed air of renunciation — every thing in Italy was a delight.

The magnificent creations of Southey's poetry — piled up, like clouds at sunset, in the calm serenity of his capacious intellect — have always been duly appreciated by poetical students and critical readers; but by the public at large they are neglected.

In pure description, — such as is not warmed by passion, or deepened by philosophical reflection, — Shelley is a great master.

In the heathen world, — where mankind had no divine revelation, but followed the impulse of nature alone, — religion was often the basis of civil government.

Demosthenes, Julius Cæsar, Henry the Fourth of France, Lord Bacon, Sir Isaac Newton, Franklin, Washington, Napoleon, — different as they were in their intellectual and moral qualities, — were all renowned as hard workers.

When we look up to the first rank of genius, — to Socrates and Plato and Pythagoras, to Paul and Luther, to Bacon and Leibnitz and Newton, — we find they are men who bow before the infinite sanctities which their souls discern.

There was a deep wisdom in the governing maxim of the old Catholic church, — though often, it must be confessed, meagrely understood and falsely applied, — that truth is to be found in a central point equally remote from divergent errors.

The poetic temperament that had led Channing to the beach in Newport, and to the willow walk in Cambridge, — thrilling his soul with the sense of beauty, with yearnings to be free from imperfection, and visions of good too great for earth, — was working strongly in him.

Truth, courage, and justice — those lion virtues that stand round the throne of national greatness — shape their blunt manners and their downright speech.

Religion — who can doubt it? — is the noblest of themes for the exercise of intellect.

I wished — oh! why should I not have wished? — that all my fellow-men possessed the blessings of a benign civilization and a pure form of Christianity.

And the ear, — that gathers unto its hidden chambers all music and gladness, — would you give it for a kingdom?

> As thus I mused amidst the various train
> Of toil-worn wanderers of the perilous main,
> Two sailors — well I marked them (as the beam
> Of parting day yet lingered on the stream,
> And the sun sunk behind the shady reach) —
> Hastened with tottering footsteps to the beach.

EXERCISE TO BE WRITTEN.

Insert in the following sentences the parenthetical dashes, with the points accompanying them when required : —

In our dwellings and in concert-rooms, ay, and in opera-houses so the theme be pure and great there is preaching as surely as within church-walls. (Remark *b*.)

Either there is a resemblance and analogy but how imperfect between the attributes of the Divinity and our conceptions of them, or we cannot have any conceptions at all. (Remark *d*.)

It is no exaggeration to say, that Milton alone has surpassed if even he has surpassed some of the noble sonnets of Wordsworth, dedicated to liberty and inspired by patriotism. (Remark *c*.)

It is when man is in his truest moods and these come never oftener than in his sorrows and self-communings that he finds himself most in harmony with nature, and most rejoices in her kindly and wholesome influence. (Remark *b*.)

When we read the maxims of La Rochefoucault which, false as they would be if they had been intended to give us a faithful universal picture of the moral nature of man, were unfortunately too faithful a delineation of the passions and principles that immediately surrounded their author, and met his daily view in the splendid scenes of vanity and ambitious intrigue to which his observation was confined it is impossible not to feel, that, acute and subtle as they are, many of these maxims must have been only the expression of principles which were floating, without being fixed in words, in the minds of many of his fellow-courtiers. (Remark *b*.)

The gods of the Greeks those graceful forms which Homer drew in verse, and Phidias realized in marble were scarcely more irrational than the objects to which, in the name of Christianity, many have paid their homage. (Remark *a*.)

When a people shall learn that its greatest benefactors and most important members are men devoted to the liberal instruction of all its classes to the work of raising to life its buried intellect it will have opened to itself the path of true glory. (Remark *c*.)

The contest between Christianity and the heathenish philosophy between the old polytheism and the new belief, a poetical mythology and a religion of morality is the most remarkable intellectual contest which has ever been exhibited and determined among the human race. (Remark *a*.)

Christianity which, as a reform lastingly affecting all the social relations of men, yet remains to be philosophically estimated (our limits forbid our entering upon that tempting field of inquiry) had sown the seeds whose fruit might supplement the pre-existing system. (Remark *g*.)

With regard to the powers of speech those powers which the very second year of our existence generally calls into action, the exercise of which goes on at our sports, our studies, our walks, our very meals, and which is never long suspended, except at the hour of refreshing sleep how few surpass their fellow-creatures of common information and moderate attainments! (Remark *b*.)

If we were to imagine present together, not a single small group only of those whom their virtues or talents had rendered eminent in a single nation, but all the sages and patriots of every country and period, without one of the frail and guilty contemporaries that mingled with them when they lived on earth; if we were to imagine them collected together, not on an earth of occasional sunshine and alternate tempests like that which we inhabit, but in some still fairer world, in which the only variety of the seasons consisted in a change of beauties and delights a world in which the faculties and virtues that were originally so admirable continued still their glorious and immortal progress does it seem possible that the contemplation of such a scene, so nobly inhabited, should not be delightful to him who might be transported into it? (Remark *b*.)

RULE V.

Ellipsis of the Adverb "Namely," &c.

The dash is commonly used where there is an ellipsis of such words as *namely, that is,* and others having a similar import.

EXAMPLES.

1. The four greatest names in English poetry are almost the first we come to, — Chaucer, Spenser, Shakspeare, and Milton.
2. Nicholas Copernicus was instructed in that seminary where it is always happy when any one can be well taught, — the family circle.
3. Gray and Collins aimed at the dazzling imagery and magnificence of lyrical poetry, — the direct antipodes of Pope.

REMARKS.

a. This rule may be properly regarded as a branch of that on page 175, in reference to significant pauses; but it is here separately introduced, in consequence of its utility, and the frequency of its application to the purpose mentioned.

b. In the first two examples, the adverb *namely,* and, in the third example, the words *which are,* might be expressed where the dash is inserted; this mark being, in such cases, unnecessary. But it will readily be seen, that, as exhibited in the briefer mode and with the rhetorical mark, the sentences are more effective than they would be if the words understood were supplied.

c. A comma is required before the dash, in accordance with the second branch of the rule, page 41, on words and phrases in apposition. The dash is annexed merely to lengthen the pause made in delivery.

d. Should the dash be necessarily used often in the same page for other purposes, it may not be improper to omit it, and to substitute a colon or a semicolon for the comma and dash, before such a specification of particulars as occurs in the first example under the rule.

e. When words after which *namely* is understood are followed by a quotation or a remark making sense in itself, the comma and dash are better omitted, and a colon substituted in their place; unless the quotation or remark commences a new paragraph, when a comma or colon and a dash are used, according to the degree of connection subsisting between the parts of the passage. — See page 138.

ORAL EXERCISE.

Why are dashes inserted in the following sentences? —

From an illusion of the imagination arises one of the most important principles in human nature, — the dread of death.

We should be enterprising in the exercise of our own minds, and in exploring the great sources of truth, — nature, man, revelation.

I am come to regard the world as an arena in which I have to do two things, — improve others, and improve myself.

Kings and their subjects, masters and slaves, find a common level in two places, — at the foot of the cross, and in the grave.

The essence of all poetry may be said to consist in three things, — invention, expression, inspiration.

Angry thoughts canker the mind, and dispose it to the worst temper in the world, — that of fixed malice and revenge.

There are two kinds of evils, — those which cannot be cured, and those which can.

I see in this world two heaps, — one of happiness, and the other of misery.

Amongst us men, these three things are a large part of our virtue, — to endure, to forgive, and ourselves to get pardon.

The orations of Cæsar were admired for two qualities which are seldom found together, — strength and elegance.

Among uncivilized nations, only one profession is honorable, — that of arms.

In 1813, Moore entered upon his noble poetical and patriotic task, — writing lyrics for the ancient music of his native country.

Milton's life was a true poem; or it might be compared to an anthem on his own favorite organ, — high-toned, solemn, and majestic.

Nearly all the evils that afflict the sons of men flow from one source, — wealth, or the appropriation of things to individuals and to societies.

It is remarked by Rousseau, that every people in the ancient world that can be said to have had morals has respected the sex, — Sparta, Germany, Rome.

The best shelter that the world affords us is the first, — the affections into which we are born, and which are too natural for us to know their worth till they are disturbed.

In my analysis of the nature of love, I have stated its two great elements, — a vivid pleasure in the contemplation of the object of regard, and a desire of the happiness of that object.

EXERCISE TO BE WRITTEN.

Insert a comma and a dash where the ellipsis of the adverb "namely," or a similar expression, occurs in the following sentences:—

The more sympathies we gain or awaken for what is beautiful, by so much deeper will be our sympathy for that which is most beautiful the human soul.

Many a brilliant reputation resembles a pageant showy and unsubstantial, attracting the acclamations of the crowd, and forgotten as soon as it has passed.

Faith builds, in the dungeon and the lazar-house, its sublimest shrines; and up, through roofs of stone, that shut up the eye of Heaven, ascends the ladder where the angels glide to and fro Prayer.

The violator of the sacred laws of justice feels, that the unhappy effects of his own conduct have rendered him the proper object of the resentment and indignation of mankind, and of what is the natural consequence vengeance and punishment.

If men would confine their talk to those subjects only which they understood, that which St. John informs us took place once in heaven would happen very frequently on earth "silence for the space of half an hour."

It is very difficult for those who, in early youth, have struggled with extreme penury, and who have been suddenly raised to affluence, not to have at their heart what may seem like original constitutional avarice to those who do not reflect on its cause a love of money, when the love of money seems so little necessary to them.

The tools of labor are a sceptre of higher empire than monarch ever swayed that of dominion over the earth and elements; they are the weapons wherewith man achieves the purest and most benignant of all conquests the subjugation of the powers of material nature to the service of humanity; and they are instruments also of the best of all worship that which a fertilized earth sends up towards a gracious Heaven.

> Friend of my bosom, thou more than a brother,
> Why wert thou not born in my father's dwelling?
> So might we talk of the old familiar faces
> How some they have died, and some they have left me,
> And some are taken from me. All are departed;
> . All, all, are gone, the old familiar faces.

RULE VI.

Subheads, &c., to Paragraphs.

The dash should be inserted between a title and the subject-matter, and also between the subject-matter and the authority from which it is taken, when they occur in the same paragraph.

EXAMPLE.

FIDELITY TO GOD. — Whatever station or rank Thou shalt assign me, I will die ten thousand deaths sooner than abandon it. — *Socrates.*

REMARKS.

a. The dash is sometimes inserted between a question and an answer, when they come together in the same paragraph; as, " Who created you ? — God."

b. So, also, the dash is useful to connect separate paragraphs, dialogues, &c., when it is deemed necessary to save room. Thus: —

"How are you, Trepid? How do you feel to-day, Mr. Trepid?"—"A great deal worse than I was, thank you; almost dead, I am obliged to you." — " Why, Trepid, what is the matter with you?"—"Nothing, I tell you, in particular; but a great deal is the matter with me in general."

c. Some writers put a dash after the name of an interlocutor, when it precedes in the same line the language which he utters. But, as the name is usually distinguished from the sentiment by its being put in Italics or in small capitals, the dash is unnecessary; as, —

Archbishop. What is your business with me, my friend?

Gil Blas. I am the young man who was recommended to you by your nephew, Don Fernando.

d. A dash is commonly inserted between the word *chapter* or *section* with its accompanying numeral, and the title of a subject, when they are placed in the same line. Thus: —

SECT. LV. — THE POWER OF IMAGINATION.

e. On the other hand, a dash is put after an expression connected in sense and construction with what follows, if the latter begins a new line; as, " Occasionally, perhaps, he was —

'Lofty and sour to them that loved him not;
But to those men that sought him, sweet as summer.' "

RULE VII.

Omission of Letters, Figures, or Words.

The dash is often used to denote an omission of letters or figures.

EXAMPLES.

1. By H——ns! . . . . for . . . . By Heavens!
2. Matt. ix. 1—6 . . . . Matt. ix. 1, 2, 3, 4, 5, 6.
3. The years 1855-56 . . . . The years 1855, 1856.

REMARKS.

a. With the exception of the dash in the ellipsis of figures, this mark may be made of various lengths, as directed by the taste of the writer or printer, or in proportion to the number of letters or words omitted.

b. When, at the beginning or end of a poetical quotation, a portion is omitted, it is recommended that a blank be left, instead of using the dash; the position of the lines sufficiently indicating the ellipsis; as, —

    Oh! It is excellent
 To have a giant's strength.

ORAL EXERCISE.

Show how the two preceding Rules, and the Remarks under them, are applicable to the insertion of the dashes found in these sentences:—

By the L——! madam, you wrong me, and the world shall know it. Though you have put me into darkness, and given your drunken cousin rule over me, yet have I the benefit of my senses as well as your ladyship.

Canon the Sixth. — All words and phrases which are remarkably harsh and unharmonious, and not absolutely necessary, may justly be judged to merit degradation. — JAMIESON: *Grammar of Rhetoric,* p. 64.

OBSEQUIES. — We celebrate noble obsequies to those we love, more by drying the tears of others than by shedding our own; and the fairest funeral wreath we can hang on their tomb is not so fair as a fruit-offering of good deeds. — *Richter.*

Q. What is the Scripture doctrine of progress? — *A.* Brethren, I count not myself to have apprehended; but this one thing I do, forgetting those things which are behind, and reaching forth to those which are before, I press towards the mark for the prize of the high calling of God in Christ Jesus. (Phil. iii. 13—15.)

> *Don.* Good-morrow, Count Erizzo: you are early.
> Are you bound to the palace?
>   *Eriz.*   Ay, Donato,—
> The common destination; but I go
> With an old friend.
>   *Don.*   What, Celso, thou turned courtier?

In the silence of evening, conscience has a distinct and audible voice. And for us, erring, sinning men, it is greatly wise to listen, —

> "To talk with our past hours,
> And ask them what report they bore to heaven,
> And how they might have borne more welcome news."

A SOFT ANSWER TURNETH AWAY WRATH. — *The Horse in the Pound, and the Cattle in the Field.* — The horse of a pious man in Massachusetts happening to stray into the road, a neighbor of the man who owned the horse put him in the pound. Meeting the owner soon after, he told him what he had done, and added, "If ever I catch him in the road hereafter, I'll do just so again." — "Neighbor," replied the other, "not long since, I looked out of my window in the night, and saw your cattle in my mowing ground; and I drove them out, and shut them in your yard; and *I'll do it again.*" Struck with the reply, the man liberated the horse from the pound, and paid the charges himself. — *Anecdotes of Kindness and Philanthropy.*

SECT. CLXXVIII. — A CONSISTENT SERVANT.

A very rich lady in Boston had in her employment a young man from the country. On certain occasions, he was instructed to inform any company who might ring at the door, that Mrs. —— was not at home.

One day, John made his reply to an intimate friend of the lady, who shortly went away, leaving a card and a promise to call again. As the card was handed to Mrs. ——, she said, "John, what did you say to the lady?" — "I told her you were not at home." — "Well, John, I hope you did not laugh?" — "Oh, no! ma'am," said John: "I never laugh when I tell a lie."

CHAPTER IV.

LETTER, SYLLABIC, AND QUOTATION POINTS.

The points treated of in the two preceding chapters have been classified into two kinds, — 1. The grammatical; and, 2. The grammatical and rhetorical. As previously stated, they are used for the purpose of developing the sense of a composition, by exhibiting the various connections and constructions of words, phrases, and clauses; and of aiding the delivery, by showing the nature of sentences, as affirmative, interrogative, emotional, parenthetic, suspensive, or broken. The marks to be considered in this chapter are —

    1. The Apostrophe . . . . [']
    2. The Hyphen . . . . [-]
    3. The Marks of Quotation . . . . [" "]

These are put into a class different from the others, because, though they serve to bring out the sense and to aid a just delivery, they do not exhibit any analysis of sentences, or point out the relation of their parts to one another, but call the attention merely to letters or syllables, as do the Apostrophe and Hyphen, or to something foreign to the meaning and construction of the passages to which they are prefixed and annexed, as is the case with the Marks of Quotation.

Sect. I. — THE APOSTROPHE.

The APOSTROPHE ['] is a mark distinguished in appearance from a comma, only in being placed above the line; but its uses are altogether different.

RULE I.

Elision of Letters, or Shortening of Words.

The apostrophe is used, chiefly in poetry and in familiar dialogue, to denote the omission of a letter or of letters.

EXAMPLES.

I've . . abbreviated for . I have.	he's . . . . . . he is.
'em . . . . them.	ne'er . . . . . . never.
i'the . . . . in the.	thou'rt . . . . . thou art
o'er . . . . over.	'tis . . . . it is.
don't . . . . do not.	who'd . . . . . . who would
'gainst . . . . . . against.	you'll . . . . . . you will.

REMARKS.

a. A word pronounced in full should not be abbreviated with the apostrophe, except in headings to column-work, where saving of room is necessary, and where the full point at the end would not indicate the word intended. — See p. 149, Remark *c.*

b. Though not, strictly speaking, abbreviations, the plurals of mere letters or of Arabic figures are formed by the insertion of an apostrophe before the *s;* as, "Mark all the *a*'s and *o*'s in your exercise." — "In this sum there are four 2's and three 5's."

c. It was once a common practice, especially in verse, to write and print *tho'* and *thro'*, instead of *though* and *through;* but these abbreviated forms are now discontinued, for the very just reason that they do not shorten the pronunciation of the words, — the chief object for which abbreviations are used. To prevent, however, the turning of a line in poetry, so as to occupy the space of two, which is offensive to the eye, *tho'* and *thro'* may occasionally be thus printed.

d. Borough, the termination of some proper names, is not unfrequently contracted into *bro* or *boro*, either with or without the addition of an apostrophe; as, *Marlbro*, *Southboro'*. If the abbreviation is made, the apostrophe should be used to indicate the omission of the last letters; but, except in lines where room must be saved, it would be much better to write and print all such words in full; as, *Marlborough*. *Edinboro'* is a barbarous corruption of *Edinburgh*, and should never deface a printed page.

e. The particle *till*, being a substitute for *until*, which is now seldom used, should not be preceded by an apostrophe.

f. The mark under notice is erroneously used in the words *to, the, heaven, power, every, threatening*, and others of a similar nature, when written, as they frequently are in verse, *t', th', heav'n, pow'r, ev'ry, threat'ning,* &c.; for, though apparently, in the full or unelided form, making a syllable additional to the number of the feet required by the verse, they are never pronounced differently from the same words in prose, nor does this pronunciation at all affect the rhythm. Indeed no elocutionist or poet deserving of the name would read the phrases, " to attain perfection " and " the accomplished sofa," in the following lines, as if written *tattain perfection, thaccomplished sofa*; though, judging from the mode in which they were originally printed (" t' attain, th' accomplished "), a reader might imagine that this absurd pronunciation was requisite. The verse in which they occur should therefore stand thus:—

> So slow
> The growth of what is excellent; so hard
> *To* attain perfection in this nether world.
> Thus, first, Necessity invented stools;
> Convenience next suggested elbow-chairs;
> And Luxury, *the* accomplished sofa next.

g. It seems to have been the practice in former times to pronounce, as an additional syllable, the *ed* in the imperfect tense of verbs, in past participles, and in participial adjectives; and hence arose the propriety, in poetical works of a bygone age, of omitting the *e* in words of this sort, and of supplying its place with an apostrophe, when the termination treated of coalesced in pronunciation with the primitive to which *d* or *ed* was attached. Now, however, that this syllable is not separately enunciated in prose,—except in *learned, beloved, cursed, winged*, when used as adjectives, and in some instances where a combination of harsh consonants necessarily requires the *ed* always to be articulated as a syllable; and except also in Sacred Scripture, portions of which should be read in a very solemn manner, — the propriety of supplying the place of the *e* with an apostrophe is exceedingly questionable. In many recent publications, therefore, the mark of elision has been thrown aside in regard to such words, and a grave accent placed on the *e* in those only which are lengthened for the sake of the rhythm; as will be seen in the following lines: —

> I *praised* the sun, whose chariot *rolled*
> On wheels of amber and of gold;
> I *praised* the moon, whose softer eye
> *Gleamed* sweetly through the summer sky;
> And moon and sun in answer said,
> " Our days of light are *numberèd*."

Some writers, however, prefer to mark the additional syllable by an acute accent or a diæresis on the vowel; as, *mailéd* or *brighténed*. But, as the acute accent is sometimes used in poetry to point out a change in the true accentuation of a word, — as *aspéct*, instead of *áspect*, — and the diæresis to separate in pronunciation two vowels coming together, — as *Danaë*, — it would be better to appropriate in verse the grave accent to the lengthening of words ending in *ed*.

h. In the preceding paragraph, we have endeavored to show the inutility of substituting the apostrophe for an *e*, in the termination *ed*, when pronounced in union with a preceding syllable. It may, however, be proper to admit, that many respectable authors and printers adopt a middle course in reference to the words under consideration. They always retain the *e* in the imperfect tense and perfect participle of those verbs whose infinitive ends in that letter, but in poetry use an apostrophe in the same forms of verbs, when the infinitive terminates with a consonant; as, "to grieve, *grieved;* to gain, *gain'd*." They also, as a matter of course, reject as useless the accent in such a word as *numberèd*, when the *ed* forms an additional syllable; the *e* being retained as an exception to their general rule, in order to show that the *ed* does not coalesce with the preceding syllable. The mode of using the vowel and the apostrophe, here adverted to, is exemplified in the following lines: —

> Ages *elapsed* ere Homer's lamp *appear'd*,
> And ages ere the Mantuan swan was heard:
> To carry nature lengths unknown before,
> To give a Milton birth, *ask'd* ages more.

i. Though but indirectly connected with punctuation, it may be remarked, that some of the past participles, having the termination *ed,* are in verse frequently written or printed with a *t,* as in the words *blest, drest, dreamt;* and this mode of spelling, though not analogical, is by no means unpleasant to the eye. In prose, however, when participles having both terminations occur, it is better to adopt that which is more usual; being, to speak generally, the regular form, *ed.*

ORAL EXERCISES.

State the reason given in the Rule for inserting an apostrophe in the words thus marked, and read them both in the elided and the full form:—

'Mid such a heavenly scene as this, death is an empty name.
Thou'lt yet survive the storm, and bloom in paradise.
Methought that I lay naked and faint 'neath a tropic sky.
If I'd a throne, I'd freely share it with thee.
That lesson in my memory I'll treasure up with care.
I might have lived, and 'joyed immortal bliss.
'Mongst horrid shapes, and shrieks, and sights unholy.
Let me thy voice betimes i'the morning hear.
Night stretches forth her leaden sceptre o'er a slumbering world.
The thing they can't but purpose, they postpone.
E'en with the tender tear which nature sheds o'er those we love.
Thou'rt neither fair nor strong nor wise nor rich nor young.
You're overwatched, my lord: lie down and rest.
Here's a marvellous convenient place for our rehearsal.
Give a single lightning glance, and he'll dwindle to a calf.
One, 'midst the forests of the West, by a dark stream is laid.
Whene'er I wander in the grove, and gaze upon the lake.
Do not ask who'll go with you: go ahead.
Tie up the knocker; say I'm sick, — I'm dead.
Go to, I'll no more of't: it hath made me mad.
If that thou be'st a Roman, take it forth.
Or in some hollowed seat, 'gainst which the big waves beat.
Faint's the cold work till thou inspire the whole.
A mingled air: 'twas sad by fits, by starts 'twas wild.
That errand-bound 'prentice was passing in haste.
You've pulled my bell as if you'd jerk it off the wire.
Of herself survey she takes, but 'tween men no difference makes.
For,'twixt the hours of twelve and one, methought I heard him shriek

THE APOSTROPHE.

Show how the insertion or the omission of apostrophes in certain words, occurring in these portions of verse, is borne out by the preceding Remarks:—

Strike — till the last armed foe expires!

Here Edwin and his Emma oft would stray,
To enjoy the coolness of the evening breeze.

The toiling ploughman drives his thirsty teams
    To taste the slippery streams.

Though darkness o'er a slumbering world
    Her sable mantle throw,
Returning splendors are unfurled,
    And all is bright below.

Unthinking, idle, wild, and young,
I laughed and talked, and danced and sung;
And, proud of health, of freedom vain,
Dreamt not of sorrow, care, or pain.

Serenity broods o'er my mind;
    For I daily pray to Heaven,
That, when the hour of death arrives,
    My sins may be forgiven.

But come, thou goddess fair and free,
In heaven ycleped Euphrosyne,
And by men heart-easing Mirth;
Whom lovely Venus, at a birth,
With two sister Graces more,
To ivy-crownèd Bacchus bore.

              Oh! when my friend and I
In some thick wood have wandered heedless on,
Hid from the vulgar eye, and sat us down
Upon the sloping cowslip-covered bank,
Where the pure, limpid stream has slid along
In grateful errors through the underwood,
Sweet murmuring, methought the shrill-tongued thrush
Mended his song of love; the sooty blackbird
Mellowed his pipe, and softened every note;
The eglantine smelled sweeter, and the rose
Assumed a dye more deep; whilst every flower
Vied with its fellow-plant in luxury
Of dress. Oh! then, the longest summer's day
Seemed too, too much in haste; still the full heart
Had not imparted half: 'twas happiness
Too exquisite to last. Of joys departed,
Not to return, how painful the remembrance!

ELISION OF LETTERS.

EXERCISE TO BE WRITTEN.

Insert the apostrophe wherever necessary; and mark a grave accent on the vowel in ED in verse, when pronounced as an additional syllable:—

As Yorkshire Humphrey, tother day,
Oer London Bridge was stumping.

That forked flash, that pealing crash,
Seemed from the wave to sweep her.

At once they sprang
With haste aloft, and, peering bright,
Descried afar the blessed sight.

For who but He that arched the skies
Could rear the daisy's purple bud,
Mould its green cup, its wiry stem,
Its fringed border nicely spin,
And cut the gold-embossed gem,
That, set in silver, gleams within?

Oer Idalia's velvet green the rosy-crowned Loves are seen

Now, brothers, bending oer the accursed loom,
Stamp we our vengeance deep, and ratify his doom.

From seventeen years till now, almost fourscore,
Here lived I, but now live here no more.

Then lighted from his gorgeous throne; for now
Twixt host and host but narrow space was left.

Approach, and read (for thou canst read) the lay
Graved on the stone beneath yon aged thorn.

Thou rather, with thy sharp and sulphurous bolt,
Splitst the unwedgeable and gnarled oak,
Than the soft myrtle.
A bearded man,
Armed to the teeth art thou: one mailed hand
Grasps the broad shield, and one the sword.

Blest be the day I scaped the wrangling crew
From Pyrrho's maze and Epicurus' sty,
And held high converse with the godlike few,
Who, to the enraptured heart and ear and eye,
Teach beauty, virtue, truth, and love, and melody.

It gazes on those glazed eyes, it hearkens for a breath;
It does not know that kindness dies, and love departs from death.

RULE II.

The Genitive or Possessive Case.

The apostrophe is used to distinguish the possessive case of nouns; which is usually formed in the singular number by adding to the nominative an *s*, with an apostrophe before it, and in the plural by simply annexing this mark.

EXAMPLES.

1. What majesty attends Night's lovely queen!
2. The Ages' voice speaks everlasting truth.

REMARKS.

a. The apostrophe is sometimes used in the singular number without the additional *s*, when the nominative ends in *s, ss, ce,* or *x*; as, "*Moses*' rod," " for *righteousness*' sake," " for *conscience*' sake," " the *administratrix*' sale." This mode of punctuation holds good chiefly in proper names having a foreign termination, and in such common nouns as are seldom used in the plural, — an exception to the rule of forming the possessive singular, which is founded on the propriety of modifying the disagreeable nature of the hissing sound.

b. Recourse, however, should not be had to the principle laid down in the preceding remark, when its adoption would cause ambiguity, or when the addition of the *s* is not offensive to a refined ear. For instance, the Italic words in the phrases, "*Burns's* Poems," "*James's* book," "*Thomas's* cloak," " the *fox's* tail," though they contain the hissing sound, are not particularly unpleasant, and are far more analogical and significant than the abbreviated forms, "*Burns*' Poems," "*James*' book," "*Thomas*' cloak," " the *fox*' tail."

c. We have no doubt that the distinctions here suggested are important, and accord with the genius of the English language; but in poetry none but the author himself should change the form of the possessive, whether written with or without the annexed *s*, as, unless the whole line were recast, such an alteration would probably mar the harmony of the verse. Even in prose, a printer should not take the liberty of changing the form of a possessive, without the consent of the author; this matter being yet a subject on which there is a difference of opinion among literary men.

d. To form the possessive case plural, the apostrophe, with an *s* after it, is added to the nominative plural, when it does not end in that letter; as, "*Men's* passions; *women's* tenderness; *children's* joys."

e. The possessive case of pronouns is formed without an apostrophe; as, —

SINGULAR.	PLURAL.	SINGULAR.	PLURAL.
Mine.	Ours.	Hers.	Theirs.
Yours.	Yours.	Its.	Theirs.
His.	Theirs.	Whose.	Whose.

Some grammarians would use the apostrophe before the *s* in *ours, yours, hers, its, theirs.* But the impropriety of this is evident from the mode in which the other pronouns in the possessive case are always written; namely, *mine, his,* and *whose;* which exhibit the case without the mark in question.

ORAL EXERCISES.

State the reason for the insertion and position of the apostrophe in these sentences: —

A man's manners not unfrequently indicate his morals.
On eagle's wings he seemed to soar. — Our enemies' resistance.
The shepherd-swain on Scotia's mountains fed his little flock.
And the Persians' gems and gold were the Grecians' funeral pyre.
We will not shrink from life's severest due. — Woman's rights.
Few columns rose to mark her patriots' last repose.
The sun is the poet's, the invalid's, and the hypochondriac's friend.
The ladies' gloves and shawls were exceedingly handsome.
Philippa was the name of Edward the Third's queen.
O majestic Night, Nature's great ancestor, Day's elder born!
He must strike the second heat upon the Muses' anvil.
Mother's wag, pretty boy, father's sorrow, father's joy.
Spirit of Good! on this week's verge I stand.
Bid them in duty's sphere as meekly move.
Why is that sleeper laid to rest in manhood's pride?
Who loves not spring's voluptuous hours, or summer's splendid reign?
Is sparkling wit the world's exclusive right?
The Turk awoke: he woke to hear his sentry's shriek.
The people's shouts were long and loud. — Thy mercies' monument.
A friend should bear a friend's infirmities. — The ox's hide.

THE APOSTROPHE.

Show how the Rule or the Remarks (pp. 204–5) *are applicable to the possessive case in the following phrases and sentences:* —

Adam's book, not Adams's: the book did not belong to Adams.
John Quincy Adams's death was no common bereavement.
Sir Humphrey Davy's safety-lamp. — Davis's Straits.
Josephus's " History of the Jews " is a very interesting work.
Andrew's hat, not Andrews's. — Andrews's " Latin Reader."
For quietness' sake, the man would not enter into any dispute.
Col. Matthews's delivery. — Matthew's Gospel, not Matthews's.
The witness's testimony agreed with the facts of the case.
Let Temperance' smile the cup of gladness cheer.
Nor roamed Parnassus' heights nor Pindus' hallowed shade.
There is no impropriety in speaking of the cockatrice's den.
I oft have sat on Thames' sweet bank to hear my friend.
Like the silver crimson shroud, that Phœbus' smiling looks doth grace.
Faustus' offence [the offence of Faustus] can never be pardoned.
After two years, Porcius Festus came into Felix's room.

EXERCISE TO BE WRITTEN.

Agreeably to the Rule and the Remarks, insert apostrophes in, or annex them to, the nouns in the possessive case which occur in the following sentences; but let the pronouns remain unmarked: —

The traveller went to lodge, not in Mr. Jacobs house, but in Mr. Jacobss. (Rule, and Remark *b*.)

I am going to the booksellers [*sing.*] to purchase Popes Homer and Drydens Virgil. (Rule.)

Procrustes bed. — Hortensius influence. — Achilles shield. — Pocahontas father. — Sophocles Greek Grammar. (Remark *a*.)

The precepts of wisdom form the good mans interest and happiness. (Rule.)

Robert Burnss prose as well as poetical writings are astonishing productions. (Remark *b*.)

Fames proud temple shines afar. — From mens experience do thou learn wisdom. (Rule, and Remark *d*.)

They applauded that conduct of his, but condemned hers and yours. The reason of its being done I cannot tell. (Remark *e*.)

He had the surgeons [*sing.*], the physicians [*sing.*], and the apothecarys advice. (Rule.)

The tendency of Dickenss genius, both in delineating the actual and the natural, is to personify, to individualize. (Remark *b*.)

Goethes "Wilhelm Meister" was the rich result of ten years labor. (Rule.)

John Parrys children played with David Parriss. — Williams wig was purchased at Mr. Williamss shop. (Rule, and Remark *b*.)

I would rather have arrived at one profound conclusion of the sages meditation in his dim study, than to win that gaze of the multitude. (Rule.)

Should you have occasion to refer, in writing or in print, to Burns sermons, meaning the sermons of Burn, you must be careful to put the apostrophe in its right place. (Rule, and comp. Rem. *b*.)

A drunkard once reeled up to him with the remark, "Mr. Whitefield, I am one of your converts." — "I think it very likely," was the reply; "for I am sure you are none of Gods." (Rule.)

I was surprised to see so many young idle sparks listening quietly and attentively to Dr. David Sparkss lecture on Drusius, Grotius, and Michaelis theological works. (Remarks *b*, *a*.)

> And still the Greek rushed on, beneath the fiery fold,
> Till, like a rising sun, shone Xerxes tent of gold. (Remark *a*.)

Education does not commence with the alphabet: it begins with a mothers look; with a fathers nod of approbation, or a sign of reproof; with a sisters gentle pressure of the hand, or a brothers noble act of forbearance; with handfuls of flowers in green dells, on hills and daisy meadows; with birds nests admired, but not touched; with humming bees and glass hives; with pleasant walks in shady lanes; with thoughts directed, in sweet and kindly tones and words, to nature, to beauty, to acts of benevolence, to deeds of virtue, to the sense of all good, and to God himself. (Rule.)

> Behold Affections garden, whose sweet flowers —
> A blending of all odors, forms, and hues —
> Were nursed by Fancy and the gentle Muse
> In heaven-born Poesys delightful bowers.
> Ye who appreciate the poets powers,
> And love the bright creations of his mind,
> Come, linger here awhile, and ye shall find
> A noble solace in your milder hours:
> Here Byrons genius, like an eagle, towers
> In dread sublimity; while Rogers lute,
> Moores native harp, and Campbells classic flute,
> Mingle in harmony, as beams with showers.
> Can their high strains of inspiration roll,
> Nor soothe the heart, nor elevate the soul? (Rule.)

Sect. II. — THE HYPHEN.

The HYPHEN [-] is sometimes employed to join the constituent parts of compound and derivative words. It is also used to divide words into syllables, for the purpose either of exhibiting the pronunciation, or of showing the simple portions into which words of more than one syllable may be resolved.

REMARKS.

a. From this explanation, it will be seen that the hyphen is used for two very different purposes, — to join and to separate. As a mark of junction, it is inserted between the simple words of which certain compounds are formed; and, in peculiar circumstances, between a preposition, or a portion of a word, and the word to which it is prefixed; as, "the inhuman and fiendish *slave-trade;*" "a man of *pre-eminence;*" "the *Neo-Platonic* philosophers." As a mark of separation, it is employed by lexicographers and by writers or printers to analyze words, and to divide them into syllables; by the former to show as accurately as possible the pronunciation, and by the latter to disunite portions of words that cannot be brought into a line of manuscript or of letterpress.

b. The distinction between a compound and a derivative word is, that the former consists of two or more simple words which are separately and commonly used in English; whereas the latter is made up of simple words, or portions of words, which are not each separately current in the language; as, *pseudo-apostle.* — See page 23, Def. XII.

c. But the simple words which make up compounds and derivatives are not always united by the hyphen; a few only of the latter being thus distinguished, and a very considerable number of the former, particularly those which form compound nouns, having coalesced so closely in pronunciation as to require them to be presented to the eye as one word. It is, therefore, a matter of importance to ascertain when it will be proper to join the parts of compounds with the hyphen, and when to unite them without this connecting mark. The mode of using the hyphen in syllabication is also attended with difficulties, which may, in a great measure, be obviated by an appeal to certain principles.

RULE I.

Compound Words.

§ I. When each of the words of which a compound is formed retains its original accent, they should be united by a hyphen.

§ II. But, when the compound word has only one accent, its parts are consolidated; being written or printed without the hyphen.

EXAMPLES.

§ I.
1. The all'-wise' God.
2. In'cense-breath'ing morn.

§ II.
1. A fortunate book'seller.
2. A mean no'bleman.

REMARKS.

a. The words "all-wise" and "incense-breathing," "bookseller" and "nobleman," are compounds, because they severally represent, not two separate ideas, but one compound idea. The primitives which enter into the composition of "all'-wise'" and "in'cense-breath'ing" retain the same accents as they had before these compounds were formed; but, as they could not be readily distinguished if written or printed closely together, the only mode of showing that they are compound is by inserting a hyphen between them. On the other hand, the simple words forming the compounds "bookseller" and "nobleman" do not both retain the accents which are heard in the phrases, "a *seller* of *books*," "a *man* who is *noble*," but so perfectly coalesce in pronunciation as to form one unbroken, continuous word, with a single accent, — *book'seller, no'bleman;* the hyphen, therefore, being unnecessary.

b. In the preceding paragraph, it was said that a compound word represents a compound idea, and not two ideas. This definition, Dr. Latham, from whom we borrowed it, illustrates (in his work on the "English Language," page 359) by the expression, "a *sharp-edged* instrument," which means an instrument with sharp edges; whereas a *sharp edged* instrument denotes an instrument that is sharp and has edges. It may not be practicable to apply the remark in each and all cases; but it is certain that compounds have often a signification very different from that which the same words convey when written apart, and that this difference should be indicated by the mode of exhibiting them. Thus, *blackbird* is properly written as one word, because it represents a particular species of birds; whereas a *black bird* means any bird that is black. A *glass-house* is a house in which glass is made, while a *glass house* is a house made of glass. The *goodman* of a house may, for aught we know, be a very bad man; and a *good man* may, for certain reasons, have no claim whatever to the civility implied in the use of the compound: yet both terms, if correctly written, will be understood. *Forget me not* literally expresses an earnest desire, on the part of a speaker or a writer, that he should be remembered; but, in a metaphorical sense, the same words, when combined, — *forget-me-not,* — denote a certain flower, emblematic of friendship or fidelity.

c. All compounds, therefore, should be so written as will best exhibit their true pronunciation, and the ideas intended to be expressed, — objects which, we have seen, may to some extent be effected either by consolidating the simples, or by uniting them with a hyphen. And here the rule already laid down might naturally be expected to come to our aid, as being founded on the characteristics and tendencies of the English language itself. But, notwithstanding the obvious worth and utility of the rule, the practice of some of our best authors and printers, as to the mode of exhibiting many of the compounds in use, is so conflicting, and the inconsistencies of perhaps all our lexicographers are so numerous, not to speak of their defect in distinguishing the compounds which have only one accent from those which have two, that it would be regarded as pedantry or presumption for a punctuator to attempt subjecting each of the compound words to the operation of the rule; and, on the other hand, it would be impracticable for him, without filling a volume, to give perfect lists of all the compounds, with the fluctuating and different modes in which they are presented in dictionaries and other books. It will therefore be our aim merely to specify some of the exceptions to the rule, and to throw out a few suggestions applicable to certain classes of compounds; recommending that, in all cases where the general and best usage as to the insertion or the omission of the hyphen cannot readily be learned, recourse be had, when the accentuation is previously known, to the rule itself.

EXCEPTIONS TO THE RULE.

d. According to the first section of the rule, those simples in a compound word which retain their original accent should be united by a hyphen. The exceptions to this principle are not very numerous, and consist chiefly — 1. Of a few compounds in common use, such as *ev′erlast′ing, not′withstand′ing*, which are universally written, at the present day, each as one unbroken word: 2. Of such as terminate in *monger;* as, *bor′oughmong′er, i′ronmong′er:* 3. Of almost all those beginning with the prepositions *over, under;* as, *o′verbal′ance, un′derstand′ing.*

e. According to the second section of the rule, when only one of the simple words retains its original accent in a compound, they are consolidated, being written without a hyphen. But to this principle there is a considerable number of exceptions, which may, however, be mostly reduced to the following classes: —

1. Those compounds in which the first of the primitive words ends, and the second begins, with the same letter; as, *book′-keeping, ear′-ring, glow′-worm, night′-time, poor′-rate, rear′-rank, rough′-hewn.* The word *oft′times*, however, is usually written without the hyphen.

2. Those compounds in which the first of two primitives ends, and the second begins, with a vowel; as, *fire′-arms, pine′-apple, peace′-offering.*

3. Those whose meaning would be obscured, or whose pronunciation would be less easily known, by the consolidation of the simples; as, *ass′-head, pot′-herb, soap′-house, first′-rate.* The reason for the division of these and similar primitives is, that the *s, t*, and *p* are pronounced separately from the *h* following them, and the *st* from the *r;* whereas, when in their usual state of combination, *sh, th, ph,* and *str* are each pronounced with one impulse of the voice.

4. All compounds ending with the word *tree;* as, *beech′-tree, date′-tree, pear′-tree, ap′ple-tree:* also those terminating with *book;* as, *day′-book, red′-book, shop′-book.*

5. Nouns formed of a verb and an adverb or preposition; as, *a break'-down, a look'-out, a start'-up:* or of a present participle and a noun; as, *dwell'ing-place, hum'ming-bird, print'ing-press, spin'ning-mill, writ'ing-school.*

6. Adjectives, or epithets, which are formed in a great variety of ways; as, *air'-built, heart'-broken; first'-born, one'-legged, two'-leaved; ill'-bred, above'-said, down'-trodden; church'-going, brain'-racking; good'-looking, hard'-working; grown'-up, unlooked'-for, unheard'-of.*

COMPOUND ADJECTIVES AND COMPOUND NOUNS.

f. An immense majority of the compound adjectives in the English language, whether with one or two accents, have their primitives united by a hyphen. A few, however, of very common occurrence, and having only one accent, are consolidated; namely, those which are the same as the one-accented compound nouns from which they have been taken; as, *high'land:* those formed from them either by adding *ed* or *ing*, or by changing *er* into these letters; as, *cob'webbed* (from *cob'web*), *shoe'making* (from *shoe'maker*): and those terminating with the words *faced, coming, holding,* and *like;* as, *bare'faced, forth'coming, slave'holding, child'like* (the word *like*, however, being preceded by a hyphen, when joined to a proper name, or to a word ending in *l;* as, *Eve'-like, owl'-like*). To which may be added the words *anoth'er, free'born, in'born, out'door.*

g. Board, house, room, side, stone, time, yard, are usually consolidated with a preceding noun if of one syllable, and are united by a hyphen to it if consisting of more than one; as, *cupboard, shovel-board; schoolhouse, senate-house; bedroom, composition-room; roadside, mountain-side; tombstone, eagle-stone; daytime, dinner-time; graveyard, timber-yard.* But the word *town-house* is commonly hyphened; so, also, *town-hall, seed-hall,* &c.

h. The compound nouns ending in the word *woman* are irregular in their form; as, *goodwoman, needlewoman, tirewoman; market-woman, oyster-woman.* If, however, these last two compounds have severally two accents, and the three preceding have each only one, they will be subject to the main rule, as given on page 209.

i. Compound nouns are sometimes formed by uniting a present participle and an adverb or preposition; as, *the coming-together, the carrying-away, the sending-off, the pulling-down, the blotting-out.* A hyphen is inserted between the parts of all such compounds, which are readily known by their taking an article before them, as in the examples here given.

NOUNS AND PRONOUNS IN APPOSITION.

j. Nouns in apposition are written and printed apart; as, *Sister Anne, Brother Marshall, Father Taylor, Professor Bush, the tyrant Nero, the poet Milton, that fellow Turpin, the lily Asphodel.* But, when put before a common noun, whether singular or plural, the words *sister, brother, fellow,* severally form part of a compound; as, *the sister-city, my brother-ministers, our fellow-men;* and, in all such cases, the hyphen should be used. *Fatherhood, brotherhood,* and *sisterhood* are not regarded as exceptions; for, according to the distinction made between compounds and derivatives, these terms will be subject to Rule II., p. 219; being each employed as one word, and without a hyphen, because the termination *hood* is not separately found, with the sense here used, in the English language.

k. The pronouns *he, she,* are commonly united by a hyphen to the nouns which they precede and qualify; as, *he-calf, she-asses.* The words *male* and *female,* when adjectives, are better put separately from the nouns which they qualify; as, *a male descendant.*

NOUNS USED ADJECTIVELY.

l. The first of two nouns, when it denotes the material or substance of which a thing is made, should stand apart from the noun which it qualifies; as, *brass pan, brick floor, glass pitcher, gold ring, granite building, mud cabin, oak chest, silver spoon, stone wall, tin basin.* But, when the nouns so coalesce in pronunciation that one of them has lost its original accent, they should be written or printed as one word; as, *rail′road, rain′drop, snow′ball.*

m. Two nouns may also be written as distinct words, when the former is put instead of an adjective; as, *an angel woman* (for *an angelic woman*), *an anniversary feast* (for *an annual feast*), *business connections* (for *mercantile* or *trading connections*), *a country trip* (for *a rural trip*), *church government* (for *ecclesiastical government*), *giant labor* (for *gigantic labor*), *gospel truth* (for *evangelical truth*), *home life* (for *domestic life*), *mountain billows* (for *huge billows*), *the north wind* (for *the northern wind*), *the west part* (for *the western part*).

n. The same remark is applicable to nouns of more than one syllable, when they are necessarily used, for want of suitable adjectives, to express the nature, quality, or some modification of the nouns before which they are placed; as, *benefit societies, evening amusements, family party, leisure hours, party strife, prose writings, summer sky, Sunday training, village maid.*

o. So, also, compound nouns, when used adjectively, are separated from the nouns which they precede or qualify; as, *pindrop silence, railway travel, a whalebone rod, the noonday sun; twenty-horse power, a custom-house officer, the council-room table.* But when the compound noun, and the simple noun which it precedes, have altogether but one accent, they should appear as one word; as, *high'wayman, domes'day-book.*

p. Two words, the last of which is a noun, though in their usual construction separate, are hyphened when put before a noun which they qualify, but are set apart from the latter; as, *high-water mark, short-metre stanzas, Sunday-school system, wild-beast skins, a bird's-eye view, a first-class car, a manual-labor business, an up-hill game, the one-hour rule.*

q. Proper names, when used as adjectives, should be separated from the words which they qualify or characterize; as, *Angola sheep, April fool, Argand lamp, Barbary horse, Bristol stone, California gold, Epsom salts, French chalk, Jamaica pepper, Jerusalem artichoke, Madeira wine, Newfoundland dog.*

NUMERAL ADJECTIVES.

r. Two numerals expressing a compound number, if in their ordinary construction, are united by a hyphen; as, *twenty-one, ninety-nine:* but if inverted, and a conjunction is placed between them, so as to constitute a phrase, they are written or printed apart; as, *three and thirty.* The word *fold* is closely annexed to the cardinals when they have only one syllable, but united to them by a hyphen when they have more than one; as, *twofold, twelvefold; thirty-fold, seventy-six-fold, two hundred-fold.* The word *penny* is subject to the same principle; as, *threepenny, fifteen-penny. Halfpenny* is an unhyphened compound; but *one penny,* two words. *Pence,* being a noun, is entirely separated from the numerals which precede it, when they consist of more than one syllable; as, *fifteen pence:* but, like the words *fold* and *penny,* it is joined without the hyphen, when they are monosyllabic; as, *fourpence, tenpence.*

s. The simple words in such terms as *one-half, two-thirds, five sixteenths,* — though, strictly speaking, not compounds, — are usually joined together by the hyphen.

t. A half-dollar, a quarter-barrel, and all such compounds, are written with a hyphen between the simple words; but, when an article or a preposition intervenes, the parts of the phrase should be separated; as, *half a pint, quarter of a pound.*

ADJECTIVES CONSOLIDATED WITH NOUNS.

u. Adjectives are not unfrequently consolidated with the nouns which they precede, when the compound thus formed admits of but one accent; as, *black'board, bluebottle, foreground, freemason, glassworks, goldsmith, hardhead, highlands, hotspur, longboat, lowlands, madhouse, mainmast, redbreast, roundhead, safeguard, stronghold, sweetbread, twelvemonth, wildfire.*

v. Freewill — having, when used adjectively, the accent on the first syllable; as, *a free'will offering* — should be written as one word; but, when employed in its proper character as a compound noun, with the accent on the last syllable, the hyphen may be inserted between its parts; as, *the doctrine of free-will'.*

w. Anybody, everybody, somebody, nobody, indicating persons, are, in this form, distinguished from the phrases *any body, every body, no body, some body,* which, as separate words, and with a pronunciation different from that of the first class, refer to inorganic substances. *Something* and *nothing* have also coalesced in pronunciation and form; but *every thing* and *any thing* (like the words *any one* and *every one*) may follow the analogy of the language, by which adjectives are separated from the nouns which they qualify.

x. When the noun which is qualified by an adjective retains its original accent, the two words should not appear as a compound, either with or without the hyphen. In the following and other phrases, therefore, which are sometimes written as compounds, the adjectives should stand apart: *Animal magnetism, armed chair, attic story, blank verse, common sense, earthen ware, good nature, good will, ill humor, old age, old maid, redeeming love, the black art.*

y. Such abbreviated sentences as *good-morning, good-night, good-by* may have a hyphen between the parts of which they consist.

NAMES OF PLACES.

z. Names of cities and other places, when formed of common nouns, are consolidated; as, *Barnstable, Bridgewater, Fairhaven, Newport, Southbridge.* When the second of the primitives is in itself a proper name, it should be set apart from the first; as, *North Britain, New York:* though, in spite of analogy, there are a few exceptions; as, *Easthampton* and *Southampton* (the *h*, in the latter word, being omitted), which usually appear as undivided words.

2 *a.* But those parts of the names of places which, according to the usual construction, are disconnected, should be united by a hyphen

when they are employed as adjectives; as, *the South-Boston foundry, the New-England people, the East-India Company.* This remark is well illustrated by Mr. Goold Brown, in his work, "The Grammar of English Grammars," p. 159: "In modern compound names, the hyphen is now less frequently used than it was a few years ago. They seldom, if ever, need it, unless they are employed as adjectives; and then there is a manifest propriety in inserting it. Thus the phrase, *the New London Bridge,* can be understood only of a new bridge in London; and, if we intend by it a bridge in New London, we must say, *the New-London Bridge.* So *the New York Directory* is not properly a directory for New York, but a new directory for York."

2 *b.* So, also, the word *street,* when forming part of a compound epithet, is connected by a hyphen with the word preceding it; as, *a Washington-street omnibus:* but, when otherwise used, it is better written or printed separately; as, *Washington Street, Boston.* The same rule will hold good in respect to such words as *place, square, court,* &c.; as, "*Howard-place* Church and *Crown-court* Chapel are situated not far from *Pemberton Square,* New Brixton."

THE POSSESSIVE CASE.

2 *c.* When the possessive case, and the word which governs it, do not literally convey the idea of property, or have lost this signification, they are connected by means of a hyphen; as, *Job's-tears, Solomon's-seal, Jesuits'-bark, bear's-foot, goat's-beard; Jew's-harp; St. Vitus's-dance, the king's-evil.* As compounds, these words do not severally denote the tears which the Arabian patriarch shed, a seal belonging to the wise Hebrew ruler, bark which is the property of Jesuits, the foot of a bear, the beard of a goat, the harp of a Jew, the dance of St. Vitus, the evil of the king. But, were the primitive words from which they are formed put separately, they would have these meanings.

2 *d.* When, however, institutions, churches, law-courts, places, rivers, &c., are called after distinguished men, the names put in the possessive case are separated from those of the objects which they characterize; as, *St. Mary's College, St. Peter's Church, St. Paul's Churchyard, Queen's Bench, Van Diemen's Land, Merchants' Exchange, the St. John's River.* The names of holydays, if similarly formed, may be written or printed in the same manner; as, *New Year's Day, All Saints' Day.* In all such phrases, the hyphen is not required, because they have severally but one signification.

2 e. If the possessive case, and the noun governing it, are used in the literal sense of the words, and have only one accent, they should be written or printed as a compound, without either apostrophe or hyphen; as, *beeswax, craftsmaster, doomsday, hogslard, kinswoman, lambswool* (but, if meaning ale mixed with sugar, &c., *lamb's-wool,* according to Remark 2 c), *newspaper, ratsbane, townsman, tradesman.*

COMPOUND PRONOUNS AND ADVERBS.

2 f. Compound pronouns have always their parts consolidated; as, *yourself, himself, herself, itself, themselves, ownself, ownselves; whoever, whomsoever, whatever, whatsoever. One's self* is probably a phrase, and not, as is sometimes written, a compound, — *oneself* or *one's-self. I myself* is also a phrase, or two words in apposition.

2 g. Compound adverbs are, generally speaking, consolidated; as, *altogether, awhile, beforehand, evermore, henceforward, indeed, instead, everywhere, nowhere, nevertheless, somehow, nowise, anywise, likewise, wherewithal, hereupon, whithersoever.* But *to-day, to-night, to-morrow,* are almost universally printed with a hyphen. So also *now-a-days;* and perhaps such words as *inside-out, upside-down.* There is a tendency on the part of American printers to spell the words *for ever* as one continuous compound; but they everywhere occur in the common version of the Bible as a phrase; and, the eye being thus accustomed to their separation, it would probably be better to retain this form. *By and by* are obviously three words, though sometimes written as a compound.

COMPOUND AND OTHER PHRASES.

2 h. All phrases which are thrown out of their usual order, and, by a strange collocation, put before the nouns which they are made to qualify, should have a hyphen between their parts; as, *some out-of-the-world place, a matter-of-fact-looking town, long-looked-for news, out-of-door business, raw-head-and-bloody-bones stories, the always-wind-obeying deep, the ever-to-be-honored Chaucer, the half-burnt-through bottom of the saucepan, well-laid-out parks.*

2 i. When epithets are formed of an adverb ending in *ly* and of a participle, the two words are usually separated without the hyphen; as, *a newly built house, a beautifully formed pen.* The reason probably is, that the structure of such adverbs does not easily admit of their junction with the words modified.

2 j. When a noun is placed before an adverb or preposition and a participle, these do not make a compound epithet, and should

therefore be written or printed as two words; as, *a catalogue well arranged, love ill requited, the place before mentioned.*

2 *k*. Words in phrases should be written and printed separately; as, *above all, after all, at second hand, balm of Gilead, cheek by jowl, in any wise* (but, without the preposition, and as an adverb, *anywise*), *might and main, rank and file, tit for tat, tooth and nail.* Of such phrases, however, as *father-in-law, attorney-at-law, commander-in chief,* the parts are usually connected by a hyphen.

2 *l*. When a compound phrase is formed of two or more words which are severally associated in sense with one term, the primitives should stand apart; as, *cannon and musket balls.* Were a hyphen inserted between "musket" and "balls," the meaning of the phrase would not be cannon-balls and musket-balls, but cannon, or large guns, and also balls for the musket. The following are additional examples: *Household and needle work; land and river travel; a chief or master builder; the watch and clock repairing business; a son and daughter in law; second, third, or fourth rate effects.* Some would insert a hyphen between the parts of the last compound, and attach it to the disjointed words; as, *iron-, cotton-, silk-, print-, and dye-works:* but, though more correct, this is a German mode of exhibiting such compounds, with which the English eye is not familiar. All difficulty would be obviated, were the phrases changed into language more grammatical.

2 *m*. All foreign phrases should be written and printed as they are found in the language from which they are taken; as, "John Sharp, Secretary *pro tempore*." — "It was a *sine qua non*, an indispensable condition, that an agreement should be entered into." — "William said in Latin, *Vade mecum*, Go with me." But such phrases, if they are used before nouns, or have been incorporated into the English language, should follow the common analogy; as, "John was elected *pro-tempore* Secretary." — "This was a *sine-qua-non* business." — "That little book is an excellent *vade-mecum*."

For further information on this difficult subject, the reader is referred to Mr. Goold Brown's invaluable work, before quoted; from which, while venturing in some respects to differ in opinion, we have derived not a little assistance as to the nature of compounds, and the forms in which they should be presented. But the subject is not exhausted; and he who, with the scholarship and industry of that gentleman, will devote himself to the classification of all the compounds in the language, would perform a good service to a branch of literature which has been sadly neglected.

RULE II.

Prefixes in Derivative Words.

§ I. If a prefix ends with a vowel, and the word with which it is combined begins with a consonant; or if the former ends with a consonant, and the latter begins with a vowel or a consonant, — the compound thus formed should appear as one unbroken word.

§ II. If, however, the prefix ends, and the word to which it is united begins, with a vowel, — both vowels being separately pronounced, — they should be connected with a hyphen.

EXAMPLES.

§ I.
1. Predetermine, resell, antedate.
2. Counteraction, multangular.
3. Supernatural, contemporaneous.

§ II.
1. Pre-occupy, re-echo, ante-act.
2. Contra-indication, retro-enter
3. Supra-orbital, co-eternal.

REMARKS.

a. When the prefix ends with a vowel, and is followed by a word beginning also with a vowel, many writers and printers place a diæresis over the latter, instead of a hyphen between them; as, *coëval.* But this mode of exhibiting derivatives does not seem to accord with the genius of the English language, which, in ordinary composition, dispenses with accentual marks. It would, therefore, probably be better to reserve the use of the diæresis for words containing two vowels separately pronounced, but not capable of being divided, except for the purpose of syllabication and at the end of a line, by the hyphen; as in *Beëlzebub*, and in borrowed foreign words.

b. The adverbs *afore* and *fore*, having now become almost obsolete as separate words, are regarded as mere prefixes; which should, therefore, without regard to accent, be subject to the present rule: as, *aforegoing, foredetermined, fore-ordained.* — See p. 208, Rem. *b.*

c. As an exception to the first section of the rule, it is worthy of remark, that a derivative which might be mistaken for a word with the same letters, but a different meaning, should be distinguished from it by the insertion of a hyphen between its parts. Thus, *re-creation*, denoting a new creation, is obviously a more appropriate form of this word than *recreation*, which, besides being differently pronounced, signifies refreshment, or relaxation after toil. Thus, also, a difference exists in meaning and pronunciation between *re-collect* and *recollect*; *re-form, re-formation*, and *reform, reformation*; which it is necessary to exhibit in corresponding modes. With the exception of such words, the manner of writing derivatives having the prefix *re* is governed by the rule.

d. Terms or epithets with prefixes of unusual occurrence, particularly if the compounds thus formed have two accents, should be excepted from the operation of the first branch of the rule; as, *astro-theology, concavo-convex, deutero-canonical, electro-magnetism*.

e. The prefixes of proper names, or words used as such, substantively or adjectively, follow both sections of the rule; as, *Antenicene, Antichrist*, &c., *Antitrinitarian, Pedobaptist, Cisalpine, Transatlantic; Anti-American, Pre-Adamic*. But the words *Neo-Platonic, Anglo-Saxon, Scoto-Hibernian*, and others of a similar kind, accord in their forms with those referred to in Remark *d*.

f. Extra is sometimes used as an adjective, and separated from the noun which it qualifies; as, *extra pay, extra work*. As a prefix in *extraordinary*, it is not followed by a hyphen, because its last letter (*a*), though coming before a vowel, is silent in pronunciation.

g. The letter *a*, when by a colloquialism it represents one of the prepositions *on, in, at, to*, should be united, without a hyphen, to the following word, if consisting of only one syllable; as, *aboard, abed, afield, apiece*.

h. Bi and *tri* are usually consolidated with the words, or parts of words, to which they are prefixed; as, *biennial; triunity, triune*.

i. Vicegerency, vicegerent, viceroyal, and *viceroyalty* are, in accordance with the rule, written each as one word. The other words, of which *vice* is a prefix, are, by almost universal custom, hyphened; as, *vice-president, vice-chancellor*, &c.

j. Bi, ante, anti, counter, contra, super, supra, semi, demi, preter, and other common prefixes, are sometimes printed with a hyphen after them; but there seem to be no just grounds for this division, except when two vowels would otherwise come together, or when a dissyllabic prefix ends with the same consonant with which the next portion of a long word begins; as, *anti-evangelical, counter-revolution*. To make any exceptions besides these, and a few others such as those noticed above, would lead to inextricable confusion.

COMPOUNDS AND DERIVATIVES. 221

ORAL EXERCISES.

Show how the Rules and the Remarks (pp. 209–20) *apply to the insertion of hyphens in certain words, or to their omission in certain phrases, which occur in the following sentences:—*

Better be trampled in the dust than trample on a fellow-creature.
Never put off till to-morrow what you can do to-day.
We have no doubt that instinct is a Heaven-ordained law.
What the nations look for is a loving and life-giving religion.
Keen-eyed revenge is riding round your ranks.
When the wind-god frowns in the murky skies.
O sailor-boy, sailor-boy! peace to thy soul!
He spoke no warrior-word, he bade no trumpet blow.
And soft-eyed cherub-forms around thee play.
The most remarkable winds are those denominated the trade-winds.
Many are the advantages of co-operation.
Self-abasement paved the way to villain bonds and despot sway.
Like ocean-weeds heaped on the surf-beaten shore.
Imagination is the truth-seeing and the beauty-seeing power.
Ben Jonson, the great dramatist, was co-eval with Shakspeare

The silver mines of Mexico and Peru far exceed in value the whole of the European and Asiatic mines.

Man possesses the great privilege of co-operating with his beneficent Creator.

Philosophy will rise again in the sky of her Franklin, and glory rekindle at the urn of her Washington.

There is little of the intellectual or moral in that sort of independence which is the proverbial characteristic of our countrymen.

Would that that noble people were re-instated in all their ancient privileges!

The instincts of multitudes feel afar the gathering earthquake, which is to swallow up caste, privileges, and unjust distinctions.

Let your lately formed engagements be fulfilled with perfect good faith.

The shrieks of agony and clang of arms re-echo to the fierce alarms her trump terrific blows.

Illiterate and ill-bred persons are apt to be verbose, contradictory, and loud in conversation.

There is a mother-heart in all children, as well as a child-heart in all mothers.

Nature cries aloud for freedom as our proper guide, our birthright and our end.

Thousands of state-projects, on the vastest scale, have been conceived, executed, and forgotten.

Deep-hearted practical faithfulness is not separable long from true-thoughted practical faith.

In the face of the young fop above mentioned was seen an impertinent smile of affectation.

They are but sluggards in well-doing who know to do good only when they have a purse in their hand.

If man could ascend to dwell at the fountainhead of truth, he would be re-absorbed in God.

In moments of clear, calm thought, I feel more for the wrong-doer than for him who is wronged.

Edward the Sixth was a boy-king and a puppet-prince, invested with supreme power, but acting without any volition of his own.

The term "bridegroom," strange as it seems, is given to a newly married man.

Education can hardly be too intellectual, unless by intellectual you mean parrot-knowledge, and other modes of mind-slaughter.

The churchyard bears an added stone; the fireside shows a vacant chair.

Columbus was for years an all but heart-broken suitor to royal stocks and stones.

Many who have worshipped within these walls are now in the higher house, in the church of the First-born.

If any one affirms that the juxtaposition of a number of particles makes a hope, he affirms a proposition to which I can attach no idea.

In shipwrecks we are furnished with some of the most remarkable examples of trust in God, of unconquerable energy, and of tender, self-sacrificing love.

The fair-weather sailor may equip himself tolerably from the storehouse of Epicurus; but stronger tackle will be needed when the masts are bending and the cordage straining in the storm.

A man of no feeling must necessarily be unhappy, since the texture of his heart affords him no superabundant sensibility for the sufferings of his fellow-creatures.

You talk of the prosperity of your city. Do not point me to your thronged streets. Is it a low-minded, self-seeking, gold-worshipping man-despising crowd which I see rushing through them?

EXERCISE TO BE WRITTEN.

In this exercise, let the compound and derivative words be written agreeably to the two preceding Rules and the Remarks:—

Genius has no chartered license to wander away from the eternal land marks of morality. (Rule I., § II.)

The selfish use rules as means of self indulgence, and the narrow minded over look the end in the means. (Rule I., §§ I. and II.)

Every rail road, connecting distant regions, may be regarded as accomplishing a ministry of peace. (Rule I., § II.)

Genius, in its highest function, cannot co exist with a corrupted moral sentiment. (Rule II., § II.)

The new moon silvered the lofty pines, and the stars twinkled with rare brilliancy from their dark blue depths. (Rule I., § I.)

He who has a good son in law has gained a son: he who has a bad one has lost a daughter. (Rule I., Remark 2 *k*.)

What is religious instruction to the vain, the frivolous, the in different, the pre occupied and fore closed mind? (Rule II.)

Is a woman ambitious to ply a black smith's hammer, when she can wield so cunningly the thin, flitting sword of the spirit? (Rule I., § II.)

The distance of the earth from the sun is, in round numbers, one hundred millions of miles; which is, of course, the radius or semi diameter of its orbit. (Rule II., § I.)

Perhaps the sermons which have cost a clergy man the least effort may some times have the most effect on his hearers. (Rule I., § II.; and Remark 2 *g*.)

The ordinary processes of direct instruction are of immense importance; but they pre suppose in the mind to which they are applied an active co operation. (Rule II., §§ I. and II.)

As some instruments are tuned with a tuning fork, some discourses seem to have been pitched with a pitch fork. (Rule I., Remark *e* 5, and § II.)

The faith of the first Christians expressed itself in vehement re action against the prevailing tendencies of an exceedingly corrupted civilization. (Rule II., § II.)

> He is gone on the mountain, he is lost to the forest,
> Like a summer dried fountain, when our need was the sorest:
> The fount, re appearing, from the rain drops shall borrow;
> But to us comes no cheering, to Duncan no morrow.
>
> (Rule I., § I.; II., § II.; I., u.)

RULE III.

The Division of Words into Syllables, according to their Pronunciation.

The hyphen is used between the syllables of a word, to exhibit, as accurately as possible, its true pronunciation; no regard being paid to the mode in which it has been formed or derived.

EXAMPLES.

hab-it	ap-a-thy	as-tron-o-my
pref-ace	pref-er-ence	an-tip-o-des
trib-ute	trin-i-ty	bi-og-ra-pher
proph-et	po-lyg-a-my	rev-e-la-tion

REMARKS.

a. A syllable is a combination of letters uttered by one impulse of the voice; as *hab* or *ha* in the word *habit*, according to the specific principle of syllabication which may be adopted. A single letter of a word, pronounced by itself, is also termed a syllable; as *i* or *o* in the exclamation *io!*

b. The mode of syllabication laid down in the rule is, unquestionably, the only one fitted for conveying the true sounds of words, or rather for making some approach to an accurate pronunciation; and all spelling-books should be constructed on this principle, — a principle which, though recommended by Dr. Lowth and adopted by lexicographers, has been neglected by some of our most popular writers of elementary works for children. It must, however, be acknowledged, that many words are divided in the same manner, whether regard be had to their pronunciation, or to the mode in which they have been formed; as, *horse-man, sa-cred, be-ing, na-tion, a-mend-ment;* and that there are others, the true sounds of which cannot be correctly shown by any kind of syllabication, without a change in the letters; such as the words *acid, docile, ancient, specify, digit, register.*

c. The rule given above is adopted by American printers in the division of such words as cannot be entirely brought into one and the same line; but the rule which follows is generally preferred by British typographers

RULE IV.

The Division of Words into Syllables, according to their Form, Derivation, or Meaning.

The hyphen is employed in words in such a manner as is best calculated to show their origin, composition, or import, and to exhibit the syllables in their neatest form.

EXAMPLES.

ha-bit	a-pa-thy	as-tro-no-my
pre-face	pre-fer-ence	an-ti-po-des
tri-bute	tri-ni-ty	bi-o-gra-pher
pro-phet	po-ly-ga-my	re-ve-la-tion

REMARKS.

a. Agreeably to this rule, and partially in accordance with that which precedes it, —

1. Compound and derivative words are resolved into their primitives; as, *school-master, hand-writing, pen-knife, snuff-box, looking-glass; arch-angel, geo-logy, theo-cracy, ortho-graphy.*

2. Prefixes, affixes, and grammatical terminations, are separated; as, *dis-continue, en-able, trans-port; shear-er, load-ed, print-ing; king-dom, false-hood, differ-ence, command-ment.*

3. Two vowels, not being a diphthong, are divided; as, *la-ity, a-eri-al, re-al, stere-otype, ri-al, pi-ety, li-on, tri-umph, co-alesce, po-et, medi-um, zo-ology, row-el, cru-elty, vacu-um.*

4. One consonant between two vowels is to be joined to the latter syllable; as, *ta-lent, fa-tal; me-lon, le-ver; spi-rit, si-lence; cy-nic, ty-ro; le-ga-cy, mo-no-po-ly.* Except *x*, and single consonants when they belong to the former portion of a derivative word; as, *ex-ile, ex-ist, ex-amine; up-on, dis-ease, circum-ambient.*

5. Two or more consonants belong to the latter syllable, when they are capable of beginning a word; as, *ta-ble, sti-fle, lu-cre, o-gle, mau-gre, stro-phe, de-stroy.*

6. But when the consonants cannot begin a word, or when the vowel preceding them is short, the first should be separated; as, *ab-bey, ac-cent, vel-lum, ab-ject, gar-den, laun-dry, pam-phlet; sac-rifice, det-riment, blas-pheme, dis-tress, min-strel.*

15

b. It is desirable that compound and derivative words should, at the ends of lines, be divided in such a manner as to indicate their principal parts. Thus, *school-master* is preferable to *schoolmas-ter*, *dis-approve* to *disap-prove*, *resent-ment* to *re-sentment*, *ortho-doxy* to *or-thodoxy*; though, as regards the analysis of words into syllables, the latter mode is unobjectionable. From the narrowness of the printed line, however, in some books, the principle recommended cannot always be adhered to.

c. The terminations *tion, sion, cial, tial,* and many others, formerly pronounced as two syllables, but now only as one, must not be divided either in spelling or at the end of a line.

d. A syllable consisting of only one letter, as the *a* in *cre-ation*, should not commence a line. This word would be better divided, *crea-tion;* and so all others of a similar kind. But such a syllable, coming immediately after a primitive, is by some printers brought to the beginning; as, *consider-able*.

e. A line of print must not end with the first syllable of a word, when it consists of a single letter; as, *a-bide, e-normous:* nor begin with the last syllable, when it is formed of only two letters; as, *nation-al, teach-er, similar-ly*. For regard should be had to the principles of taste and beauty, as well as to the laws of syllabication.

f. Three or more successive lines should not end with a hyphen. A little care on the part of the compositor will, in general, prevent an appearance so offensive to a good eye. Divisions, indeed, except for purposes of spelling and lexicography, should take place as seldom as possible.

EXERCISES TO BE WRITTEN.

Divide the following words agreeably to both the preceding Rules; namely, according to their pronunciation, and according to their composition or derivation:—

Habit, vivid, considerable, speculative, philosophy, modification, govern, individual, phenomenon, knowledge, elaborate, academical, progress, critical, vacuum, labyrinth, animal, physiology, revelation, constituent, reciprocally, vigor, accredited, curiosity, magnificent, privacy, cherish, valuable, apology, idolater, equilibrium, solemn, separate, metaphysics, liberal, modern, preface, gratify, biography, literature, nominal, philanthropy, theocracy, barometer, preparation, figure, natural, prelude, clamor, reformation, metropolis, represent, recognize, rhetoric, diminish, articulate, peasant, antipodes, misery,

SYLLABICATION.

recriminate, floriferous, desolate, preference, dedicate, bibliopolist, eloquent, irregular, ventriloquist, memorable, reputation, doxology, conspiracy, general, desultory, contribute, omnivorous, typographer, oblivion, democracy, polygamy, citizen, stenography, parish, talent, melodist, borough, prisoner, promise, clever, metal, discrimination, theology, cylinder, paradise, monitory, solitude, sycophant, nobility, cavalcade, rivulet, profitable, integrity, relative, jealous.

Insert the hyphen in those places only in which the division appears best at the end and the beginning of lines, according to the Remarks, p. 226: —

Philosophy, intermediate, theology, magnificence, venturesome, biographer, questionable, lithography, professing, zoology, demigod, personate, widowhood, kaleidoscope, periphrasis, supervisor, geology, animation, abhorrence, government, tautology, permanent, classical, forgetfulness, superficial, congenial, circumstances, metamorphosis, subdivision, patronage, subordinate, beneficent, resistless, sufficient, superhuman, pantheism, disappointment, typographical, microscope, disinterestedness, benevolence, superficial, contradiction, sensibility, happiness, misanthropy, imperfect, circumference, counteracting, disproportionately, excitement, semicircle, predominate, artificial, portfolio, equilibrium, manufacture, preternatural, nomenclature, supernumerary, terraqueous, malefactor, primogeniture, resemble, suicide, transaction, intercept, education, counterfeit, superlative, transgression, supernatural, predestinate, typography, polysyllable, introduction, confident, philology, sympathy, misinform, spiritless, provision, appearance, belonging, cleverness, uniform, outnumber, bedchamber, gardening, fishmonger, disrespectful, plenipotentiary, doctorship, neighborhood, bedlamite, nonconformity, nightingale, antediluvian, parsonage, correspond, forgetfulness, superabundant, metaphorically, hydrophobia, antitrinitarian, putrefaction, alteration, haughtiness, semidiameter, improvement, proposition, serpentine, disjunction, intercourse, animalcule, bookselling, commonwealth, colloquial, reasoning, polyglot, puerility, correctness, understanding, preliminary, qualification, attaining, composition, commencement, incompetence, exclusive, disapprobation, adventure, introduction, gentleman, trinity, acquaintance, consciousness, transubstantiation, considering, persuasion, trigonometry, parallelogram, successfully, improper, diffidence, moreover, inference, hydrostatics, recollection, ameliorative, authorities, unwilling, autocrat, accelerate, emolument, carnivorous, emaciated.

Sect. III.— MARKS OF QUOTATION.

Marks of Quotation [" "] are employed to show that the words of an author or a speaker are quoted. These marks consist of two inverted commas placed at the beginning, and two apostrophes at the end, of a quotation.

RULE I.

Words borrowed from a Speaker or an Author.

A word, phrase, or passage, belonging to another, and introduced into one's own composition, is distinguished by marks of quotation.

EXAMPLE.

To one who said, " I do not believe there is an honest man in the world," another replied, " It is impossible that any one man should know all the world, but quite possible that one may know himself."

REMARKS.

a. When a writer repeats his own language, and wishes to draw to it particular attention, he properly uses the same marks as he would employ were he transcribing the sentiments of another. Thus, if the author of the present work wished again to give directions on the grammatical points usually required before extracts, he might, instead of referring merely to page 108, copy from it the rule and certain comments, prefixing and appending the marks under notice, as follow: " A short quotation, or any expression that resembles a quotation, is separated by a comma from the clause which precedes it." " If, however, quotations or remarks extend to two or more sentences, and are formally or specially introduced, a colon is preferable." "When an indirect quotation or a remark is preceded by a very brief clause, the comma is not required."

b. Marks of quotation may be omitted where the matter taken is not given in the exact words of the author; as, —

Socrates said that he believed in the immortality of the soul.

In the direct form, the sentence would be correctly written thus:—

Socrates said, "I believe that the soul is immortal."

c. It is usual to omit the quotation-marks when a mere phrase or saying from a foreign language is distinguished by Italics; as, —

Nil mortalibus arduum est is a bold but encouraging assertion.

d. In old works, it was a common practice to introduce all extracts from Scripture in Italic characters; but, except when there is a necessity for calling particular attention to certain words or expressions, authors now generally and very properly prefer using marks of quotation; as, —

One of the evangelists says, "Jesus wept."

e. Titles of books, and names of ships, &c., are sometimes written without the inverted commas, and put in Italic characters; as "Falconer, the author of *The Shipwreck,* embarked on board the *Aurora* frigate in the year 1769, and was supposed to have perished with the vessel at sea." But, as Italics give an irregular look to a printed page, quotation-marks are preferable; as, —

We may justly regard "Paradise Lost" as one of the noblest monuments of human genius.

f. In speaking of certain words or phrases, some authors put them in Italics. Others, however, prefer placing them within marks of quotation; and, for the reason given in Remark *e,* this is the more eligible mode of exhibiting them; as, —

We find the word "pharisaical" very useful in our modern speech.

g. When an example or an extract, particularly if in verse, is begun in a new line, and set in a smaller type, the marks of quotation are by some writers dispensed with. In cases, however, of this kind, perhaps the generality of authors and printers use the inverted commas and the apostrophes, agreeably to the rule; and this usage is recommended, except in works containing numerous quotations, which are well known to be such, as in the present book.

RULE II.

One Quotation within another.

When one quotation is introduced within another, the included one should be preceded by a single inverted comma, and closed by a single apostrophe.

EXAMPLES.

1. When treating of Christian orators, Maury asks the following apposite questions: "What is this you call eloquence? Is it the wretched trade of imitating that criminal, mentioned by a poet in his satires, who 'balanced his crimes before his judges with antithesis'? Is it the puerile secret of forming jejune quibbles; of rounding periods; of tormenting one's self by tedious studies, in order to reduce sacred instruction into a vain amusement?"

2. In describing the vast influence of a perfect orator over the feelings and passions of his audience, Sheridan forcibly says, "Notwithstanding the diversity of minds in such a multitude, by the lightning of eloquence they are melted into one mass; the whole assembly, actuated in one and the same way, become, as it were, but one man, and have but one voice. The universal cry is, 'Let us march against Philip; let us fight for our liberties; let us conquer or die!'"

REMARKS.

a. Double marks should be used before and after a quotation inserted in that which has been introduced into an extract; as, "Channing, the friend of humanity in every condition and under every garb, says, 'When I consider the greater simplicity of their lives, and their greater openness to the spirit of Christianity, I am not sure but that the "golden age" of manners is to begin among those who are now despaired of for their want of refinement.'"

b. Some writers and printers observe the following direction, in preference to the rule given in the text: That a single inverted comma should be prefixed to a single quotation occurring in composition, and a single apostrophe annexed to it; but that two inverted commas should be introduced before, and two apostrophes after, another quotation occurring within the primary one; as, 'There are times when the spirit, oppressed with pain, worn with toil, tired of tumult, sick at the sight of guilt, wounded in its love, baffled in its hope, and trembling in its faith, almost longs for the "wings of a dove, that it might fly away," and take refuge amidst the "shady bowers," the "vernal airs," the "roses without thorns,"· the quiet, the beauty, the loveliness, of Eden.' But the great objection to this mode of setting off extracts is, that, by using single marks to the quotations which are of primary importance, and double to those which are merely secondary, we exhibit the former less prominently than the latter.

c. The marks under consideration may with propriety be omitted in some instances, where several quotations are so much involved one within another, that the insertion of all the inverted commas and the apostrophes would tend to obscure the meaning of the entire passage; as, —

In the New Testament we have the following words: "Jesus answered the Jews, 'Is it not written in your law, — I said, Ye are gods?'"

By considering the example itself as an extract, there will be found here no fewer than five quotations; and yet, though two only are set off with quotation-marks, the passage is perhaps more intelligible, and to the eye certainly less offensive, than if printed thus: " In the New Testament we have the following words: ' Jesus answered the Jews, " Is it not written in your law, — ' I said, " Ye are gods " ' ? " ' " Ridiculous as it may appear, this mode of exhibiting quotations is only the application of the principle contained in the rule, but carried out beyond its legitimate purpose and extent.

d. Indeed, in quoting from such texts of Scripture as contain citations from other books of the sacred canon, it is usual to present them as they appear in the Common Version, — without any quotation-marks in the body of the passage; as, —

St. Paul thus expresses himself: "Therein is the righteousness of God revealed from faith to faith; as it is written, The just shall live by faith. For the wrath of God is revealed from heaven against all ungodliness, and unrighteousness of men, who hold the truth in unrighteousness." In another place the apostle says, "David also describeth the blessedness of the man unto whom God imputeth righteousness without works, saying, Blessed are they whose iniquities are forgiven, and whose sins are covered. Blessed is the man to whom the Lord will not impute sin. Cometh this blessedness, then, upon the circumcision only?" &c.

But the exhibiting of a quotation within a quotation without the inverted commas, though more pleasing to the eye, is less accurate, than it would be if they were used in a single form, as in the passage above, lines six and seven of Remark c.

e. See page 156, Remark *f*; and page 161, Remark *e*.

RULE III.

Extracts composed of Successive Paragraphs.

When an extract is composed of successive paragraphs, each is commenced with inverted commas; but the apostrophes are not used till the quotation finally terminates.

EXAMPLE.

To exemplify this rule, a passage, consisting of more than one paragraph, may be taken from an essay by Godwin:—

"No subject is of more importance, in the morality of private life, than that of domestic or family life.

"Every man has his ill humors, his fits of peevishness and exacerbation. Is it better that he should spend these upon his fellow-beings, or suffer them to subside of themselves?

"It seems to be one of the most important of the arts of life, that men should not come too near each other, or touch in too many points. Excessive familiarity is the bane of social happiness."

REMARKS.

a. When phrases or sentences in an extract consist of portions not connected in the discourse or book from which they have been taken, each portion should begin and end with the quotation-marks, as in those cited on p. 228, Remark *a*; unless several points (....) are inserted to indicate the omission, in which case it will be sufficient to put the marks of quotation at the beginning and the end of the whole extract, if it is contained in one paragraph.

b. In the leading articles of newspapers, and sometimes in books, when particular attention would be drawn to an extract embodied in the text, the inverted commas are placed at the beginning of each line of the quotation; as, Slavery must fall, because it stands in
" direct hostility to all the grand movements, principles, and reforms
" of our age; because it stands in the way of an advancing world.
" One great idea stands out amidst the discoveries and improvements
" of modern times. It is, that man is not to exercise arbitrary,
" irresponsible power over man." But, except in the more transient class of publications, this mode of exhibiting extracts is now seldom used.

QUOTATIONS.

ORAL EXERCISE.

Show how the Rules and the Remarks (pp. 223–30) *apply to the use or omission of quotation-marks in the following sentences:* —

The psalmist says again, " I am a stranger with thee and a sojourner, as all my fathers were."

When Fénélon's library was on fire, " God be praised," said he, " that it is not the dwelling of a poor man!"

I repeat what I said on a former occasion, that " no man can be happy who is destitute of good feelings and generous principles."

" There is but one object," says St. Augustine, " greater than the soul; and that one is its Creator."

Plato, hearing that some asserted he was a very bad man, said, " I shall take care so to live that nobody will believe them."

" Let me make the ballads of a nation," said Fletcher of Saltoun " and I care not who makes its laws."

" Any man," it has been well said, " who has a proneness to see a beauty and fitness in all God's works, may find daily food for his mind even in an infant."

A minister of some experience remarks, " I have heard more than one sufferer say, ' I am thankful; God is good to me; ' and, when I heard that, I said, ' It is good to be afflicted.' "

The celebrated and ingenious Bishop of Cloyne, in his " Principles of Human Knowledge," denies, without any ceremony, the existence of every kind of matter whatever.

After Cicero, the literary history of the Romans is written in one line of Tacitus, *Gliscente adulatione, magna ingenia deterrebantur;* " As adulation increased, great minds were deterred."

A being crowned with all the blessings which men covet and admire, — with youth, health, beauty, rank, genius, and fame, — writes four cantos of melodious verse to prove that he is the most miserable of mortals.

Trench well says, " What a lesson the word ' diligence ' contains! How profitable is it for every one of us to be reminded, — as we are reminded when we make ourselves aware of its derivation from *diligo,* ' to love,' — that the only secret of true industry in our work is love of that work ! "

To the man who walks among the flowers which he has tended, —

" Each odoriferous leaf,
Each opening blossom, freely breathes abroad
Its gratitude, and thanks him with its sweets."

EXERCISE TO BE WRITTEN.

Insert the marks of quotation agreeably to some of the directions given in pp. 223-32.

Johnson's Lives of the English Poets may justly be considered as the noblest specimen of elegant and solid criticism which any age has produced. (Rule I. and Remark *e.*)

Terrific examples of license and anarchy in Greece and Rome are quoted to prove, that man requires to be protected from himself; forgetting the profound wisdom wrapped up in the familiar inquiry, *Quis custodiet ipsos custodes?* Who shall guard the keepers? (Rule I. and Remark *c.*)

An eloquent preacher asks, Who would not far prefer our wintry storm, and the hoarse sighings of the east wind, as it sweeps around us, if they will brace the mind to nobler attainments, and the heart to better duties? [The author of this passage quotes the phrase, "the hoarse sighings of the east wind."] (Rule II.)

What is the soul? was a question once put to Marivaux. — I know nothing of it, he answered, but that it is spiritual and immortal. — Well, said his friend, let us ask Fontenelle, and he will tell us what it is. — No, cried Marivaux: ask anybody but Fontenelle; for he has too much good sense to know any more about it than we do. (Rule I.)

D'Alembert congratulated a young man very coldly, who brought him the solution of a problem. I have done this to have a seat in the Academy, said the young man. — Sir, answered D'Alembert, with such motives you will never earn one. Science must be loved for its own sake, and not for the advantage to be derived. No other principle will enable a man to make true progress. (Rule I.)

The following sarcastic rules for behavior are said by Goldsmith to have been drawn up by an indigent philosopher: —

1. If you be a rich man, you may enter the room with three loud hems, march deliberately up to the chimney, and turn your back to the fire.

2. If you be a poor man, I would advise you to shrink into the room as fast as you can, and place yourself, as usual, upon a corner of a chair, in a remote corner.

3. If you be young, and live with an old man, I would advise you not to like gravy. I was disinherited myself for liking gravy. (Rule III.)

CHAPTER V.

MISCELLANEOUS MARKS AND CHARACTERS.

In addition to the sentential points and marks treated of in the preceding pages, there are other characters, sometimes occurring in English composition, which will now be explained.

I. BRACKETS, or CROTCHETS [ ], are employed for the same purpose nearly as the marks of parenthesis; but they are usually confined to words, phrases, or sentences, inserted in or appended to a quotation, and not belonging to it; as, " The captain had several men died [who died] in the ship."

Brackets are chiefly intended to give an explanation, to rectify a mistake, or to supply an omission. But they are also sometimes used in dictionaries and in poetry to separate such words as are put, for the saving of room, into lines to which they do not belong; and in psalms and hymns to include verses that may be omitted by a congregation. They are used, besides, in a single form, in printed dramas, to note the entrance or the departure of certain characters; as, " [*Exeunt* Portia and Nerissa."

Marks of parenthesis and the brackets are often employed indiscriminately; but the following rule, from Parker's " Exercises in Rhetorical Reading," will aid the pupil in distinguishing the difference as to their application: " Crotchets [the writer means marks of parenthesis] are used to enclose a sentence, or part of a sentence, which is inserted between the parts of another sentence: brackets are generally used to separate two subjects, or to enclose an explanation, note, or observation, standing by itself."

The grammatical punctuation of the words or sentences enclosed by brackets, and of the context, when they require such pointing, should be the same as that adopted in respect to the parenthesis, and to the clauses between which it is inserted. — See pp. 168–70.

Dashes are sometimes used, one before the first bracket, and another after the second, to lead the eye from the preceding portion of the main sentence to the latter. They may with propriety be introduced in such passages as the following: "I know the banker I deal with, or the physician I usually call in, — [' There is no need,' cried Dr. Slop (waking), 'to call in any physician in this case.'] — to be neither of them men of much religion."

II. A COMMA INVERTED ['] is sometimes used instead of a very small *c*, in many proper names beginning with *Mac;* as, *M'Donald*, the abbreviation of *Macdonald.*

This mark seems to be getting out of use; authors and printers now generally preferring the *c*, either on or above the line, as in *McKenzie, McFarlane.*

The same mark is sometimes annexed to the letter *O* in proper names; as, *O'Neil:* but an apostrophe is more frequently used, and is more correct; as, *O'Neil.*

III. TWO COMMAS [„] are occasionally employed to indicate that something is understood which was expressed in the line and word immediately above; as, —

    John Jones, Esq. . . . . Plymouth.
    John Smith, Esq. . . . . „

By many printers the commas are inverted [thus, "]; but the mode of using them here presented, which was once very common, is a more exact imitation of handwriting.

Names of different persons, though spelled in the same way, — as the word "John" in the preceding lines, — are commonly repeated.

IV. The INDEX, or HAND, points out a passage to which special attention is directed; as, "☞ All orders will be promptly and carefully attended to."

V. THREE STARS, placed in this form [*⁎*], or N.B., the initials of *nota bene*, "mark well," are sometimes used for the same purposes as the index.

<small>The characters explained in the two preceding paragraphs are employed chiefly in cards, handbills, advertisements, and catalogues; seldom in books.</small>

VI. The CARET [‸] is used, only in manuscript, to show where a letter or a word was accidentally omitted, but which has afterwards been placed over the line; as, —

p   are
Disapointments and trials often blessings in disguise.
‸   ‸

VII. The BRACE [⏞] is used to connect a number of words with one common term; as, —

3 barleycorns ⎫   ⎧ 1 inch ⎫
12 inches .... ⎬ are equal to ⎨ 1 foot ⎬ long measure.
3 feet ..... ⎭   ⎩ 1 yard ⎭

This character is often found serviceable in lists of articles and in tabular matter, where the object is to save room, or to avoid repetition. The inside of a brace should, as in the example, be turned to that part of the matter which contains most lines.

The brace was once generally used to bind together a triplet, or three lines of poetry having the same rhyme; but this practice is becoming obsolete.

A brace is sometimes put in the side-margin of a page to separate dates, when placed there, from the text.

VIII. Marks of Ellipsis are formed by means of a long dash, or of a succession of points or stars [——, ... , * * * *], of various lengths; and are used to indicate the omission of letters in a word, of words in a sentence, or of sentences in a paragraph; as, —

    1. C——s is not uniformly distinguished for dignity, wisdom, patriotism or philanthropy.

    2. If the great have no other glory than that of their ancestors; if their titles are their only virtues, ... their birth dishonors them, even in the estimation of the world.

    3. Some persons believe that there are no longer any duties to be fulfilled beyond the tomb; and there are but few who know how to be friends to the dead. * * * * * * * * The name of our friends, their glory, their family, have still claims on our affection, which it would be guilt not to feel. They should live still in our heart by the emotions which subsist there; in our memory, by our frequent remembrance of them; in our voice, by our eulogiums; in our conduct, by our imitation of their virtues.

In the first example, " C——s " is substituted for *Congress;* in the second, a single clause is omitted; and, in the third, several sentences are left out by the transcriber. Periods are considered much less offensive to the eye than asterisks.

To avoid repetitions in catalogues, a dash is sometimes used instead of the word or words immediately above; as, —

    Pope's Works, with Notes and Illustrations, 6 vols. calf.
    ——— Rape of the Lock, and other Poems.

For other elliptical uses of the dash, see pp. 175, 191, and 195.

IX. Leaders are dots or periods, used in contents and indexes of books, and in similar matter, to lead the eye to the end of a line, for the completion of the sense; as, —

	Page.
Comma	27
Semicolon	113
Colon	129
Period	142

ACCENTS AND OTHER MARKS. 239

X. ACCENTS. — There are three marks, termed *Accents*, placed over the vowels; namely, the Acute [´], as in *fáncy;* the Grave [`], as in *fàvor;* and the Circumflex [ˆ], as in *fâll*. The acute accent commonly represents a sharp, the grave a depressed, and the circumflex a broad sound.

<small>The grave accent is sometimes placed in verse over the vowel *e*, to show that it must be fully pronounced; as, *cankerèd, Dircè*. See p. 199, Remark *g*.

These characters are also used to denote the inflections of the voice, according to the system invented by Walker; and for various purposes in the Latin, French, and other languages.</small>

XI. MARKS OF QUANTITY. — There are other three marks, indicating the pronunciation, which are sometimes classed among the accents; namely, the Long [¯], as in *rōsy;* the Breve, or Short [˘], as in *fŏlly;* and the Diæresis [¨], as in *aërial*.

<small>The diæresis is usually placed over the latter of two vowels, and denotes that they are to be pronounced separately.</small>

XII. The CEDILLA is a mark resembling a comma placed under the letter ç, when it has the sound of *s* before *a* or *o*, in words taken from the French; as, *façade*.

XIII. THE TILDE [˜] is an accentual mark, placed over *n* in Spanish to give that letter a liquid sound; as, *señor*, sir.

<small>If great accuracy is required, all such words should be thus printed when occurring in English composition.</small>

XIV. MARKS OF REFERENCE. — The Asterisk, or Star [*], the Obelisk, or Dagger [†], the Double Dagger [‡], the Section [§], Parallel Lines [‖], and the Paragraph [¶], are used, in the order here presented, when references are made to observations or notes in the margin.

When references are numerous, the above marks, when they have been all used in one and the same page, and others are required, should be doubled or trebled; as, **, †††.

But, for purposes of reference, many authors prefer lowercase Italic letters or Arabic figures, enclosed by marks of parenthesis (a) or (1): some using the letters throughout the alphabet, or the figures as far as 10 or 100 inclusive, then beginning again with (a) or (1); and others commencing each page with the first letter or figure.

As, however, all the above marks have a rather clumsy appearance, particularly when they often occur in the same page, it has, in more recent times, been regarded as an improvement to use, in their order, letters or figures of a smaller size, technically called, from their standing above the line, *Superiors*; as, ^{a} or ^{1}. If the notes are placed in the margin, it is recommended that the letter ^{a} or figure ^{1} be the first reference of every page in which notes occur; but that figures, and not letters, be employed in regular succession, as far as required, if the notes are introduced at the end of the volume.

The ASTERISK is used in some dictionaries to note, either that a word is of Greek origin, or is distinguished by some other peculiarity; and the OBELISK, that a word or phrase is barbarous or obsolete. In Roman-Catholic church-books, the asterisk is used to divide each verse of a psalm into two parts, showing where the responses begin. The obelisk is inserted, instead of the proper square cross, in those places of the printed prayers and benedictions where the priest is to make the sign of the cross. It is also used in the briefs of the pope, and in the mandates of archbishops and bishops, who put this symbol immediately before the signature of their names.

The mark termed the SECTION [§] is sometimes employed, as in Locke's "Essay on the Human Understanding," to divide books or chapters into smaller portions; and that called the PARAGRAPH [¶] occurs frequently in the authorized version of the Bible.

CHAPTER VI.

GENERAL EXERCISES,

PUNCTUATED ACCORDING TO THE PRINCIPLES LAID DOWN IN THE PRESENT WORK.

THE following Exercises are presented in the hope, that they will be not only perused as a source of pleasure and general improvement, but also studied with relation to the art which they are meant to exemplify. This can be done in one of two ways: The reader may, in passing from one sentence to another, assign, either mentally or to a teacher, the reasons for the punctuation adopted, by referring to the rules or the remarks which are laid down in the preceding pages as applicable to each separate case. Or he may write out the exercises, one at a time, without any points whatever; and, in the course of a day or two, take his transcribed copy, and, without aid from the book, insert such marks as he thinks will best exhibit the grammatical structure of the composition, the connections or relations subsisting between the various parts of its sentences, and the sense which the author intended to express. He may then compare his manuscript with the print, in order to ascertain in what respects they correspond or differ; introducing the points which he has omitted, or rectifying the errors he has made. If the defects or mistakes are numerous, he should carefully transcribe the exercise a second time.

The Index, at the end of the book, will enable the pupil, when his memory fails him, to discover any particular rule or remark to which he may have occasion to refer.

I. — PRIDE AND HUMILITY.

Pride and humility are always relative terms. They imply a comparison of some sort with an object higher or lower; and the same mind, with actual excellence exactly the same, and with the same comparative attainments in every one around, may thus be either proud or humble, as it looks above or looks beneath. In the great scale of society, there is a continued rise from one excellence to another excellence, internal or external, intellectual or moral. Wherever we may fix, there is still some one whom we may find superior or inferior; and these relations are mutually convertible as we ascend or descend. The shrub is taller than the flower which grows in its shade; the tree, than the shrub; the rock, than the tree; the mountain, than the single rock; and above all are the sun and the heavens. It is the same in the world of life. From that Almighty Being who is the Source of all life, to the lowest of his creatures, what innumerable gradations may be traced, even in the ranks of excellence on our own earth! each being higher than that beneath, and lower than that above; and thus, all to all, objects at once of pride or humility, according as the comparison may be made with the greater or with the less.

Of two minds, then, possessing equal excellence, which is the more noble, — that which, however high the excellence attained by it, has still some nobler excellence in view, to which it feels its own inferiority; or that which, having risen a few steps in the ascent of intellectual and moral glory, thinks only of those beneath, and rejoices in an excellence which would appear to it of little value if only it lifted a single glance to the perfection above? Yet this habitual tendency to look beneath, rather than above, is the character of mind which is denominated "pride;" while the tendency to look above, rather than below, and to feel an inferiority, therefore, which others perhaps do not perceive, is the character which is denominated "humility." Is it false, then, or even extravagant, to say that humility is truly the nobler; and that pride, which delights in the contemplation of abject objects beneath, is truly in itself more abject than that meekness of heart which is humble because it has greater objects, and which looks with reverence to the excellence that is above it, because it is formed with a capacity of feeling all the worth of that excellence which it reveres? . . .

The accomplished philosopher and man of letters, to whom the great names of all who have been eminent in ancient and modern times, in all the nations in which the race of man has risen to glory, are familiar, almost like the names of those with whom he is living in society, — who has thus constantly before his mind images of excellence of the highest order, and who, even in the hopes which he dares to form, feels how small a contribution it will be in his power to add to the great imperishable stock of human wisdom, — may be proud indeed; but his pride will be of a sort that is tempered with humility, and will be humility itself if compared with the pride of a pedant or sciolist, who thinks, that, in adding the result of some little discovery which he may have fortunately made, he is almost doubling that mass of knowledge in which it is scarcely perceived as an element.

Pride, then, as a character of self-complacent exultation, is not the prevailing cast of mind of those who are formed for genuine excellence. He who is formed for genuine excellence has before him an ideal perfection, — that *semper melius aliquid*, — which makes excellence itself, however admirable to those who measure it only with their weaker powers, seem to his own mind, as compared with what he has ever in his own mental vision, a sort of failure. He thinks less of what he has done than of what it seems possible to do; and he is not so much proud of merit attained, as desirous of a merit that has not yet been attained by him.

It is in this way that the very religion which ennobles man leads him, not to pride, but to humility. It elevates him from the smoke and dust of earth; but it elevates him above the darkness, that he may see better the great heights that are above him. It shows him, not the mere excellence of a few frail creatures, as fallible as himself, but excellence, the very conception of which is the highest effort that can be made by man: exhibiting thus constantly what it will be the only honor worthy of his nature to imitate, however faintly; and checking his momentary pride, at every step of his glorious progress, by the brightness and the vastness of what is still before him.

May I not add to these remarks, that it is in this way we are to account for that humility which is so peculiarly a part of the Christian character, as contrasted with the general pride which other systems either recommend or allow? The Christian religion is, indeed, as has been often sarcastically said by those who revile it, the religion of the humble in heart; but it is the religion of the humble, only because it presents to our contemplation a higher excellence than was ever before exhibited to man. The proud look down upon the earth, and see nothing that creeps upon its surface more noble than themselves: the humble look upward to their God.

THOMAS BROWN.

II. — ABOU BEN ADHEM.

Abou Ben Adhem (may his tribe increase!)
Awoke one night from a deep dream of peace,
And saw within the moonlight of his room,
Making it rich and like a lily in bloom,
An angel writing in a book of gold.
Exceeding peace had made Ben Adhem bold;
And to the presence in the room he said,
"What writest thou?" The vision raised its head,
And, with a look made of all sweet accord,
Answered, "The names of those who love the Lord."
"And is mine one?" asked Abou. "Nay, not so,"
Replied the angel. Abou spoke more low,
But cheerly still; and said, "I pray thee, then,
Write me as one that loves his fellow-men."
The angel wrote, and vanished. The next night
It came again, with a great wakening light,
And showed the names whom love of God had blest;
And, lo! Ben Adhem's name led all the rest.

LEIGH HUNT.

III. — PANEGYRIC ON ENGLAND.

No character is perfect among nations, more than among men: but it must needs be conceded, that, of all the states of Europe, England has been, from an early period, the most favored abode of liberty; the only part of Europe, where, for any length of time, constitutional liberty can be said to have a stable existence. We can scarcely contemplate with patience the idea, that we might have been a Spanish colony, a Portuguese colony, or a Dutch colony. We can scarcely compare with coolness the inheritance which was transmitted to us by our fathers, with that which we must have received from almost any other country, — absolute government, military despotism, and the "holy inquisition." . . . . What hope can there be for the colonies of nations which possess themselves no spring of improvement, and tolerate none in the regions over which they rule; whose administration sets no bright examples of parliamentary independence; whose languages send out no reviving lessons of sound and practical science, . . . of manly literature, of sound philosophy; but repeat, with every ship that crosses the Atlantic, the same debasing voice of despotism, bigotry, and antiquated superstition?

What citizen of our republic is not grateful, in the contrast which our history presents? Who does not feel, what reflecting American does not acknowledge, the incalculable advantages derived to this land out of the deep fountains of civil, intellectual, and moral truth, from which we have drawn in England? What American does not feel proud that his fathers were the countrymen of Bacon, of Newton, and of Locke? Who does not know, that, while every pulse of civil liberty in the heart of the British empire beat warm and full in the bosom of our ancestors, the sobriety, the firmness, and the dignity, with which the cause of free principles struggled into existence here, constantly found encouragement and countenance from the friends of liberty there? Who does not remember, that, when the Pilgrims went over the sea, the prayers of the faithful British confessors, in all the quarters of their dispersion, went over with them, while their aching eyes were strained till the star of hope should go up in the western skies? And who will ever forget, that, in that eventful struggle which severed these youthful republics from the British crown, there was not heard, throughout our continent in arms, a voice which spoke louder for the rights of America, than that of Burke or of Chatham within the walls of the British Parliament.

and at the foot of the British throne? No: for myself, I can truly say, that, after my native land, I feel a tenderness and a reverence for that of my fathers. The pride I take in my own country makes me respect that from which we are sprung. In touching the soil of England, I seem to return, like a descendant, to the old family seat; to come back to the abode of an aged and venerable parent. I acknowledge this great consanguinity of nations. The sound of my native language, beyond the sea, is a music to my ear, beyond the richest strains of Tuscan softness or Castilian majesty. I am not yet in a land of strangers, while surrounded by the manners, the habits, and the institutions under which I have been brought up. I wander delighted through a thousand scenes, which the historians and the poets have made familiar to us, of which the names are interwoven with our earliest associations. I tread with reverence the spots where I can retrace the footsteps of our suffering fathers: the pleasant land of their birth has a claim on my heart. It seems to me a classic, yea, a holy land; rich in the memory of the great and good, the champions and the martyrs of liberty, the exiled heralds of truth; and richer as the parent of this land of promise in the West.

I am not — I need not say I am not — the panegyrist of England. I am not dazzled by her riches, nor awed by her power. The sceptre, the mitre, and the coronet, — stars, garters, and blue ribbons, — seem to me poor things for great men to contend for. Nor is my admiration awakened by her armies mustered for the battles of Europe, her navies overshadowing the ocean, nor her empire grasping the farthest East. It is these, and the price of guilt and blood by which they are too often maintained, which are the cause why no friend of liberty can salute her with undivided affections. But it is the cradle and the refuge of free principles, though often persecuted; the school of religious liberty, the more precious for the struggles through which it has passed; the tombs of those who have reflected honor on all who speak the English tongue; it is the birthplace of our fathers, the home of the Pilgrims, — it is these which I love and venerate in England. I should feel ashamed of an enthusiasm for Italy and Greece, did I not also feel it for a land like this. In an American, it would seem to me degenerate and ungrateful to hang with passion upon the traces of Homer and Virgil, and follow without emotion the nearer and plainer footsteps of Shakspeare and Milton. I should think him cold in his love for his native land who felt no melting in his heart for that other native country which holds the ashes of his forefathers. EDWARD EVERETT.

IV. — THE PEN AND THE PRESS.

Young Genius walked out by the mountains and streams,
Entranced by the power of his own pleasant dreams,
Till the silent, the wayward, the wandering thing
Found a plume that had fallen from a passing bird's wing:
Exulting and proud, like a boy at his play,
He bore the new prize to his dwelling away;
He gazed for a while on its beauties, and then
He cut it, and shaped it, and called it a Pen.

But its magical use he discovered not yet,
Till he dipped its bright lips in a fountain of jet;
And, oh! what a glorious thing it became!
For it spoke to the world in a language of flame;
While its master wrote on, like a being inspired,
Till the hearts of the millions were melted or fired:
It came as a boon and a blessing to men, —
The peaceful, the pure, the victorious Pen.

Young Genius went forth on his rambles once more,
The vast, sunless caverns of earth to explore;
He searched the rude rock, and with rapture he found
A substance unknown, which he brought from the ground;
He fused it with fire, and rejoiced at the change,
As he moulded the ore into characters strange,
Till his thoughts and his efforts were crowned with success,
For an engine uprose, and he called it the Press.

The Pen and the Press, blest alliance! combined
To soften the heart, and enlighten the mind;
For that to the treasures of knowledge gave birth,
And this sent them forth to the ends of the earth:
Their battles for truth were triumphant indeed,
And the rod of the tyrant was snapped like a reed;
They were made to exalt us, to teach us, to bless,
Those invincible brothers, — the Pen and the Press.

John Critchley Prince.

V. — A TASTE FOR READING.

We cannot linger in the beautiful creations of inventive genius, or pursue the splendid discoveries of modern science, without a new sense of the capacities and dignity of human nature, which naturally leads to a sterner self-respect, to manlier resolves and higher aspirations. We cannot read the ways of God to man as revealed in the history of nations, of sublime virtues as exemplified in the lives of great and good men, without falling into that mood of thoughtful admiration, which, though it be but a transient glow, is a purifying and elevating influence while it lasts. The study of history is especially valuable as an antidote to self-exaggeration. It teaches lessons of humility, patience, and submission. When we read of realms smitten with the scourge of famine or pestilence, or strewn with the bloody ashes of war ; of grass growing in the streets of great cities ; of ships rotting at the wharves ; of fathers burying their sons ; of strong men begging their bread ; of fields untilled, and silent workshops, and despairing countenances, — we hear a voice of rebuke to our own clamorous sorrows and peevish complaints. We learn that pain and suffering and disappointment are a part of God's providence, and that no contract was ever yet made with man by which virtue should secure to him temporal happiness.

In books, be it remembered, we have the best products of the best minds. We should any of us esteem it a great privilege to pass an evening with Shakspeare or Bacon, were such a thing possible. But, were we admitted to the presence of one of these illustrious men, we might find him touched with infirmity, or oppressed with weariness, or darkened with the shadow of a recent trouble, or absorbed by intrusive and tyrannous thoughts. To us the oracle might be dumb, and the light eclipsed. But, when we take down one of their volumes, we run no such risk. Here we have their best thoughts, embalmed in their best words ; immortal flowers of poetry, wet with Castalian dews, and the golden fruit of wisdom that had long ripened on the bough before it was gathered. Here we find the growth of the choicest seasons of the mind, when mortal cares were forgotten, and mortal weaknesses were subdued ; and the soul, stripped of its vanities and its passions, lay bare to the finest effluences of truth and beauty. We may be sure that Shakspeare never out-talked his Hamlet, nor Bacon his Essays. Great writers are indeed best known through their books. How little, for instance, do we know of the life of Shakspeare; but how much do we know of him! . .

For the knowledge that comes from books, I would claim no more than it is fairly entitled to. I am well aware that there is no inevitable connection between intellectual cultivation, on the one hand, and individual virtue or social well-being, on the other. "The tree of knowledge is not the tree of life." I admit that genius and learning are sometimes found in combination with gross vices, and not unfrequently with contemptible weaknesses; and that a community at once cultivated and corrupt is no impossible monster. But it is no overstatement to say, that, other things being equal, the man who has the greatest amount of intellectual resources is in the least danger from inferior temptations, — if for no other reason, because he has fewer idle moments. The ruin of most men dates from some vacant hour. Occupation is the armor of the soul; and the train of Idleness is borne up by all the vices. I remember a satirical poem, in which the Devil is represented as fishing for men, and adapting his baits to the taste and temperament of his prey; but the idler, he said, pleased him most, because he bit the naked hook. To a young man away from home, friendless and forlorn in a great city, the hours of peril are those between sunset and bedtime; for the moon and stars see more of evil in a single hour than the sun in his whole day's circuit. The poet's visions of evening are all compact of tender and soothing images. It brings the wanderer to his home, the child to his mother's arms, the ox to his stall, and the weary laborer to his rest. But to the gentle-hearted youth who is thrown upon the rocks of a pitiless city, and stands "homeless amid a thousand homes," the approach of evening brings with it an aching sense of loneliness and desolation, which comes down upon the spirit like darkness upon the earth. In this mood, his best impulses become a snare to him; and he is led astray because he is social, affectionate, sympathetic, and warm-hearted. If there be a young man thus circumstanced, within the sound of my voice, let me say to him, that books are the friends of the friendless, and that a library is the home of the homeless. A taste for reading will always carry you into the best possible company, and enable you to converse with men who will instruct you by their wisdom, and charm you by their wit; who will soothe you when fretted, refresh you when weary, counsel you when perplexed, and sympathize with you at all times.

GEORGE S. HILLARD

VI. — RELATIVE PERFECTION.

There is a relative, as well as a more general, perfection in man, which must not be lost sight of in examining the question of his proper vocation in life. There is required of him, not only a culture of his whole being as a man, but also a diligent and faithful adaptation of certain of his powers to the particular circumstances in which he is placed. Life's purpose is only adequately accomplished in discharging both these claims; and, indeed, the more limited service is a necessary condition of the general development. You find yourself, then, occupying a given position in the world. It has its appointed duties, its special opportunities of usefulness, trials also, difficulties and temptations of its own. Take your lot as it is assigned you, without murmuring. Make the best of it; and, if in the eyes of men it seems unhonored and unenviable, ennoble it by your own spirit, and work your way through it, by character and honest industry, to something better and happier. If, on the other hand, you find it accord with your inclination, and open before you a fair prospect of worldly advancement, be assured there is nothing irreligious in honorably aiming at success and eminence in it, and still less in openly avowing that such is your object. Every pursuit which conduces to the welfare of the world has its appropriate honor attending it; and a genuine virtue is developed by enthusiasm for what is highest in our own line of action. You may treat life as a problem, which has to be wrought out to a successful result, with certain moral conditions attached to it. Do not, because it looks difficult, timorously shrink from attempting the solution; but work through every part of it, whether you get the whole result or not, without violating one of its moral conditions. Draw the utmost from it that it will yield for temporal prosperity, for social weight and position, for honor, usefulness, mental culture, and refined enjoyment, consistently with the strictest integrity, with health and the exercise of the affections, with a remembrance of the end of life and a cheerful submission to the divine will. Whatever your vocation in life, — whether you labor with the head or with the hand; whether you write books, or manufacture cloth; whether your ships cross every sea, or your whole stock in trade is contained within the four walls of your humble shop; whether you sit on the bench of justice, or earn your honest wages from week to week, — honor your work as assigned you by God, who regards not its subject-matter, but the spirit in which it is performed; and, as in his sight, with a loyal and devoted heart, strive to be outdone by no one in the completeness and efficiency of its execution.

This is the healthy view of our human world. Contentment, comfort, abundance, depend on its wide diffusion. It would put every one in his proper place, and fit him with his proper task. It would let none be idle, and leave none in want. It would abolish useless privilege, and bring all under the constraint of wholesome duty. This view reconciles earth and heaven. While we are in the world, it makes us, in the best of senses, friends with the world, but not less fitted for heaven when we pass away. It is also the honest and sincere view. Thousands who disown it act upon it; and none more so, and with a keener eye even to selfish advancement, than some who put forth an exclusive claim to the religious character. Such is the course of action which contributes to relative perfection, by linking our individual lives through specific duties with the general well-being of the world.

JOHN JAMES TAYLER.

VII. — LABOR NOT LOST.

A genial moment oft has given
    What years of toil and pain,
Of long industrious toil, have striven
    To win, and all in vain:
Yet count not, when thine end is won,
    That labor merely lost;
Nor say it had been wiser done
    To spare the painful cost.

When, heaped upon the altar, lie
    All things to feed the fire,
One spark alighting from on high,
    The flames at once aspire:
But those sweet gums and fragrant woods,
    Its rich materials rare,
By tedious quest o'er lands and floods
    Had first been gathered there.

R. C. TRENCH

VIII. — ANCIENT AND MODERN WRITERS.

The classics possess a peculiar charm, from the circumstance that they have been the models, I might almost say the masters, of composition and thought in all ages. In the contemplation of these august teachers of mankind, we are filled with conflicting emotions. They are the early voice of the world, better remembered and more cherished still than all the intermediate words that have been uttered; as the lessons of childhood still haunt us when the impressions of later years have been effaced from the mind. But they show with most unwelcome frequency the tokens of the world's childhood, before passion had yielded to the sway of reason and the affections. They want the highest charm of purity, of righteousness, of elevated sentiments, of love to God and man. It is not in the frigid philosophy of the Porch and the Academy that we are to seek these; not in the marvellous teachings of Socrates, as they come mended by the mellifluous words of Plato; not in the resounding line of Homer, on whose inspiring tale of blood Alexander pillowed his head; not in the animated strain of Pindar, where virtue is pictured in the successful strife of an athlete at the Isthmian games; not in the torrent of Demosthenes, dark with self-love and the spirit of vengeance; not in the fitful philosophy and intemperate eloquence of Tully; not in the genial libertinism of Horace, or the stately atheism of Lucretius. No: these must not be our masters; in none of these are we to seek the way of life. For eighteen hundred years, the spirit of these writers has been engaged in weaponless contest with the Sermon on the Mount, and those two sublime commandments on which hang all the law and the prophets. The strife is still pending. Heathenism, which has possessed itself of such siren forms, is not yet exorcised. It still tempts the young, controls the affairs of active life, and haunts the meditations of age.

Our own productions, though they may yield to those of the ancients in the arrangement of ideas, in method, in beauty of form, and in freshness of illustration, are immeasurably superior in the truth, delicacy, and elevation of their sentiments; above all, in the benign recognition of that great Christian revelation, the brotherhood of man. How vain are eloquence and poetry, compared with this heaven-descended truth! Put in one scale that simple utterance, and in the other the lore of antiquity, with its accumulating

glosses and commentaries, and the last will be light and trivial in
the balance. Greek poetry has been likened to the song of the
nightingale, as she sits in the rich, symmetrical crown of the palm-
tree, trilling her thick-warbled notes; but even this is less sweet
and tender than the music of the human heart.

CHARLES SUMNER.

IX. — THE TRUE SOURCE OF REFORM.

The great element of reform is not born of human wisdom; it
does not draw its life from human organizations. I find it only in
Christianity. "Thy kingdom come," — there is a sublime and
pregnant burden in this prayer. It is the aspiration of every soul
that goes forth in the spirit of reform. For what is the significance
of this prayer? It is a petition that all holy influences would penetrate and subdue and dwell in the heart of man, until he shall think
and speak and do good from the very necessity of his being. So
would the institutions of error and wrong crumble and pass away
So would sin die out from the earth; and, the human soul living
in harmony with the divine will, this earth would become like
heaven.

It is too late for the reformers to sneer at Christianity; it is fool-
ishness for them to reject it. In it are enshrined our faith in human
progress, our confidence in reform. It is indissolubly connected with
all that is hopeful, spiritual, capable, in man. That men have misunderstood it and perverted it, is true. But it is also true that the
noblest efforts for human melioration have come out of it, have been
based upon it. Is it not so? Come, ye remembered ones, who sleep
the sleep of the just, who took your conduct from the line of Christian philosophy! — come from your tombs, and answer.

Come, Howard! from the gloom of the prison and the taint of
the lazar-house, and show us what philanthropy can do when imbued
with the spirit of Jesus. Come, Eliot! from the thick forest where
the red man listens to the word of life; come, Penn! from thy sweet
counsel and weaponless victory, — and show us what Christian zeal
and Christian love can accomplish with the rudest barbarians or the
fiercest hearts. Come, Raikes! from thy labors with the ignorant
and the poor, and show us with what an eye this faith regards the
lowest and least of our race; and how diligently it labors, not for

the body, not for the rank, but for the plastic soul that is to course the ages of immortality.

And ye, who are a great number, — ye nameless ones, — who have done good in your narrower spheres, content to forego renown on earth, and seeking your reward in the record on high! come, and tell us how kindly a spirit, how lofty a purpose, or how strong a courage, the religion ye professed can breathe into the poor, the humble, and the weak.

Go forth, then, Spirit of Christianity! to thy great work of reform. The Past bears witness to thee in the blood of thy martyrs, and the ashes of thy saints and heroes. The Present is hopeful because of thee. The Future shall acknowledge thy omnipotence.

E. H. CHAPIN.

X. — GREAT MEN GENERALLY GOOD.

(See p. 124.)

Those who have shone in all ages as the lights of the world; the most celebrated names that are recorded in the annals of fame; legislators, the founders of states, and the fathers of their country, on whom succeeding ages have looked back with filial reverence; patriots, the guardians of the laws, who have stemmed the torrent of corruption in every age; heroes, the saviours of their country, who have returned victorious from the field of battle, or, more than victorious, who have died for their country; philosophers, who have opened the book of nature, and explained the wonders of almighty power; bards, who have sung the praises of virtue and of virtuous men, whose strains carry them down to immortality, — with a few exceptions, have been uniformly on the side of goodness, and have been as distinguished in the temple of fame. It was one of the maxims which governed their lives, that there is nothing in nature which can compensate wickedness; that, although the rewards and punishments which influence illiberal and ungenerous minds were set aside; that, although the thunders of the Almighty were hushed, and the gates of paradise were open no more, they would follow religion and virtue for their own sake, and co-operate with eternal Providence in perpetual endeavors to favor the good, to depress the bad, and to promote the happiness of the whole creation.

JOHN LOGAN.

APPENDIX.

APPENDIX.

I. — USES OF CAPITAL LETTERS.

Though the subject of capital letters is but indirectly allied to punctuation, it may be suitable here to lay down a few principles, useful to all who are desirous of combining taste and propriety in their compositions, especially to persons likely to become in any way connected with the public press. It was formerly the custom to use capitals with greater frequency and less discrimination than it is at the present day; almost every noun, nay, in some cases almost every word of the slightest importance, having had its initial thus distinguished. The following is a moderate specimen of the style alluded to, taken from Clarendon's "History of the Rebellion," where he treats of Lord Strafford's death: —

"Thus Fell the greatest Subject in power, and little inferior to any in Fortune that was at that time in any of the three Kingdoms; Who could well remember the time when he led those People who then pursued him to his Grave. He was a man of great Parts, and extraordinary Endowments of Nature; not unadorned with some addition of Art and Learning, though that again was more improved and illustrated by the other."

But as this practice was to a great extent arbitrary, and did not possess the advantage of either ornament or utility, the use of capital letters is now very properly limited to the applications about to be mentioned.

RULE I.

The First Word of a Book, Tract, &c.

The first word of every book, tract, essay, &c., and of their great divisions, — chapters, sections, paragraphs. and notes, — must commence with a capital letter.

REMARKS.

a. Numerous exemplifications of the rule will be found in the present or any other work.

b. Phrases or clauses, when separately numbered, begin each with a capital letter; as, "The reproach of barbarism may be incurred in three different ways: 1. *By* the use of words entirely obsolete; 2. *By* the use of words entirely new; or, 3. *By* new formations and compositions from simple and primitive words in present use."

RULE II.

The First Word after a Full Point.

The first word after a period, and after a note of interrogation or exclamation when grammatically equivalent to a period, should begin with a capital; as, —

1. Let the tone of your conversation be invariably benevolent. Differ without asperity; agree without dogmatism. Kind words cost no more than unkind ones.

2. What is it that keeps men in continual discontent and agitation? It is, that they cannot make realities correspond with their conceptions.

3. Fair, fair, shall be the flowers that spring over thy tomb, dear, gentle Ella! Sweet shall be the song — sweet as thine own — that shall lure the wanderer to the spot where thy urn receives the tears of the stranger.

REMARKS.

a. Some writers and printers always commence with a capital letter the word immediately following a colon; but this should take place only when required by other rules.

b. When the period is a mark for an abbreviated word or phrase which does not end a sentence, the following word is commenced, not with a capital, but with a small letter; as, "Franklin had the degree of LL.D. *conferred* on him by the University of St. Andrew's, Scotland." Here it will be seen, that the initial of "conferred" is small. The word "Andrew's," indeed, though coming after an abbreviation, is put with a capital; but this, of course, arises from the fact that "St. Andrew's" is a proper name.

c. When two or more sentences, of an exclamatory or interrogative kind, are closely connected in sense and construction, all of them, except the first, begin with a small letter; as, "How ugly a person appears, upon whose reputation some awkward aspersion hangs! and how suddenly his countenance clears up with his character!"—"What child is there, who, in a toyshop, does not prefer the gaudiest toy, if all other circumstances of attraction be the same? or, rather, to what child are not this very glare and glitter the chief circumstances of attraction? and in what island of savages have our circumnavigators found the barbarian to differ in this respect from the child?" In the passages just cited, the words "and," "or," which follow the note of exclamation and of interrogation, are begun with small letters, because these marks are equivalent, not to full points, but to semicolons.

RULE III.

Appellations of God and Christ.

Names of the Deity and of Jesus Christ must commence with a capital letter; as, —

1. Jehovah, Lord, God; Creator, Father, Preserver, Governor; the Eternal, the Almighty, the All-wise; the Supreme Being; the Holy Spirit.
2. The Messiah, the Anointed; the Son, the Saviour, the Redeemer; the Holy One; Prophet, Teacher, Master; Judge of the world.

REMARKS.

a. Some of these and similar words are begun, sometimes with a capital, and sometimes with a small letter, according to the sense in which they are taken. Thus, *God*, with a large initial, is the name of the Supreme Being; *god*, with a small character, an appellation used occasionally of men, angels, and false divinities; as, "The Lord is a great *God* above all *gods*."

b. With initial capitals, *Lord* and *King* are applied to God and Christ; with a small *l* and *k*, the same words denote men having authority and power. Thus, in the Apocalypse, our Saviour is called "Lord of lords, and King of kings;" and, in the Old Testament, a great sovereign is styled a "king of kings."

c. From the vagueness of the ideas represented by the word *nature*, it is difficult to lay down any precise rule as to the mode of writing or printing it. In general, it should begin with a small *n;* as, "He looks through *nature* up to *nature's* God;" except when strongly personified, or when clearly used of the intelligent Principle of the universe.

d. Providence, with an initial capital, denotes the infinitely good Being who provides for the wants of his creatures; but, when beginning with a small *p,* it means either divine superintendence or human foresight. So, *Heaven,* with a capital *H,* signifies God, the Sovereign of *heaven,* or of the celestial regions.

e. The adjectives *divine, heavenly, eternal, universal, providential,* and others of a similar kind, when applied to God, his attributes, or his agency, are sometimes written initially with capitals; but, unless when particularly emphatic, small letters are preferable, because the names of the Deity occurring in the connection sufficiently indicate the Being referred to.

f. As exceptions to Remark *e,* the epithets occurring in *First Cause, Divine* or *Supreme Being, Almighty God, Infinite One,* should begin with large letters, because universal custom favors this mode of writing. The adjective *Most High* or *Highest* should also appear with an initial capital, when the noun which it qualifies is not used.

g. When the attributes of the Deity or of the Saviour are expressed, not by adjectives, but, in the Hebrew style, by nouns, — as, *Father of mercies, God of wisdom, Prince of peace,* instead of *the merciful Father, the wise God, the peaceful Prince,* — they should begin, like the adjectives, with small letters, as here exemplified.

h. The appellation *Son of man,* when applied to Christ, whether by way of eminence or of humility, is probably better printed, not "Son of Man" or "son of man," but as it appears in the common version of the Bible, and in the first line of this remark.

i. The word *Spirit,* and the phrases *Holy* or *Divine Spirit, Holy Ghost, Spirit of God,* are usually capitalized, whether said of the Deity or of his gifts and influences. Some writers, however, restrict the capitals to these terms when they have a personal import, but use small letters when they signify merely divine inspiration or heavenly aid. As the mode of exhibiting these words is as much a matter of theology as of taste, authors should be particularly careful to write the initials as they wish them to be printed.

j. Pronouns referring to God and Christ should not begin with capitals, unless they are used emphatically without a noun. Hymns and prayers are often disfigured by the unnecessary use of these letters, as in the following lines: —

> These are Thy glorious works, Parent of good,
> Almighty! Thine this universal frame,
> Thus wondrous fair: Thyself how wondrous then! —

which would lose none of their true grandeur, if more simply printed: —

> These are thy glorious works, Parent of good,
> Almighty! thine this universal frame,
> Thus wondrous fair: thyself how wondrous then!

RULE IV.

Titles of Honor and Respect.

Titles of honor and respect, either descriptive of persons in exalted stations or addressed to them, usually begin with capital letters; as, —

1. Her Majesty, His Honor, Your Royal Highness, Your Grace.
2. My Lord, my Lady; dear Sir, respected Madam or Friend.
3. The President of the United States.
4. His Excellency the Governor of Massachusetts.

REMARKS.

a. In the rules and reports of societies, institutions, &c., names indicating office should begin with capitals; as, *Chairman, President, Vice-President, Treasurer, Secretary, Committee, Directors, Board of Managers.* So also, when used in a specific sense, the words *Report, Society, Institution, Corporation, Constitution, Commonwealth, State, University, College, Academy, School, Congress, Parliament, Legislature,* &c. In the plural number, or when used in a general sense, such words are properly put in small characters.

b. The *pope; his* or *her majesty; king, queen; duke, duchess; lord, lady; sir, madam; president, governor,* and words of a similar kind, should be written or printed with small initials, when they occur very frequently, or without any particular expression of honor. When prefixed to proper names, however, they are always begun with capitals; as, *President Jefferson, Governor Winthrop, Professor Longfellow, Lord Brougham, Countess of Blessington, Queen Victoria the Emperor Napoleon, Pope Pius IX.*

c. So, also, *father, mother; brother, sister; uncle, aunt,* &c., commence with capital letters when put before proper names; as, *Aunt Dorothy, Brother Gray.* But the term *father,* when applied to any of the early orthodox writers of the Christian Church, is begun with a capital, whether it be or be not prefixed to a proper name; as, " Even the soundest of the *Fathers* held some opinions inconsistent with the doctrines of the gospel."

RULE V.

Names of Persons, Places, &c.

All proper names, whether of animate or inanimate existences, begin with capitals; as, —

    1. Jupiter, Juno; Pompey, Penelope; William, Sarah.
    2. America, Europe; France, Spain, Great Britain.
    3. New York, Philadelphia; London, Edinburgh, Broadway.
    4. The Atlantic, the Red Sea, Lake Erie, the Alps.
    5. January, Monday, Christmas, Good Friday, Easter.

REMARKS.

a. When the word *devil* is used of Satan, it may begin with a capital; as, *the Devil and his angels.* But when employed of demoniacal agents or of wicked men, whether in the singular or the plural number, it commences with a small letter.

b. The words *heaven, hell, paradise, the celestial and the infernal regions,* representing either states of mind or places of reward and punishment, usually begin with small letters; but *Elysium, Tartarus,* and *Pandemonium,* with capitals.

c. Appellatives, merely expletory, coming before proper names, are begun with small letters; but, when put immediately after them, they are distinguished by capitals; as, *the river Thames, the city of London; London City, the Thames River.*

d. When *North, South, East, West,* &c., denote certain countries of which we are accustomed to speak, or the people who reside in certain parts of the globe or in districts of our own land, they are written or printed with initial capitals; as, " This man's accent shows that he belongs to the *South.*" But, when they refer to places or things as being more to the north, south, &c., than others, these words are begun with small letters; as, "London is situated *east* of Windsor."

e. Sunday, as one of the days of the week, always has an initial capital; while, on the contrary, *sabbath,* or *sabbath-day,* is perhaps more frequently written and printed with a small *s* than with a large one. The initials in *Lord's Day, New Year's Day,* &c., are usually capitalized.

RULE VI.

Nouns and Adjectives derived from Proper Names.

Gentile nouns, adjectives derived from gentile nouns, and nouns or adjectives formed from proper names, begin with capitals; as, —

1. A Hebrew, a Greek, a Roman, a German, a Spaniard, a Frenchman.
2. Hebrew, Grecian, Roman, Italian, French, Spanish, American.
3. A Christian, a Brahmin, a Mahometan; Augustan, Elizabethan.

REMARKS.

a. Names of sectaries, whether formed from proper nouns or otherwise, should begin with capitals; as, "Good men are found among Christian denominations of the most opposite doctrines, — among Roman Catholics and Protestants, Athanasians and Arians, Trinitarians and Unitarians, Lutherans, Calvinists, Arminians, and Universalists." So, also, when used adjectively; as, *the Wesleyan doctrines; Papal, Protestant, and Episcopal ceremonies.*

b. A few adjectives and common nouns, derived from proper names, are usually printed with small initials; as, *godlike, stentorian, hermetical, hymeneal, prussic; epicure, epicurism; philippic, simony, jalap, damask, cashmere* (shawl), *china* (ware), *guinea* (a coin), *turkey* (a fowl), *champagne* (wine). These and similar words are so written, because usually little or no reference is made to the proper names from which they were derived.

c. For the same reason, the verbs *to hector, to philippize, to romance, to galvanize, to japan,* should be written with small letters. But, on account of their more obvious allusion to the proper names whence they have been taken, *Judaize* and *Christianize* are better written or printed with initial capitals. The compounds *unchristian, antichristian,* &c., are, however, done with small characters.

RULE VII.

Words of Primary Importance.

Words of primary importance, especially if they indicate some great event, or remarkable change in religion or government, are commenced with capital letters; as, —

1. The Reformation, effected mainly by Luther, is one of the most wonderful events in modern times.
2. Glorious New England! around thy hills and mountains cling, like gathering mists, the mighty memories of the Revolution.

REMARKS.

a. The use of capitals in important words and phrases seems to be, in some measure, a matter of mere taste or caprice. Channing not unfrequently represents the greatest of his great ideas by words having initial capitals; Carlyle, and other imitators of German thought and expression, employ them superabundantly, and with little discrimination; while others are particularly careful that the uniformity which is so desirable in a printed page be marred as little as possible by the practice referred to.

b. Every noun or leading word in the titles of books and other publications must begin, wherever it occurs, with a capital letter; as, " Gray's ' Elegy in a Country Churchyard ' is perhaps the finest poem of the kind in the English or any other language."

c. Terms denoting the records of the Jewish and Christian revelations are distinguished by initial capitals; as, *the Scriptures, the Holy Bible, the Sacred Writings, the Old and the New Testament.* But the phrase *word of God,* when employed in this sense, is begun with a small letter; while the term *Word,* or " Logos," as used by St. John in the introduction to his Gospel, and so much discussed by divines, is generally written and printed with a capital.

d. The word *gospel* has a small letter for its initial when it means the religion of Jesus, but a capital when it denotes one of the four Gospels; as, *the Gospel of Matthew.* So, also, the term *revelation* when denoting the divine instructions contained in the Bible, begins with a small letter; but, used of the Apocalypse, or *Revelation* of St. John, it must be distinguished with a capital.

e. The word *church*, when used by itself or in a general sense, should begin with a small letter; but, when connected with an adjective indicating a particular body of Christians, it should commence with a capital; as, *the Protestant Church.*

f. So, also, the term *catholic*, whether as a noun or an adjective, should be written and printed with a small *c*, when it is used of all Christians, or of men of liberal and tolerant principles; but with a capital when significant merely of the Romish community.

g. For the sake of uniformity, the names *Gentile, Heathen,* and *Pagan,* so often occurring in connection with *Jew*, should, when used as nouns, begin with capitals; but, when employed adjectively, with small letters. The words *orthodoxy, orthodox; heterodoxy, heterodox; heresy, heretic, heretical; mysticism, mystic, mystical; atheism, atheist, atheistic; pantheism, pantheist, pantheistic; deism, deist, deistical; rationalism, rationalist, rationalistic; supernaturalism, supernaturalist; transcendentalism, transcendentalist, transcendental; spiritualism, spiritualist,* are usually put with small characters. The term *Orthodox,* however, when used of any particular section of the orthodox body of Christians, should begin with a capital letter; as, *the Orthodox Congregationalists.* — See p. 263, Remark *a.*

h. Designations of political parties should commence each with a capital letter; as, *Whig, Tory, Federalist, Democrat, Republican, Conservative, Radical, Free Soiler.*

i. In advertisements, handbills, and cards, the principal words — such as the names of the arts and sciences, and nouns occurring in a list of articles — are properly begun with capitals.

RULE VIII.

The Pronoun I, and the Interjection O.

The pronoun *I,* and the interjection *O,* should invariably be written or printed in capitals; as, —

With three steps I compass thy grave, O thou who wast so great before!

REMARKS.

a. The interjection *oh* should never, as is sometimes done, be put with an initial capital, except at the beginning of a sentence, or of a line in verse.

b. For the modes of using the two words *O* and *oh,* see page 160, Remark *c.*

RULE IX.

Commencement of Lines in Verse.

The first word of every line in poetry is begun with a capital letter; as,—

> No eye beheld when William plunged
> Young Edmund in the stream;
> No human ear but William's heard
> Young Edmund's drowning scream.

REMARKS.

a. The initial letter in the first word of a poetical quotation, though not beginning a line, should be capitalized; as, " One of the most illustrious names in the literary annals of Europe is that of Spenser,—

> ' That gentle bard,
> Chosen by the Muses for their page of state.' "

b. In humorous verse, when a portion of a word is put at the end of one line, and the other portion at the beginning of the next, the latter should be put with a small initial; as,—

> Paganini, Paganini!
> Never was there such a geni-
> us before as Paganini.

RULE X.

Prosopopœia, or Personification.

Nouns that represent inanimate beings as persons should begin with capitals; as,—

> Better to sit in Freedom's hall,
> With a cold, damp floor, and a mouldering wall,
> Than to bend the neck or to bow the knee
> In the proudest palace of Slavery.

REMARKS.

a. According to this rule, all such words as *the Muses, the Graces, the Furies, the Fates*, should be distinguished by capitals. When " the graces " is used of certain moral affections, a common *g* is properly used.

b. So, also, *Spring, Summer, Autumn, Winter; the Sun, the Earth, the Moon,* and *the Stars,* should each begin with a capital when they are personified, but with a small letter when they are used in ordinary composition. In works on astronomy, it is better to capitalize them.

c. The rule should be applied with some discrimination. It is only when the figure *prosopopœia* is uncommonly vivid that the noun should have its initial with a capital letter; there being a tendency, even in the most inanimate compositions, to impart a certain degree of life and energy to the representatives of our thoughts. But, though in numberless instances it would be improper to capitalize such words, the more glowing personifications of the poet and the orator ought unquestionably to be so distinguished.

RULE XI.

Quotations, Examples, &c.

The first word of every quotation, example, precept, or question, introduced in a direct form, must begin with a capital letter; as, —

1. Bushnell well remarks, "Hitherto, the love of passion has been the central fire of the world's literature."

2. These two questions, "What are we?" and "Whither do we tend?" will at times press painfully upon thoughtful minds.

REMARKS.

a. When a quotation is introduced by the conjunction *that,* or is brought in obliquely or indirectly, a small letter is preferable; as, "It is well said by a celebrated writer, that, '*precious* as thought is, the love of truth is still more precious.'" — "Happy those who, '*dying,* leave no line they wish to blot'!" — "This great patriot bequeathed to his heirs the sword which he had worn in the war for liberty, and charged them '*never* to take it from the scabbard but in self-defence, or in defence of their country and her freedom.'"

b. Examples, consisting of mere words or phrases, may have small letters for their initials, when they do not commence new lines, or are not formally introduced with the words "as follows," or with a similar expression. Numerous illustrations of this remark may be seen in pages 211–20.

RULE XII.

Capitals used instead of Figures.

Numbers are sometimes written or printed wholly in capitals, as representative characters. Thus, —

I. is used instead of one, or first; IV. for four, or fourth; XI. for eleven, or eleventh; XX. for twenty, or twentieth; XL. for forty, or fortieth; &c.

REMARKS.

a. Some writers refer to passages in books by putting the numbers of the volume, part, chapter, &c., in capital letters, and also by capitalizing the first letter in the name of the division specified; as, "Campbell on the Four Gospels, Vol. I. Diss. V. Part IV. Sect. II. Page 218." But, when such references are numerous, small letters are preferable, because they have a neater appearance; as, "Campbell on the Four Gospels, vol. i. diss. v. part iv. sect. ii. page [or p.] 218."

b. For the punctuation, see pp. 150-1, Rule V. and Remarks.

RULE XIII.

Titlepages, Inscriptions, &c.

Titlepages of books, and heads of chapters, sections, articles, &c., are, with some few exceptions, put entirely in capitals. Unless very long, dedications of printed works, and inscriptions on monuments, are commonly distinguished in the same manner.

REMARKS.

a. The first word in a book or chapter is usually put in small capitals, with the exception of the initial letter, which should have a common-size capital.

b. Capitals or small capitals are also used, either singly or otherwise, as abbreviations of titles and other words, and as representative signs, particularly in works of art and science, such as chemistry, mechanics, arithmetic, grammar, music, &c. Many of these will be exhibited in the article beginning on page 272.

In concluding these rules and remarks on the use of capitals, we would suggest that authors either note accurately and consistently the words which they mean to be so distinguished, or allow the printer to exercise his own taste and judgment. By this means, not only would a great loss of time be saved to the workman, but the work itself would have a neater and more uniform appearance.

In manuscript, words or sentences meant to be printed in CAPITALS are distinguished by having three lines drawn under them; in SMALL CAPITALS, by two lines; and in *Italics*, by one.

II. — ITALIC CHARACTERS.

Characters called *Italics*, and printed in this form, are used chiefly to point out emphatical expressions, or to distinguish foreign words and phrases. In the common version of the Scriptures, however, words are so printed to show that they have nothing corresponding to them in the original Hebrew or Greek, but were inserted by the translators to complete or explain the sense.

It is quite impracticable to lay down definite and unvarying rules in respect to all the circumstances under which it is proper to use Italic letters. Their employment was at one time exceedingly common; all proper names, and almost all words of more than ordinary significance, having been written or printed in this manner. A sparing use of Italics is, however, strongly recommended to authors and typographers; for it is obvious, that, as there are in composition innumerable shades and degrees of emphasis, a prodigal introduction of words of a sloping character would tend rather to confound the sense and perplex the reader, than to elucidate the meaning, or to assist in discriminating the relative importance which should be attached to different sentiments.

In all works, however, which treat of matters relating to science, art, or language, where it is necessary to adduce words and phrases in illustration of certain principles, or to employ them in technical senses, the use of Italic characters is indispensable. In the present treatise, it will be seen that they are freely and unavoidably used.

III. — TERMS RELATING TO BOOKS.

CAPTIONS and SUBHEADS are words or expressions that stand above chapters, sections, and paragraphs, for the purpose of indicating their contents. SIDEHEADS are of a similar nature, but put in the first line of the paragraph or paragraphs to which they refer. RUNNING TITLES — or, as they are sometimes called, *headlines* — are such words or phrases as are placed at the top of the page. All these are printed usually in capital or small-capital letters; sometimes, especially in magazines, in Italics.

Signatures are the letters of the alphabet, used by English printers in the foot-margin of certain pages, as a guide to direct the bookbinder in arranging and folding the sheets. The letter B is put at the bottom of the first sheet or half-sheet which comes immediately after the titlepage, preface, and contents; C, at that of the second; and so on throughout the alphabet, with the exception of J, V, and W. If the number of pages require more signatures than the alphabet will indicate, the letters are doubled or trebled, or a numeral is prefixed to them; as, A a, B b; 2 A, 2 B; 3 A, &c. Figures, or numeral characters (1, 1*; 2, 2*; &c.), being more convenient than letters, are used for the same purpose by American printers. But in catalogues, and other publications in which figures often occur, capitals or small capitals are, for distinction's sake, preferable.

Names of Various Sizes of Books. — *Folio* denotes a sheet of paper folded into two leaves, making four pages; *quarto*, or, as abbreviated, 4to or 4°, is a sheet divided into four leaves, or eight pages; *octavo*, 8vo or 8°, a sheet into eight leaves, or sixteen pages; *duodecimo*, 12mo or 12°, a sheet into twelve leaves, or twenty-four pages. So, also, sixteens, 16mo or 16°; eighteens, 18mo or 18°; twenty-fours, 24mo or 24°; thirty-twos, 32mo or 32°; forty-eights, 48mo or 48°; sixty-fours, 64mo or 64°, are the several designations of sheets when folded into sixteen, eighteen, twenty-four, thirty-two, forty-eight, and sixty-four leaves; making each twice the number of pages.

IV. — ABBREVIATIONS AND REPRESENTATIVE LETTERS.

The following is perhaps the largest list of miscellaneous abbreviations that has yet been published; but its chief value consists in affording to writers and printers an opportunity of selecting those modes of abbreviating words which seem best fitted for the purposes they may have in view. To further this object, the compiler has presented the various forms in which any given word or phrase has been employed, where more than one has been in use; appending a dagger (†) to such as appear unsuitable, either in consequence of their being already employed for other words, because they are less intelligible than they should be, or have but slight authority for their adoption. But the mark is not intended to imply, that these should never be preferred; for cases will arise, where, from the connection or the narrowness of the printed line, it may be desirable to use them. To those abbreviations, however, which are regarded as unfit to appear under any circumstances, but which are used by some writers, he has put a double dagger (‡).

It need scarcely be said, that only a few of the abbreviations here exhibited should appear in ordinary composition. But they are very serviceable in catalogues, directories, tabular lists of articles, and family registers; and in works on grammar, lexicography, arithmetic, geography, &c.; where certain terms often occur, and their full spelling would impede the course of a reader, or swell the size of a book. There are also some words and phrases, which, wherever they may occur, whether in works relating to science and art or to general literature, are commonly written as abbreviations. These are either mostly a few Latin words, which, without being Anglicized, are found useful in supplying the place of circumlocutions in the language; as, &c., instead of "and other persons" or "things:" or they are titles prefixed to proper names; as, "Mr. Richardson, Dr. Finlay, Capt. Jameson," &c.: or are terms made use of in reference to passages in books; as, "See pp. 500, seq.; and comp. sect. 6."

When referring, in notes or at the beginning or end of extracts, to works that are well known, it is usual to abbreviate the longer words in their titles; as, "Gibbon's Hist. of the Dec. and Fall of the Rom. Emp., vol. ii. p. 288." In the list will be found abbreviations of only some American and British periodicals; for it would be a vain attempt to give more than a few specimens of the abbreviations adopted in the names of such publications, and altogether impossible to exhibit those used in the names of books in general. Indeed, such abbreviations are quite too much in vogue; and it is recommended, that, in all cases where the common reader is supposed to be unacquainted with the works to which reference is made, the titles be printed in full, or at least such portions as will clearly indicate what the writer intends. In treatises, however, addressed merely to the learned professions, it may be sufficient generally to indicate authorities by the first letter or letters in each word. Copious lists of those relating to botany, law, and organic remains, will be found in Savage's " Dictionary of the Art of Printing," pp. 59–81, 430–37, and 548.

When the names of the books of Scripture are specified with chapter and verse, they should, except those of but one syllable, be given in their abbreviated forms; as, " Gen. xlix. 26. Matt. vii. 28." When spoken of without reference to any particular passage, the names should be spelled out; as, " The Gospel of Matthew is the first book in the New Testament."

The more common baptismal names, if put in lists where the saving of room is an object, should be printed with such portions as will lead to a true knowledge of them. They may all, indeed, be severally abbreviated with only the initial letter, when the persons whom they represent are so well known that no mistake can readily take place, or when it is deemed of little importance whether they be known or not. But in books in which elegance of composition, intelligibility of sense, or uniformity of printing, is desirable, the names of persons, at least those by which they are commonly designated, ought to appear in full. Names of ladies should, if possible, be so given.

Titles of eminent men, when put immediately after their names, are almost universally abbreviated; as, " Walter Kinderhook, D.D." But, when the titles are predicated of persons, they are better written in full; as, " The Rev. Joshua Rankin is a Doctor of Divinity; and Matthew Finlayson, Bachelor of Arts."

To preclude mistakes, the names of cities, towns, and other places, should not, if avoidable, be abbreviated.

The names of states and kingdoms should also be written or printed in full, unless they occur in tabular matter or in geographical books where the abbreviations have been previously explained; or unless they are placed immediately after the names of cities, &c.; as, "There being a Boston in *England* as well as in *Massachusetts*, besides several others in the United States, be careful that, in addressing any letter to a place bearing that name, you state its proper destination, and say either ' Boston, *Eng.*;' ' Boston, *Mass.*;' ' Boston, *N. Y.*;' or ' Boston, *O.*;' as the case may require."

With the exception of May, June, and July, and perhaps also March and April, the names of the months should be abbreviated when they stand in connection with the day of the month; as, "Dec. 25, 1854." In all other instances, they should, if possible, be spelled out; as, "Robert Burns was born in the month of January, 1759."

All words which, when abbreviated, are shortened only by one letter, should be written or printed in full. *Jb.* for "Job," *Jno.* for "John," and *dy.* for "day," are, obviously, improper and unnecessary.

The usual abbreviations made use of in works on chemistry and in medical prescriptions, &c., will be found inserted in the following table; but a more complete list appears in Savage's "Dictionary of Printing," pp. 237–44, 481–84.

Some abbreviations are used only in the middle of sentences, and begun with small characters; others, as the initials of titles, are always printed in capitals; while others, again, appear sometimes with initial capitals, and sometimes with initial small letters. When there are two modes of printing them, both will be found exhibited in the table, that the eye may be accustomed to both forms; but the mode of using them will depend on the principles laid down in the article on capitals, pp. 257–68.

To an author who finds it necessary to adopt abbreviations not in common use, it is recommended that he present, at the beginning of his treatise, a list of all that may be required for his purpose, with the requisite explanations; and that, if at all practicable, he preserve the same forms throughout the work.

Contractions formed by the insertion of apostrophes — as, *Sup't* for "Superintendent," or *Veg'ta's* for "Vegetables" — are altogether excluded from the following list, because deemed fit to be used only in cases of extreme necessity. So, also, those contractions which sometimes appear at the foot of advertisements, but which are not meant to be read by the public; as, "isF&Tu&osMWThSattf;" a direction which would have a more common-sense-like appearance, if it stood thus: "i.F.&Tu. & o.M.W.Th.S. t.f.;" and be better adapted to express the meaning, — "To be inserted inside on Friday and Tuesday, and outside on Monday, Wednesday, Thursday, and Saturday, till forbidden."

As the exhibiting of Latin abbreviations, unless used in English composition, falls not within the scope of the present work, it will be sufficient merely to refer to the Latin dictionaries for those pertaining to the classics; and to Savage's book, already mentioned, pp. 204 and 689–700, for such as are used in Domesday-Book and in the old Public Records.

ABBREVIATIONS AND CONTRACTIONS.

A. — Five hundred (*anc.*).
A̅. — Five thousand (*anc.*).
A. — Augustus; Aulus.
A. — Accepted; Answer.
A.† or a.† — Adjective.
A. or a. — Afternoon.
A.† a.† or ac. — Acre, acres.
A. A. P. S. — American Association for the Promotion of Science.
A. A. S. — *Academiæ Americanæ Socius*, Fellow of the American Academy (of Arts and Sciences).
A.A.S.S. — *Americanæ Antiquarianæ Societatis Socius*, Member of the American Antiquarian Society.
A.B. — *Artium Baccalaureus*, Bachelor of Arts.
Ab. or ab. — About.
Abbr. or abbr. — Abbreviated.
A.B.C.F.M. — American Board of Commissioners for Foreign Missions.
Abl. or abl.; Ab.† or ab.† — Ablative (case).
Abp. or Archb.† — Archbishop.
Absol. or absol. — Absolute.
A. C. — *Ante Christum*, before Christ.
A.C. — Archchancellor.
Ac. or ac. — Acre, acres.
Acc. or acc.; Ac.† or ac.† — Accusative (case).
Acct. or acct. — Account.
A.C.S. — American Colonization Society.

A.D. — *Anno Domini*, in the year of our Lord; Archduke.
Ad lib. or ad lib. — *Ad libitum*, at pleasure.
Adj. or adj. — Adjective.
Adjt. — Adjutant.
Adjt.-Gen. — Adjutant-General.
Adm. or Adml.† — Admiral, Admiralty.
Adm. Co. — Admiralty Court.
Admr. — Administrator.
Admx. — Administratrix.
Ad v. or ad v. — *Ad valorem*, at the value.
Adv. — Advent; Advocate.
Adv. or adv. — Adverb.
Æt. or æt.; Æ.† or æ.† — *Ætatis*, of age, aged.
A. & F. B. S. — American and Foreign Bible Society.
A.F.† or A. fir. — Firkin of ale.
Af. — Africa.
Ag. — Argentum (Silver).
Agric. — Agriculture.
Agt. — Agent.
A.H. — *Anno Hegiræ*, in the year of the Hegira.
A. H. M. S. — American Home Missionary Society.
Al. — Aluminum.
Ala. or Al.† — Alabama.
Ald. — Alderman or Aldermen.
Alex. — Alexander.
Alt. or alt. — Altitude.
A.M. — *Anno mundi*, in the year of the world.
A.M. — *Artium Magister*, Master of Arts.

A.M., A.M. or a.m. — *Ante meridiem*, before noon, morning.
Am.† or Amer. — America.
Am. or Amer.† — American.
Am. Alma. — American Almanac.
Am. Inst. of Instruc. — American Institute of Instruction.
Am. Quar. Obs. — American Quarterly Observer.
Am. Quar. Reg. — American Quarterly Register.
Am. Quar. Rev. — American Quarterly Review.
Amb. — Ambassador.
AMM. — *Amalgama*, amalgamation.
Amst. — Amsterdam.
An. — *Anno*, in the year.
An. A. C. — *Anno ante Christum*, in the year before Christ.
Anal. — Analysis.
Anal. Mag. — Analectic Magazine.
Anat. — Anatomy.
Anc. or anc. — Ancient, anciently.
And. — Andrew.
Ang.-Sax. — Anglo-Saxon.
Ann. Reg. — Annual Register.
Anom. or anom. — Anomalous.
Anon. or An.† — Anonymous.
Ans. — Answer.
Ant. — Antiquities.
Anth. — Anthony.
Antw. — Antwerp.
Aor. or aor. — Aorist.
A.O.S.S. — *Americanæ Orientalis Societatis Socius*, Member of the American Oriental Society.
Ap. — Apostle; Appius.
ap.† — *Apud*, in the writings of; as quoted by.
Ap.† Apr or Apl.† — April.

A.P.G. or Ast. P.G.† — Professor of Astronomy in Gresham College.
Apo. or apo. — Apogee.
Apoc. — Apocalypse.
A.R. — *Anna Regina*, Queen Anne.
A.R. — *Anno regni*, in the year of the reign.
Ar. or ar.; Arr.† or arr.† — Arrived, arrivals.
Arab., Arn.† or Ar.† — Arabic.
Arch. — Archibald.
Arch. — Architecture.
Archb.† — Archbishop.
Arith. — Arithmetic.
Ark. — Arkansas.
Arm. — Armoric; Armenian.
A. R. R. — *Anno regni regis*, in the year of the reign of the king.
Arrond. or arrond. — Arrondissement.
A.R.S.S. — *Antiquariorum Regiæ Societatis Socius*, Fellow of the Royal Society of Antiquaries.
Art. or art. — Article.
As. — Arsenic.
As.† — Asia.
A. S. A. — American Statistical Association.
A. S. S. U. — American Sunday School Union.
Ass.‡ Asst.† or Assist. Sec. — Assistant Secretary.
Astrol. — Astrology.
Astron. — Astronomy.
A.T. — Archtreasurer.
A.T.S. — American Temperance Society.
A. T. S. — American Tract Society.

Att. — Attic.
Atty. or Att.† — Attorney.
Atty.-Gen. — Attorney-General.
Attys. — Attorneys.
Au. — *Aunes*, French ells.
Au. — *Aurum* (Gold).
A. U. A. — American Unitarian Association.
Aub. Theol. Sem. — Auburn Theological Seminary.
A.U.C. — *Anno urbis conditæ*, in the year after the building of the city (Rome).
Aug. — August; Augustus.
Aust. or Austr.† — Austria, Austrian.
Austral. — Australasia.
Auth. Ver. — Authorized Version (of the Bible).
Av. or av.† — Average; avenue.
Avoir. or av.† — Avoirdupois.
B. — Three hundred (*anc.*).
B̄. — Three thousand (*anc.*).
B. — *Basso*, bass.
B. — Boron.
B. or b.; Bk.† or bk.† — Book.
B. or b. — Bay; born.
B.A. — Bachelor of Arts.
B.A. — British America.
Ba. — Barium.
Bail. or bail. — Bailiwick.
Bal. — Balance.
Bank. Mag. — Banker's Magazine.
Bar. — Baruch.
Bar. or bar. — Barleycorn.
Bar.† bbl.‡ or bl. — Barrel.
Bart. or Bt.† — Baronet.
B.C. — Before Christ.
B.C.L. — Bachelor of Civil Law.
B.D. — *Baccalaureus Divinitatis*, Bachelor of Divinity.
Bd. or bd. — Bound

Bds. or bds. — Boards (bound in).
Benj. or Ben.† — Benjamin.
Berks. — Berkshire.
B. & L. D. — Duke of Brunswick and Lüneburg.
B. F. or B. fir. — Firkin of beer.
Bi. — Bismuth.
Bib. Sac. — Bibliotheca Sacra.
Bk. — Bank.
Bk.† or bk.† — Book.
B.LL. — *Baccalaureus Legum*, Bachelor of Laws.
Bl. or bl. — Barrel.
Bls. or bls.; Bbl. or bbl. — Barrel.
Blackw. Mag. — Blackwood's Magazine.
B.M. — *Baccalaureus Medicinæ*, Bachelor of Medicine.
B.M. — British Mail.
B.M. — British Museum.
Bor. or bor. — Borough.
Bos. — Boston.
Bot. — Botany.
Bp. — Bishop.
B.R. — *Banco Regis*, or *Reginæ*, the King's or Queen's Bench.
Br. — Bromine.
Br. or br. — Brig.
Br. — Brother. Brs. — Brothers.
Braz. — Brazil.
Brig. — Brigade; Brigadier.
Brig.-Gen. — Brigadier-General.
Brit. or Br.† — British.
Brit. Alma. — British Almanac.
Brit. Crit. — British Critic.
Brit. Mus. — British Museum.
Brit. Quar. Rev. — British Quarterly Review.
Brit. and For. Rev. — British and Foreign Review.
Bro. — Brother. Bros. — Brothers.
Br. Univ. — Brown University.

Brus. — Brussels.
Brux. — Bruxelles.
Bt.† — Baronet.
Bu. or bu.; Bush.† or bush.† — Bushel, bushels.
Bucks. — Buckinghamshire.
B.V. — *Beata Virgo*, Blessed Virgin.
B.V. — *Bene vale*, farewell.
C. — Cæsar; Caius.
C. — Carbon.
C. — A hundred; a century.
C̄. — A hundred thousand (*anc.*).
CC. — Two hundred.
CCC. — Three hundred.
CCCC.† or CD.—Four hundred.
C. or c. — Cape.
C. or c. — *Centum*, a hundred.
C. or c. — Cent, cents.
C. or c. — Centime, centimes.
C. or c. — Coomb, coombs.
C.† or c.†; Ch.‡ or ch.‡; Chap. or chap. — Chapter, chapters.
C.† or c.†; Cor. or cor. — Corner.
C.† or c.†; Cub. or cub.—Cubic.
c. — Childless.
Ca. — Calcium.
Cæs. Aug. — Cæsar Augustus.
cæt. par. — *Cæteris paribus*, other things being equal.
Cal. — *Calendæ*, the Calends.
Cal. — California.
Cam. — Cambridge.
Can. — Canada.
Can. or can. — Canton (a portion of territory).
Cant. — Canticles.
Cap. or cap. — Capital.
Caps. — Capitals.
Cap. or cap. — *Caput, capitulum*, chapter.
Capt. — Captain.

Capt.-Gen. — Captain-General.
Car. — Carpentry.
Car. or car. — Carat or carats.
C.A.S. — *Connecticuttensis Academiæ Socius*, Fellow of the Connecticut Academy.
Cash. — Cashier.
Cath. — Catherine; Catholic.
C.B. — Cape Breton.
C.B. — Companion of the Bath.
C.C. — Caius College; County Commissioner; County Court.
C.C.‡ — Account Current.
C.C.C. — Corpus Christi College.
CCIƆƆ. — Ten thousand.
CCCIƆƆƆ. — A hundred thousand.
C.C.P. — Court of Common Pleas.
CD. — Four hundred.
Cd. — Cadmium.
C.E. — Canada East.
C.E. — Civil Engineer.
Ce. — Cerium.
Cel. or Celt.† — Celtic.
Cen. — Century.
Cent. — *Centum*, a hundred.
Cf. or cf. — *Confer*, compare.
C.H. — Court-house.
Ch. — China.
Ch.‡ or ch.‡—Chapter, chapters.
Ch. or ch. — Chain, chains.
Ch. or ch. — Child or children.
Ch. or C.† — Church.
Ch. Ch.† or C. Ch. — Christ Church.
Ch.† or Chal. — Chaldee.
Ch.† or ch.†; Chal. or chal. — Chaldron or chaldrons.
Chanc. — Chancellor.
Chap. or chap. — Chapter, chap- [ters.
Chas. — Charles.

Chem. — Chemistry.
Chris. Ex. — Christian Exami-[ner.
Chris. Month. Spec. — Christian Monthly Spectator.
Chris. Quar. Spec. — Christian Quarterly Spectator.
Chris. Rev. — Christian Review.
Chron. — Chronicles.
Chron. — Chronology.
Chs. — Churches.
CIƆ. (contracted, M.). — A thou-[sand.
Cic. — Cicero.
Circ. — Circle or circles.
Cit. — Citizen.
C.J. — Chief Justice.
C.J.C. — Caius Julius Cæsar.
Cl. — Chlorine.
Cl. — Claudius; Clergyman.
Cl.† or Clk. — Clerk.
Cl. Dom. Com. — Clerk of the House of Commons.
Cld. or cld. — Cleared.
CM. — Nine hundred.
Cn. — Cnæus.
Co. — Company; Cobalt.
Co. or co.; Cy.† or cy.†—County.
Coch. — *Cochleare*, a spoonful.
Col. — Colonel; Colossians.
Col. — Column.
Cold.† or cold.† — Colored.
Coll. — Collector.
Coll. — *Collega*, Colleague.
Coll. — *Collegium*, College.
Com. — Commerce; Committee; Commentary; Commissioner; Commodore.
Com. or com. — Commune.
Comdg. — Commanding.
Com. Arr. — Committee of Arrangements.
Comp. or comp. — Compare; compound.

Compar. or compar.; Comp.† or comp.† — Comparative.
Com. Ver. — Common Version (of the Bible).
Con.† or con.†; Conj. or conj. — Conjunction.
Con. or con. — Connective.
Con. — *Contra*, against, in opposition.
Con. Cr. or C.C.† — Contra credit.
Conch. — Conchology.
Cong. or C. — Congress.
Cong. — *Congius*, a gallon.
Conj. or conj. — Conjunction.
Conn. or Con.† — Connecticut.
Const. or Cons.† — Constable; Constitution.
Contr. or contr. — Contraction.
Cop. — Coptic.
Cor. — Corinthians.
Cor. or cor. — Corner.
Corn. — Cornish.
Corol. — Corollary.
Cor. Sec. or Secy.† — Corresponding Secretary.
C.P. — Common Pleas.
C.P. — Court of Probate.
C.P.S. — *Custos Privati Sigilli*, Keeper of the Privy Seal.
C.R. — *Carolus Rex*, King Charles.
C.R. — *Custos Rotulorum*, Keeper of the Rolls.
C.R.P. — *Calendarium Rotulorum Patentium*, Calendar of the Patent Rolls.
Cr. — Chromium.
Cr. — Creditor; credit.
Crim. Con. — Criminal conversation.
Crit. — Criterion, criteria.
Crit. Rev. — Critical Review.

C.S. — Court of Sessions.
C.S. — *Custos Sigilli*, Keeper of the Seal.
Ct. — Count.
Ct.† or Conn. — Connecticut.
Ct. or ct. — Cent; Court.
Cts. or cts. — Cents.
Cu. — Cuprum (Copper).
Cub. or cub. — Cubic.
curt. or cur.† — Current.
C.W. — Canada West.
Cwt. or cwt. — Hundred-weight.
Cy.† or cy.† — County.
Cyclo. — Cyclopedia.
D. — Decius; Dutch.
D. — Didymium.
D. — Five hundred.
D̄. — Five hundred thousand.
D. or d. — Decime, decimes.
D. or d. — *Denarius*, a penny.
D. or d. — *Denarii*, pence.
D. or d. — Denier, deniers.
D. or d. — Died.
D.† or d.†; Di. or di. — Dimes.
D.† or d.†; Deg. or deg. — Degree or degrees.
D.† or d.†; Diam. or diam. — Diameter.
D. or d.; da.† dy.‡ — Day, days.
da.† or dr. — Daughter.
Dan. — Daniel; Danish.
Dart. — Dartmouth.
Dat., dat. or D. — Dative (case).
D. B. or Domesd. B. — Domesday-book.
D.C. — *Da Capo*, again.
D.C. — District of Columbia.
D.C.L. — Doctor of Civil Law.
D.D. — *Divinitatis Doctor*, Doctor of Divinity.
Dea. — Deacon.
Dec. — December.

Dec. or dec. — Declension.
Dec. or dec. — Declination.
Deg. or deg. — Degree, degrees.
Del. — Delaware; Delegate.
Del. or del. — *Delineavit*, drew.
Dem. — Democrat, Democratic.
Dem. or dem. — Demonstrative (pronoun).
Den. — Denmark.
Dep. — Deputy.
Dept. or dept.; Dep.† or dep.† — Department.
Deut. — Deuteronomy.
D.F. — Dean of Faculty.
Dft. or Deft.† — Defendant.
D.G. — *Dei gratiá*, by the grace of God.
D.G. — *Deo gratias*, thanks to God.
Diam. or diam. — Diameter.
Dict. — Dictator; Dictionary.
Dim. or dim. — Diminutive.
Dis. or dis. — Distance, distant.
Disc. or disc.; Disct.† or disct.;† Dis.† or dis.† — Discount.
Diss. or diss. — Dissertation.
Dist. or dist. — District.
Dist.-Atty. — District-Attorney.
Div. — Division.
Div. or div. — Dividend.
D.M. — Doctor of Music.
Do. or do. — *Ditto*, the same.
Doct.† D.‡ or Dr. — Doctor.
Dol., dol., or doll.† — Dollar.
Dols. or dols. — Dollars.
D.O.M. — *Deo optimo maximo* to God, the best, the greatest.
Dor. — Doric.
Doz. or doz. — Dozen, dozens.
D.P. — Doctor of Philosophy.
Dpt. — Deponent.
Dr.‡ — Dear.

Dr. — Debtor; Doctor.
Dr. or dr. — Dram, drams.
dr. — daughter.
D.T. — *Doctor Theologiæ*, Doctor of Divinity.
Dub. — Dublin.
Dub. Univ. Mag. — Dublin University Magazine.
D.V. — *Deo volente*, God willing.
Dwt. or dwt. — Pennyweight.
Dy.‡ or d. — Day, days.
E. — Two hundred & fifty (*anc.*).
E.‡ — Earl.
E. (*after titles*). — Edinburgh.
E. — Erbium; East.
E. by S. — East by south.
E. or e. — Eagle, eagles.
E. or e. — Ecu, ecus.
ea. — Each.
East. Isl. — Eastern Islands.
E.B. — English Bible (common).
Eben. — Ebenezer.
Ecc.† or Eccles. — Ecclesiastical.
Eccl. — Ecclesiastes.
Ecclus. — Ecclesiasticus.
Eclec. Mag. — Eclec. Magazine.
Eclec. Rev. — Eclec. Review.
Ed. — Editor. Eds. — Editors.
Ed.† or ed.† — Edition.
Edin. or Ed.† — Edinburgh.
Edit. or edit. — Edition.
Edm. — Edmund.
Edw. — Edward.
E.E. — Errors excepted.
E.E. — Ell or ells English.
E. Fl. — Ell or ells Flemish.
E. Fr. — Ell or ells French.
E.G.‡ or E. g.; e. g. or ex. g.† — *Exempli gratiâ*, for example.
Eg.† — Egypt.
E.I. — East Indies.
E.I.C. — East-India Company.

E.I.M. Coll. — East-India Military College.
Elec. — Electricity.
Eliz. — Elizabeth.
E. lon. — East longitude.
E.N.E. — East-north-east.
Ency. — Encyclopedia.
Eng. — England, English.
Engd. or engd. — Engraved.
Ent. — Entomology.
Ent. or ent. — Entrance. [nary.
Env. Ext. — Envoy Extraordi-
Ep. or Epis.† — Epistle.
Eph. — Ephesians; Ephraim.
E.S. — Ell or ells Scotch.
E.S.E. — East-south-east.
Esq. — Esquire.
Esqs. — Esquires.
Esth. — Esther.
E.T. — English Translation
et al. — *Et alibi*, and elsewhere.
et al. — *Et alii*, and others.
et seq. — *Et sequentia*, and what follows.
etc.† or &c. — *Et cæteri, et cæteræ, et cætera*, and others; and so forth.
Eth. — Ethiopic.
Evang. — Evangelical.
Eve.† or eve.;† Even. or even. - Evening.
Ex. — Example.
Exc. — Excellency; Exception.
Exch. — Exchequer.
Exclam. — Exclamation.
Exec. or Exr.† — Executor.
Exec. Com. — Executive Committee.
Execx. — Executrix.
Exod. or Ex.† — Exodus.
Exon. D. — Exeter Domesday book.

Ez. — Ezra.
Ezd. — Ezdra.
Ezek. — Ezekiel.
F. — Fluorine.
F. — Forty (*anc.*).
F̄. — Forty thousand (*anc*).
F. or f. — Feminine (gender).
F. or f. — *Fiat*, let it be made.
F. or f. — Florin, florins.
F.† f.† Fr. or fr. — Franc, francs.
F.† or f.;† Ft. or ft. — Foot, feet.
F., Fr.† Fri. or Frid.† — Friday.
Fa.† Fl.† Fla. or Flor. — Florida.
Fahr. — Fahrenheit.
Far. or f. — Farthing, farthings.
F.A.S. — Fellow of the Antiquarian Society.
Fath. or fath.; Fth.† or fth.† — Fathom or fathoms.
F.D. — *Fidei Defensor*, Defender of the Faith.
F.† or Fl. E. — Flemish ell or ells.
Fe. — Ferrum (Iron).
Feb. — February.
Fem. or fem.; F. or f. — Feminine.
ff. — The Pandects.
F.E.S. — Fellow of the Entomological Society.
F.G.S. — Fellow of the Geological Society.
F.H.S. — Fellow of the Horticultural Society.
Fig. or fig. — Figure, figures.
Fig. or fig. — Figuratively.
Fin. — Finland.
Finn. — Finnish.
Fir. or fir. — Firkin, firkins.
Fl. or fl. — Flourished.
Fl. E. — Flemish ell or ells.
Flor. or Fla. — Florida.
F.L.S. — Fellow of the Linnæan Society.

F. or f. m. — *Fiat mixtura*, let a mixture be made.
Fol. or fol.; Fo.† or fo.†; F.‡ or f.‡ — Folio, folios.
For. — Foreign.
For. Quar. Rev. — Foreign Quarterly Review.
Fort. — Fortification.
Fr. — France, French.
Fr.† or Fran. — Francis.
Fr. or fr. — Franc, francs.
fr. or f.† — From.
F.R.A.S. — Fellow of the Royal Astronomical Society.
Fras. Mag. — Fraser's Magazine.
Fr. E. — French ell or ells.
Fred. — Frederic or Frederick.
Freq. or freq. — Frequentative.
F.R.G.S. — Fellow of the Royal Geographical Society.
Fri. — Friday.
F.R.S. — Fellow of the Royal Society.
F.R.S. E. — Fellow of the Royal Society, Edinburgh.
F.R.S. L. — Fellow of the Royal Society, London.
F.R.S.L. — Fellow of the Royal Society of Literature.
F.S.A. — Fellow of the Society of Arts.
F. or f. s. a. — *Fiat secundum artem*, make it according to art.
F.S.A. E. — Fellow of the Society of Antiquaries, Edinburgh.
Ft. or ft. — Foot, feet.
Ft. or ft. — Fort.
Fth.† fth.† — Fathom, fathoms.
Fur. or fur. — Furlong, furlongs.
Fut. or fut. — Future (tense).
F.Z.S. — Fellow of the Zoological Society.

ABBREVIATIONS.

G. — Four hundred (*anc.*).
G̅. — Forty thousand (*anc.*).
G. — Gaius; Gellius.
G. — Glucinum; Genitive (case).
G. or g. — Guinea, guineas.
G. or g. — Gulf.
G.‡ Ger. or Germ.† — Germany, German.
Ga. or Geo. — Georgia.
Gal. — Galatians.
Gal. or gal. — Gallon, gallons.
Gall.† or gall.† — Gallon, gallons.
G.B. — Great Britain.
G.C.B. — Grand Cross of the Bath.
G.C.H. — Grand Cross of Hanover.
Gen. — General; Geneva.
Gen. — Genesis (Book of).
Gen. or gen. — Genitive (case).
Gent. — Gentleman.
Gent. Mag. — Gentleman's Magazine.
G. gr. or g. gr. — Great gross.
Geo. — George; Georgia.
Geog. or Geo.† — Geography.
Geol. — Geology.
Geom. — Geometry.
Ger. — Germany, German.
Ger. or ger. — Gerund.
Gi. or gi. — Gill, gills.
Gib. — Gibraltar.
Glas. — Glasgow.
Goth. or Go.† — Gothic.
Gött. — Göttingen.
Gov. — Governor.
Gov.-Gen. — Governor-General.
G.R. — *Georgius Rex*, King George.
Gr. — Greek.
Gr. or gr. — Grain, grains.
Gram. — Grammar.

Griesb. — Griesbach.
Gro. or gro. — Gross.
Grot. — Grotius.
Gtt. or gtt. — *Gutta*, a drop.
Gtt. or gtt. — *Guttæ*, drops.
Guin. or guin. — Guinea, guineas.
H. — Two hundred (*anc.*).
H̅. — Two hundred thousand.
H. — Hydrogen.
H. or h. — Harbor, height.
H. or h. — Hour, hours.
h. — Husband.
Hab. — Habakkuk.
Hag. — Haggai.
Ham. Coll. — Hamilton College.
Hants. — Hampshire.
Harv. or Har.† — Harvard.
H.B.C. — Hudson's Bay Company.
H.B.M. — His or Her Britannic Majesty.
Hdkf. or hdkf. — Handkerchief.
h.e. — *Hoc est*, that is, or this is.
Heb. — Hebrew; Hebrews.
Hebr.† — Hebrew; Hebrews.
H.E.I.C. — Honorable East-India Company.
Hep. sulph. — Hepar sulphuris.
Her. — Heraldry.
Hf.-bd. or hf.-bd. — Half-bound.
Hg. — Hydrargyrum (Mercury).
Hhd. or hhd.; Hd.† or hd.† — Hogshead, hogsheads.
Hil. — Hilary.
Hind. — Hindostan.
Hist. — History; Historical.
H.J.S. — *Hic jacet sepultus*, Here lies buried.
H.M. — His or Her Majesty.
H.M.P. — *Hoc monumentum posuit*, erected this monument.
H.M.S. — His or Her Majesty's Ship or Service.

Hon. — Honorable.
Hond.† or hond.† — Honored.
Hort. — Horticulture.
Hos. — Hosea.
H.P. — Half-pay.
H.R. — House of Representatives.
H.R.E. — Holy Roman Emperor.
H.R H. — His Royal Highness.
H.R.I.P. — *Hic requiescit in pace*, Here rests in peace.
Hrs.† or hrs.;† H. or h. — Hours.
H.S. — *Hic situs*, Here lies.
hum. or humb. — Humble.
Hund. or hund.; Hun.† hun.† — Hundred, hundreds.
I. — Iod'ne.
Ī. — One thousand (*anc.*).
I. II. III. — One, two, three; or first, second, third.
I.† Is.† or Isl. — Island.
Ia.† In.‡ or Ind. — Indiana.
Ib. or ib.; Ibid.† or ibid.† — *Ibidem*, in the same place.
IƆ.† (by contraction, D.). — Five hundred.
IƆC.† or DC. — Six hundred.
IƆCC.† or DCC. — Seven hundred.
IƆCCC.† or DCCC. — Eight hundred.
IƆCCCC.† or DCCCC. — Nine hundred.
IƆƆ. — Five thousand.
IƆƆƆ. — Fifty thousand.
Icel. or Ice.†—Iceland, Icelandic.
Ich. — Ichthyology.
Id. or id. — *Idem, eadem; iidem, eædem*, the same (author or authors).
I.e. or i.e. — *Id est*, that is.
I.H.S. — *Jesus hominum Salvator*, Jesus, the Saviour of men.

IIII.† or IV. — Four; fourth.
ij. — Two (*med.*).
Ill. — Illinois.
Illus. — Illustration.
Imp. or imp. — Imperial.
Imper. or imper. — Imperative (mood).
Imperf. or imperf.; Impf.† or impf.† — Imperfect (tense).
Impers. or impers.; Imp.† or imp.† — Impersonal (verb).
In. or in. — Inch, inches.
Inch. — Inchoative (verb).
incog. — *Incognito*, unknown.
Incor. or incor. — Incorporated.
Ind. — India, Indian; Indiana.
Ind. Ter. — Indian Territory.
Indef. or indef. — Indefinite.
Indic. or indic.; Ind.† or ind.† — Indicative (mood).
Infin. or infin.; Inf.† or inf.† — Infinitive (mood).
in lim. — *In limine*, at the outset.
in loc.† — *in loco*, in the place; on the passage.
I.N.R.I. — *Jesus Nazarenus, Rex Judæorum*, Jesus of Nazareth, King of the Jews.
Ins. — Inspector.
Ins.-Gen. — Inspector-General.
Insep. or insep. — Inseparable.
inst. — Instant, of this month.
Int. or int. — Interest.
Interj. or interj.; Int.† or int.† — Interjection.
in trans. — *In transitu*, on the passage.
Io. — Iowa.
Ion. — Ionic.
I.O.O.F. — Independent Order of Odd Fellows.
Ipecac. — Ipecacuanha.

Ir. — Iridium.
Ir. — Irish.
Ire. or Ir.† — Ireland.
Irreg. or irreg. — Irregular.
Isa. — Isaiah.
Isl. or isl.; Is.† is.† l.† — Island.
It. or Ital.† — Italy.
Ital. or It.† — Italian; Italic.
Itin. — Itinerary.
IV. — Four or fourth.
IX. — Nine or ninth.
J. — Judge; Julius.
j. — One (*med.*).
J.A. — Judge-Advocate.
Jac. — Jacob.
Jam. — Jamaica.
Jan. — January.
Jap. — Japan.
Jas. or Ja.† — James.
J.C. — Julius Cæsar.
J.C.D. — *Juris Civilis Doctor*, Doctor of Civil Law.
J.D. — *Jurum Doctor*, Doctor of Laws.
Jer. — Jeremiah.
J.H.S. — *Jesus hominum Salvator*, Jesus, the Saviour of men.
Jno.‡ — John.
Jona. — Jonathan.
Jos. — Joseph.
Josh. — Joshua.
Jour. — Journal.
J.P. — Justice of the Peace.
J. Prob. — Judge of Probate.
J.R. — *Jacobus Rex*, King James.
Jr.† jr.†; Jun. or jun. — Junior.
J.U.D. or J.V.D. — *Juris utriusque Doctor*, Doctor of both Laws (of the Canon and the Civil Law).
Jud. — Judith.
Judg. — Judges

Judge-Adv. — Judge-Advocate.
Jul. — Julius.
Jul.‡ — July.
Jul. Per. — Julian Period.
Jun.‡ — June.
Jun. — Junius.
Jun. or jun. — Junior.
Jus. or Just.† — Justice.
Jus. P. — Justice of the Peace.
Just. — Justinian.
K. — Kalium (Potassium).
K. — King.
K. — Two hundred & fifty (*anc.*).
K̄. — Two hundred and fifty thousand (*anc.*).
K.A. — Knight of St. Andrew, in Russia.
K.A.N. — Knight of Alexander Newski, in Russia.
Kan. — Kansas.
K.B. — King's Bench.
K.B. — Knight of the Bath.
K.B.A. — Knight of St. Bento d'Avis, in Portugal.
K.B.E. — Knight of the Black Eagle, in Prussia.
K.C. — King's Council.
K.C. — Knight of the Crescent, in Turkey.
K.C.B. — Knight Commander of the Bath.
K.C.H. — Knight Commander of Hanover.
K.C.S. — Knight of Charles III. of Spain.
K.E. — Knight of the Elephant, in Denmark.
Ken.† or Ky. — Kentucky.
K.F. — Knight of Ferdinand of Spain.
K.F.M. — Knight of St. Ferdinand and Merit, in Sicily.

APPENDIX.

K.G. — Knight of the Garter.
K.G.C. — Knight of the Grand Cross.
K.G.C.B. — Knight of the Grand Cross of the Bath.
K.G.F. — Knight of the Golden Fleece, in Spain.
K.G.H. — Knight of the Guelph of Hanover.
K.G.V. — Knight of Gustavus Vasa of Sweden.
K.H. — Knight of Hanover.
Kil. or kil. — Kilderkin, kilderkins.
Kingd. or kingd.; Km.† or km.† — Kingdom.
K.J. — Knight of St. Joachim.
K.L. or K.L.A. — Knight of Leopold of Austria.
K.L.H. — Knight of the Legion of Honor.
K.M. — Knight of Malta.
Km.† or km.† — Kingdom.
K. Mess. — King's Messenger.
K.M.H. — Knight of Merit, in Holstein.
K.M.J. — Knight of Maximilian Joseph of Bavaria.
K.M.T. — Knight of Maria Theresa of Austria.
K.N. — Know Nothing.
Knick. — Knickerbocker.
K.N.S. — Knight of the Royal North Star, in Sweden.
Knt., Kt.† or K.† — Knight.
K.P. — Knight of St. Patrick.
K.R.E. — Knight of the Red Eagle, in Prussia.
K.S. — Knight of the Sword, in Sweden.
K.S.A. — Knight of St. Anne of Russia.

K.S.E. — Knight of St. Esprit, in France.
K.S.F. — Knight of St. Fernando of Spain.
K.S.F.M. — Knight of St. Ferdinand and Merit, in Naples.
K.S.G. — Knight of St. George of Russia.
K.S.H. — Knight of St. Hubert of Bavaria.
K.S.J. — Knight of St. Januarius of Naples.
K.S.L. — Knight of the Sun and Lion, in Persia.
K. S. M. & S. G. — Knight of St. Michael and St. George of the Ionian Islands.
K.S.P. — Knight of St. Stanislaus of Poland.
K.S.S. — Knight of the Southern Star of the Brazils.
K.S.S. — Knight of the Sword, in Sweden.
K.S.W. — Knight of St. Wladimir of Russia.
K.T. — Knight of the Thistle.
Kt.† — Knight.
K.T.S. — Knight of the Tower and Sword, in Portugal.
K.W. — Knight of William of the Netherlands.
K.W.E. — Knight of the White Eagle, in Poland.
Ky. — Kentucky.
L. — Fifty or fiftieth.
L̄. — Fifty thousand (anc.).
L. — Latin; Lucius; Lithium.
L. (after titles). — London.
L. or l. — Lake; lane.
L. or l. — Line, lines; link, links.
L.† or l.;† Lea. or lea.; Leag.† or leag.† — League, leagues.

ABBREVIATIONS.

L. or l. ; Lib. or lib. — *Liber*, book.
L.‡ or l.;‡ Lib.‡ or lib.;‡ Lb., lb. or ℔. — *Libra* or *libræ*, pound or pounds in weight.
L.† £, or l.† — *Libra* or *libræ*, pound or pounds sterling.
La. — Lantanum.
La. or Lou.† — Louisiana.
Ladp. — Ladyship.
Lam. — Lamentations.
Lat. — Latin.
Lat. or lat. — Latitude.
Lb., lb. or ℔. — Pound or pounds weight.
L.C. — Lord Chancellor.
L.C. — Lower Canada.
l.c. — *Loco citato*, in the place cited.
l.c. — Lowercase.
L.C.J. — Lord Chief Justice.
L.D. — Lady-Day.
Ld. or L.† — Lord.
Ldp. or Lp.† — Lordship.
Lea. or lea. — League, leagues.
Leg. — Legate.
Legis. or Leg.† — Legislature.
Leip. — Leipzig or Leipsic.
Lev. — Leviticus (Book of).
Leyd. — Leyden.
L.I. — Long Island.
Li. or L. — Lithium.
Lib. — Librarian.
Lib. or lib. — *Liber*, book.
Lieut. or Lt.† — Lieutenant.
Lieut.-Col.—Lieutenant-Colonel.
Lieut.-Gen. — Lieutenant-General.
Lieut.-Gov. — Lieutenant-Governor.
Lit. — Literary.
Lit. — Literary Magazine.

Lit. or lit. — Literally.
Liv. or Liverp.; Lpool.† or Lpl.‡ — Liverpool.
Liv. or liv. — Livre, livres.
LL.B. — *Legum Baccalaureus* Bachelor of Laws.
LL.D. — *Legum Doctor*, Doctor of Laws.
l. l. — *Loco laudato*, in the place quoted.
L.N.E.S. — Ladies' Negro Education Society.
Lon. or lon.; Long.† or long.† — Longitude.
Lond. or Lon.† — London.
Lou.† — Louisiana.
L.P. — Large paper.
L.S. — *Locus sigilli*, place of the seal.
L.S. — Left side.
L. s. d. — Livres, sous, deniers.
L.† or £, s. d. — Pounds, shillings, pence.
Lt.† — Lieutenant.
Lt. Inf. — Light Infantry.
LX. — Sixty or sixtieth.
LXL. — Ninety (*anc.*).
LXX. — Seventy or seventieth.
LXX.—The Septuagint (Version of the Old Testament).
LXXX. — Eighty or eightieth.
M. — *Mille*, a thousand.
M̄. — Million.
M. — Manlius; Marcus.
M. — Martius; Mutius.
M. or Mon. — Monday.
M. or Mons. — Monsieur.
M.† or Marq. — Marquis.
M. or m. — *Manipulus*, handful.
M. or m.—*Mensurá*, by measure.
M. or m. — *Mixtura*, a mixture.
M. or m. — Mix.

M. or m. — Mile, miles.
M.† M. or m. — *Meridies*, noon.
M. or m.; Mas.† or mas.;† Masc. or masc.—Masculine (gender).
M.† or m.;† Mi. or Mi. — Mill, mills.
M. or m.; Min. or min. — Minute, minutes.
M.† m.;† Mo. or mo. — Month, months.
m. — Married.
M.A. — Master of Arts.
M.A. — Military Academy.
Ma. — Minnesota.
Ma. or Mg. — Magnesium.
Macc. or Mac.† — Maccabees.
Mad. — Madam.
Mad. — Madrid. [sity.
Mad. Univ. — Madison University.
Mag. — Magazine.
Maj. — Major.
Maj. Gen. — Major-General.
Mal. — Malachi.
M.A.L.A. — Mechanic Apprentices' Library Association.
Mam. — Mamercus.
Man. — Manasses (Book of).
Manch. — Manchester.
Mar.† — March.
March. — Marchioness.
Marg. Tran. — Marginal Translation.
Marq. — Marquis.
Masc. or masc. — Masculine.
Mass. or Ms.† — Massachusetts.
Math. — Mathematics; Mathematician.
Matt. or Mat.† — Matthew.
M.B. — *Medicinæ Baccalaureus*, Bachelor of Medicine.
M.B. — *Musicæ Baccalaureus*, Bachelor of Music.

M.C. — Master-Commandant.
M.C. — Member of Congress.
M.D. — *Medicinæ Doctor*, Doctor of Medicine.
Md. — Maryland.
Mdlle. or Mlle.† — Mademoiselle.
Me. — Maine.
Meas. — Measure.
Mech. — Mechanics.
Med. — Medicine.
Med. or med. — Medical.
Mem. — *Memento*, remember.
Mem. — Memorandum, Memoranda.
Merc. — Mercury.
Messrs. or MM.† — Messieurs, Gentlemen.
Met. — Metaphysics.
Metaph. — Metaphor. [rically.
Metaph. or metaph. — Metaphorically.
Meteor. — Meteorology.
Meth. — Methodist.
Mex. — Mexico or Mexican.
Mg. — Magnesium.
M.-Goth. — Mœso-Gothic.
M.H.S. — Massachusetts Historical Society.
M.H.S. — Member of the Historical Society.
Mi. or mi. — Mill, mills.
Mic. — Micah.
Mich. — Michael; Michaelmas.
Mich. — Michigan.
Mid. — Midshipman.
Mid. or mid. — Middle (voice).
Mil. — Military.
Min. — Mineralogy.
Min. or min. — Minute, minutes.
Min. Plen. — Minister Plenipotentiary.
Miss. or Mi.† — Mississippi.
Miss. Sta. — Missionary Station.

M. L. A. — Mercantile-Library Association.
Mls.† or mls.† — Mills.
MM.† — Messieurs, Gentlemen.
MM. — Two thousand.
Mme. — Madame.
M.M.S. — Moravian Missionary Society.
M. M. S. S. — *Massachusettensis Medicinæ Societatis Socius*, Fellow of the Massachusetts Medical Society.
Mn. — Manganese.
Mo. — Missouri.
Mo. — Molybdenum.
Mo. or mo. — Month, months.
Mob. — Mobile.
Mod. — Modern.
Mon. — Monday.
Mons. — Monsieur, Sir.
Morn. or morn. — Morning.
M.P. — Member of Parliament.
M.P. — Member of Police.
Mr. — Mister.
M.R.A.S. — Member of the Royal Asiatic Society.
M.R.C.S. — Member of the Royal College of Surgeons.
M. R. I. — Member of the Royal Institution.
M.R.I.A. — Member of the Royal Irish Academy.
Mrs. — Mistress.
M.R.S.L. — Member of the Royal Society of Literature.
M.S. — *Memoriæ sacrum*, Sacred to the memory.
M.S. — Mood-stem.
MS. — *Manuscriptum*, Manuscript. MSS. — Manuscripts.
Ms.† — Massachusetts.
Mt. -- Mount or mountain.

M.T.C. or M. Tull. Cic. — Marcus Tullius Cicero.
Mus. — Museum; Music.
Mus. D. — Doctor of Music.
M.W. — Most Worthy.
M.W.S. — Member of the Wernerian Society.
Myth. — Mythology.
N. — Nine hundred (anc.).
N̄. — Nine thousand (anc.).
N. — Nitrogen; North.
N., Nom. or nom. — Nominative.
N. or n. — Name, noun.
N. or n.; Neut. or neut.—Neuter.
N. or n. — Note, notes.
N.† n.;† Na. or na. — Nail, nails.
N.‡ or n.;‡ No. — Number.
n. — Near.
N.A. or N. Am.† — North America, North American.
Na. — Natrium (Sodium).
Na. or na. — Nail, nails.
Nah. — Nahum.
Nat. — National; Natural.
Nath. — Nathanael or Nathaniel.
Naut. — Nautical.
N.B. — New Brunswick.
N.B. — North Britain.
N.B. — *Nota bene*, mark well.
N. Brit. Rev. — North-British Review.
N.C.† — New Church.
N.C. — North Carolina.
N.E. — New England.
N.E. — North-eȧst.
Neb. — Nebraska.
N. Eng.— New-Englander (*pub.*).
Neh. — Nehemiah.
nem. con. or nem. diss. — *Nemine contradicente*, or *nemine dissentiente;* no one opposing unanimously.

Neth. — Netherlands.
Neut. or neut.— Neuter (gender).
New Test. or N. T. — New Testament.
N.F. — Newfoundland.
N.H. — New Hampshire.
N H. H. S. — New-Hampshire Historical Society.
Ni. or Nk. — Nickle.
N.J. — New Jersey.
N.L. or N. lat. — North latitude.
N. l. or n. l. — *Non liquet*, it does not appear.
Nl.† or nl.† — Nail.
Nls.† or nls.† — Nails.
N.M. — New Mexico.
N.N.E. — North-north-east.
N.N.W. — North-north-west.
N.O. — New Orleans.
No. or no.‡ — *Numero* or *nombre*, number. Nos. — Numbers.
Nom. or nom. — Nominative.
Nov. — November.
N.P. — New Providence.
N.P. — Notary Public.
N.S. — New Style (after 1752).
N.S. — Nova Scotia.
N.T. — New Testament.
n.u. — Name or names unknown.
Num. — Numeral.
Num. or Numb.† — Numbers (Book of).
Numer. — Numerator.
Nux vom. — Nux vomica.
N.V.M. — Nativity of the Virgin Mary.
N.W. — North-west.
N.Y. — New York.
N.Y.H.S. — New-York Historical Society.
N.Y. Rev. — New-York Review.
N. Zeal. — New Zealand.

O. — Ohio.
O. — Eleven (*anc.*).
O̅. — Eleven thousand (*anc.*).
O. — Oxygen.
O_3, 3O†, or OOO†. — Three atoms of oxygen.
Ob. or ob. — *Obiit*, he or she died.
Obad. — Obadiah.
Obj. or ob.† — Objection.
Obj. or ob.† — Objective (case).
Obs. — Observation.
Obs. — Observatory.
Obs. or obs. — Obsolete.
Obt.† or obedt. — Obedient.
Oct. — October.
O.F. — Odd Fellow, or Odd Fellows.
Old Test. or O.T. — Old Testament.
Olym. — Olympiad.
Op. or op. — Opposite.
Opt. — Optics.
Opt. or opt.; Optat.† or optat.† — Optative (mood).
Or. — Oregon.
Ord. — Ordinary.
Ornith. — Ornithology.
O.S. — Old Style (before 1752).
Os. — Osmium.
O.T. — Oregon Territory.
O.T. — Old Testament.
O.U.A. — Order of United Americans.
Oxf. — Oxford.
Oxon. — *Oxonia, Oxonii*, Oxford.
Oz. or oz. — Ounce, ounces.
P. or G. — Four hundred (*anc.*).
P̅. — Four hundred thousand.
P. — Phosphorus.
P. — Publius.
P.† or p. — Page.
P. or p. — Pint, pints; pole, poles.

P. or p. — *Particula* or *pugillus*, what is taken between the fingers.
P.† or p.;† Part. or part. — Participle.
P.† p.;† Pi. or pi. — Pipe, pipes.
P.† Pop. or pop. — Population.
P.A. or p.a. — Participial adjective.
Pa.† or Penn. — Pennsylvania.
P.Æ. or p. æq. — *Partes æquales*, equal parts.
Pal. — Palestine.
Pamph. — Pamphleteer.
Par. — Paragraph.
Par. or par. — Parish.
Par. Pas. — Parallel passage or passages.
Parl. — Parliament.
Parl. or parl. — Parliamentary.
Part. or part. — Participle.
Partic. or partic. — Particle.
Pash. or pash. — Pashalic.
Pass. — Passive (voice).
Payt. — Payment.
Pb. — Plumbum (Lead).
P. C. — *Patres Conscripti*, Conscript Fathers; Senators.
P.C. — Privy Counsellor.
Pd. — Palladium.
Pd. or pd. — Paid.
P.E.I. — Prince Edward Island.
Pen. or pen. — Peninsula.
Penn. — Pennsylvania.
Pent. — Pentecost.
Per. — Persia or Persian.
per an.—*Per annum*, by the year.
per ct.† or per cent. — *Per centum*, by the hundred.
Perf. or perf.; Pf.† or pf.† — Perfect (tense).
Peri. — Perigee.

Pers. or pers. — Person.
Pers. or pers. pron. — Personal pronoun.
Persp. — Perspective.
Pet. — Peter.
Pf.† or pf.† — Perfect (tense).
Ph. D. or P. D.† — *Philosophiæ Doctor*, Doctor of Philosophy.
Phil. — Philip; Philippians.
Phil. — Philosophy.
Phil. or phil. — Philosophically.
Phila. or Phil.† — Philadelphia.
Philem. — Philemon.
Phil. Mag. — Philosophical Magazine.
Philom. — *Philomathes*, a lover of learning.
Philomath. — *Philomathematicus*, a lover of mathematics.
Phil. Trans. — Philosophical Transactions.
Phosph. — Phosphorus.
Phren. — Phrenology.
P.H.S. — Pennsylvania Historical Society.
Pi. or pi. — Pipe, pipes.
Pinx. or pxt.† — *Pinxit*, painted.
Pk. or pk. — Peck.
Pks. or pks. — Pecks.
Pl. or pl. — Place.
Pl. or pl. — Plate or plates.
Pl. or pl.; Plur. or plur.— Plural.
Pl. or Pt.† — Platinum.
Plup. or plup.; Plupf.† or plupf.† — Pluperfect.
Plff. — Plaintiff.
Plur. or piur. — Plural.
P.M. — Postmaster.
P.M. — Passed Midshipman.
P.M.† P.M. or p.m. — *Post meridiem*, afternoon, evening.
P.M.G. — Postmaster-General.

P.M.G. — Professor of Music in Gresham College.
P.O. — Post-Office.
Poet. or poet. — Poetically.
Pop. or pop. — Population.
Port. — Portugal or Portuguese.
Posit. or posit. — Positive.
Pot. or pot. — Pottle, pottles.
P.P. — *Pulvis patrum*, the Jesuits'-bark in powder.
P.P.C. — *Pour prendre congé*, to take leave.
Pp. or pp. — Pages.
P. p. or p. p. — Past participle.
P. pr. or p. pr. — Participle present.
Ppt. or ppt. — *Præparatus*, prepared.
P.R. — *Populus Romanus*, the Roman people.
P.R. — Porto Rico.
pr.‡ — *Per*, by the.
Pr. or pr. — Pronounce.
Pr.† or pr.† — Province.
Pr.† or pr.†; Pron. or pron. — Pronoun.
Pr.† or pr.;† Pret. or pret. — Preterite (tense).
Pr. p. or pr. p. — Present participle.
P.R.A. — President of the Royal Academy.
Pref. — Preface.
Prep. or prep. — Preposition.
Pres. or pres. — Present (tense).
Pres. — President.
Presid. — Presidency.
Pret. — Preterite (tense).
Prim. or prim. — Primary.
Prob. — Problem.
Prof. — Professor.
Pron. or pron. — Pronoun

Pron. or pron. adj. — Pronominal adjective.
Prop. — Proposition.
Prot. — Protestant.
Pro tem. — *Pro tempore*, for the time being.
Prov. — Proverbs; Provost.
Prov. or prov. — Province.
prox. — *Proximo*, next (month).
Prp.† or prp.† — Preposition.
P.R.S. — President of the Royal Society.
Prus. — Prussia or Prussian.
P.S. — Particle-stem.
P.S. — *Post scriptum*, Postscript
P.S. — Privy Seal.
Ps. — Psalm or Psalms.
P.T. or p. t. — Post-town.
Pt.† — Platinum.
Pt. or pt. — Part; port; point.
Pt. or pt. — Pint.
Pts. or pts. — Pints.
P. Th. G. — Professor of Theology in Gresham College.
P.V. or p.v. — Post-village.
Pub. — Publisher; Publication; published.
Pub. Doc. — Public Documents.
Puls. — Pulsatilla.
Pun. or pun. — Puncheon · puncheons.
Pwt. or pwt. — Pennyweight, pennyweights.
Q. — Five hundred (*anc.*).
Q̄. — Five hundred thousand.
Q. — Quintus; Quintius.
Q. — Queen.
Q., Ques. or Quest.† — Question.
Q. or q. — *Quadrans*, a farthing; *quadrantes*, farthings.
Q.‡ or q.‡ Qu.† or qu.;† Qy. or qy. — *Quære*, inquire; query.

ABBREVIATIONS.

q. — *Quasi*, as it were.
Q.B. — Queen's Bench.
Q.C. — Queen's College.
Q.C. — Queen's Counsel.
Q. d. or q. d. — *Quasi dicat*, as if he should say; *quasi dictum*, as if said; *quasi dixisset*, as if he had said.
Q.E. or q.e. — *Quod est*, which is.
Q.E.D. — *Quod erat demonstrandum*, which was to be proved.
Q.E.F. — *Quod erat faciendum*, which was to be done.
q. l. — *Quantum libet*, as much as you please.
Q. Mess. — Queen's Messenger.
Qm. or qm. — *Quomodo*, how, by what means.
q. p. or q. pl. — *Quantum placet*, as much as you please.
Qr. or qr. — Quarter.
Qrs. or qrs. — Quarters.
Q.S. — Quarter Sessions.
q. s. — *Quantum sufficit*, a sufficient quantity.
Qt. or qt. — Quart.
Qts. or qts. — Quarts.
Quar. or Qu.† — Quarterly.
Ques. — Question.
Quint. — Quintilius.
q. v. — *Quantum vis*, as much as you will.
q. v. — *Quod vide*, which see.
Qy. or qy. — Query.
R. — Eighty (*anc.*).
R̄. — Eighty thousand (*anc.*).
R. — *Recipe*, take.
R. — *Regina*, Queen.
R. — *Rex*, King.
R. — Rhodium.
R.‡ or Rem.—Remark, Remarks.
R.† or Russ. — Russia, Russian.

R. or r. — River.
R. or r. — Rod, rods.
R. or r. — Rood, roods.
R.† or r.‡ — Rule.
r. — Resides; retired; rises.
R.A. — Royal Academy.
R.A. — Royal Academician.
R.A. — Royal Arch.
R.A. — Royal Artillery.
R.A. — Russian America.
Rad. — Radical.
Rd.† or rd.† — Rod; rood.
R.E. — Royal Engineers.
Re. or re. — Removed.
Rec. — Recipe.
Recd. — Received.
Recpt.‡ — Receipt.
Rec. Sec. or Secy.† — Recording Secretary.
Rect. — Rector.
Ref. — Reformation; Reformed.
Ref. Ch. — Reformed Church.
Ref. or ref. — Reference.
Reg. — Register, Registry.
Reg. Prof. — Regius Professor
Regr. — Registrar.
Regt. — Regiment.
Rel. or rel. pron.; Rel. or rel. pr.† — Relative pronoun.
Rem. — Remark or remarks.
Rep. — Reporter.
Rep. — Representative.
Repub. or Rep.† — Republic
Rev. — Reverend; Revelation.
Rev. — Review.
Rhet. — Rhetoric.
R.I. — Rhode Island.
R.I.H.S. — Rhode-Island Historical Society.
Richd. — Richard.
R.M. — Royal Marines.
R.N — Royal Navy.

R.N.O.—*Riddare af Nordstjerne*, Knight of the Order of the Polar Star.
Ro. — *Recto*, right-hand page.
Robt. — Robert.
Rom. — Romans (Book of).
Rom. Cath. — Roman Catholic.
R.P. — *Regius Professor*, the King's Professor.
R.P. — *Respublica*, Republic.
R.R. — Railroad.
R.S. — Right side.
R.S.S. — *Regiæ Societatis Socius*, Fellow of the Royal Society.
Rt. Hon. — Right Honorable.
Rt. Rev. — Right Reverend.
Rt. Wpful. — Right Worshipful.
Ru. — Runic.
Russ. — Russia or Russian.
R.W. — Right Worthy.
R.W.O. — *Riddare af Wasa Orden*, Knight of the Order of Wasa.
S. — Sextus; seven (*anc.*).
S. — Solo (*in Italian music*).
S. — Stem (of a word).
S. — Sulphur; Sunday.
S. or So.† — South.
S.‡ or s.‡ — See.
S. or s. — Set, sets; sign, signs.
S. or s. — *Solidus*, a shilling.
S. or s. — *Solidi*, shillings.
S. or s. — Sou, sous.
S. or s.; Sec. or sec. — Second, seconds.
S. or s.; Sec.† or sec.;† Sect. or sect. — Section.
SS. or ss.; Sects. or sects. — Sections.
S.‡ or s.;‡ Ser. or ser. — Series.
S.† or s.:† Sing. or sing. — Singular (number)

S.† or s.;† Subst or subst. — A substantive (noun).
S.† s.;† SS. or ss. — *Semis*, half.
s.‡ ss.† sc. or scil. — *Scilicet*, to wit, namely.
s.a.—*Secundum artem*, according to art.
S.A. or S.Am.†—South America.
Sam. — Samaritan; Samuel.
Sansc. or Sans.† — Sanscrit.
S.A.S.—*Societatis Antiquariorum Socius*, Fellow of the Society of Antiquarians.
Sat. or Sa.† — Saturday.
Sax. — Saxon.
Sax. Chron. — Saxon Chronicle.
Sb. — Stibium (Antimony).
S.C. — *Senatûs Consultum*, a decree of the Senate.
S.C. — South Carolina.
Sc. or sc.; Scr.† or scr.† — Scruple, scruples.
Sc. or sc. — *Sculpsit*, engraved.
sc. or scil. — *Scilicet*, namely.
S. caps. — Small capitals.
Sch. or sch.; Schr.† or schr.‡ — Schooner.
Schs. or schs. — Schooners.
Sci. — Science.
Scip. — Scipio.
Sclav. — Sclavonic.
Scot. — Scotland.
Scot. — Scotch or Scottish.
Sc. Pen. — Scandinavian Peninsula.
Sculp. or sculp. — *Sculpsit*, (he or she) engraved.
S.E. — South-east.
Se. — Selenium.
Schol. — *Scholium*, a note.
Schol. — *Scholia*, notes.
Sec. or sec. — Second, seconds

ABBREVIATIONS.

Sec.† — Section.
Sec. or Secy.† — Secretary.
Sec. Leg. — Secretary of Legation.
Sect. or sect. — Section.
Sects. or sects. — Sections.
Select. — Selection or selections.
Sen. — Senate; Senator.
Sen. or sen. — Senior.
Sept. or Sep.† — September.
Sept. — Septuagint.
seq. or sq.† — *Sequente*, and in what follows.
seqq. or sqq.† — *Sequentibus*, and in the following (places).
Ser. or ser. — Series.
Serg. — Sergeant.
Serg.-Maj. — Sergeant-Major.
Serj. — Serjeant.
Serv. — Servius.
Servt. — Servant.
Sex. — Sextus.
S.G. — South Georgia.
Shak. — Shakspeare.
S.H.S. — *Societatis Historiæ Socius*, Fellow of the Historical Society.
Si. — Silicium or Silicon.
Sic. — Sicily or Sicilian.
Sim. or sim. — Similarly.
Sing. or sing. — Singular.
S. Isl. — Sandwich Islands.
S.J.C.—Supreme Judicial Court.
S.L. — Solicitor at Law (Scot.).
S.L. or S. lat. — South latitude.
Sld. or sld. — Sailed.
S. L. P.q. Preston. Soc. Hon. — *Societatis Literariæ Philosophicæque Prestonensis Socius Honorarius*, Honorary Member of the Literary and Philosophical Society of Preston.

S.M. Lond. Soc. Cor. — *Societatis Medicæ Londonensis Socius Cor.* Corresponding Member of the London Medical Society.
Sn. — Stannum (Tin).
s. n. — *Secundum naturam*, according to nature.
So.† — South.
Soc. Isl. — Society Islands.
Sol. — Solomon.
Sol. — Solicitor; Solution.
Sol.-Gen. — Solicitor-General.
S. of Sol. — Song of Solomon.
South. Lit. Mess. — Southern Literary Messenger.
South. Quar. Rev. — Southern Quarterly Review.
S.P. or s. p. — Seaport.
S.P. or s. p. — *Sine prole*, without issue.
Sp. — Spain or Spanish.
S.P.A.S.— *Societatis Philosophicæ Americanæ Socius*, Member of the American Philosophical Society.
S.P.G. — Society for the Propagation of the Gospel.
Sp. or sp. gr. — Specific gravity.
S.P.Q.R. — *Senatus Populusque Romanus*, the Senate and Roman people.
Sq. or sq. ft. — Square foot, feet.
Sq. or sq. in. — Square inch or inches.
Sq. or sq. m. — Square mile or miles.
Sq. or sq. r. — Square rood or roods.
Sq. or sq. yd. — Square yard.
Sq. or sq. yds. — Square yards.
sq.† — In what follows.
sqq.† — In the following (places).

Sr. — Strontium. Sr.‡ — Sir.
S.R.I. — *Sacrum Romanum Imperium*, the holy Roman empire.
S.R.S. — *Societatis Regiæ Socius*, Fellow of the Royal Society.
S.S. — Sunday School.
SS. or ss. — Sections.
SS. or ss. — *Semis*, half.
SS.† or ss.† — *Scilicet*, to wit.
S. S. C. — Solicitor before the Supreme Courts (Scotland).
S.S.E. — South-south-east.
S.S.W. — South-south-west.
St. — Saint.
St. or st. — Street; Strait.
Stat. — Statute or statutes.
S.T.D. — *Sanctæ Theologiæ Doctor*, Doctor of Divinity.
Ster. or ster.; Stg.† or stg.† — Sterling.
S.T.P. — *Sanctæ Theologiæ Professor*, Professor of Divinity.
Sts. or sts. — Streets.
Subj. or subj.; Subjunct.† or subjunct.† — Subjunctive.
Subst. or subst. — Substantive.
Suff. or suff. — Suffix.
Su.-Goth. — Suio-Gothic.
Sulph. — Sulphur or sulphurous.
Sup. — Supplement.
Super. or super. — Superfine.
Superl. or superl. — Superlative.
Supt. — Superintendent.
Surg. — Surgeon; Surgery.
Surg.-Gen. — Surgeon-General.
Surv. — Surveyor.
Surv.-Gen. — Surveyor-General.
Sus. — Susannah.
S.W. — South-west.
Sw. — Sweden or Swedish.
Switz. — Switzerland.
Syr. — Syria or Syriac.

T. — A hundred and sixty (*anc.*).
T̄. — A hundred and sixty thousand (*anc.*).
T. — Technical (term).
T. — Tenor (*in music*).
T. — Titus; Titius; Tullius.
T.† or Tur. — Turkey or Turkish.
T. — *Tutti*, the whole band after a solo.
T. or t.; Tn.† or tn.† — Town, township.
T. or t.; Tom.† or tom.† — Tome, tomes.
T. or t. — Ton, tons; tun, tuns.
T. or tr. — *Trillo*, a shake.
Ta. — Tantalum (Columbium).
Te. — Tellurium.
Tenn. or Ten.† — Tennessee
Ter. — Territory.
Term. — Termination.
Tex. — Texas.
Text. Rec. — *Textus Receptus*, the Received Text.
Th. — Thorium.
Th.† Thu.† Thurs. — Thursday.
Theo. — Theodore.
Theol. — Theology, Theological.
Theoph. — Theophilus.
Theor. — Theorem.
Thess. — Thessalonians.
Thos. — Thomas.
Thurs. — Thursday.
Ti. — Titanium.
Tier. or tier. — Tierce, tierces.
Tim. — Timothy.
Tit. — Titus.
T.O. — Turn over.
Tob. — Tobit.
Tom.† or tom.† — Tome, tomes
Tonn. or tonn. — Tonnage.
Tr. — Terbium.
Tr. or tr. — Transpose.

Tr. — Trustee. Trs. — Trustees.
Tr. Brit. Mus. — Trustee of the British Museum.
Trans. or Tr.† — Translator.
Trans. or Tr.† — Translation.
Trans. or trans. — Translated.
Treas. or Tr.† — Treasurer.
Trin. — Trinity.
T.S. — Tense-stem, or stem of the perfect tense.
Tues. or Tu.† — Tuesday.
Tur. — Turkey or Turkish.
Turnp. — Turnpike.
Tut. — Tutor.
Typ. — Typographer.
U. — Uranium.
U.C. — Upper Canada.
U. E. I. C. — United East-India Company.
U.J.C. — *Utriusque Juris Doctor*, Doctor of both Laws.
ult. — *Ultimo*, last; of the last month.
U.K. — United Kingdom.
um. — Unmarried.
Univ. — University.
U.S. — United States.
U.S.A. — United States-Army.
U.S.A. — United States of America.
U. S. Lit. Gaz. — United-States Literary Gazette.
U.S.M. — United-States Mail.
U.S.M. — United-States Marines.
U.S.N. — United-States Navy.
U.S.S. — United-States Ship.
u. s. — *Ut supra*, as above.
V. — Five or fifth.
V̄. — Five thousand (*anc.*).
V. — Vanadium.
V. — Victoria.
V. — Violin. VV. — Violins.

V. or v. — Verb.
V.‡ or v.;‡ Ver. or ver. — Verse, verses. vv.† — Verses.
V. or v.; Vi.† or vi.;† Vid.‡ or vid.‡ — *Vide*, see.
V.† or v.;† Vil. or vil. — Village.
V., Voc. or voc. — Vocative.
V.† or v.;† Vol. or vol. — Volume.
v., vs. or vers. — *Versus*, against.
Va. — Virginia.
Vat. — Vatican.
v. a. — Verb active.
v. aux. — Verb auxiliary.
v. def. — Verb defective.
v. dep. — Verb deponent.
V.C. — Vice-Chancellor.
V. D. M. — *Verbi Dei Minister*, Minister of God's Word.
Ven. — Venerable.
Ver. or ver. — Verse, verses.
vers. — *Versus*, against.
V. g. or v. g. — *Verbi gratiá*, for example.
VI. — Six or sixth.
VII. — Seven or seventh.
VIII. — Eight or eighth.
VIIII.† or IX. — Nine or ninth.
Vice-Pres. or V.P.† — Vice-President.
v. imp. — Verb impersonal.
v. in. or v. i.†— Verb intransitive.
v. irr. — Verb irregular.
Vil. or vil. — Village.
Visc., Vis. or V.† — Viscount.
viz. or vi.‡ — *Videlicet*, to wit namely.
v. n. — Verb neuter.
Vo. — *Verso*, left-hand page.
Voc. or voc. — Vocative (case)
Vol. or vol. — Volume.
Vols. or vols. — Volumes.

V. R. — *Victoria Regina*, Queen Victoria.
v. r. — Verb reflective.
v. tr. — Verb transitive.
Vt. — Vermont.
Vul. — Vulgate (Version).
Vulg. or vulg. — Vulgar (expression).
W. — Welsh; West.
W. — Wolfram (Tungsten).
w. — Wife.
W. or Wed. — Wednesday.
W.† or w.;† Wk. or wk. — Week.
Wash. — Washington.
West. Res. Coll. — Western Reserve College.
Westm. Rev. — Westminster Review.
w.f. — Wrong font.
Whf. or whf.; Wf.† or wf.† — Wharf.
W.I. or W. Ind.† — West Indies or West India.
Wis. or Wisc. — Wisconsin.
Wisd. — Wisdom (Book of).
Wks. or wks. — Weeks.
W. lon. — West longitude.
Wm. or Will.† — William.
W.M.S. — Wesleyan Missionary Society.
W.N.W. — West-north-west.
Wp. — Worship.
Wpful. — Worshipful.
W.S. — Writer to the Signet.
W.S.W. — West-south-west.
W.T. — Washington Territory.
Wt. or wt. — Weight.
X. — Ten or tenth.
⋈. — A thousand (*anc.*).
Ẋ. — Ten thousand (*anc.*).
XI., XII. — Eleven, twelve.
XIII. — Thirteen.

XIIII.† or XIV. — Fourteen.
XV., XVI. — Fifteen, sixteen.
XVII. — Seventeen.
XVIII. or XIIX.‡ — Eighteen.
XVIIII.† or XIX. — Nineteen.
XX. — Twenty.
XXI. — Twenty-one.
XXII. — Twenty-two.
XXX. — Thirty.
XXXX.† or XL. — Forty.
XC. or LXL.† — Ninety.
X.† or Xt.† — Christ.
Xmas.† or Xm.† — Christmas.
Xn.† or Xtian.† — Christian.
Xnty.† or Xty.† — Christianity.
Xper.† — Christopher.
Y. — A hundred and fifty (*anc.*).
Ȳ. — A hundred and fifty thousand (*anc.*).
Y. — Yttrium.
Y.† y.† or yr. — Year.
Y.B. or Yr.-Bk. — Year Book.
Yd. or yd. — Yard.
Yds. or yds. — Yards.
y.† or yᵉ.† — The.
yᵐ.† — Them.
yⁿ.† — Then.
yʳ.† — Their; your.
yˢ.† — This.
yᵗ.† — That.
Yrs. or yrs. — Years.
Yrs.† — Yours.
Z. — Two thousand (*anc.*).
Z̄. — Two millions (*anc.*).
Z. or Zr. — Zirconium.
Zech. — Zechariah.
Zeph. — Zephaniah.
Zn. — Zinc.
Zoöl. — Zoölogy.
&. — And.
&c. or etc. — *Et cæteri, et cæteræ, et cætera*, and the rest.

V. — MEDICAL, ARITHMETICAL, ALGEBRAIC, AND GEOMETRICAL SIGNS.

℞	. . .	*Recipe*, take of.
ß	. . .	*Semis*, half.
ā, or aa	. . .	*Ana*, equal parts of each.
℔	. . .	Pound.
ʒ	. . .	Ounce.
ʒ	. . .	Dram.
℈	. . .	Scruple.
℟	. . .	*Per*, each.
@	. . .	At or to.
$	. . .	Dollar or dollars.
£	. . .	Pound or pounds sterling.
/	. . .	Shilling or shillings.
+	. . .	*Plus*, more, in addition.
—	. .	*Minus*, less, in subtraction.
×	. . .	Into, in multiplication.
÷	. . .	By, in division
=	. . .	Equal to.
: :: : .	. .	Signs in proportion.
√ ᵛ√	. .	The radical sign in evolution.
ⁱⁿ	. . .	Sign in evolution.
∽	. . .	Unknown difference; similitude.
◻	. . .	Regular quadrangle.
△	. . .	Triangle.
∠	. . .	Angle.
∟	. . .	Right angle.
⊥	. . .	Perpendicular.
▭	. . .	Rectangle.
>	. . .	Greater than.
⊏	. . .	Greater than.
<	. . .	Less than.
⊐	. . .	Less than.
—:	. . .	The difference, or excess.
~	. . .	The difference, or excess.
∥	. . .	Parallelism.
≚	. . .	Equiangular.
⧻	. . .	Geometrical proportion.
≎	. . .	Equivalent.
∫	. . .	Sum or integral.
ε	. . .	Residual.
∴	. . .	Whence.
±	. . .	Positive or negative
∞	. . .	Infinitely large.
∝	. . .	Proportional to.
○	. . .	Circle, or 360°.
°	. . .	Degree.
′	. . .	Minute of arc.
″	. . .	Second of arc.
π	. . .	Ratio between diam and circumference
e	. . .	Napier's base.

VI. — ASTRONOMICAL CHARACTERS.

I. THE TWELVE SIGNS OF THE ZODIAC.

♈ .. *Aries*, the Ram.	♎ .. *Libra*, the Balance.
♉ .. *Taurus*, the Bull.	♏ .. *Scorpio*, the Scorpion.
♊ .. *Gemini*, the Twins.	♐ .. *Sagittarius*, the Archer.
♋ .. *Cancer*, the Crab.	♑ .. *Capricornus*, the Goat.
♌ .. *Leo*, the Lion.	♒ .. *Aquarius*, the Waterman.
♍ .. *Virgo*, the Virgin.	♓ .. *Pisces*, the Fishes.

II. THE PLANETARY SIGNS.

☿ ..... Mercury.	⚳ ..... Iris.*
♀ ..... Venus.	⚘ ..... Flora.*
⊕ ..... Earth.	⚶ ..... Metis.*
● ..... Moon.	⚵ ..... Parthenope.*
♂ ..... Mars.	⚴ ..... Clio.*
⚳ ..... Ceres.*	⚸ ..... Irene.*
⚴ ..... Pallas.*	♃ ..... Jupiter.
⚵ ..... Juno.*	♄ ..... Saturn.
⚶ ..... Vesta.*	♅ ..... Uranus.
⚷ ..... Astræa.*	♆ ..... Neptune.
⚸ ..... Hebe.*	☉ ..... Sun.

III. THE LUNAR SIGNS.

● ..... New Moon.	○ ..... Full Moon.
◐ ..... First Quarter.	◑ ..... Last Quarter.

IV. ASPECTS OF THE PLANETS.

☌ ..... Conjunction.	✶ ..... Sextile.
☍ ..... Opposition.	☊ ..... Ascending Node.
△ ..... Trine.	☋ ..... Descending Node.
□ ..... Quartile.	⊕ ..... Part of Fortune.

* These and the other asteroids are now more commonly designated by a ○ inclosing the number indicating the order of their discovery.

HINTS

on

THE PREPARATION OF "COPY,"

AND ON

PROOF-READING.

In preparing and bringing out a book for publication, a great number of persons are employed; each of them having to use more or less the brain, the hand, and the eye; to call into action the principles of mind, mechanism, and taste; to occupy, in short, his special department of duty and toil. For our present purpose, however, we will mention only three agents who play a prominent though an unequal part in the production of a book, and who have particularly to do with the mode in which it is executed. These are the author, the compositor, and the proof-reader; the producer of the ideas, the arranger of the types, and the corrector of the typographic errors.

Let us suppose, then, that the writer of a work, instead of transcribing it as many times as would be requisite for the perusal of his friends or his fellow-men, is desirous of saving himself this trouble, and of having a large number of copies put into their hands by means infinitely more rapid; namely, through the agency of the printing-press. Before, however, taking this step, he will ascertain whether his manuscript — or, as it is technically called, "the copy" — be in a suitable condition for being made out by the compositor and the proof-reader. If it consists of orations, discourses, lectures, or poems, certain portions of which have, for his own accommodation in delivery, been underlined, but which are not to be printed in Italics or small capitals, he will carefully expunge all such marks. He will examine if proper names and foreign or technical expressions, supposing them to occur, have been correctly spelled and clearly written; rectifying the inaccuracies, and making the obscure perfectly plain and legible. He will dot the i's, and cross the t's, which, in the haste of composition, may have been left imperfect; change such capital I's and J's as may be confounded with each other; and re-form whatever letters may be blurred or ill-shapen, particularly the s's in the terminations of plural nouns. He will see whether the interlineations, if there be any, have been introduced with sufficient distinctness. Should he make additions in the margin, or on the opposite or a separate leaf, he will mark with a caret the place of insertion, and say whether they are designed as text for the body of the matter, or as notes for the foot of the page; putting such or any other direction within a circle, that it may be readily noticed. If points have been omitted, he will supply them; if erroneously made, correct them. All words and phrases, which, for his own ease, he has abbreviated, he will write in full; and at the commencement of any sentence meant to begin a new paragraph, but not distinctly exhibited as such, he will put the mark (¶) appropriated for that purpose.

If, however, after all this care, an author find, on re-inspection, that the manuscript cannot without difficulty be deciphered, he will either fairly transcribe it himself, or cause it to be transcribed by a good penman. He, or his amanuensis, will write on only one side of the paper, and mark the number of each page, that the copy may admit of being cut into portions; put, if necessary, into the hands of several compositors; and, after having been set up, be re-arranged in its proper order. He will see that the orthography, the capitals, and the points, which were perhaps imperfectly attended to in the original manuscript, be all conformed to the best usages of the present day. He will distinguish the paragraphs by commencing each in a new line, and putting its first word at a greater distance from the edge of the paper, at the left hand, than the other lines, to prevent sentences which should be separated from being brought together, or those which should be joined from being separated. On no account should the paragraphing be left to the compositor; it being unreasonable to expect him to perform a species of work for which no remuneration is given, and which peculiarly devolves on the writer himself.

In the observations just made, we have assumed that an author takes all possible care to make his manuscript clear and legible; and, no doubt, many literary gentlemen are not ashamed to do their own work, instead of leaving it to be done, at the imminent hazard of mistakes, by the compositor and the proof-reader. But it is a well-known fact, at least to those conversant with subjects relating to the press, that manuscripts designed for publication are often found written so carelessly, or with so little regard to any system of capitalizing and punctuation, as to render the labor of printing them vexatious, unsatisfactory, and unproductive, — first to the compositor, who, after coming to many a dead halt, and troubling *ad nauseam* his fellow-workmen, in attempting to decipher the copy, is obliged to creep his "slow length along," with all the patience that may be supplied by the prospect of miserable earnings; then to the corrector of the press, who, whatever may be his literary qualifications, is certainly not familiar with the *unexpressed* thoughts of authors, and cannot find an explanation of their flourishes, their half-written words, or their peculiar hieroglyphics, in any of the dictionaries at his command; and lastly to the master-printer, whose material is blocked up by the slow progress of the work in question, and whose pockets sometimes suffer from the cancelling of pages, which is not unfrequently as much attributable to scratches of the pen as to " errors of the press," — as much owing to the carelessness of the author or his amanuensis, as to the incompetency of the printer or his workmen. We do not mean to apologize for the blunders of compositors, or to excuse the negligence and ignorance of proof-readers, but merely to express our sense of the injustice done to the profession of typography, when authors who have written illegibly, or who have themselves examined the proof-sheets without detecting mistakes, throw the whole responsibility on the shoulders of others.

As a justification of our hardihood in thus laying down to authors instructions so minute and yet so obvious, we quote a paragraph, which has recently appeared in an English newspaper, showing the gross carelessness and utter want of thought manifested, on the part of some writers, in preparing their works for publication. The case referred to is, indeed, an extreme one; but its main feature — the illegibility of the copy — unhappily characterizes the manuscripts of many other distinguished men.

> "The late Sharon Turner, author of the 'History of the Anglo-Saxons,' who received three hundred a year from Government as a literary pension, wrote the third volume of his 'Sacred History of the World' upon paper which did not cost him a farthing. The copy consisted of torn and angular fragments of letters and notes; of covers of periodicals, — gray, drab, or green, — written in thick, round hand over a small print; of shreds of curling paper, unctuous with pomatum or bear's grease; and of the white wrappers in which his proofs were sent from the printers. The paper, sometimes as thin as a bank-note, was written on both sides; and was so sodden with ink, plastered on with a pen worn to a stump, that hours were frequently wasted in discovering on which side of it certain sentences were written. Men condemned to work on it saw their dinner vanishing in illimitable perspective, and first-rate hands groaned over it a whole day for tenpence. One poor fellow assured the writer of this paper, that he could not earn enough upon it to pay his rent, and that he had seven mouths to fill besides his own In the hope of mending matters in some degree, slips of stout white paper were sent frequently with the proofs; but the good gentleman could not afford to use them, and they never came back as copy."

Satisfied that the manuscript is in a fit state to be read, the author employs a letterpress printer, giving him such directions as he thinks are necessary. The copy is then delivered to the compositor, whose province it is to put in type what the author has written. As soon as the workman has finished the setting-up of some eight, twelve, or more pages, according to the size of the paper to be used, and has arranged them in such a way that they may all be printed together, he obtains a "proof," or impression in ink, of the matter he has set up; and then lays it, along with the copy, on the corrector's desk.

The obtaining of this proof-sheet implies, that the work of "composition," or the arrangement of the types, is to some extent imperfect or erroneous; that the matter set up is not a true counterpart of the original; that blunders have been made, as even by the best of compositors they will be made, in a variety of particulars which need not here be enumerated.

Unless, from instructions previously received, or from an inspection of the manuscript, he has reason to believe that the author has a peculiar and unalterable taste in regard to certain minutiæ, — such as the style of type in titles and heads of chapters, the orthography, punctuation, use of capitals, &c., — the proof-reader, if faithful to his duty, proceeds to the labor of correction on the principle of endeavoring to render the work of the compositor, where changes are necessary, as neat, accurate, and consistent in its parts, as possible. He begins by writing the phrase "First Proof" on the upper margin of the first page. He then examines the folios and the signatures, the captions and the subheads; notices whether the pages are of equal or proper lengths, and if the lines are straight or crooked; inspects the spacing, or blank, between the words and sentences, that they may have regularity of appearance; and peruses the whole sheet more or less rapidly, — putting his corrections in the margin, as exemplified at the end of the present work. All this should be the first thing done in proof-reading; but, from carelessness or from a supposed want of time, it is commonly left undone, except so far as the duty can be performed in the next process, about to be described.

The manuscript is now put into the hands of an intelligent boy, one who is able to read it aloud clearly and accurately. The corrector of the press has the proof-sheet before him, and, if he have gone through the process just mentioned, has no occasion, when making fresh marks, to stop the reader of the copy, unless there be some peculiar difficulty. His chief aim is to make the print an accurate representation of the author's writing, or mode of expression: but his attention is also devoted to the spelling of the words in accordance with some authorized standard; and to the punctuation, that it may develop the construction of the sentences, and the meaning intended. He is not usually expected, nor indeed is it his province, to change the ideas, to improve the style, or, except merely in a lapse of the pen, to correct grammatical blunders. But should there occur any obscurities in the writing, or any errors or inelegances in the language, he may put a *Qy.* ("query") in the margin, and leave the suggestions to be made in the next proof.

In reading the manuscript, the boy should pronounce with an additional syllable such proper names as have a final *e*, to distinguish them from those which want this letter; reading, for instance, *Browne, Deane, Greene*, each as two syllables, and sounding the *e* so as to be plainly heard. He should lay the accent on the last syllable of proper names having two consonants of the same kind, to distinguish them from those which have only one; as, *Bennett*. But all uncommon or difficult words, whose constituent letters cannot be known by any mode of pronunciation, he should spell throughout; as, *Samson, Sampson; Taylor, Tayler; Thomson, Thompson.* When *viz.* is written for "namely," and &c. for "and so forth," he should give each word such a pronunciation as will exhibit the mode in which it is to be printed; as *viz,* in conformity with its spelling, for the former, and *et cetera* for the latter. At the beginning of every paragraph, except the first, he should say "Paragraph." At the commencement of each quotation that has quotation-marks, he should say "Turn," and, at the end of it, "Close;" meaning by the former expression that a quotation in the manuscript is preceded by *turned* or inverted commas, and by the latter that it is *closed* or finished by apostrophes. In reading words which have a single line drawn under them, he should, instead of saying "Italics," which would mar the sense, gently strike the desk, making one tap simultaneously with the pronunciation of each word; unless a long sentence is Italicized, when the naming of "Italics" before the passage, and "Roman" after it, will be a sufficient token where it begins and ends. To indicate such words as are meant to be printed on capitals or small capitals, he should say "Caps." or "Small caps.," as the case requires. That the corrector may conveniently inspect the manuscript when it is hard to make out, the boy should sit at his left hand.

When the proof-sheet has been carefully read in the manner spoken of, the corrector inserts in the manuscript a bracket between the last word of the printed sheet and the first of the next; and, over these, the paging, the signature, and, if requisite, the number of volume; as, "[Page 9, Sig. 2, vol. i.;" or "[Page 9, Sig. C;" so that no mistake may be committed in beginning to set or make up the pages that immediately follow. He then cuts off the portion of the manuscript which is marked as above, and returns it at once with the proof-sheet to the compositor, whose business it is to make his work correspond accurately with the corrections marked. Having performed this duty, the compositor has another impression taken of his pages, which he delivers, along with the former one, to the proof-reader.

And now begins another process on the part of the corrector of the press, by his writing on the newly printed sheet the words "Second Proof." After placing the two proofs in juxtaposition, he minutely compares them, in order to ascertain whether all the errors that had been marked have been corrected in the type; re-marking those which may have been neglected, transcribing the *queries* from the first proof, and making such suggestions as he thinks proper. Should the establishment have another proof-reader, he transfers to him the second proof, with the manuscript, to be examined again, and, if necessary, recorrected. If, however, there is only one reader, he should with unwearied eye peruse it afresh; mark in the margin whatever errors may have escaped his notice in the previous reading, or been made by the compositor in the transference of the corrections; and send the proof-sheet immediately to the writer of the work, unless the errors are so numerous as to require additional labor and a third proof.

If the author be a thoughtful man, he will take care that no unnecessary delay occur in the performance of his duty; for, though it may possibly be a matter of little importance to the public or himself when his book will make its appearance, it is of the utmost moment to the printer and his workmen that their material be not blocked up, or their time frittered away. He therefore proceeds at once to the inspection of his proof-sheet; to the task of examining every page, line, word, letter, point, with a keen and scrutinizing eye. In this he has in view one at least of two objects, — to ascertain whether the compositor and the proof-reader have left any errors uncorrected, or whether he himself, in the preparation of his manuscript, has been sufficiently careful to express his ideas in the clearest and most accurate manner. Indeed, to ensure the highest degree of correctness, he should have both objects in view; for even if the writer have genius or great learning, and the printer be a man of talent and taste, it is not to be supposed, that these qualities, so desirable in authorship and typography, will have made either of them immaculate. It is therefore probable that both parties have more or less erred. The spelling or the punctuation may be sometimes erroneous; the capitalizing and Italicizing may be susceptible of improvement; inelegances may be noticed, improprieties perceived, or grammatical inaccuracies detected, which, either in the warmth of composition or in a premature haste for going to press, were before concealed. Suggestions, too, may appear in the margin, which, though made by the office-corrector in the modest form of queries, are worthy, at least for courtesy's sake, of being attended to by the author; who should either adopt them, and expunge, in every case, the word "*Qy.;*" make, if thought preferable, a different change; or erase both the query and the suggestion, — instead of leaving them, as is sometimes done, in the margin, to try the printer's patience, and to baffle his skill and ingenuity in ascertaining what is meant.

But an author may be capable of rectifying all these mistakes, and yet, from his inexperience or his heedlessness, he may note them down in the proof-sheet in such a way as to render them either invisible or illegible, and thus defeat his own purposes. To prevent this result, he should mark his corrections, not with a pencil, but with a pen; and place them, not between the printed lines, but in the margin, exactly opposite where the changes required are to be made. In short, to preclude the probability of additional or different mistakes, it should be his aim to use the very marks which the printer employs, and in a similar way. To facilitate an object so essential, we present two pages (*see* pp. 320-21); the one exhibiting a proof, when read and marked, of work such as may proceed from the hands of a compositor; the other, as it would appear after the corrections have been duly made in type. The former is called a "foul proof," because it contains a far greater number of mistakes than could be made by a skilful and attentive workman; but it is purposely thus presented, in order that an author may see at once the whole of the marks which are adopted, and be enabled to write in the same manner those required in his own proof.

We may add, for the information of young writers, and to deter them from making changes out of mere caprice, that the transferring of these to type is a matter of considerable labor; and that alterations, when numerous, will form a rather heavy item in the printer's bill. To save, however, as much of this expense as possible, an author may, by a little manœuvring, often substitute, in room of what he erases, just as much as would fill up the space, or expunge as great an amount of matter as he wishes to introduce.

Having finished the reading and correcting of his proof-sheet, the author should write on the lower margin of the last page, either the words " Revise wanted," indicating that he must have another proof, in order to compare it with the former, and to see whether all the pages are correct, before being printed; or the term " Press," showing that, after the alterations have been made in the metal, and read again by the office proof-reader from another impression, there will be no occasion for himself to see a revise, but that the form of pages may be put to press. This impression is usually termed a " Press-proof," and so marked at the top of the first page.

When the form has gone to press, the first fair-printed sheet, called a " Revise," is shown to the proof-reader, who compares it with the press-proof, and cursorily examines the folios, the foot-lines, and the sides of the pages, to ascertain whether any types have fallen out or been broken, or any " bites " have been made, in the last processes.

All the operations described may be regarded as only one of the stages made in the progress of a work through the press. The same course has to be performed with the remainder of the book, before it meets the approving smile, the condemnatory voice, or the silent indifference, of the mighty Public, — before it shine as a beautiful and benignant sun in the firmament of literature, or glimmer like a taper through its little night, shedding for a moment its delusive rays on the step of the benighted traveller, but soon to be extinguished and forgotten amid the effulgence of meridian day.

In these suggestions we have said nothing of the processes adopted in correcting a proof taken from reprinted, magazine, or newspaper matter. But it will be easy for the printer to modify these in accordance with the nature of the work, with the views of parties having over it literary control, or with the amount of time given for bringing out the publication. This much, however, may be said, in justice to authors who have no opportunity of superintending the press, that the same degree of accuracy should be ensured in the second and following editions of their books as in the first; and, in relation to journals, that if an article, poem, or advertisement is worth the perusal of the public, it surely deserves to be exhibited in a form not altogether disgraceful to taste and letters.

VIII. — EXPLANATION OF PROOF-MARKS.

To enable the young author to write his corrections in the proof-sheet, so as to be readily seen and understood by the compositor, we now enter on an explanation of the marks used in pages 320–21, and to which some allusions were made in the preceding article: —

In page 269, it is said that capital letters are indicated by three horizontal lines drawn beneath a word meant to be so printed; small capitals, by two lines; and Italics, by one. This is illustrated in page 320, — in the title of the piece, the printed lines numbered 1, 23, and the last line; where the abbreviated words, *Caps.*, *S. Caps.*, and *Ital.*, are written in the margin, exactly opposite where the corrections are to be made in type.

If a word or phrase has been erroneously put in capitals or small capitals, instead of common letters, the change is indicated by writing in the margin, as in No. 2, the abbreviation *l. c.* (for "lower-case letters").

To correct a wrong letter, point, or other character, a line is drawn slopingly through it; to correct a wrong word or phrase or two wrong letters, across them; and the right letter, point, word, or phrase, or the appropriate mark, is written in the margin, opposite the error. See Nos. 2, 5, 6, 9—11, 14, 16—19, 27, 29.

When letters, words, points, characters, or spaces have been omitted, a caret is put where they are to be introduced; the corrections, as before, being written in the margin. See Nos, 3, 4, 7, 13, 15, 17, 24, 27.

A line drawn in a sloping direction from right to left is put after all the points written in the margin; with the exception of the period, which is placed within a circle, and of the apostrophe, reference-marks, and superiors, which are inserted in a figure resembling a capital V. The lines are used to separate one mark from another with which it is unconnected, or to attract the eye to corrections, which, from their smallness, are liable to be overlooked. See Nos. 2, 9, 13, 15—17, 29.

If a space is wanting between two words, a mark like that opposite Nos. 3 and 27 is put in the margin. But, if letters that should join are separated, the mark ⌣ must be used, both under them and in the margin opposite, agreeably to No. 28.

A little line is written under letters or other printed characters that are inverted, broken, or dirty, and also under those which are too large or too small, as in Nos. 5 and 24. To draw attention to an inverted letter, a mark resembling the figure 9, but sloped, is written in the margin, No. 5; to a bad or foul type, a small cross, like an Italic *x*, No. 24; and to a character of an improper size, the abbreviation *w.f.*, denoting a wrong font, No. 25.

When a word, character, or point is erased, a *d*, written with a line through it from the top, similar to that opposite Nos. 6, 11, 17, 22, 29, and appropriately called a *dele* ("strike out"), is placed in the margin.

If a space sticks up between two words, a mark like a double dagger should be put opposite, as in No. 19.

Should two words be transposed, note the mistake by drawing a line over the first word, and continuing it under the second; and by placing the abbreviation *tr.* ("transpose") in the margin, as in No. 21. If the misplaced word belongs to a different line of print, encircle the word, and draw a line from it to the place where it should be inserted. When several words are to be transposed, indicate the order by placing the figures 1, 2, 3, &c., over them, and by drawing a line under them; *tr.* being, as in the other modes of transposition, written in the margin.

Should a character, word, or phrase be struck out that is afterwards approved of, dots are placed under it, and the Latin direction *Stet* ("let it stand or remain") placed in the margin, as in No. 23.

When lines of print are close that should be separate, write in the margin the term *Lead* or *Leads*, according to Nos. 13, 14; and, when lines are apart that should be close, say, *Dele lead*, using, however, the peculiar mark for the first of these words, in accordance with Nos. 23, 24.

When several words or lines have been left out, they should be written at the side, top, or bottom of the page, as is most convenient, and a line drawn from the place where they are to be introduced, to the first word of the written phrase or passage, as exemplified in No. 24. But, if more matter is to be inserted than can be contained in the margin, the direction *See Copy* and the folio of the manuscript should be written within a circle, opposite the line where the omission has been made.

In the left-hand margin of Nos. 8 and 9 occurs the direction, *No break;* and, in that of No. 12, the mark ¶. The former denotes that the sentences between which a line is drawn are to be put in one and the same paragraph; and the latter, that the passage preceded by the crotchet [is to begin a *new* paragraph. The last mark is also used for a different purpose, as in No. 1, where the first word is to be brought to the commencement of the line, without being indented.

If a line is irregularly spaced, as in No. 26, — that is, if some of the words are too close, and others too wide apart, — let the direction *Space better* be written opposite, in the margin.

When the reader of the proof-sheet is doubtful as to the spelling of any word, or the correctness of any expression, he writes on the opposite margin the abbreviation *Qy.* (for *query*), with his suggestion; as exemplified in No. 26, where the *e* in the first syllable of Shakspeare's name is queried, and the suggestion made, by the appropriate mark, that the letter be deled, or struck out.

Crooked letters or words are noticed, as in Nos. 28—30, by means of horizontal lines [═══] drawn above and below them, and also in the margin.

Corrections are usually placed in the margin to the right, as being more convenient to the hand of the proof-reader and the eye of the compositor; the left-hand margin being appropriated to directions and marks for which there is little room in the opposite margin. All the corrections or emendations should be put in the order in which they occur, as marked in Nos. 1, 2, 5, 8, 9, 11. 17, 19, 23, 24, 26, 27, 29.

SPECIMEN OF PROOF-SHEET.

TYPOGRAPHICAL MARKS EXEMPLIFIED.

WORTH OF HUMAN NATURE.

1. Where, unreasonable complainer! dost thou stand, and what
2. is around thee? The world spreads before thee its sublime
3. mysteries, where the thoughts of sages lose themselves in won-
4. der; the ocean lifts up its etrnal anthems to thine ear; the
5. golden sun lights thy path; the wide heavens stretch them-
6. selves above thee, and worlds rise upon worlds, and systems
7. beyond systems, to infinity; and dost thou stand in centre of
8. all this, to complain of thy lot and place?
9. Pupil of that infinite teaching, minister at Nature's great
10. altar! child of heaven's favor! ennobled being! redeemed
11. creature! must thou pine in moping and envious melancholy,
12. amidst the plenitude of the whole creation? But thy neigh-
13. bor is above thee, thou sayest. What then? What is that to
14. thee? What though the shout of millions rose around him?
15. What is that to the million voiced nature that God has given
16. thee? That shout dies away into the vacant air; it is not his,
17. but thy nature, thy favored, sacred, and glorious nature, is
18. thine — it is the reality, to which praise is but a fleeting breath.
19. Thou canst meditate the things which pplouse but cele-
20. brates.
21. In that thou art a man, thou art exalted infinitely above what
22. any man can be, in that that he is praised. I would rather be
23. the humblest man in the world, than barely be thought greater
24. than the greatest. Not one of the crowds that listened to
25. the eloquence of Demosthenes and Cicero, — not one who has
26. bent with admiration over the pages of Homer and Shake-
27. speare, — not one who followed in the train of Cæsar or of
28. Napoleon, would part with the humblest power of thought,
29. for all the fame that is echoing over the world, and through
30. the ages.

Dewey.

The beggar is greater as a man, than
is the man merely as a king.

PRECEDING PAGE AFTER CORRECTION.

WORTH OF HUMAN NATURE.

Where, unreasonable complainer! dost thou stand, and what is around thee? The world spreads before thee its sublime mysteries, where the thoughts of sages lose themselves in wonder; the ocean lifts up its eternal anthems to thine ear; the golden sun lights thy path; the wide heavens stretch themselves above thee, and worlds rise upon worlds, and systems beyond systems, to infinity; and dost thou stand in the centre of all this, to complain of thy lot and place? Pupil of that infinite teaching! minister at Nature's great altar! child of Heaven's favor! ennobled being! redeemed creature! must thou pine in sullen and envious melancholy, amidst the plenitude of the whole creation?

"But thy neighbor is above thee," thou sayest. What then? What is that to thee? What though the shout of millions rose around him? What is that to the million-voiced nature that God has given *thee?* That shout dies away into the vacant air; it is not his: but thy *nature* — thy favored, sacred, and glorious nature — is thine. It is the reality, to which praise is but a fleeting breath. Thou canst meditate the things which applause but celebrates.

In that thou art a man, thou art infinitely exalted above what any man can be, in that he is praised. I would rather *be* the humblest man in the world, than barely *be thought* greater than the greatest. The beggar is greater as a man, than is the man merely as a king. Not one of the crowds that listened to the eloquence of Demosthenes and Cicero, — not one who has bent with admiration over the pages of Homer and Shakspeare, — not one who followed in the train of Cæsar or of Napoleon, would part with the humblest power of thought, for all the fame that is echoing over the world and through the ages.

Dewey.

INDEX.

A.

Abbreviations require periods after them, 148, 149. Remarks on the various modes of forming, 272-276. List of, 277-300. Words in copy, not meant to be printed as abbreviations, should be written in full, 304.

"Above all," as an adverbial phrase, pointed with a comma, 72, *a*.

Absolute phrases, 69, 70.

Accents, 239, X.

"Accordingly," 72, *a*.

Adjectives, two, without a conjunction between them, 33, 34, *d—g*.

Adjectives in a series, 39, *e, f*. Consolidated with nouns, 215.

Adjectival phrases, 22, VI.; 59, 60, *j—m*; 69, 70.

Adverbs, 29, *d*; 30, *j*; 33, *d*; 34, *e, j*; 38, *e, f*; 52, *g* 1; 59, *i*; 72-74; 217, 2 *i* and *j*.

Adverbial phrases, 22, VI.; 72-74.

Affirmative words quoted in an interrogative form, 156, *f*. Quoted in an exclamatory form, 161, *e*.

"Again," with or without a comma, in accordance with the connection, 72, *a, b*. Followed by a colon, when referring to several sentences, 131, *e*.

Algebraic signs, list of, 301.

"Also," 73, *e*.

"And," between two words of the same part of speech, 28-30. Occurring in a series of words, 37, 38. Between phrases or clauses in the same construction, 98, 99. Between two short clauses, a verb understood in the last, 104, *c*. Between two clauses, the last being added as an explanation, 113, 114. Beginning sentences, 143, *e*.

Antithetic or contrasted words and expressions, 45-47; 79, *f*; 104, 105; 113, 114.

Apostrophe, rules and remarks on the, with exercises, 198-207. Improperly used in certain abbreviations, 149, *e*; 198, 199, *c—f*; 276. Marks the possessive case, 204, 205; 216.

Appellations of God and Christ, initial letters in the, 259, 260.

Appellatives before and after proper names, initials of, 262, *e*.

Apposition, 23, X.; 41-43; 213.

Apprentices to the printing-business counselled, 11.

Arabic figures, how pointed, 112; 149, *e*; 150, IV Dash supplying the place of, 195. Plurals of, how formed, 198, *b*. Small, or superiors, for references, 240.

Arithmetic, the points to be used in books of, 141, *a*.

Arithmetical signs, 301.

"As," signifying *in the manner in which*, 89, *c*; 105, *d*.

"As—as," "as—so," the correlatives, 93, *a*; 94, *c*.

"As well as," between two words mutually related, 45, *e*. Between a word and a phrase, or between two phrases, 46, *e*.

"As yet," and similar phrases, 72, *a*

"As," "namely," &c., 128; 138, d.
Asterisk, the uses of the, 240. The three asterisks, 237, V.
Astronomical characters, list of, 302.
"At present," 72, a.
Authors, the duty of, to point their manuscripts well, 7, 8; 304, 305. Are assisted in composition by an acquaintance with the art of punctuation, 7, 8. If considerate, they prepare "copy" so as to be perfectly legible, 304–306. And correct the proof-sheets with all possible care, adopting the precise marks used by printers, 312, 313.

B.

"Because," the comma sometimes omitted before, 89, c.
"Besides," used as a preposition or a conjunction, 74, j.
Bible references, how pointed, 100, j; 150, V., 1; 151, b, c. Chapters of the Bible referred to by numeral letters, 151, b.
Blank at the beginning of a poetical quotation, when the first portion is omitted, 195, b.
Blunders in sense caused by a habit of careless punctuation, 3–5, 18. In printing, often caused by illegible writing, 306.
Books, terms relating to, 270, 271. Captions, subheads, sideheads, and running titles, 270. Signatures, and names of sizes of volumes, 271.
"Boro'," better spelled out, 190, d.
"Both—and," the correlatives, 29, g; 94, h.
Brace, for what purpose used, 237.
Brackets, the manner of applying them, 170, j; 235.
Broken sentences, 175.
"Brothers" in a firm, 41, c.
"But," between two words contrasted or mutually related, 45, c.
Between a word and a phrase, or between two phrases, 46, e. Between two short clauses, in the last of which a verb is understood, 104, c. Between two clauses, the latter being added by way of contrast, 113, 114. Commencing sentences, 142, 143. In the sense of *except*, 79, g.
"But also," 35, l.
"But has," meaning *as not to have*, 93, b.

C.

Capitals, their uses and applications, 257–269. Used as reference-signs and dominical letters, 149, f. The points put after representative or numeral capitals, 149, f; 151, a. Capitals used instead of Arabic figures, 150, V, 2; 268, XII. In titlepages, inscriptions, &c., 268, XIII. Words wholly in capitals and small capitals, how distinguished in manuscript, 269.
Captions, or headings, 147, 270.
Caret, its form and use, 237, VI.; 304.
Catalogues, words or phrases in, often followed by a period, 147. Names omitted in, sometimes supplied by two commas or by long dashes, 236, III., and 238, VIII. Leaders in, 238, IX. Abbreviations serviceable in, 272.
"Catholic," the initial letter of, 265, f.
Cedilla, the, 239, XII.
Change of subject, abrupt, preceded by a dash, 175.
Chanting service in the Liturgy, a colon inserted in each verse of, 141.
"Chapter," a dash commonly put after the word and its numeral, 194, d.
Chapters of the Bible referred to by numeral letters, 150, V., 1; 151, b
"Church," initial of, 265, e.

Clauses, definition of, 21, V. Relative, 57-60. Parenthetical or Intermediate, 64. Vocative, 68. One clause depending on another, 89, 90. Correlative, 93, 94. In the same construction, 98; 100, k, l. One having a verb understood, 104, 105. Clauses preceding quotations or remarks, 108, 109; 138. United by conjunctions, 113, 114. Divisible into simpler portions, 100, l; 116, 117. Series of, having a common dependence, 120, 121. Complete, but followed by a remark, inference, or illustration, 130, 131. Constituting members, 134, 135. Interrogative, 155, 156. Exclamatory, 159-161. In parentheses, 168, 169. Concluding, on which other expressions depend, 178.

Colon, rules and remarks on the, with exercises, 129-141.

Comma, rules and remarks on the, with exercises, 27-112. An inverted, sometimes used instead of a small c, 236, II.

Commas, two, used under names to avoid repetition, 236, III. Inverted, double or single, as quotation-marks, 228, 230.

Commencement of a broken quotation in verse, blank at the, 195, b.

Complete sentences, 142, 143.

Compositors, a knowledge of punctuation necessary to, in their business, 8, 9. Their skill in the art conducive to mental vigor, 9-11.

Compound sentences, what they are, 21, III.

Compound and derivative words, distinction between, 23, XII.; 208, b.

Compound words, rule and remarks on, 209-218. Exceptions to the rule, 211, 212. Compound adjectives and compound nouns, 212. Nouns and pronouns in apposition, 213. Nouns used adjectively, 213, 214. Numeral adjectives, 214. Adjectives consolidated with nouns, 215. Names of places, 215, 216. The possessive case, 216, 217. Compound and other phrases, 217, 218. Exercises on, 221-223.

Conjoined members of sentences, 134, 135.

Conjunctions to be pointed, when separated by other words from the parts to which they belong, 65, d. Joining words of the same part of speech, 28-30; 37, 38. Between contrasted or related words and phrases, 45, 46, c, e, f, g, j. Used as adverbs, 73, h, i. As correlatives, 93, 94. Joining phrases and words, 98, 99. Joining clauses, 89, 90, e, f; 104, c; 108, 109, d, e; 113, 114. Joining sentences, 126, c. Beginning sentences, 134, b; 143.

"Consequently," how punctuated, 72, a.

Construction of a sentence, what it is, 23, XIII. Illustrated, 98, a.

Contents of books, chapters, or sections, how pointed, 148, b.

Contractions and abbreviations, remarks on, 272-276. Table of, 277-300.

Contrasted words and expressions, 45-47; 79, f; 104, 105; 113, 114.

Co-ordinate or consecutive clauses, 22, V.; 100, k.

Copy, hints on the preparation of, 303-307.

Corrector of the press, duties of a, 11, 12; 308-315.

Correlative clauses and words explained, 21-23, V. and IX. Their punctuation, 93, 94.

Crotchets, or brackets, 170, j; 235

D.

Dagger, the uses of the, 240.
Dash, rules and remarks on the, with exercises. 174-196. What points, if any, are used with dashes, 175, *a*, *b*; 178, *a*; 182, *a—c*; 186, 187; 191, *c*.
Dates 79, *j*; 80, *k*; 100, *j*; 112; 149, *e*; 150, 151; 195; 275.
Decimals, pounds and shillings, how pointed, 150. IV.
Definition of the art of punctuation, 2, 19.
Definitions of terms used in the present work, 20-23.
Dependent clauses, 21, 22, V.; 89, 90; 120, 121.
Derivative words, how distinguished from compounds, 23, XII.; 208, *b*. Prefixes in, 219, 220. Exercises on derivatives and compounds, 221-223.
Designations of religious and political parties, initial letters of the, 263, *a*; 265, *e—h*.
"Devil" and "devils," the initials of, 262, *a*.
Diæresis, use of the, 200, *g*; 219, *a*; 239, XI.
"Divine," "Divine Being," &c., the initial letters of, 260, *e*, *f*.
Division of words into syllables, according to their pronunciation, 224. According to their form, derivation, or meaning, 225. At ends of lines, 226. Exercises on the, 226, 227.
Dominical letters, pointed not as abbreviations, but signs, 149, *f*.
'Doubtless," 72, *a*, *b*.

E.

Echo, or rhetorical repetition, 182, 183. What points are used with the dash after it, 182, *a—c*. Echo of the thought, 183, *e*.

"Ed," "èd," &c., the termination of participles in verse, 199-201. *g—i*.
"Either," "even," beginning a final phrase, 79, *c*.
"Either—or," the correlatives, 29, *g*; 94, *h*.
Elision of letters in poetry and dialogue, 198, 199.
Ellipsis of "namely," "that is," &c., 191. Of letters, figures, or words, 195; 238, VIII. Of words at the beginning of poetical quotations, 195, *b*. Marks of, how formed, 195; 238, VIII.
Epigrammatic sentences, 175.
"Eternal," the initial letter of, as an adjective applied to God, 260, *e*.
"Ev'ry," the apostrophe in, 199, *f*.
Example, the punctuation of words introducing an, 128, 138, 191. A poetical, marked with inverted commas, 229, *g*. The initial letter of the first word in an, 267, XI.
Exclamation, the note of, rule and remarks on, with exercises, 159-163. Sometimes improperly used, 159, *a*; 161, *d*.
Exercises on the definitions, 24, 25. On the comma, 31, 32; 35, 36; 39, 40; 43, 44; 47-49; 54-56; 61-63; 66, 67; 68; 70, 71; 74-77; 80-82; 86-88; 90-92; 95-97; 100-103; 105-107; 109-111; 112. On the semicolon, 114, 115; 117, 118; 122; 126, 127; 128. On the comma and the semicolon, 119; 123, 124. On the colon, 131-133; 136; 139, 140. On the semicolon and the colon, 137. On the period, 143-146; 151, 152. On the notes of interrogation and exclamation, 157, 158; 162, 163; 164-166. On the marks of parenthesis, 171-173. On the dash, 176, 177; 179, 180; 183-185; 188, 189; 192; 195, 196. On the semicolon

and dash, 181. On the dash and its accompanying point, 189, 190; 193. On the apostrophe, 201-203; 205-207. On the hyphen, 221-223; 226, 227. On marks of quotation, 233, 234. General, 241-254.

Explanation of proof-marks, 316-318.

"Expression," meaning of the word, 22, VII.

Expressions, inverted, 83-85. Correlative, 93, 94. Divided into simpler parts, 116, 117. Having a common dependence, 120, 121; 178. In the form of questions, 155, 156. Indicating passion or emotion, 159-161.

Extracts, consisting of words or expressions, 228-231. Composed of successive paragraphs, 232.

F.

"Father," "Fathers," distinctions made in the initials of, 260, g; 262. c.

Figures, Arabic, how punctuated, 112; 150. IV. Not abbreviations, 149, e; 150, IV.

Final phrases, 70, g; 78-80. Clauses, 89, 90.

"First," "finally," "for the most part," often pointed with commas, 72. a.

"First Cause, Father of mercies," the initials of, 260, f, g.

First word in a book, tract, &c., 258, I. In phrases or clauses separately numbered, 258, I., b. After a period, or note of interrogation or exclamation, 258, II. b; 259, c.

"For," between two clauses, the latter being explanatory, 113, 114. Beginning sentences, 134, b; 143, e.

Foreign words that have been Anglicised by contraction, 149, d.

"Formerly," often unpointed, 72, c.

G.

General exercises, 241-254.

Genitive case, rule and remarks on the sign of the, with exercises, 204-207.

Geographical and geometrical signs, 301.

"God," when used with a capital, and when with a small initial, 259, a.

"Gospel," initial of, varied in accordance with its meaning, 264, d.

Governing words, the last of two or more, 33, d; 34, e; 38, g.

Grammar, some acquaintance with, necessary to a knowledge of punctuation, 20.

Grammatical punctuation different from rhetorical, 15-17; 27, 28.

Grammatical points, rules and remarks on the, with exercises, 26-152.

Grammatical and rhetorical points, rules and remarks on the, with exercises, 153-196.

H.

Hand, or index, 237, IV.

Headings and subheads, 147, 270.

Heads of chapters, sections, articles, put entirely on capitals or small capitals, 268, XIII.

"Heaven," not to be printed *heav'n*, 199, f. The initial letter of, 260, d; 262, b.

"Heavenly" should have a small initial, 260, e.

"Hence," "here," 73, e, f.

"However," the pointing of, as a conjunction and an adverb, 73, h.

Hints on the preparation of copy, and on proof-reading, 303-315.

"Holy Spirit," "Holy Ghost," the initials of, usually put in capitals. 260, i.

"How," 109, g; 160, b

INDEX.

Hyphen, rules and remarks on the, with exercises, 208-227. As used in compound words, 209-218. In derivatives, 219, 220. In syllabication, 224-226.

I.

" I. e.," " that is," 123; 138, *d*.
" If," 89, *a*, *e*; 109, *g*.
Imperative absolute, 69, *b*.
Importance of punctuation, 1-18.
' In conclusion," when put at the beginning of a paragraph, 131, *e*.
' In fine," " in short," " in truth," " in general," &c., usually pointed with commas, 72, *a*.
" In order that," 90, *g*, *h*.
" In order to," 79, *i*.
" Indeed," as an adverb and as a conjunction, 73, *h*.
Independent phrases, 69, 70.
Independent sentences, 142.
Index, or hand, use of the, 237, IV.
Indirect quotations, questions, &c., 108, *c*; 109, *g*; 155, *b*; 229, *b*.
" Indisputably," 72, *a*.
" Infinite One," begun with capital letters, 260, *f*.
Initial letters of words, when to be capitalized, 257-267.
Inscriptions, capitals and small capitals used in, 268, XIII.
Institutions, principal words in the rules and reports of, 261, *a*.
Interlineations to be made in copy with great distinctness, 304.
Interlocutors, names of, 194, *c*.
Intermediate words, phrases, and clauses, 22, VIII.; 46, *j*; 50, *c*; 57, *b*; 58, *e*; 64, 65; 69, *d—f*; 72, XI., *d*; 73, *g—i*; 186, 187.
Interrogation-point, rules and remarks on the, with exercises, 154-158.
Inverted expressions, 83-85. When the comma should be omitted in, 84, *d*; 85, *f*. When inserted, 84, *e*; 85, *g*.
Italics, how distinguished in manuscript, 269. To be sparingly used. 223, *d—f*; 269, 270.

K and L.

" King," sometimes put with a capital *K*, and sometimes with a small one, 259, *b*; 261, *b*.
Language, oral, rendered more expressive by variation of tones, inflections, and pauses, 1, 2. Written or printed, elucidated by points, 2.
Larger portions of sentences, 116, 117.
Leaders, or dots, 238, IX.
Letter-writers cause trouble by their loose style of pointing, 5.
Letter, syllabic, and quotation points, rules and remarks on the, with exercises, 197-234.
Letters of the alphabet, sometimes signs, not abbreviations, 149, *f*. Used instead of Arabic figures or numeral words, 150, 151.
" Lord," " lady," initials of, 259, *b*; 261, IV., *b*.
Lunar signs, 302.

M.

" Madam," the initial of, 261, IV., *b*.
Marks, not pointed as abbreviations, 150, IV.
Marks, miscellaneous, explanation of, 235-240. Arithmetical and other, 301.
Marks of parenthesis, rule and remarks on the, with exercises, 167-174.
Marks of quotation, rules and observations on the, with exercises, 228-234.
Marks, typographical, explained and exemplified, 316-321.

Mathematical signs, 301.
Medical signs, 301.
Members of sentences, explanation of, 21, IV. Conjoined, 134, 135.
Miscellaneous abbreviations, list of, 277–300.
Miscellaneous marks, 235–240.
"More, greater, &c.,—than," the correlatives, 93, *a*; 94, *d, e.*
"More, the,—the better," the correlatives, 93, *a.*
"Most High," "Highest," applied to God, begin with capitals, 260, *f.*

N.

Ñ, the Spanish, 239, XIII.
"Namely," 128; 138, *d*; 191.
Names of the grammatical points, and whence borrowed, 26. Of interlocutors, the dash unnecessary after, 194, *c.* Of persons and places begun with capital letters, 262. Compound, of places, 215. Names of sizes of books, 271.
"Nature," with a capital or a small *n*, 260, *c.*
"Neither—nor," the correlatives, 29, *g*; 93, *a*; 94, *h.*
"No," when equivalent to a sentence, 130, *d.*
Nominative and verb, 50–54. Absolute or independent, 69, *a, c.*
Nominative clause, what it is, 21, V.; 50, *a.* Phrase, 22, VI.; 50, *a.*
"Nor," between two words of the same part of speech, 28, 29. In a series of words, 87, 88. As a correlative, 93, *a*; 94, *h.* Between phrases and words in the same construction, 98, *b*; 99, *g.* Between two short clauses, a verb being understood in the latter, 104, *e.*
"Not," between two words contrasted or mutually related, 46, *d.* Preceding the first of two contrasted words or phrases, 46, *f, h.* and *i.*
Notes of interrogation and exclamation, difference between the, 154. Rules and remarks on the, with exercises, 155–166.
"Notwithstanding," 74, *j.*
Nouns in apposition, 41, 42; 213. In the possessive case, 204, 205; 216. Compound, 212. Used adjectively, 213. Gentile, initials of, 263.
"Now," as an adverb and a conjunction, 73, *h.*
"Now and then," 72, *a.*
Number of a house or shop and the name of street, 100, *j.*
Numeral adjectives, with respect to the hyphen, 214.
Numeral figures and words, how pointed, 112.

O.

"O" and "oh," in what they differ, and how pointed, 160, *c.*
Obelisk, or dagger, 240.
Objections to the study of punctuation answered, 12–14.
Objective absolute or independent, 69, *f.*
"Of," having before it a verb understood, 105, *e.*
"Of late," "of course," &c., 72, *a.*
"Of which," "of whom," 59, *h.*
Omission of "namely" or "that is," 191. Of letters, figures, or words 195; 239, VIII. Of words in the first line of a poetical quotation, 195, *b.*
"On the one hand," "on the contrary," &c., 72, *a.*
"Once more," put at the beginning of several sentences, 131, *e.*
"Or," 28–30; 37, 38; 94, *h*; 98–100, *b, g, i*; 104, *e.*
"Orthodox," initial of, 265, *g.*

P

"Pagan," initial of, 265, g.
Pairs, words in, united by conjunctions, 38, i, j; 99, i. Contrasted by prepositions, 46, g.
Paragraph-mark, 240, 304.
Paragraphs sometimes connected by a dash, 194, b. To be distinctly marked in manuscript, 304, 305.
Parallel lines, 240, 301.
Parentheses and parenthetical expressions, difference between, 64, a, b.
Parenthesis, marks of, rules and observations on the, with exercises, 167–173. How points are to be used with, 168, 169.
Parenthetical words and expressions, 22, VIII.; 46, j; 50, c; 57, b; 64, 65; 69, d—f; 186, 187. The commas often omitted before and after short, 65, e.
Participles used relatively, 60, j—m.
Participial phrases, 22, VI.; 69, 70.
Particulars of a series, 23, XI.; 37, 38; 58, d; 98, 99; 120, 121; 125, 126.
Pauses marked and unmarked, 15, 16; 51, 52.
"Perhaps," 72, c, d.
Period, rules and remarks on the, with exercises, 142–152.
Persons and places, initial letters of the names of, 262.
Phrase, definition of a, 22, VI.
Phrases in apposition, 41–43. In contrast, 45–47. Adjectival, participial, and absolute, 69, 70. Adverbial, 72. Final, 78–80; 70, g. Inverted, 83–85. Having the import of conditional clauses, 85, g; 89, b. In the same construction, 98–100. In titlepages, catalogues, &c., 147. Distinguished by Italics or by inverted commas, 229.
Planetary signs and aspects, 302.

Plurals of letters of the alphabet and of Arabic figures, 198, b. Of nouns and pronouns in the possessive case, 205. All plural nouns to be clearly written in copy, 304.
Poetical quotations beginning with a broken line, 195. b.
Poetry requires more semicolons and colons than prose, 125, b. When to be marked with inverted commas, 229, g.
Points, enumeration of the, 26, 153, 197.
Political parties, initials of the names of, 265, h.
Possessive case, 42, h; 204, 205; 216, 217.
"Power" not to be written pow'r, 199, f.
Prefixes in derivative words, 219, 220.
Prepositions, two, joined by "and," "or," "nor," 29, b.
Primitive word, what it is, 23, XII.
Pronoun I, and interjection O, 265.
Pronouns in appositional phrases, 41, 42. In the possessive case, 205, e. Referring to God and Christ, 261, j.
Pronouns, relative, 57–59.
Proof-readers, a knowledge of punctuation indispensable to, 11, 12.
Proof-reading, hints on, 308–315.
Proof-marks explained. 316–319. Exemplified, 320. Corrected, 321.
Proper names in apposition, 41, 42. In an address, 68. In signatures to documents, 147, 148. When pronounced in accordance with their abbreviated forms, 149, g. In the possessive case, 204, 216. The simples of, when to be consolidated, and when to be hyphened, 215. 216. To be correctly spelled and clearly written in copy, 302.

INDEX. 331

Prosopopœia, or personification, 266, 267.

"Providence" and "providential," the initials of, 260, *d*, *e*.

Punctuation, its importance, 1-17. What it is, and what its aim, 2, 19. Useful to all, but much neglected, 3-5. Even by authors and printers, 5, 6. Means of acquiring a knowledge of its principles, 6, 7. Appeal, on its behalf, to authors, journeymen compositors, apprentices, and proof-readers, 7-12. Objections to the study of it stated and answered, 12-14. Its essential principles fixed, 14. Imperfectly treated by grammarians, 14. Regarded by speakers in a false light, 15. Confounded with rhetorical, 15, 16. Determined chiefly by grammatical principles, 16, 17. Illustrated, 4, 18. Exemplified in general exercises, 241-254.

Q.

Qualifying words, two, without a conjunction, 33, *d*; 34, *e—g*. Three, 38, *e*, *f*.

Quantity, marks of, 239, XI.

Questions, 154-156. Indirect, 155, *b*. Assertive in form, 156, *c*. Containing an affirmative quotation, 156, *f*. Introducing quotations, 156, *g*.

Question and answer in the same paragraph, 194, *a*.

Quotations, clauses preceding, 108; 138; 191, *e*.

Quotations, read as interrogatory, which were originally affirmative, 156, *f*. Indirect, 229, *b*; 267, *a*. Quotations within, 230, 231. The initial in the first word of, 267, XI.

Quotation, the marks of, rules and observations on, with exercises, 228-234.

R.

Reader of proof-sheets, matters to be attended to by the, 11, 12; 308-315.

Reading-boy, directions to the, in reading copy aloud, 309, 310.

Reference-marks, 240.

References to books, chapters, and verses in the Bible, 100, *j*; 151, *b*, *c*; 274. To other works, 268, XII., *a*; 273.

Relative clause, definition of a, 21, V. Explaining the antecedent, 57, § I., and *a*, *b*. Restricting the antecedent, 57, § II., and *a*; 58, *c*. Whose antecedent consists of particulars, 58, *d*.

Relative pronoun followed by an expression enclosed by commas, 58, *e*. Separated by several words from its grammatical antecedent, 58, *f*; 59, *g*. "Of which," "of whom," 59, *h*. Adverb put for a preposition and relative, 59, *i*. Relative and verb understood, 59, *j*; 60, *l*, *m*. Present participle used for a relative and verb, 60. *k*. The relative only understood, 60, *n*. "Such as," denoting *that which*, 60, *o*.

Remarks, short, 108, 109.

Remarks formally introduced, 138.

Repetition of nominative in a different form, 53, *g* 8, *h*. Of words or phrases, 34, *i*, *j*; 182, 183.

Representative letters, and abbreviations, 272-300.

"Revelation," initial of the word, 264, *d*.

Rhetorical punctuation contrasted with grammatical, 15-17.

Rules and reports of societies, initial letters of the principal words in, 261, *a*.

Running titles, or headlines, explanation of, 270, III.

S.

"Scriptures" and "Sacred Writings," initials of, 264, c.
"Section," the dash put after the number of, in a headline, 194, d.
Section-mark, 240.
Semicolon, rules and remarks on the, with exercises, 113–128.
Sentences defined, 20, I. and II.; 21, III. Consisting each of two clauses joined by "for," "but," or "and," 113. Short, slightly connected in sense or in construction, 125, 126. Complete and independent, 142. Interrogative and exclamatory, 154–161. Used as parentheses, 169, f—h. Broken and epigrammatic, 175.
Series, the term, defined, 23, XI.
Series of words of the same part of speech, 37, 38. Of phrases and clauses, 98, 99. Of expressions having a common dependence, 120, 121; 178.
Short quotations or remarks, 108, 109; 228, 229; 267, XI., a, b.
Short sentences, slightly connected, 125, 126.
Sideheads and subheads, 194, 270.
Signatures to documents, how punctuated, 147, 148.
Signatures, letters of the alphabet or Arabic figures for the accommodation of the bookbinder, 271.
Significant pauses, 175; 191, a.
Signs, medical, arithmetical, algebraic, and geometrical, 301. Astronomical, 302.
Simple word, what it is, 23, XII.
Simpler parts into which expressions are sometimes divisible, 116, 117.
Sizes of books, names of various, 271.
"So—as," "so—that," the correlatives, 93, a; 94, e, f, g.
Societies, principal words in the rules and reports of, 261, a.

"Son of man," when used of Christ how to be written and printed, 260, h.
Songs, ballads, and hymns, often pointed with semicolons and colons, 125, b.
Specification of subjects, or names of things, 128; 138, d, e.
Specimen of proof-sheet, 320, 321.
"Spirit," "Holy Spirit," and "Spirit of God," usually begun with capital letters, 260, i.
Star, or asterisk, 240.
Stars, the three, or N.B., 237, V.
Subject and predicate, 50–54. With separable or inseparable adjuncts, 50, 51. Exceptions to the rule on the, 52, 53. Subject repeated, 54, g 8, h. The copula, or a verb in the infinitive mood, 54, j. Abrupt change of subject, 175.
"Such as," denoting *that which*, 60, o.
"Such—as" and "such—that," the correlatives, 93, a; 94, f.
"Sunday" and "sabbath," the initials of, 263, e.
Superior figures and letters, used as references, 240.
Suspension of sense, 175, 191.
Syllabication, rules and remarks on, 224–226. Exercises on, 226, 227.

T.

Table of abbreviations, 277–300. Of signs and characters, 301, 302.
Technical expressions to be correctly spelled and clearly written in copy, 304.
"Terms" and "expressions," how used in the present work, 22, VII.
Terms relating to books, their sizes, &c., 270, 271.
Terminations "ed," "èd," "'d," and "t," the participial, occurring in poetry, 199, g; 200, 201.

"Th'," and "t'," the elision of the *e* and *o* in, unnecessary, 199, *f*.
"That," denoting purpose or design, 90, *f*. Introducing a quotation or a remark, 108, 109, *a—e*; 267, *a*.
"That is," "to wit," &c., 72, *a*; 128; 138, *d*; 191.
"The more—the better," 93, *a*.
"Then," "now," "too," "therefore," 73, *h*, *i*.
"There" and "here," 73, *f*.
"Though," between two words contrasted or mutually related, 45, *c*. Preceding the first of two contrasted words or phrases, 46, *f*.
"Though—yet," the correlatives, 93, *a*.
"Though" and "through," improperly contracted *tho'*, *thro'*, 198, *c*.
Three stars, how used, 237.
"Till," not preceded by an apostrophe, 199, *e*.
Titles of eminent men, abbreviated, 148, *a*; 274.
Titles of honor and respect, initial letters in, 261, 262.
Titles of books, names of ships, &c., to be quoted, 229, *e*.
Titles of books, initials of the leading words in, 264, *b*.
Titlepages, authors' names in, how pointed, 147. Words in, displayed entirely with capitals and small capitals, 268, XIII.
"To," signifying *in order to*, 79, *h*.
"To-day" and "to-morrow," commonly used without points, 74, *l*.
"To proceed," "to conclude," "to sum up all," introducing a paragraph, 70, *i*; 131, *e*.
"To wit," 128; 138, *d*.
Transposed or inverted expressions, 83–85.
Two words, of the same part of speech, connected by the conjunctions "and," "or," "nor," 28–30. Not connected by a conjunction, 33–35.
Two brief phrases, united by "and," "or," "nor," 98, *b*; 99, *c*.
Two clauses, one depending on the other, 89, 90. Joined by "and," "or," "nor," "but;" a verb being understood, 104, *c*. United by "for," "but," or "and," 113, 114. Related, but not joined by a conjunction, 130, 131.
Two conjoined members of sentences, 134, 135.
Typographical marks explained, 316–318. Exemplified, 320. Corrected, 321.

U and V.

Uses of capital letters, 257–269. Of Italics, 269, 270.
Verb and its nominative, 50–54. Understood, 104. 105.
"Viz." or "namely," preceding an example or a specification of particulars, 128; 138, *d*. Understood, 191.
Vocative words and expressions, usually pointed with commas, 68, IX. When denoting strong emotion, with notes of exclamation, 68, *a*; 160, *c*. The personal pronoun in vocative expressions, 42, *j*.

W.

"What," "when," "where," indicating indirect questions or remarks, 109, *g*.
"What," used in an exclamatory sense, 160, *b*.
"When," "where," "wherever," &c., in the latter of two clauses, 89, *c*, *d*.
"Whether—or," the correlatives, 94, *k*.
"Without doubt," 72. *a*.

"Word," the initial of, when denoting either the Logos or the Bible, 264, c.

Words in a series, 37, 38. In apposition, 41–43. In contrast, or having a mutual relation to others, 45–47. Correlative, 93, 94. Omitted, 79, 80, j, k; 104, 105; 191; 195. Numeral, when they are to be preferred to Arabic figures, 112, c; 149, e. Specification of words, 128. Words thrown obliquely into the body of a sentence, 168–170. Repeated rhetorically, 182, 183. Compound, 209–218. Derivative, 219, 220. Borrowed from a speaker or an author, 228–231. Words of primary importance, initial letters in, 264, 265.

Y and Z.

"Yes," "no," when equivalent to sentences, how pointed, 130, d.

"Yesterday," not separated by a comma, 74, l.

"Yet," between two words contrasted or mutually related, 45, e. Between two contrasted words, the first preceded by *though*, 46, f

Zodiac, signs of the, 302

THE END.

25TH EDITION, PAGES XII. AND 334, 16MO.

Treatise on English Punctuation;

DESIGNED FOR

LETTER-WRITERS, AUTHORS, PRINTERS, AND CORRECTORS OF THE PRESS; AND FOR THE USE OF SCHOOLS AND ACADEMIES.

WITH AN APPENDIX,

CONTAINING

Rules on the Use of Capitals, a List of Abbreviations, Hints on Preparing Copy and on Proof-reading, Specimen of Proof-Sheet, &c.

BY JOHN WILSON.

NOTICES OF PRECEDING EDITIONS.

This is undoubtedly the most complete work yet published on the subject, both as regards the amount of instruction conveyed, and the lucid arrangement adopted; and we cannot commend it too highly for general use, the more especially as the typographical execution of the work is so superior. — *Norton's Literary Gazette* for March 15, 1855.

Rarely have we seen a book so attractive to the eye. Its rules of punctuation are, in the main, accurate and perspicuous, — far superior to any other system of directions which we have read on this theme. The volume contains much information on the *minutiæ* of literature, with which every scholar ought to be familiar, but of which many eminent authors are lamentably ignorant. We know not where so many particulars relating to the *finish* of copy for the press can be learned. A study of this volume would save youthful scholars from many careless and uncouth habits of writing. The spirit and genius of the English language are intimately connected with some of the questions involved in an accurate punctuation. He who can punctuate accurately can write perspicuously. — *Bibliotheca Sacra*, April, 1855.

A treatise that proposes to familiarize the principles of Punctuation, easily accessible in price and readily intelligible in its composition, cannot be other than welcome to all who write or print; and Mr. Wilson's is certainly the most comprehensive and the most instructive that has come under our observation. . . . It is prepared with great care and good judgment, and no printing-office ought to be without it; as, from its simple arrangement, the compositor and reader will be enabled in an instant to solve any doubt that may arise in the course of their labors. In schools and families, it cannot fail to be useful, equally to teacher and pupil; and even the accomplished author may read it with advantage. Mr. Wilson has done good service to literature by this little volume; and we thank him for it. — *London Critic*

It is an excellent work for schools and academies, and for those who would become self-taught. — *Christian Freeman.*

We have never before met with any work on Punctuation which gave us so great satisfaction as this. — *The Student.*

The best book [on Punctuation] to be recommended is this by Mr. Wilson: there is no other so elaborate and trustworthy. — *Ladies' Repository.*

This is a valuable manual. . . . The work of Mr. Wilson is well calculated to supply the want, which has long been felt to exist, of a suitable text-book upon Punctuation. — *Boston Daily Journal.*

We advise any one, who wishes to understand thoroughly the whole art and mystery of Punctuation and Proof-reading, to get this volume. — *Christian Register.*

A more elegantly printed book than this little volume it would be difficult to find. Mr. Wilson has evidently bestowed upon it the best workmanship of his hand, as well as of his mind. — *Boston Post.*

This treatise of Mr. Wilson, a thorough practical printer, is the best we have ever seen, and in fact the only one we have ever seen worth having. — *Chronotype.*

We invite attention to this truly admirable work. It is one which no printer can afford to want, while to ordinary English scholars its importance is incalculable. — *Belfast (Ire.) News-Letter.*

A work which should be in the possession of every student who aspires even to write a letter. . . . It is a perfect guide in all matters covered by the title. — *Water-cure Journal.*

This is a useful and valuable work on English Punctuation, and every one can read it with profit and pleasure. . . . The subject is treated in an agreeable, instructive, and entertaining manner. — *Boston Daily Atlas.*

A very useful and carefully executed treatise on a subject justly claiming attention, and commonly too much neglected. . . . The classes are so large who feel their want of this kind of instruction, that we must anticipate for our author the success which its merits deserve. — *London Inquirer.*

This work seems to us worthy of being in the hands of every letter-writer, author, printer, editor, and teacher. . . . The work of Mr. Wilson shows much familiarity with the principles of language, and the examples with which he illustrates his text are well chosen. — *Springfield Daily Republican.*

This is a very neatly printed volume, on a subject much neglected, and very imperfectly understood, even by accomplished scholars. . . . This treatise appears to have been prepared with great care and accuracy, and deserves a circulation as wide as the country. — *Liberator.*

From a careful examination of the work, we hesitate not to pronounce it one of the most valuable treatises in the English language. We trust it will be adopted as a text-book in all the institutions in the country. — *Prisoners' Friend.*

If every author and letter-writer could be put in possession of this perfect little work, printers and correctors of the press would canonize Mr. Wilson forthwith; for it would create a new era in their profession. — *Monthly Religious Magazine.*

The whole system is so simply and thoroughly explained in this book of Mr. Wilson's, that any one may clearly comprehend the whole system of Punctuation by a careful perusal and study of this book. We warmly recommend it to all persons. — *Newport Daily News.*

This very excellent work should be in the hands of every aspirant to a true and correct method of English Punctuation. . . . The Appendix and Hints on Proof-reading, with an exemplification of typographical marks, are alone worth the price of the book. — *New-York Day-book.*

My dear Sir, — I have carefully read your volume on English Punctuation, and consider it a most excellent treatise. It places the whole subject upon which you write on a surer basis than any work I have ever before seen. — *Extract of a Letter from the Rev. R. C. Waterston.*

Dear Sir, — Many thanks for your excellent "Treatise on English Punctuation." We have long needed a work which could show the philosophy and common sense of this department of letters. Your book meets the want fully. It is a most scholar-like production, and I hope every writer will be familiar with it. — *Extract of a Letter from the Rev. Charles Brooks.*

We remember purchasing an English edition of this work some years since, and prizing it so highly that we tried several times, without success, to replace it, after it had disappeared from our collection. . . . Not only to professional authors, teachers, and letter-writers, but to the intelligent public at large, this work especially commends itself. — *Boston Transcript.*

. . . Such was the experience, also, of a graduate from our excellent University, who said that he had acquired more useful hints on Punctuation from a few moments given to the perusal of this book in the intervals of leisure, than he had from all the attention, voluntary or acquired, of an entire course of collegiate study. — *Evening Traveller.*

It contains all the necessary directions for self-taught writers and editors, a very large class in this country, and is a book of a kind absolutely necessary to be read by every type-setter and proof-reader who intends to be master of his art. . . . Every person, who intends publishing his own productions or those of others, should have Mr. Wilson's book upon his writing-desk. — *American Whig Review.*

It is the best book on the subject with which we are acquainted. The rules are deduced from the best usage, and commend themselves to the judgment of practical men, and men of taste. The directions for Proof-reading and Correcting, appended to the main work, are concise and clear. . . . We would recommend to every person, who in public or private writes the English language, to procure a copy of this treatise. — *Quincy Patriot*

NOTICES.

Dear Sir, — We have used your "Treatise on Punctuation" in my school for more than two years, as the text-book on that subject. I feel it due to you to say, that it has given me great satisfaction. In its arrangement, its fulness, in the great number of exercises, and the demand which they make on the learner for study, and in its completeness, your work seems to me to be all that could be desired in such a treatise. — *From N. Tillinghast, Esq., Principal of the Normal School at Bridgewater*, Jan. 18, 1851.

Our educational library has lately been enriched by a copy of Wilson's "Treatise on English Punctuation." We have read it through with great pleasure, and find little or nothing in it opposed to our own notions, but much that will be useful to us and to every teacher and author. . . . The definitions are generally clear and simple, and the exercises such as are appropriate and sufficient: any one of ordinary intelligence can understand them.

Besides valuable instruction in regard to Punctuation, there is much other matter, which none but a practised proof-reader could give. — *Common-school Journal*.

Mr. Wilson has just issued another volume, to be very earnestly recommended to all. . . . The Appendix, among other useful matter, contains capital and much-needed remarks and directions on Proof-reading. We have heard good judges speak of this manual as an "authority;" and such is our own opinion. Were it thoroughly studied and followed, what improvements would follow in all manner of manuscripts! what songs of joy would resound throughout the printing establishments of the land! and what blessed changes for the better would be witnessed in periodicals and newspapers! It is an excellent book for schools, and no family should be without it for purposes of reference. — *New-York Christian Inquirer*.

In itself a most beautiful specimen of the noble art of printing, this book is designed to secure accuracy, elegance, and lucidness in works that issue from the press. . . . All necessary information upon this important subject will be found, presented in a very simple and forcible way, in Mr. Wilson's "Treatise on Punctuation." It is an exceedingly valuable book; and a copy of it should be at the service of every one who is directly or indirectly interested in the large subject of which it treats, — all who have to write important letters, records, and documents, as well as those who write for the press . . . Its title is a very full exposition of its contents; and a reader of it will be equally surprised and instructed by the amount of knowledge which its perusal will impart. We heartily commend it to the masters and pupils of all our high schools and academies. — *Christian Examiner*.

POTTER, AINSWORTH, & COMPANY,

NEW YORK AND CHICAGO.

www.ingramcontent.com/pod-product-compliance
Lightning Source LLC
Chambersburg PA
CBHW030306240426
43673CB00040B/1080